GENDER, LAW AND MATERIAL CULTURE

This interdisciplinary volume discusses the division of the early modern material world into the important legal, economic, and personal categories of mobile and immobile property, possession, and the rights to usufruct.

The chapters describe and compare different modes of acquisition and intergenerational transfer via law and custom. The varying perspectives, including cultural history, legal history, social and economic history, philosophy, and law, allow for a more nuanced understanding of the links between the movability of an object and the gender of the person who owned, possessed, or used it. Case studies and examples come from a wide geographical range, including Norway, England, Scotland, the Holy Roman Empire, Italy, Tyrol, the Ottoman Empire, Greece, Romania, and the European colonies in Brazil and Jamaica. By covering both urban and rural areas and exploring all social groups, from ruling elites to the lower strata of society, the chapters offer fresh insight into the division of mobile and immobile property that socially and economically posed disadvantages for women.

By exploring a broad scope of topics, including landownership, marriage contracts, slaveholding, and the dowry, this book is an essential resource for both researchers and students of women's history, social and economic history, and material culture.

Annette Caroline Cremer is an assistant professor in the history faculty at Giessen University, Germany. She has published several books in the fields of material culture research, European cultural history in the seventeenth and eighteenth centuries, court culture, and gender history.

GENDER, LAW AND MATERIAL CULTURE

Immobile Property and Mobile Goods in Early Modern Europe

Edited by Annette Caroline Cremer

Routledge
Taylor & Francis Group
LONDON AND NEW YORK

First published 2021
by Routledge
2 Park Square, Milton Park, Abingdon, Oxon OX14 4RN

and by Routledge
52 Vanderbilt Avenue, New York, NY 10017

Routledge is an imprint of the Taylor & Francis Group, an informa business

British Library Cataloguing-in-Publication Data
A catalogue record for this book is available from the British Library

Library of Congress Cataloging-in-Publication Data
Names: Cremer, Annette Caroline, editor.
Title: Gender, law, and material culture : immobile property and mobile goods in early modern Europe / edited by Annette Caroline Cremer.
Description: Milton Park, Abingdon, Oxon ; New York, NY : Routledge, 2021. | Includes bibliographical references and index. | Contents: Gifts, symbolic values and strategies—Women' s access to immobile property—Women, law and property in colonial contexts—Women and property in transitory zones—Synthesis.
Identifiers: LCCN 2020020327 | ISBN 9780367371777 (paperback) | ISBN 9780367371791 (hardback) | ISBN 9780429352980 (ebook)
Subjects: LCSH: Property—Europe—History. | Women—Legal status, laws, etc.—Europe—History.
Classification: LCC KJC1255 .G46 2021 | DDC 346.40409/031—dc23
LC record available at https://lccn.loc.gov/2020020327

ISBN: 978-0-367-37179-1 (hbk)
ISBN: 978-0-367-37177-7 (pbk)
ISBN: 978-0-429-35298-0 (ebk)

Typeset in Bembo
by Apex CoVantage, LLC

CONTENTS

FIGURES

TABLES

CONTRIBUTORS

Siglinde Clementi studied history at the University of Vienna, Austria, where she also received her PhD. She is the Vicedirector of the Competence Center for Regional History of the Free University of Bolzano, Italy, and is head of the research area on gender and women's history. Her research field comprises gender and women's history, history and anthropology, microhistory, history of the body and medicine in the early modern period, social and cultural history of nobility, and regional history of Tyrol.

Annette Caroline Cremer, MA, PhD, read art history and English language and literature at Cork, Ireland, and Marburg, Germany. She became a research assistant (April 2008 to March 2013) at the International Graduate Centre for the Study of Culture (GCSC) of Giessen-University, where she earned her doctorate in cultural studies, writing her dissertation on an eighteenth-century dollhouse collection as three-dimensional ego document. She has worked as Akademischer Rat (Assistant Professor) at the Historical Institute of JLU Giessen since April 2013. In September 2018, she was appointed Visiting Fellow, History Department, Cambridge, United Kingdom. She has published several books in the fields of material culture research, European cultural history in the seventeenth and eighteenth centuries, court culture, and gender history.

Evdoxios Doxiadis is an associate professor in history at Simon Fraser University, Canada. His research is on Greek, Balkan, and Mediterranean history, with a focus on the eighteenth and nineteenth centuries and a particular interest in questions of gender, law, state formation, and minorities. He has published two monographs: *The Shackles of Modernity: Women, Property, and the Transition from the Ottoman Empire to the Modern Greek State 1750–1850* (2011) and *State, Nationalism* *and the Jewish Communities of Modern Greece* (2018). He also co-edited with Aimee Placas the volume *Living under Austerity: Greek Society in Crisis* (2018).

Ida Fazio is Full Professor of Early Modern History at the University of Palermo, Italy, where she teaches economic and social history and gender history. She is Editor in Chief of *Genesis. Rivista della società italiana delle storiche*, the academic journal of Italian women historians. Her research interests focus on women's and gender history, where she explores the transmission of property in early modern and modern Italy and Sicily, and on the economic and social history of urban provisioning systems and wheat trade in the seventeenth to nineteenth centuries, focussing on legal and illegal trade networks in the southern Mediterranean.

Fatma Gül Karagöz studied law at Galatasaray University, Turkey. After completing her law internship at the İstanbul Bar Association in 2006, she decided to follow an academic path and obtained her master's degree in Ottoman history at Bilkent University in 2010. She obtained her PhD in 2018 in public law at İstanbul University, Turkey. She worked as a research assistant at Bahçeşehir University between 2009 and 2013. Since 2013, she continues her research and teaches at Galatasaray University. Karagöz is specialised in early modern Ottoman law. Her studies are mostly focussed on land law, property relations, and codification of law.

Margareth Lanzinger is a professor of social and economic history (sixteenth to nineteenth centuries) at the University of Vienna, Austria. She was a visiting professor at the Free University of Berlin (2011) and at Leibniz University Hannover (2013–2014). Her research interests are kinship, marriage, property and the power of disposal, inheritance, marital property regimes, legal and administrative practices, relations between norms and practice, the construction of heroes and heroines, and historiographic topics.

Janine Maegraith studied history and history of science and technology at the University of Stuttgart, Germany, where she obtained her PhD. She was a postdoctoral research associate at the University of Cambridge and is currently a research associate at the University of Vienna, Austria, working on the project The Role of Wealth in Defining and Constituting Kinship Spaces from the Sixteenth to the Eighteenth Century. Her research interests are early modern history of Central Europe, focussing on social, economic, and legal history; consumption; and gender studies.

Rebecca Mason is an Economic History Society Power Fellow at the Institute of Historical Research in London, United Kingdom. Her PhD was funded as part of the Arts and Humanities Research Council project *Women Negotiating the Boundaries of Justice: Britain and Ireland, c.1100–1750* at the University of Glasgow. She is an historian of gender and law, with a special focus on the legal activities and property rights of married women in early modern Scotland. She has published on married women's legal rights to paraphernalia and the impact of gender and marital status when accessing justice in seventeenth-century Glasgow.

Susann Anett Pedersen is a PhD student at the Norwegian University of Science and Technology, where she also earned her master's degree in 2012. She is an historian with a particular interest in economic and social history, and her research explores women's ownership and management of landed property in late mediaeval Norway.

Nicoleta Roman is a researcher at the Nicolae Iorga-Institute of History, Romanian Academy, and New Europe College–Institute for Advanced Study, both in Bucharest, Romania. She obtained her PhD at the University of Bucharest, writing her dissertation on women in nineteenth-century Wallachia, published under the title *Deznădăjduită muiere n-au fost ca mine. Femei, onoare şi păcat în Valahia secolului al XIX-lea* (*Women, honour and sin in 19th century Wallachia*), Humanitas, 2016. As a historian, she extended her interests towards the history of childhood, welfare systems, and legal and material cultures in Southeastern Europe and has published in various peer-reviewed international journals, including *The History of the Family*, *Popolazione e Storia*, and *Annales de Démographie Historique*.

Luisa Stella de Oliveira Coutinho Silva studied law and psychology at the Center Universitary of João Pessoa and the Federal University of Paraíba, Brazil, and obtained her master's degree and PhD at Lisbon University, Portugal, in legal history. Her research fields comprise legal history of the Portuguese Empire and women's history. She is currently working on the legal history of the Christian century in Japan as a member of the broader research project Glocalising Normativities by the Max Planck Institute for European Legal History, Frankfurt, Germany.

Amelie Stuart studied philosophy and sociology and obtained her doctoral degree in philosophy in 2019 at the University of Graz, Austria. Her main research interests are theories of ownership and property, feminist philosophy, and postmodern political philosophy. She is a postdoctoral researcher at the University of Leipzig, Germany, and is currently working on cultural practices of inheritance and the limits of ownership.

Christine Walker is an assistant professor of history at Yale-NUS College, Singapore. She received a PhD from the University of Michigan (2014), an MA from the University of Connecticut (2007), and a BA from Yale University (2000). She specialises in the history of colonialism, gender, and slavery in the Atlantic World. Her current work, which focusses on women's involvement in slavery, will be published in the book *Jamaica Ladies: Female Slaveholders and the Creation of Britain's Atlantic Empire* (Chapel Hill: University of North Carolina Press) in June 2020.

ACKNOWLEDGEMENTS

This volume is the result of the interdisciplinary and international conference *Movable Goods and Immovable Property. Gender, Law and Material Culture in Early Modern Europe (1450–1850)*, held 19–21 July 2018 at the German Historical Institute London. This was also the 9th Conference of the European network *Gender Differences in the History of European Legal Cultures*, founded by Professor Emerita Heide Wunder in 2000.

The German Historical Institute London kindly agreed to host the conference, and I am deeply grateful to Hannes Ziegler (GHI London) for his help and support in preparing, organising, and convening the event. The conference audience was an inspiring mixture of established as well as young scholars from social and economic history, legal history, cultural history, and law, coming from places around the world, including Scotland, Singapore, Germany, Turkey, Portugal, Austria, Italy, France, Greece, United Kingdom, Poland, Sweden, and the United States, and dealing with localities in Europe and its colonies during early modernity. The event was, in every sense of the word, truly international and truly interdisciplinary. Both presented a challenge in respect to terminology, methodology, and general approach. Some but not all of the papers presented at the conference are included in this volume. Nonetheless, all have strongly gained from presenting and discussing their work. Therefore, I would like to thank all participants for their contributions and participation during the conference. I especially would like to thank Amy Erickson (Cambridge) for her keynote "The Social Capital and Physical Assets of Craftswomen in Early Modern London" and Grethe Jacobsen, Anna Bellavitis, and Heide Wunder for their constant support. I would also like to thank Torsten dos Santos Arnold, Julia Hinze, Katja Berndt, Sarah Noske, and Lena Frewer for their help during the editing process.

Annette Caroline Cremer, Giessen/Germany, June 2020

PART I

Introduction

Men, women, property, law, and custom

FIGURE 1.1 Early modern Germany, Guillaume de L'Isle, Philippe Buache, *Carte d'Europe*, 1769 (detail).

Source: Library of Congress Geography and Map Division, Washington, D.C., U.S.A., public domain, G5700 1724. L5 TIL, http://hdl.loc.gov/loc.gmd/g5700.ct000045 (15.02.2020, 12:45 CET).

1

GENDER, LAW, AND MATERIAL CULTURE

Annette Caroline Cremer

I. The tooth of a hippo as gendered item?

In 1716, Countess Auguste Dorothea of Schwarzburg (1666–1751), member of the high nobility and widow of the late ruler over a small earldom in today's Thuringia, Germany, appeared as litigant before the *Reichshofrat* (Aulic Council), the Supreme Court of the Holy Roman Empire in Vienna. The premature death of her husband, Count Anton Günther II (1653–1716), had left her without issue. Now, as a childless widow she had to fight for her dowry against the interests of the agnate heirs. Auguste claimed housing and financial support that she was entitled to according to the marriage contract from 1684. To that extent, the case seems rather ordinary. But she also claimed specific items from the residency the couple had inhabited, among them items from the collection in the cabinet of curiosities, such as a petrified piece of wood "since it resembled a jewel"; a camera obscura and microscope "since they contained a mirror"; a papyrus with Chinese letters declared "a historical book, made for the perusal of women"; and a Roman oil lamp that "looked like a portable chandelier". Finally, she claimed the tooth of a hippo and argued *ex negative* that "there was no proof that it had stemmed from a male animal".[1] It is not the items she claims for herself, but the way she argues that leaves us slightly puzzled. I want to use this curious example of a court case as a point of departure to explain the connexions between the keywords and concepts that form the core of this volume – namely, gender, law, and material culture.

Auguste's claims were informed by early modern Saxonian law and contemporary ideas in respect to the ordering of things as part of the male or female sphere of the material world. Objects that were legally considered part of the female sphere were called *Gerade*, which stemmed from a Middle High German term meaning "utensils" or "tools". The *Gerade* can be traced back to the thirteenth century as a part of female property.[2] In force in northern parts of the Holy Roman Empire, it stayed in use for several hundred years, until the middle of the nineteenth century, exceeding the introduction of the General Prussian Law in 1794. Paragraph 206 of the Prussian Law still states that within marriage, apart from wedding gifts and property secured by a premarital contract, subject to the wife's assets were only those objects "which, by their very nature, are dedicated to the use of women", emphasising their habitual use.[3] Comprehensive descriptions of what were considered items of the *Gerade* appear as entries in mid-eighteenth- to mid-nineteenth-century German encyclopaedias.[4] The rules of the *Gerade* were also included in the popular handbook *Frauenzimmer-Lexicon* (*Curious Women's Dictionary*), first published in 1715 and intended "for women's usage and entertainment". The book included a detailed description of the specific items that counted as part of the *Gerade* in conjunction with topics such as the history of famous women and medical treatment and recipes.[5] The *Gerade*, so it seems, was part of a common pattern of agency and a matter of regular debate among women. Exact knowledge of what was to be considered part of it was key.

TABLE 1.1 Items of the *Gerade* understood as "female" objects as defined in Johann Heinrich Zedler's *Universal Lexicon* (1735) and Johann Georg Krünitz's *Oekonomische Encyklopädie* (1779).

- CLOTHING from wool, linen, and silk, including underwear, sleeping gown, and trousers
- RIBBONS, bonnets, gloves, stockings, shoes, and buckles that go with them as well as fans and veils
- CHESTS and coffers with lids
- All BOXES and cases in which female property was stored, and then if only the widow had the keys to them, but not inside walls and only if inside the cases were less general heritage pieces than *Gerade* pieces, according to their value
- Squeezing MACHINE for tablecloths and other textiles
- THREAD but not from wool
- Unused SILK and embroidery
- All harvested LINEN and FLAX but not hemp
- MIXED TEXTILES, including cotton and linen textiles
- BEDS and mattresses on which she herself, the children, and the servants have slept or those used for travel, as long as she had the keys to them, but not those used for guests
- Any CUSHIONS in daily use
- Any LINENS used as bedcovers, tablecloths, handkerchiefs, towels, aprons, scarfs, or sleeves
- All CURTAINS, carpets, and tapestries used daily by the wife
- Any FEATHERS
- BATHING towels, basin, and cauldron, but not the bathtub
- All blankets, SADDLE for horse-riding
- All CHANDELIERS and candleholders made of silver, tin, brass, or crystal that are not tied to the wall even if the name of the husband was imprinted on them, including the objects on which they stand (gueridons), but not large chandeliers hanging from the walls or ceilings or those that were bought by the husband for special occasions and not for daily usage

- Washing CAULDRON "within the wall or freely standing"
- All JEWELLERY
- Small IMAGES of emperors, kings, electors, and so on
- WATCHES when used as part of female attire
- Little POTS with balsam and RINGS, but not the signet ring unless adorned with gemstones
- SOAP in vessels
- All BOOKS the woman has read, together with the furniture they are stored in or set on (repository or table)
- All "items that belong to female work": SPINNING WHEELS, lace pillows, all items connected to weaving, sewing, and knitting, including scissors
- MIRRORS in daily use but not those in the salon or bought for special decoration by the husband
- All SHEEP of female sex, all geese and ducks
- The horse-drawn CARRIAGE used by the wife, but without the horses

Source: © Annette Caroline Cremer.

The *Gerade* was defined as a set of objects that was considered female property and was to be extracted from the estate *before* the general Saxon laws of distribution in hereditary succession applied. Traditionally, what was to be divided in accordance with its rule consisted in part of tools habitually used and all movable objects controlled by females and necessary for household chores. It also included such items that women had produced as well as all textiles in the house, clothing, mattresses, jewellery, mirrors, and chandeliers and also portraits of female family members and, in general, the female share of livestock. The *Gerade* varied in its details in accordance with local ordinances and depended on the social status of the persons concerned.[6] The reason for the invention of the *Gerade*, so contemporaries argued, was the fact that daughters were excluded from their natural heritage by the sons since they did not benefit from the male form of the *Gerade*, called *Hergewedde*, which referred to male clothing, tools, and weapons handed down from father to son or next male heir. By contrast, the *Gerade* generally excluded sons, but with a telling exception: Sons who had become clergymen were also entitled to claim their share of the *Gerade*.[7] While the male form (*Hergewedde*), which implied compulsory armed service, fell out of use in the seventeenth and eighteenth centuries, the *Gerade* stayed in use. Clearly, not all objects of the material world had a specific "gender"; nonetheless, parts of the material world were obviously understood as "female" or "male". The gender category was defined by its visual characteristics (portraits of women), sex (female livestock), control (lock and key), homemade character, or object in daily use.

Early modern Europe had clear associations between men, women, and objects. The object types that functioned almost as an icon of the female gender role in all social groups were the spindle and distaff. The allegorical connotation of the spindle and distaff operated in three ways: First, as an expression of the clearly gendered household chore of spinning, the objects as such, because of their repetitive usage by women, were "gendered" as female. Second, as spinning formed the economic basis of many women in the pre-industrial home production of textiles, it stood for the industriousness of and capacity for self-subsistence of its owner. Third, it turned into a symbol of female virtue, so much so that even the Habsburg princess Marie Christine depicted herself using it. The spindle and distaff were objects integral to every household and can be traced from the lowest to the highest social levels (see Figures 1.2–1.4). They also appear in several fairy tales as attributes of female

FIGURE 1.2 Michael Sweerts, *An Old Woman Spinning*, 1646–1648.

Source: © The Picture Art Collection / Alamy Stock Photo.

FIGURE 1.3 Jean-Baptiste-Siméon Chardin, *The Diligent Mother*, oil on canvas, 50 × 39.5 cm.

Source: © Artokoloro / Alamy Stock Photo.

virtuousness and diligence, such as Old Mother Frost or Rumpelstiltskin by the Brothers Grimm. In early modern Germany, the spindle and distaff were, without any doubt, part of the gendered pre-inheritance of the *Gerade*.

Still, to reflect on the "gender" of an object seems irritating, as objects as such are neither male nor female. It is their connotation – an applied meaning that

FIGURE 1.4 German: Marie Christine von Habsburg-Lothringen: *Erzherzogin Marie Christine im weißen Kleid*. Gouache; English: Archduchess Marie Christine of Austria (1742–1798), daughter of Franz I, Stephan of Lorraine, Holy Roman Emperor, and Maria Theresia, Empress of Austria and Hungary, spouse of Albert, Prince of Saxony (1738–1822). Self-portrait. *c.* 1765. Marie Christine of Austria.

Source: © The Picture Art Collection / Alamy Stock Photo.

derives from a repetitive usage in a certain way and by a certain group of people – that ascribes to things a gender. A stomacher in the eighteenth century was clearly part of a woman's attire and was thus coded as a "female" object. A stomacher worn by a man on stage in Shakespearean England, where women as artists were forbidden, was still a female garment and a costume, indicating that the actor wearing it represented a female character. A man wearing a stomacher in the twenty-first century is playfully criticising the binary division of humans' biological sex and either represents a deconstruction of the visual code for male/female or states an appropriation of "femininity". The meaning of a "gendered" object clearly depends on its precise contexts of usage.

I.a Categories of objects: Mobile and immobile

The early modern material world was classified not only by its alleged gender but also by a second category in respect to its *movability*:

> [T]hings are by the law . . . distributed into two kinds; things real, and things personal. Things real are such as are permanent, fixed and immoveable, which cannot be carried out of their place; as lands and tenements; things personal are goods, money, and all other moveables; which may attend the owner's person wherever he thinks proper to go.[8]

General as well as legal understanding categorised objects under two rubrics, seemingly in respect to their intrinsic properties, as mirrored by the citation of William Blackstone. This basic division followed an alleged "nature of an object"[9] and defined objects as either immobile ("real") or movable – terms still partly reflected in our modern language (German *Immobilie* for "real estate" or the French *biens meubles*). The German legal dictionary documents the use of these terms since the thirteenth century – almost parallel to the appearance of the term *Gerade*.[10] According to the famous German *Universal Lexicon*, an encyclopaedia from the mid-eighteenth century, immobile goods were described as anything that "*cannot* or *may not* be moved". Within this category were so-called "standing goods", such as houses, stables, and cellars, or "lying goods", such as fields, pastures, forests, ponds, and gardens. Yet not only did the houses and lands count as immovable but also everything that derived from them, such as privileges, interests, rent, and crops or fruit prior to being harvested. In spite of this apparently clear-cut differentiation, the typology of defining objects as immobile exceeded by far the general characteristic of "not movable". It also included movable items and *simply defined them as immobile* because the general division was oriented towards the functioning of an economic system as an entity. For example, as part of immovable property, genuinely movable items were sometimes counted, such as instruments necessary for brewing beer in a brewery or beds in a house used as a hotel.[11] Serfs who belonged to an estate also counted as immobile as well as objects defined as indivisible in the form of an entail (e.g. the books in a library).[12]

Once labour in the form of harvesting had been applied to fields and pastures, the same items – crops and fruit – counted as *mobile*. In fact, by applying physical work or changing its physical condition – i.e. from a green fruit on an apple tree with no economic value to a mature and merchantable or edible item – an object changed into an altogether different object with another quality or character. Movable goods, in principle, included everything that *moved by itself* – for example cattle – or that *could be moved* from one place to another by others without being destroyed – for example cash, household effects, and personal chattels.[13] In general, one could say that the fundamental division ran between the house and what was inside. The definition of the two categories also referred to the spatial hierarchy between people and things: In respect to their movability, mobile goods were subordinate to people's abodes, whereas real estate defined people's whereabouts.

But what exactly was to be considered immobile or mobile property was part of an intensive debate until the mid-nineteenth century – for example whether trade commodities counted as mobile.[14] Within this system of classification, the windmill presented a severe problem of definition, as it was rooted to the ground, yet nonetheless moved by itself. Water in rivers and wells also presented a problem since its general characteristic was its movability. To keep it part of the concept of real estate, it was argued that the soil under the river or well was immobile and thus so was the water on top of it.[15] No wonder then that this basic division of the material world led to jurisdictional disputes.

By their nature, such different categories of "objects" like land, buildings, a pig, tools, furniture, or a pot (within the same social and economic level) greatly differed in quality and meaning as well as in price of acquisition, size, permanence, economic value, and degree of attention needed for maintenance. A pot or a pig was far more easily replaced compared with a house. Fields or meadows secured farming and space to graze the cattle. A house meant protection and shelter against weather and cold and had a symbolic meaning for the identity of a family. As Raffaela Sarti stated, "[T]here were . . . those who linked their whole identity to their house. One might say there were houses that had a family, rather than the other way round."[16] But an empty house without basic furniture and chattels did not function as a place for survival and living. Movables represented the means of housekeeping and the processing of vegetables and meat and small comforts. *Normatively*, the house – associated with protection and shelter – and the sphere outside of it were attributed to men as the head of the family, while everything inside the house – housekeeping and nutrition – was attributed to women.

The grouping of the material world stemmed not only from the different value, durability, and meaning but also from an understanding of life as complementary spheres of men and women. The normative division of space of agency or spheres translated to the combination of gender and specific tasks; tasks became attached to certain tools or objects, which, in consequence, led to the attribution of a certain gender to specific items. The division ran along practical lines of responsibilities for areas and between experts at different kinds of tasks. Each new generation grew into practiced competences, which then reaffirmed the person-object relation. Each transfer process cemented it further. So, the ideas about separated tasks inspired a gendered behavioural pattern, which was then associated with certain categories of objects. The case of the *Gerade* and its male counterpart, the *Hergewedde*, testifies to the fact that objects became regarded as male or female. As a general tendency, under Saxonian law and the territories that applied it, real estate was perceived or connoted as "male" property and mobile property, in accordance with its specific category and use, as either "female" or "male".

In consequence, the general principle of movability as the fundamental pattern of differentiation was mixed and even overruled by the attribution of gender to an item. Amazingly, objects that by their nature *could not move or should not be moved*, e.g. a basin firmly tied to the wall or floor for the laundering of textiles, were considered undoubtedly a part of female household responsibility and (very hard to believe) could be pulled out and handed to the next female kin.[17] In this case, the gendering of an object overruled the condition that its transfer should never harm the physical integrity of the house. Here, the category "gender" is more important than the category "movability" as a characteristic of an item. A second example shows that the internal logic of the *Gerade* as a gender-based classificatory system of objects linked to movability was not always coherent since, for example, the lying-in furniture in which women gave birth, definitely gendered as female and mobile, *did not* count as *Gerade* and had to stay in the house. Lying-in furniture was defined as immobile, although it was clearly movable by its nature. This hints at the important role of the continuity of the agnate lineage and the perception of a strong link between children and fathers.

Early modern societies operated mostly within a recognisable system of visual patterns that indicated the gender and age of a person, their geographical origin, and their social rank and occupation. Within this system of placement and ranking of each person, apart from habits, posture, and practices, objects such as clothing and housing plus the type, and especially the material, of objects inside played an essential role. It was the meaning and connotation of every object that made the world "readable".[18] The gendering of the material world was deeply rooted within the contemporary understanding of the gender divide that applied to complementary roles and responsibilities in accordance with the assumed natural capacities and competences or naturalised gender prejudices. The

> dualistic gender system has often been associated with other dichotomies, such as body/spirit, public/private, nature/culture, light/dark, . . . sun/moon [and was] viewed as divinely created. Which has enabled people to view the male/female dichotomy also as natural or divinely ordained. This dichotomy . . . has generally been viewed as a hierarchy, with the male linked with the stronger and more positive element . . . and the female with the weaker and more negative one.[19]

The divide went even further to arrive at an understanding of the material world that was not only socially coded but also defined as belonging to either the male or the female sphere. Following the dualistic line of argument of Merry Wiesner-Hanks, we could now associate close links between the categories "male-strong-immobile property" and "female-weak-mobile goods". So, when thinking about people and things, one should consider the precise legal context as it shapes its appropriation, emotional attachment and (economic) use.

I.b Legal relations between objects and persons: Property, possession, and usufruct

So far I have used the term *property* as a placeholder for a complex system of diverse kinds of legal relations between a person and an object, which are defined as property, possession, and usufruct. The term *property* indicates the legal right of ownership as an absolute form of power over something. This includes, for example, the right to dispose of an object. The property relation is the greatest possible extent of power over any item, large or small. The term *possession* refers to the actual and practical power over something. To give an example, the owner of a house holds it as property (freehold); the tenant of a house is in possession of it (copyhold). Possession implies limited power over an object, but it indicates who practically controls it. The third term is the so-called *usufructus*. A proprietor theoretically has three different sorts of rights in respect to his property, which are expressed by the Latin terms *usus*, *fructus*, and *abusus*. *Usufructus* means that the proprietor passes on the first two rights – *usus* and *fructus* – to another person (often for as long as a lifetime) and keeps only his third right. The term *usufruct* means to be allowed to use something without any further rights to it but with the obligation to keep up its value.[20]

I.c Sources and social strata

The sources we draw upon to investigate what people owned are ego documents – such as letters and diaries, marriage contracts and protocols, death inventories, wills, payrolls, tax books, court records, and images and paintings depicting early modern life – although highly constructed. Likewise, all kinds of objects that have come down to us, either in the form of real estate or conserved by national heritage programmes, serve as sources. Finally, we can use furniture, clothes, and the like, which are protected and displayed in museums of cultural history. The question of the sources brings us to the question of whose property and distribution pattern we can examine at all. Obviously, it applies only to those groups of society who owned at least some property and for whom the necessity arose to give written evidence of what they owned.[21] However, some exceptions did exist. When the obligation to register an official "marriage protocol" in the eighteenth century was introduced in the principality of Hesse-Kassel, inventories of people's belongings followed a set order for each material and painstakingly documented everything people did *not* own.

In 1804, Georg Bernhard, groom of the princely stables in Kassel, registered his deceased wife's property in the presence of his mother and a notary. The inventory shows that she owned neither immobile property nor money nor gold nor silver but had a few household items of tin, copper, and brass; a considerable amount of iron items for cooking; diverse pieces of wooden furniture, such as a bed, cupboard, and chest; a porcelain dish for drinking coffee; two mirrors and four wine glasses; bedding, such as linen bedclothes; and very few items of clothing.[22]

In some areas, the obligation to register enables us to access the lower strata of society, if sedentary. It implies that we omit those people all over Europe and its colonial parts without a fixed home who were migrating constantly as well as the truly poor in urban areas and those in the countryside who owned no more than they could carry.[23] Thus, the main targets of our discourse are those groups of the population who owned at least a little, such as sharecroppers, peasants, farmers, and domestic servants; the petit bourgeois, such as craftsmen, teachers, and retail tradesmen; the bourgeois, such as physicians, lawyers, and scholars; and court or state officials, the gentry, the patricians, and the nobility.

I.d Connexion between gender, movability and law

Of great importance is the idea that the definition of an object as immovable or movable and the three different ways to relate to objects legally – property, possession, and usufruct – are interwoven and mixed with the aforementioned categories of the gender of a person and the gender of objects. The connexion between being male and female, gendered movable and immovable items, and legal regulations becomes most sharply contoured at the moment of the transfer of property.[24] The plurality of partly competing – even contradictory – legal norms under canon law, Roman law, and common law as well as of local varieties and of the application of customs in Europe and the division of norm and practice has been widely acknowledged.[25] Although there have been many exceptions, in general the inheritance pattern was gendered and favoured firstborn sons.[26] The ordinary inheritance line in patrilineal heritage systems usually allocated immobile property to male family members, while mobile goods could be distributed among heirs according to locally and nationally diverse regulations. Therefore, the debate and decision about what counted as mobile and immobile was at the core of inheritance practices.

I.e An experiment: Degrees of personal attachment?

The concept of property has meaning far beyond its legal properties. Legal conditions (property, possession, and usufruct) shaped the way people related to things. The way a person is legally entitled to an object now or in the near or far future surely influences the way it is handled, preserved, or simply used. But how does one relate to something that is not one's own? At a certain biographical stage, before marriage, many men and women worked as servants or day labourers, mainly operating with things, objects, and tools they did not own.[27] Most likely, this daily handling to fulfil a given task involved action that was largely unconscious. Let us speculate on the personal consequences of a legally shaped relation between people and things and reflect on the possibility of personal attachment to things by looking at an image.

This German painting from around 1900 imitates Dutch genre painting of the Golden Age of the seventeenth century (see Figure 1.5). It shows an elderly female servant cleaning the collection of precious silver objects of her employers. Although we are looking at a cleverly constructed painting, the situation depicted, people handling things they did not own, must have happened numerous times in reality. What might be the emotional relation of this (imagined) person in respect to the silver she has to polish but that she will never own? Pride on behalf of such a task? Admiration? Envy? To clean silver takes a lot of time, during which she could marvel over the beauty of the items, their condition, or their value or even muse about theft. Apart from the silver objects, we could ask if the dress she wears is her own property or has been given to her by her employers. If so, does she wear it with pride?[29] And what might have been the relation of the imaginary housewife in respect to the family heirloom of her husband? Silver objects that represented the wealth of her family and that she might proudly present when having guests but that she would never own nor pass on? And what about the respective children who grew up, taking in the material atmosphere with unconscious nonchalance or ignorance while small because the silver simply was part of a "bunch" of things present at home? What was the relation of the son who would at some stage be told that one day all of this would be his as undivided treasure of the family? What was the relation of the father towards the silver objects that might have been handed down over generations as an embodiment of the family's long-lasting success and as a monetary resource if need be? Although mobile in principle, such silver items usually were seen as belonging to the house as indivisible family treasure (if they had not been part of the woman's dowry).

Legally, objects remained within the ownership of a person until the moment of death. But the abstract value of things and the social capital they carried could be transferred beforehand as a "promise". The material and symbolic value of an object was conveyed towards its (future) owner associatively. This differentiation between the true object and its properties adds meaning to the principal idea that the material world shapes the identity, social placement, and sense of the self, as cultural anthropologists have argued.[30] The option to view things as extensions or attributes of men and women was formed fundamentally by the legal relations between objects and persons.

Nonetheless, the meaning of property for the identity of a person was limited. It has to be considered beside strong elements of identity that originated from the personal status as unmarried, married, and widowed and from women's and men's

FIGURE 1.5 Alphons Spring, *A Cleaning Day* (*Ein Putztag*), 1898 (Munich, Neue Pinakothek).

Source: © Archive of the History of Art Department of LMU Munich.[28]

fields of expertise in respect to tasks or work and the place in society a person held. To reflect on the personal or emotional attachment of persons in the early modern era to things is highly speculative, as it cannot be supported by written evidence. The consequences of legal property relations are difficult to grasp beyond the obvious economic aspects. We cannot as yet prove the hypothesis that legal relations did indeed give rise to options of emotional attachment.

I.f Permanently reassembling

In practice, the custom of *Gerade* must have led to a permanent reassembling and recombination of mobile and immobile property.[31] In general, items that counted as *Gerade* were introduced by the paraphernalia each generation of women would bring into the house of her husband or the neo-local home, thereby leaving her own material and visual and, in higher strata, even her personal aesthetic mark. In the frequent occurrence of death, these objects as well as acquired pieces were redistributed. The idea of familial or dynastic tradition was nevertheless conveyed by the remaining *in situ* of all items that had a ritual value. What might the house have looked like once the *Gerade* objects had been taken away? What implications did this have on both sides, male and female? On the one hand, a widower would be left with a house and bare furniture without cushions, tables without cloths, beds without mattresses, walls with empty spots, and just one set of dishes. The material layout of the house in its barren state obviously pointed to a man's personal status as a widower. On the other hand, the widow or next female kin would have more mattresses, textiles, pots, and female livestock without the room to use, display, or breed them. For both parties, the items missing conveyed the lack of the person needed to complete the household. The material consequences of the *Gerade* could have appeared as described, but they also depended on the age of the person when widowed, whether she or he was a mother or father, and the familial structure on both sides. Nonetheless, mobile and immobile property stood as a symbol for the female and male part of life. In a way, the separation and redistribution of the material world, the mobile and immobile property, encouraged men and women to seek new partners.

To get back to my introductory example, having looked at the perception of a gendered material world, we are now able to evaluate Auguste's argument regarding the objects from the couple's mutual collectables she claimed, i.e. the piece of wood, the microscope, the papyrus, the Roman oil lamp, and the tooth of the hippo. Her key argument was the aspect of *habitual female daily usage* or the appointment of a certain *gender category* to each object, which led in principle to a legitimate claim. In respect to the microscope she defined as a mirror, the ancient papyrus she defined as a book, the ancient lamp she defined as a bedside lamp, and the tooth of a hippo as a form of female livestock, her claims certainly were far-fetched and a peculiar application of the *Gerade*. Nonetheless, in general, she won her case in court, and the family of her late husband had to pay large sums as dowry and for maintenance.[32] But in respect to the objects in question, she might have failed since Auguste never learned to read Chinese and probably never used the Roman oil lamp from the *Kunstkammer* collection to light her chamber. Unfortunately, we do not know if her claims were granted, but it is highly unlikely they were. Nevertheless, her *argument* followed both law and custom.

II. The content and aims of this book

This volume on gender, law, and material culture tries to bring together different fields of research. The term "gender" primarily points to a social and cultural construction of a fundamental difference and inequality between men and women.[33] The term "law" brings in the state or government as regulator of society, while "custom" refers to interfamilial or interpersonal levels of negotiation. The combination of the terms "gender" and "law" appears in the context of marriage, perceived as the state's nucleus and central social institution, and touches on individual persons being caught between *oikos* and *polis*. Marriage as favoured biographical model and as the political core of society lies at the heart of the division of property.[34] To reflect on the combination of "marriage" and "objects" leads to research on household economy and marital goods, and to reflect on "economy" and "objects" results in research on consumerism. Anglo-American archaeology and cultural anthropology, as disciplines with a genuine interest in things as sources, have been connecting the two analytical categories of gender and material culture since the mid-1990s.[35] Historians in France and Italy became interested in material culture from the 1980s on, and their research became accessible to a wider international audience with Daniel Roche's *A History of Everyday Things* (2000) and Raffaella Sarti's *Europe at Home* (2002), which both integrated gender as an aspect of the material world.[36] John Styles's *The Dress of the People* (2007), Ulinka Rublack's *Dressing Up* (2010), Ludmilla Jordanova's *The Look of the Past* (2012), and Renata Ago's *Gusto for Things* (2013) – in respect to the methodology of material culture research and the interpretation of the material world, be it on the basis of written, pictorial, or material evidence – became highly influential in the field, especially in respect to the research beyond elites.[37] Material culture research in the context of early modernity has focussed on different geographical areas; on the reconstruction of households; on specific categories of objects, such as clothing, shoes, or china; and on things as commodities, tracing the beginning of fashion, taste, and the consumer societies, in which a firm position has been attributed to gender.[38]

The chapters in this book look at the division of the early modern material world into the legally, economically, and personally important categories of mobile and immobile property and possession as well as the rights to usufruct. They describe different modes of acquisition and intergenerational transfer via law and (often differing) custom and investigate the social and economic consequences that derive from the links that were established between the categories of movability of an object and the gender of the person who owned, possessed, or used it. The contributions look at the normative order of different codes of law and their appropriation and at practical solutions that often differed widely from the norm. The focus of the volume is on women, as the abstract division of mobile and immobile property socially and economically posed disadvantages for women more than men. The connexion between men and property seems to be the expected "standard case" of distribution, as in most – but not all – areas of the early modern world, inheritance laws privileged husbands over wives, brothers over sisters, and firstborn over all other siblings.[39] If law did not fundamentally privilege men over women, sometimes custom did (see Tyrol). Custom (visible to us, i.e. by way of wills and contracts) partly stood over or against the law or interpreted it.

In respect to the topic of this volume, there are two ways to approach the treatment of property: From practical handling within tradition and custom that gradually was codified into law and from abstract discourse on the idea of property. Both are necessary to understand why rules developed in precisely the way they did. Theory certainly has its foundation in observation of gender-related practices, whereas theoretical or academic concepts entered the letters of the law.

Only seldomly do we come across explicit personal praise of objects by which we can clearly deduce their meaning for each family, family member, or person. Nonetheless, we may assume a strong personal relation of people to their goods and estates because of their economic, social, and possibly emotional or memorial value. We have to learn to read between the lines of sources by which we can trace their mere existence. The bulk of objects become visible principally at the moment of transfer from one owner to the next in legal documents. Many appear in the context of marriage and death; dowry and marriage contracts, inventories, and wills thus form major types of sources. They have been repeatedly used as sources for social and economic history or gender history.[40]

The authors in this book come not only from ten different countries but also from different disciplinary backgrounds and perspectives: Cultural history, legal history, social and economic history, philosophy, and law. The case studies and examples in this book come from Norway and Scotland, Tyrol, the Holy Roman Empire and Italy, Greece, Romania and Turkey under Ottoman rule, and Brazil and Jamaica as Portuguese and English colonies. Although comparative in approach, the perspective remains "Eurocentric". The authors cover urban and rural areas and look at all social groups, from ruling elites to the lower strata of society, and their access to different kinds of property.

But what *is* property as such? How did the concept of property come about and why is it acceptable that things are yours and not mine? And why (once I learned the difference between "yours" and "mine" as a child) do I – do we all – agree to this fact in principle?[41] The philosopher Amelie Stuart's (Erfurt) contribution is central to this volume, as she establishes the basis of our thinking on the relation between people and things – namely, the normative justification of private property as such and how, according to early modern political philosophy, this property could be acquired. Starting from the progressive writings of the Venetian Modesta Pozzo in 1600 on the issue of women and property, she demonstrates that canonical texts of political philosophy still mainly read today refer only to men as relevant subjects. By looking at two highly influential exemplary property theories of John Locke and Jean-Jacques Rousseau, she analyses the sources in respect to the original difference between common property and private property, how "private property" has been valued morally, and the "(im-)possibility of women owning private property". The author convincingly shows how early modern ideas about the two genders, their attributed "nature", and their appointed places in the spheres of the public and the household are deeply intertwined with law and custom. These ideas led to (or mirrored) a gender inequality regarding ownership rights, as the hierarchy between the sexes was translated into the ordering of goods to men and women and gendered property rights and, in consequence, shaped inheritance patterns. The author emphasises that the canonical texts are understudied in respect to women's property rights, as are their "gender biases, inconsistencies and ambivalences", and that other, less popular texts such as Pozzo's should be taken into consideration when thinking about early modern concepts of property rights.

Part II deals with gifts, symbolic values, and strategies. It covers the late fourteenth to the early seventeenth century in Norway, Scotland, and Tyrol. The historian Susann Anett Pedersen (Trondheim) takes us to fifteenth century Norway and looks at the legal institution of "gifts" between couples of the landowning elite during their lifetime. Although governed by Copenhagen, Norway had its own law code. In general, both partners in the countries' elites contributed mobile and immobile property to the marriage. In Norway, property within marriage was held separately and would automatically be redistributed to the respective heirs of each spouse after death, but it could also be held jointly. If couples entered a "joint property of halves", the surviving spouse would keep half the property, while the heirs of the deceased would be entitled to the other half. The practice of gift-giving (also common in Sweden and in Iceland) was mutual. It could range from sentimental but valuable items such as jewels or silver to large estates; it could come as factual exchange of material goods, as rights to usufruct, or as an abstract promise for the future. Often, gifts contained the transfer of real estate to women. By looking at contracts, donation letters, and court proceedings she investigates gendered aspects of marital gift exchange. In her central case study, a politically loaded court case between members of the highest Norwegian elites, the allodial land in question and one of the largest estates in Norway, after twenty years of conflict, was retrieved from the widow by force, as the court could not come to a verdict. The cases mentioned show that women did indeed own, possess, and use land.

The sources of the historian Rebecca Mason (London) stem from the early modern era in Glasgow, a vibrant city of international trade that doubled its population during the seventeenth century. Scots law presented a mixture of Roman, civil, canon, and custom law. In Scotland, heritable land mainly stayed undivided and was left to the firstborn son, with daughters only entitled to inherit this property upon the absence of brothers. Scottish women (who retained their natal surname in marriage) were often given mobile goods in lieu of land. In contrast to the Norwegian example, the author looks at movable goods and assets of the middling to lower strata of society. She conducts a quantitative analysis of approximately 6,000 final wills and testaments accompanied by inventories that were drawn either before death, containing a will, or after death, registered by the surviving spouse or kin, in Glasgow's commissary court (Reformed Church). Although there was a difference between testate and intestate succession, both procedures contained inventories of woman's properties. By a close examination of one hundred final wills and testaments, she accesses married women's property in detail. She investigates what kinds of goods married women possessed; how they bequeathed them to their husbands, children, and kin; and how the practice reflects their ideas of ownership. Mason's findings show a gendered pattern of property possession within marriage and beyond. Similar to the German custom and the Norwegian example, Scots singled out "the best" items that were appointed to the eldest son before the distribution of property. This insightful study shows that even though the majority of movable goods, such as livestock, household furnishings, kitchen utensils, and money, were understood as owned by the husband, they appeared as women's property in intestate inventories, and explicitly by way of wills women claimed and distributed them as their own.

The historian Siglinde Clementi (Bolzano) examines the relations between women, men, and property within a group of landed Tyrolean nobles (among others the families of Wolkenstein-Trostburg, Welsperg, and Spaur) who, as barons, certainly were part of the social elites but nonetheless depended on the ruling elites of the princes of the Holy Roman Empire. Tyrol in the sixteenth and seventeenth centuries constituted a "hybrid" space, in a cultural, political, and legal sense, in which traditions and rules from German-speaking lands to the north and Italy to the south overlapped. The flexibility of the legal culture and custom becomes evident as the author compares regional and transregional marriages. Marriage contracts, receipts, letters of renunciation, widows' endowments, and private correspondences allow the researcher to access the family's strategies to protect and convey property. Despite the fundamentally patrilineal pattern in the background of an elite that largely depended on allodial property or fiefdoms, Clementi argues that the symbolic meaning, which she calls the "ideational component" of the material objects, requires greater attention. Marriage and its legal prerequisites, such as the marriage contract, can be identified as the crucial moment in which the material value of property is thoroughly scrutinised and compared and the abstract qualities of objects or land as well as the connotations and meanings of dynastic identity they carry become visible. Since property and possession, as well as usufruct, for both men and women carry social and cultural capital within their respective social ranks and as markers of distinction towards other ranks, they are turned into material representations of dynastic "honour".

Part III brings together two case studies from the seventeenth and eighteenth centuries and reflects on the question of if and how access to land was enhanced or restricted to women. The social and economic historian Janine Maegraith (Vienna/Cambridge) links fences, as common material surroundings and part of everyday life in both the countryside and towns, to "legal, social, institutional, and political conditions for women's access to landed property". Fences define spaces, block pathways, and keep spheres apart. They do so in a very unobtrusive manner and are hardly consciously realised. Their legal status in respect to mobility or immobility in early modern times is unclear. The fence represented (and still does) the border of the land and forms part of the real estate but certainly could be dismantled and moved. In rural Tyrol, a landscape characterised by farmhouses in an Alpine region, fences as "material signifiers of property" structured space and separated common ground from privately owned land. Ownership of land has been predominantly associated with men, as inheritance patterns privileged sons over daughters in respect to its transfer. In this sense, a fence as a gender-neutral type of object turns into a visual representation of gender inequality and unequal division of economic chances and social status, as landownership formed the core of a society that was still largely based on subsistence farming. The author studies women's access to landed property in the late sixteenth and early seventeenth centuries by investigating purchase deeds of real estate from the town court of Brixen and the manorial court of Sonnenburg. She correlates types of landed property (building, farms, and land) with the gender of buyers and sellers and thus shows statistically considerable market participation by women in Sonneburg of ten percent at the beginning of the seventeenth century and their complete disappearance as active buyers and sellers in 1670. Maegraith assumes that limited access to credit markets and obstacles created by practices of inheritance prevented women from access to landed property and deprived them of its social and economic benefits.

Fatma Gül Karagöz looks at law and custom in respect to immobile property in the Ottoman Empire during the first half of the eighteenth century. Her sources are comprised of court records from two towns in rural areas: Vidin (in today's Bulgaria) in the far northwest, near the border of the Habsburg Empire, and Antakya (the famous Antiochia) in the south, near the border with Syria. In both Sharia courts, more than one-third of the cases concerning property rights of real estate involved women. The Ottoman code of law recognised two kinds of immobile property. On the one hand, gardens or buildings could be privately owned and alienated in accordance with the desire of their owners, male or female, and had to be distributed after standard inheritance patterns. On the other hand, all agricultural land in general remained the property of the state and came under the rights of usufruct. Because of the war and climate-induced crisis of the seventeenth century, the land was deserted, and the empire lacked subjects to maintain farm produce. As a consequence, the rights to usufruct were expanded to women, who now could claim empty land or become the beneficiaries of the transfer of usufruct rights. As both forms of property rights had to follow different procedures of transfer, this led to complex legal situations. Frequently, the land would come under the right of usufruct, while the buildings or trees upon it would be privately owned. Although Ottoman law in general prescribed the marital separation of goods, men were privileged over women, both in the context of the transfer of private property (sons always received double the share of daughters) and in respect to usufruct rights. The findings seem to suggest a tendency towards monetisation of privately owned real estate and indirect activity of women as usufruct owners.

Part IV looks at the relation between women and property in the two colonial contexts of Jamaica and Brazil. In respect to private law, both the English and Portuguese colonies partly transferred law and custom from England and Portugal to the colonies, only to adopt them to local realities. Thus, both case studies present examples in which custom and practices deviated from European law and thereby developed different patterns of property transfer and a "more equal" distribution of wealth between men and women. Both examples were slaveholding societies based on ideas of ethnic inequality and whose economies depended on the exploitation of African or indigenous people. The system's continuity was secured by legally defining slave status as hereditary and by objectifying enslaved people, treating them as movable assets. While Jamaica was a melting pot of various denominations of colonisers and ethnically diverse slaveholders, Brazil's elite was predominantly Roman Catholic. The mixture of the slaveholder society, the geographical conditions of each place, the high mortality rates, and the influence of various denominations led to similar but different developments that brought about a change in gender roles, allowing women far more control of their property and more economic independence.

The historian Christine Walker (Singapore) looks at Jamaica during its time as an English colony, from 1655 until the abolition of slavery in 1834, focussing on the eighteenth century. In her thorough investigation of wills and testaments, she claims that by simply categorising enslaved people as movable property rather than as part of the real estate, it was much easier to convey captives to women. Although Jamaica in law and practice differed from the coverture regime and inheritance pattern of English common law, it was still more popular to transfer landed property to men and movable property to women. As a new and valuable form of movable property, slaves comprised large parts of women's wealth. In a convincing estimation, Walker states that eighty percent of women were slaveholders and had their share of both the cruelty of slaveholding and the economically profitable exploitation of captives. On average, a female colonist in Jamaica had nearly twenty times as much property as a Briton and enjoyed extensive legal authority. She argues that this developed out of the necessity to perpetuate the mechanism of the slaveholding society, which led as a result to an empowerment of women in Jamaica.

In her contribution, the lawyer Luisa Stella de Oliveira Coutinho Silva (Frankfurt/Main) takes us to Brazil during its period as a Portuguese colony, from the mid-sixteenth to early nineteenth century. As a political strategy, Portugal divided the colony into administrative districts. With the aim of economically developing and best exploiting the country, heritable pieces of land (*sesmarias*) were granted to individuals by the king. The author shows that women of all ages claimed control of land and privileges that their fathers held for their own benefit through different laws of succession. They succeeded as both independent possessors of immobile estates and legitimate heirs to titles and offices, the latter of which would turn into an abstract form of a dowry and was handed over to the future husband. Special attention is drawn to "virginity" as a legal status, for the loss of which women could sue the man in question for a dowry appropriate to her "social value". The author investigates women as landholders, the possession of privileges as part of women's dowries, and slaves as property legally categorised as half-movables. Her primary sources are women's letters to the Portuguese crown that claim the confirmation of land grants. Her examples demonstrate the importance of the dowry in the colonial context, highlight strategies of property transfer in cases of cocubinage and illegitimate children via gifts and transfer during one's lifetime, and illustrate female mutual support via final wills and testaments against the prescribed inheritance order of the letter of the law.

Part V presents examples from the early to third quarter of the nineteenth century and looks at the monetisation of property in geographically, politically, and culturally transitory zones. Not surprisingly, the nineteenth century – as a transitory phase in respect to nation-building, urbanisation, changing work conditions, changing family structures, and bourgeois gender-related behavioural concepts – established global markets and a blossoming consumer society with the quickly changing tastes and fashion, especially in urban contexts, across Europe. This affected not so much the immobile object world but the esteemed durability of most types of objects within the category of movable objects.[42] This led to a devaluation of movables, a decrease within formerly flourishing second-hand markets, and a steeper time curve in the life cycle of each object, ranging from praised newly acquired to out-of-use and superfluous items.[43] The smaller the item, the more movable and the faster the process of its substitution. Furniture, such as a four-poster bed, might survive the use of more than one generation; clothing and accessories, by contrast, were subject to quickly changing tastes. Textiles could be reused and adapted to a more modern style, handed down to younger relatives, or turned into rags and finally end up as part of paper production. This devaluation process might have been true as a general tendency but was surely not the case for valuables such as jewellery, which functioned as capital treasury, or emotionally loaded family relics. The function of an immobile object was basically unaltered in respect to shelter, economics, and even material representation of a family's origin. But while the value of a house, farmland, or meadow retained its value, the value of mobile assets decreased considerably. The stomacher that had been part of the trousseau became unimportant in itself and was replaceable by any other stomacher as fashion, social status, and the rules of decorum might dictate. Because of this development, the abstract monetary value of a mobile item became more important than the item as such. In consequence, by translating objects into monetary values, sources show a monetisation of mobile goods. Certainly, in times of need, mobile goods have always presented the easiest access to cash; mobile property can be sold or pawned, and the money gained by the sale can be used for an altogether different purpose.[44] The legally enforced monetary evaluation of property adhered to the state's wish to exert more control and paid tribute to societies that became more dynamic and flexible in every aspect of living. Slowly, this turned mobile items into abstract values. This was definitely true for urban contexts and towns, but as expected, development in rural areas was delayed. The southern Italian, Greek, and Romanian examples all represent transitory zones or use examples from border regions between different countries, cultures, and landscapes.

The historian Ida Fazio (Palermo) looks at a small, secluded community on the volcanic island of Stromboli, located far from the coast of Sicily and reachable only by boat. In this part of the Kingdom of Sicily, women in the nineteenth century outnumbered men. The combination of these aspects created a climate that provided fertile ground for the coexistence of several legal systems and a number of local customary laws. The author's findings point to a differentiated treatment of immobile property according to social class: While peasants tended to include houses in dowries to attract young workers, the higher the social status, the more likely the estate would be handed down to firstborn sons. By looking at judicial proceedings, marriage contracts, wills, post-mortem inventories, and travel reports from the early nineteenth century, she manages to shed light on the daily life of women of the lower classes and on their relationship with mobile goods of all kinds. In a microanalysis, she studies an exceptional court case brought before the court of the Kingdom of Sicily in 1811, which reveals the collaboration of pirates ransacking ships in the Tyrrhenian Sea and several inhabitants of Stromboli, where the illegal cargo was regularly discharged. The combined analysis of the different sources reveals women as landowners and owners of objects and tools for agriculture and fishing. It shows the active participation of women in all areas of the economic life on the island, legal or illegal, and their intense trading activity via boats within this "border economy". Fazio's thorough and thoughtful contribution and her intricate example are emblematic of the intended approach of this volume. She questions our traditional modes of analysis of written sources and calls for a new and a subtle "reading between the lines" if we want to investigate the relation between people and objects in history. We should turn our attention to "ephemeral traces", as Fazio phrases it, and to habit and custom, such as the informal maintenance and administration practices of the time.

In his example, the historian Evdoxios Doxiadis' (Vancouver) focusses on Greece in the early nineteenth century. The author compares the dowry custom of Ottoman Greece before 1829 to legally enforced practices after the Greek Revolution in 1821 and the foundation of the Greek monarchy in 1832. The bankrupt Greek state introduced a stamp duty on marriage contracts in 1843. This had three severe consequences: Many of the poorer couples avoided official contracts, only women who had a marriage contract could legally claim their dowry at court, and the mobile and immobile dowry was given a monetary value. By looking at court cases and marriage contracts of different regions, the author argues that during the nineteenth century, the stamp duty led to a monetisation of property and, eventually, to an alienation of women from their property that in fact resembled an expropriation and disinheritance. Before the revolution, a wide range of heritage and dowry patterns existed regionally, from equal division among all siblings to privileging the youngest daughter.

The historian Nicoleta Roman (Bucharest) looks at one hundred dowry contracts drawn up in the third quarter of the nineteenth century in the courts of two towns, Pitești and Câmpulung, in Wallachia in today's Romania in order to access information on the property of women of the "middling classes" who entered marriage. The province of Wallachia was sandwiched between the Habsburg, Russian, and Ottoman empires, by which it was controlled politically, but it adhered to the

Orthodox Church. In Wallachia, cultural and legal traditions of Eastern and Western models and customs were merged together. In a phase of transfer from ecclesiastical to state control, the obligation to register women's dowries was introduced in the eighteenth century and legally enforced in the nineteenth. The dowry contract not only explicitly listed traditional mobile goods, animals, and money but also frequently included immobile goods such as houses and shops as well as gypsy slaves, who were seen as a kind of immobile yet animated object. Forty-one percent of the dowry contracts included gypsy slaves as property. In the dowry contracts analysed, while immobile property was never given a monetary value, all mobile items of the dowry needed to be valued in monetary terms. Once registered, the sum entered in the dowry contract was legally protected, i.e. from the husband's debts, and could be reclaimed when widowed. Thus, one of the couple's many strategies was to enlarge the sum entered to protect the husband's property within the institution of the dowry. By empirically analysing all mobile goods entered in the dowry contracts, the author establishes an image of a hybrid culture that dwelled between custom and law, tradition and modernity, East and West. Items varied between old and new and between homemade and luxury, showing a trickle-down effect. In total, the mobile and immobile goods demonstrate a consumption pattern of a new type of bourgeoisie that was on the lookout for different cultural models viewed against the backdrop of the tradition and custom of the region.

Part VI, presented by the historian Margareth Lanzinger (Vienna), concludes our volume and represents a synthesis. It draws on all topics and themes that have appeared throughout the book and bridges different geographical areas in a diachronic, comparative way. Her highly intricate contribution states that we should not investigate mobile and immobile property separately, but rather should understand them as interconnected and interrelated categories, deeply embedded in historical contexts in need of consideration. The author points to the fact that the categories as such changed over time and were flexible to a certain extent. Mobile and immobile property created a basis for subsistence: Both entailed legal properties, and both could be containers of value and status symbols. Although normative literature has paid less attention to mobile goods, both forms of property could symbolise a family's origin and its continuation. The multitude of contents hidden beneath the term "immobile" have an indicatory function of their owners or occupants and social milieu and functioned as primary economic resources. But we should take into consideration, as the author analyses, that only by the end of the Middle Ages and the beginning of the era of early modernity did landed property become heritable. Nonetheless, ownership models such as tenure and copyhold remained valid. To own or not to own landed property shaped inner-familial power relations and indicated "situated practices based on particular concepts of gender". The important question, according to Lanzinger, is thus, Who had access to what kind of immobile property? The relation or even gaps between norm and practice were of utmost importance and opened up options for agency. As the marital property regime was at the centre of the distribution pattern, she compares systems of separation to systems of joint property regimes and the consequences for the agnate and cognate lineage. Of all the known types of movables, from clothing to weapons, the family documents we use as sources themselves deserve attention insofar as they represent an understudied category of objects. Within movable goods, the bed had a special symbolic value for the married couple. Lanzinger points to the fact that mobile goods needed to be replaced far more often due to their lack of durability, which touched on market issues. She also raises the question of the legal status of movables and suggests that many, despite their official status, were of a more "tenurial nature". An indicator of ownership was the visibility of the relation between people and things in everyday contexts that could be observed by neighbours. In many regions it was women's physical control over things locked away in a drawer, to which they held the key, that proved ownership. After looking at possible modes of transfer, she investigates the social and economic networks of relations each object is inscribed in and the ambivalence and flexibility of the typology as such. The increase in simply defining certain assets as movable led to a strengthening of couples, women, and secondborn sons. But what are the links between landed property and mobile goods? The dowry or marriage portion was understood as a loan and could be turned into landed property or the usufruct thereof. Mobile and immobile goods could be linked by credit relations. Mobile possessions could also be exchanged "for guarantees of provision". Also, mobile goods were gradually understood as integral components of the house and slowly turned into monetary assets. The categorising of objects became even more difficult once confronted with debts and the question as to whether work tools of proto-industry were to be considered mobile or immobile. The author concludes that we should not apply a polar view regarding the categories examined in this book, but rather what is necessary is a multi-dimensional and nuanced approach. She emphasises her hope for a "productive exchange between social, economic, and legal history and material culture studies", with which I can wholeheartedly agree.

III. Terminology, maps, and drawings

The incredible chance to compare different legal cultures in different countries and social strata in early modernity also has its pitfalls. English, as the unifying language of this volume, does not offer terminology that explains the different meanings of terms, say in Greek, Romanian, or Portuguese. The term "dowry" appears in each chapter, but it does not always mean "dowry" in the English sense. It can imply paraphernal goods as well as a bridal gift or morning gift, or it can refer to capital reserved for widowhood. What the term "dowry" means in each case has to be established from its precise social, local, and legal context.

Most of the chapters are accompanied by a map, indicating the geographical area and localities focussed on; as far as possible, we also integrated schematic drawings of heritage models favoured in each example to faciliate the comparison between legal and cultural landscapes represented in this book.

Notes

1 ThStA Gotha, Geheimes Archiv, B IV 67–72, vol. II, 294, 308–310. I am grateful to Prof. Dr. Dr. h.c. Heide Wunder for her inspiring comments. All translations of German originals by the author.

2 *Sachsenspiegel*, Erstes Buch, Landrecht, Artikel 3–5, C.V., folio 11v; see www.sachsen spiegel-online.de/export/index.html (accessed 20 February 2020).

3 *Allgemeines Landrecht für die Preussischen Staaten, Zweyte Auflage*, Berlin 1794 [Decker], Zweyter Theil: Von der Ehe, §. 206. "Lawfully Entrusted Assets Included What According to Its Nature Is Reserved for Use by the Wife", https://opinioiuris.de/quelle/1623#Fuenfter_Abschnitt._Von_den_Rechten_und_Pflichten_der_Eheleute_in_Beziehung_auf_ihr_Vermoegen (accessed 20 February 2020).

4 Zedler, Johann Heinrich, *Grosses vollständiges Universal Lexicon aller Wissenschafften und Künste*, Halle und Leipzig 1732–1754 [Zedler], vol. 10 (1735), col. 1043–1051, www.zedler-lexikon.de/ (accessed 20 February 2020); Johann Georg Krünitz, *OekonomischeEncyklopädie*, Berlin 1773–1858 [Pauli], vol. 17 (1779), col. 365–369, www.kruen itz1.uni-trier.de/home.htm (accessed 20 February 2020).

5 Gottlieb Siegmund Corvinus, *Nutzbares, galantes und curiöses Frauenzimmer-Lexicon*, Leipzig 1715 [Gleditsch], "Gerade", Col. 653–659, further editions 1739 and 1773.

6 Karin Gottschalk, "Does Property Have a Gender? Household Goods and Conceptions of Law and Justice in Early Modern Saxony", in: *Medieval History Journal* 8, 1 (2005), pp. 7–24. Also see Karin Gottschalk, *Eigentum, Geschlecht, Gerechtigkeit. Haushalten und Erben im frühneuzeitlichen Leipzig*, Frankfurt am Main 2003 [Campus]. Saxon law considered cattle and horses who were daily grazing on pasture part of the *Gerade*, but only if they were not used to pull a carriage. Sheep and pigs were defined as part of the morning gift and fell under a different distribution rule. The same was true for geese and ducks, who were commonly counted as *Gerade*. Other than in the noble context, beehives or bellows and other items belonged to the *Gerade* in the town of Halle, but only in contexts of the peasantry. Zedler, *Universal Lexicon*, vol. 10, Col. 1043–44. See also the contribution of Lanzinger in this volume.

7 "The priest has an equal share with his sister in the mother's *Gerade*", *Sachsenspiegel*, Book 1, V.3.

8 William Blackstone, *Commentaries on the Laws of England*, 2nd book, Of the Rights of Things, Oxford 1766 [Clarendon], "Of real property and first of corporeal hereditaments", p. 16.

9 "Natur der Sache", Krünitz, *OekonomischeEncyklopädie*, "Mobilien", vol. 92 (1803), col. 215–252, 223.

10 Deutsches Rechtswörterbuch online, https://drw-www.adw.uni-heidelberg.de/drw-cgi/zeige?index=woerterbtext&term=immobilibus (accessed 20 February 2020).

11 Zedler, *Universal Lexicon*, vol. 17, col. 1048.

12 Krünitz, *OekonomischeEncyklopädie*, "Mobilien", vol. 92, col. 240.

13 Zedler, *Universal Lexicon*, vol. 9, col. 102.

14 Krünitz, *OekonomischeEncyklopädie*, "Mobilien", vol. 92, col. 216.

15 Blackstone, *Commentaries*, p. 18.

16 Raffaella Sarti, *Europe at Home. Family and Material Culture 1500–1800*, New Haven and London 2002 [Yale University Press], p. 38.

17 "wash basins, whether embedded in the wall/ floors or not", Krünitz, *Oekonomische Encyklopädie*, vol. 17, col. 367.

18 Giorgio Riello and Ulinka Rublack (eds.), *The Right to Dress: Sumptuary Laws in a Global Perspective, c. 1299–1800*, Cambridge and New York 2019 [Cambridge University Press].

19 Merry Wiesner-Hanks, "Difference and Similarity: A Global Perspective", in: Grethe Jacobsen and Heide Wunder (eds.), *East Meets West: A Gendered View of Legal Tradition*, Kiel 2015 [Solivagus], pp. 206–226.

20 On the concept of usufruct, see Henry Goudy, "Roman Law", in: *Encyclopædia Britannica*, Cambridge 1911, vol. 23, p. 569, https://en.wikisource.org/wiki/1911_Encyclop%C3%A6dia_Britannica/Roman_Law (accessed 20 February 2020).

21 John Styles, *The Dress of the People. Everyday Fashion in Eighteenth-Century England*, New Haven and London 2007 [Yale University Press], cf. p. 4 on the limitations of inventories in respect to research on the poor.

22 Inventory 1804, "1) Immobilibus (nil), 2) Capitalien (= assets, nil), 3) Baarschaften (= Cash, nil), 4) Gold (nil), 5) Silber (= Silver, nil)", Property of Johanna Bernhard née Wolfing, 2 March 1804, Kassel (Hess.StAM, Protokolle 2 Kassel A2 vol. 9). See Jochen Ebert, "und baten ihr Ehe-Verlöbnis edictmäßig ad Protocollum zu nehmen". Eheprotokolle als sozial- und wirtschaftshistorische Quelle", in: Alexander Jendorff and Andrea Pühringer (eds.), *Pars pro toto. Historische Miniaturen zum 75. Geburtstag von Heide Wunder*, Neustadt Aisch 2014 [Schmidt], pp. 213–226.

23 Sarti, *Europe at Home*, p. 38.

24 Back in 1766, William Blackstone wrote "neither does any thing vary more than the right of inheritance under different national establishments". Blackstone, *Commentaries*, p. 12.

25 Karin Gottschalk (ed.), *Gender Difference in European Legal Cultures – Historical Perspectives*, Stuttgart 2013 [Steiner]; Grethe Jacobsen and Heide Wunder (eds.), *East Meets West: A Gendered View of Legal Tradition*, Kiel 2015 [Solivagus]; Anna Bellavitis and Beatrice Zucca Micheletto (eds.), *Gender, Law and Economic Well-Being in Europe from the Fifteenth to the Nineteenth Century – North Versus South?* Abingdon 2019 [Routledge].

26 "[I]n real estates, males are prefer(r)ed to females . . . in the division of personal estates, the females of equal degrees are admitted together with the males". Blackstone, *Commentaries*, p. 13. Legally, in the Holy Roman Empire two patterns of inheritance existed, the first of which was primogeniture, in which the lion's share of the parents' property was conveyed to one descendent ony – usually the firstborn but also possibly the lastborn (ultimogeniture). The second model distributed all parental property equally between siblings, mobile and immobile (real division). Both models had large impacts not only on the economic and social options of each person but also on the structuring of the landscape. In the northwest of the empire, large agrarian estates dominated, while in the middle and southwest small and even inefficient pieces of land shaped the landscape. Still, early modern patterns of succession are visible in the cultural layout of our landscapes even today.

27 Hanna Östholm and Cristina Prytz, "Less Than Ideal? Making a Living Before and Outside Marriage", in: Maria Ågren (ed.), *Making a Living, Making a Difference. Gender and Work in Early Modern European Society*, Oxford 2017 [Oxford University Press], pp. 103–126.

28 Foto © Archiv des Instituts für Kunstgeschichte der LMU München. See Horst Ludwig *et al.*, *Münchner Maler im 19. Jahrhundert*, vol. IV, Munich 1983 [Bruckmann], p. 192.

29 For a discussion of involuntary object usage, see Roger Carles Richardson, *Household Servants in Early Modern England*, Manchester 2010 [Manchester University Press], pp. 96–123; Styles, *Dress of the People*, chapters 15–17. "Many things people used, treated and spoke of as their own were supplied to them on terms which removed choice [. . .] in other words, we need to recognise the diversity of means by which they sustained an engagement with things." Styles, *Dress of the People*, p. 321.

30 Mary Chan and Nancy E. Wright, "Marriage, Identity and the Pursuit of Property in Seventeenth-Century England: The Cases of Anne Clifford and Elizabeth Wiseman", in: Nancy E. Wright and Margaret W. Ferguson (eds.), *Women, Property, and the Letters of the Law in Early Modern England*, Toronto 2004 [Toronto University Press], pp. 162–182, p. 163; Martine Segalen, "Material Conditions of Family Life", in: David Kertzer and Marzio Barbagli (eds.), *Family Life in the Long Nineteenth Century 1789–1913*, New Haven and London 2002 [Yale University Press], pp. 3–39.

31 Stefan Brakensiek, "Generationengerechtigkeit? Normen und Praxis im Erb- und Ehegüterrecht 1500–1850: eine Einführung", in: Stefan Brakensiek, Michael Stolleis and Heide Wunder (eds.), *Generationengerechtigkeit? Normen und Praxis im Erb- und Ehegüterrecht 1500–1850*, Berlin 2006 [Duncker & Humblot], (Zeitschrift für historische Forschung: Beiheft 37), pp. 1–21, p. 18.
32 Annette Caroline Cremer, *Mon Plaisir. Die Puppenstadt der Auguste Dorothea von Schwarzburg (1666–1751)*, Weimar and Vienna 2015 [Böhlau], pp. 170–191.
33 See the discussion of the terminology and historical fields in Merry Wiesner-Hanks, *Gender in History*, Oxford 2001 [Blackwell].
34 Silvana Seidel Menchi (ed.), *Marriage in Europe, 1400–1800*, Toronto and London [University of Toronto Press] 2016; Grethe Jacobsen, Helle Vogt, Inger Dübeck and Heide Wunder (eds.), *Less Favored- More Favored. Proceedings from a Conference on Gender in European Legal History, 12th-19th Centuries*, Copenhagen 2004, http://www5.kb.dk/da/nb/publikationer/fundogforskning-online/less_more/ (accessed 20 February 2020).
35 Roberta Gilchrist, *Gender and Material Culture: The Archaeology of Religious Women*, London and New York 1994 [Routledge]; Katharine Martinez (ed.), *The Material Culture of Gender, the Gender of Material Culture* [Henry Francis du Pont Winterthur Museum], Winterthur 1997 [University Press of New England]; Moira Donald and Linda Hurcombe (eds.), *Gender and Material Culture in Archaeological Perspective*, Basingstoke 2000 [Macmillan]; Jane Eva Baxter, *The Archaeology of Childhood: Children, Gender, and Material Culture*, Walnut Creek, CA 2005 [AltaMira Press].
36 Daniel Roche, *A History of Everyday Things: The Birth of Consumption in France, 1600–1800*, Cambridge 2000 [Cambridge University Press]; Sarti, *Europe at Home*, 2002.
37 Styles, *The Dress of the People*; Ulinka Rublack, *Dressing Up. Cultural Identity in Renaissance Europe*, Oxford 2010 [Oxford University Press]; Ludmilla Jordanova, *The Look of the Past: Visual and Material Evidence in Historical Practice*, Cambridge 2012 [Cambridge University Press]; Renata Ago, *Gusto for Things: A History of Objects in Seventeenth-Century Rome*, Chicago 2013 [Chicago University Press].
38 Evelyn Welch, *Shopping in the Renaissance. Consumer Cultures in Italy 1400–1600*, New Haven, CT and London 2005 [Yale University Press]; Giorgio Riello, *A Foot in the Past. Consumers, Producers and Footwear in the Long Eighteenth Century*, Oxford 2006 [Oxford University Press]; John Styles and Amanda Vichery (eds.), *Gender, Taste, and Material Culture in Britain and North America 1700–1830*, New Haven and London 2006 [Yale University Press]; Hannah Greig, Jane Hamlett and Leonie Hannan (eds.), *Gender and Material Culture in Britain since 1600*, London 2015 [Macmillan]; Frank Trentmann, *Empire of Things. How We Became a World of Consumers from the Fifteenth Century to the Twenty-first*, London 2016 [Allen Lane]; Antony Buxton, *Domestic Culture in Early Modern England*, Woodbridge 2015 [Boydell & Brewer] (Studies in Early Modern Cultural, Political and Social History, v. 24).
39 Some areas in the Holy Roman Empire privileged the youngest son or daughter (see Jürgen Schlumbohm, *Lebensläufe. Familien, Höfe, Die Bauern und Heuerleute des Osnabrückischen Kirchspiels Belm in proto-industrieller Zeit, 1650–1860*, Göttingen 1994 [Vandenhoeck & Ruprecht]), while other areas divided the property among all heirs (male and female) equally in principle (see David Warren Sabean, *Kinship in Neckarhausen, 1700–1870*, Cambridge 1998 [Cambridge University Press]; *Property, Production, and Family in Neckarhausen, 1700–1870*, Cambridge 1990 [Cambridge University Press]).
40 See the comprehensive bibliography in the introduction of Bellavitis and Micheletto (eds.), *Gender, Law and Economic Well-Being*, pp. 21–28; Peter N. Miller, "About an Inventory. A Conversation Between Natalie Zemon Davis and Peter N. Miller", in: Deborah Krohn and Peter N. Miller (eds.), *Dutch New York, Between East and West, The World of Margrieta van Varick*, New Haven, CT 2009 [Yale University Press], pp. 117–129.
41 Knud Haakonssen, "Early-modern Natural Law", in: George Duke and Robert P. George (eds.), *Cambridge Companion to Natural Law Jurisprudence*, Cambridge 2017

[Cambridge University Press], pp. 76–102; John J. Coughlin, *Law, Person, and Community. Philosophical, Theological, and Comparative Perspectives on Canon Law*, Oxford 2012 [Oxford University Press].
42 Jacobsen and Wunder (eds.), *East Meets West*, Introduction, pp. 9–22, p. 14.
43 Asa Briggs, *Victorian Things*, London 1990 [Penguin].
44 Matteo Pompermaier, "Women and Credit in Eighteenth-century Venice: A Preliminary Analysis", in: Anna Bellavitis and Beatrice Zucca Micheletto (eds.), *Gender, Law and Economic Well-Being in Europe from the Fifteenth to the Nineteenth Century – North Versus South?* Abingdon 2019 [Routledge], pp. 183–199.

Bibliography

Archival sources and manuscripts

Germany, Gotha, Thüringisches Staatsarchiv, Geheimes Archiv, B IV 67–72, vol. II. (=ThStA Gotha).
Germany, Marburg, Hessisches Staatsarchiv, Protokolle 2 Kassel A2 Bd. 9 (=Hess. StAM).
Repgow, Eike von, *Sachsenspiegel*, Herzog August Library Wolfenbüttel, Cod. Guelf. 3.1, 2 August, www.sachsenspiegel-online.de/export/index.html (accessed 20 February 2020).

Sources

Allgemeines Landrecht für die Preussischen Staaten, Zweyte Auflage, Berlin 1794 [Decker], https://opinioiuris.de/quelle/1622 (accessed 20 February 2020).
Blackstone, William, *Commentaries on the Laws of England, 2nd book, Of the Rights of Things*, Oxford 1766 [Clarendon].
Corvinus, Gottlieb Siegmund, *Nutzbares, galantes und curiöses Frauenzimmer-Lexicon*, Leipzig 1715 [Gleditsch].
Deutsches Rechtswörterbuch online, vol. I–XIII, Berlin 1932–1956, Heidelberg 1957–2020 [Heidelberger Akademie der Wissenschaften], https://drw-www.adw.uni-heidelberg.de/drw-cgi/zeige (accessed 20 February 2020).
Krünitz, Johann Georg, *Oekonomische Encyklopädie*, Berlin 1773–1858 [Pauli], www.kruenitz1.uni-trier.de/home.htm (accessed 20 February 2020).
Zedler, Johann Heinrich, *Grosses vollständiges Universal Lexicon aller Wissenschafften und Künste*, Halle und Leipzig 1732–1754 [Zedler], www.zedler-lexikon.de/ (accessed 20 February 2020).

Research bibliography

Ago, Renata, *Gusto for Things. A History of Objects in Seventeenth-Century Rome*, Chicago 2013 [University of Chicago Press].
Ågren, Maria (ed.), *Making a Living, Making a Difference. Gender and Work in Early Modern European Society*, Oxford 2017 [Oxford University Press].
Ågren, Maria and Amy Louise Erickson (eds.), *The Marital Economy in Scandinavia and Britain 1400–1900*, Aldershot 2005 [Taylor & Francis].
Andersen, Per (ed.), *Law and Marriage in Medieval and Early Modern Times*, Copenhagen 2012 [DJOEF].
Batchelor, Jennie and Cora Kaplan (eds.), *Women and Material Culture, 1660–1830*, Basingstoke 2007 [Palgrave Macmillan].

Baxter, Jane Eva, *The Archaeology of Childhood: Children, Gender, and Material Culture*, Walnut Creek, CA 2005 [AltaMira Press].

Bellavitis, Anna and Beatrice Zucca Micheletto (eds.), *Gender, Law and Economic Well-Being in Europe from the Fifteenth to the Nineteenth Century – North versus South?* Abingdon 2019 [Routledge].

Brakensiek, Stefan, "Generationengerechtigkeit? Normen und Praxis im Erb- und Ehegüterrecht 1500–1850: eine Einführung", in: Stefan Brakensiek, Michael Stolleis and Heide Wunder (eds.), *Generationengerechtigkeit? Normen und Praxis im Erb- und Ehegüterrecht 1500–1850*, Berlin 2006 (Zeitschrift für historische Forschung: Beiheft, 37) [Duncker & Humblot], pp. 1–21.

Briggs, Asa, *Victorian Things*, London 1990 [Penguin].

Buck, Andrew, *Women, Property, and the Letters of the Law in Early Modern England*, 2nd ed., Toronto 2014 [University of Toronto Press].

Buxton, Antony, *Domestic Culture in Early Modern England*, Woodbridge 2015 [Boydell & Brewer].

Chan, Mary and Nancy E. Wright, "Marriage, Identity and the Pursuit of Property in Seventeenth-Century England: The Cases of Anne Clifford and Elizabeth Wiseman", in: Nancy E. Wright and Margaret W. Ferguson (eds.), *Women, Property, and the Letters of the Law in Early Modern England*, Toronto 2004 [Toronto University Press], pp. 162–182.

Coughlin, John J., *Law, Person, and Community. Philosophical, Theological, and Comparative Perspectives on Canon Law*, Oxford 2012 [Oxford University Press].

Cremer, Annette Caroline, *Mon Plaisir. Die Puppenstadt der Auguste Dorothea von Schwarzburg (1666–1751)*, Weimar and Vienna 2015 [Böhlau].

Derix, Simone and Margareth Lanzinger (eds.), *Housing. Capital, Resource and Representation*, Berlin 2017 [Degruyter], www.degruyter.com/downloadpdf/books/9783110532241/9783110532241-001/9783110532241-001.pdf.

Donald, Moira and Linda Hurcombe (eds.), *Gender and Material Culture in Archaeological Perspective*, Basingstoke 2000 [Macmillan].

Ebert, Jochen, ". . . und baten ihr Ehe-Verlöbnis edictmäßig ad Protocollum zu nehmen". Eheprotokolle als sozial- und wirtschaftshistorische Quelle", in: Alexander Jendorff and Andrea Pühringer (eds.), *Pars pro toto. Historische Miniaturen zum 75. Geburtstag von Heide Wunder*, Neustadt Aisch 2014 [Schmidt], pp. 213–226.

Erickson, Amy Louise, *Women and Property in Early Modern England*, London 1995 [Routledge].

French, Katherine L., "Genders and Material Cultures", in: Judith Bennett and Ruth Mazo Karras (eds.), *The Oxford Handbook of Women and Gender in Medieval Europe*, Oxford 2013 [Oxford University Press], pp. 197–212.

Gilchrist, Roberta, *Gender and Material Culture. The Archaeology of Religious Women*, London and New York 1994 [Routledge].

Glendon, Mary, *The Transformation of Family Law. State, Law, and Family in the United States and Western Europe*, Chicago 1989 [University of Chicago Press].

Gottschalk, Karin, *Eigentum, Geschlecht, Gerechtigkeit. Haushalten und Erben im frühneuzeitlichen Leipzig*, Frankfurt am Main 2003 [Campus].

———, "Does Property Have a Gender? Household Goods and Conceptions of Law and Justice in Early Modern Saxony", in: *Medieval History Journal* 8, 1 (2005), pp. 7–24.

———, (ed.), *Gender Difference in European Legal Cultures – Historical Perspectives*, Stuttgart 2013 [Steiner].

Goudy, Henry, "Roman Law", in: *Encyclopædia Britannica*, Cambridge 1911, https://en.wikisource.org/wiki/1911_Encyclop%C3%A6dia_Britannica/Roman_Law (accessed 20 February 2020).

Greig, Hannah, Jane Hamlett and Leonie Hannan (eds.), *Gender and Material Culture in Britain since 1600*, London 2015 [Macmillan].

Haakonssen, Knud, "Early-modern Natural Law", in: George Duke and Robert P. George (eds.), *Cambridge Companion to Natural Law Jurisprudence*, Cambridge 2017 [Cambridge University Press], pp. 76–102.

Howell, Martha C., *The Marriage Exchange. Property, Social Place, and Gender in Cities of the Low Countries, 1300–1550*, Chicago and London 1998 [University of Chicago].

Jacobsen, Grethe, Helle Vogt, Inger Dübeck and Heide Wunder (eds.), *Less Favored - More Favored*, Proceedings from a Conference on Gender in European Legal History, 12th–19th Centuries, Copenhagen 2004, http://www5.kb.dk/da/nb/publikationer/fundog forskning-online/less_more/ (accessed 20 February 2020).

Jacobsen, Grethe and Heide Wunder (eds.), *East Meets West: A Gendered View of Legal Tradition*, Kiel 2015 [Solivagus].

Jordanova, Ludmilla, *The Look of the Past: Visual and Material Evidence in Historical Practice*, Cambridge 2012 [Cambridge University Press].

Kuehn, Thomas, *Family and Gender in Renaissance Italy, 1300–1600*, Cambridge 2017 [Cambridge University Press].

Ludwig, Horst, *Münchner Maler im 19. Jahrhundert*, vol. IV, Munich 1983 [Bruckmann].

Martinez, Katharine (ed.), *The Material Culture of Gender, the Gender of Material Culture [Henry Francis du Pont Winterthur Museum]*, Winterthur 1997 [University Press of New England].

Miller, Peter N., "About an Inventory. A Conversation Between Natalie Zemon Davis and Peter N. Miller", in: Deborah Krohn and Peter N. Miller (eds.), *Dutch New York, Between East and West, the World of Margrieta van Varick*, New Haven, CT 2009 [Yale University Press], pp. 117–129.

Östholm, Hanna and Cristina Prytz, "Less Than Ideal? Making a Living before and Outside Marriage", in: Maria Ågren (ed.), *Making a Living, Making a Difference. Gender and Work in Early Modern European Society*, Oxford 2017 [Oxford University Press], pp. 103–126.

Pompermaier, Matteo, "Women and Credit in Eighteenth-Century Venice: A Preliminary Analysis", in: Anna Bellavitis and Beatrice Zucca Micheletto (eds.), *Gender, Law and Economic Well-Being in Europe from the Fifteenth to the Nineteenth Century – North versus South?* Abingdon 2019 [Routledge], pp. 183–199.

Richardson, Roger Carles, *Household Servants in Early Modern England*, Manchester 2010 [Manchester University Press].

Riello, Giorgio, *A Foot in the Past. Consumers, Producers and Footwear in the Long Eighteenth Century*, Oxford 2006 [Oxford University Press].

Riello, Giorgio and Ulinka Rublack (eds.), *The Right to Dress: Sumptuary Laws in a Global Perspective, c. 1299–1800*, Cambridge and New York 2019 [Cambridge University Press].

Roche, Daniel, *A History of Everyday Things: The Birth of Consumption in France, 1600–1800*, Cambridge 2000 [Cambridge University Press].

Rublack, Ulinka, *Dressing up. Cultural Identity in Renaissance Europe*, Oxford 2010 [Oxford University Press].

Sabean, David Warren, *Property, Production, and Family in Neckarhausen, 1700–1870*, Cambridge 1990 [Cambridge University Press].

———, *Kinship in Neckarhausen, 1700–1870*, Cambridge 1998 [Cambridge University Press].

Sarti, Raffaella, *Europe at Home. Family and Material Culture 1500–1800*, New Haven and London 2002 [Yale University Press].

Schlumbohm, Jürgen, *Lebensläufe. Familien, Höfe, Die Bauern und Heuerleute des Osnabrückischen Kirchspiels Belm in proto-industrieller Zeit, 1650–1860*, Göttingen 1994 [Vandenhoeck & Ruprecht].

Segalen, Martine, "Material Conditions of Family Life", in: David Kertzer and Marzio Barbagli (eds.), *Family Life in the Long Nineteenth Century 1789–1913*, New Haven and London 2002 [Yale University Press], pp. 3–39.

Seidel Menchi, Silvana (ed.), *Marriage in Europe, 1400–1800*, Toronto and London 2016 [University of Toronto Press].

Spence, Cathryn, *Women, Credit, and Debt in Early Modern Scotland*, Manchester 2016 [Bonnier].

Stolleis, Michael, *Öffentliches Recht in Deutschland. Eine Einführung in seine Geschichte (16.-21. Jahrhundert)*, Munich 2014 [Beck].

Styles, John, *The Dress of the People. Everyday Fashion in Eighteenth-Century England*, New Haven and London 2007 [Yale University Press].

Styles, John and Amanda Vichery (eds.), *Gender, Taste, and Material Culture in Britain and North America 1700–1830*, New Haven and London 2006 [Yale University Press].

Trentmann, Frank, *Empire of Things. How We Became a World of Consumers from the Fifteenth Century to the Twenty-first*, London 2016 [Allen Lane].

Welch, Evelyn, *Shopping in the Renaissance. Consumer Cultures in Italy 1400–1600*, New Haven, CT and London 2005 [Yale University Press].

Wiesner-Hanks, Merry, *Gender in History*, Oxford 2001 [Blackwell].

———, "Difference and Similarity: A Global Perspective", in: Grethe Jacobsen and Heide Wunder (eds.), *East meets West: A Gendered View of Legal Tradition*, Kiel 2015 [Solivagus], pp. 206–226.

Wright, Nancy E. and Margaret W. Ferguson (eds.), *Women, Property, and the Letters of the Law in Early Modern England*, Toronto 2004 [Toronto University Press].

2

EARLY MODERN POLITICAL PHILOSOPHY ON RIGHTS OF OWNERSHIP

Amelie Stuart

ABSTRACT

One of the main questions of political philosophy concerns the justification of private property and its legitimate ownership. Most of the early modern contractarian theories placed the issue of private property at the centre of their argument. It was used to justify the sovereign's rule and authority as well as the citizens' duty to obey. In this context, I will look at two dimensions of legitimate ownership: First, how the right to private property was *normatively* justified in early modern contractarianism and, second, in which ways private property in the form of material goods could be legitimately acquired according to these theories. After closely examining each of these two positions regarding the rights of ownership and the normative value they place on private property, I will continue to look at the status of women in two exemplary property theories. John Locke and Jean-Jacques Rousseau presented several influential hypotheses concerning the status of women and their place in society and in the household. I will conclude by critically assessing both lines of argument, especially with regard to their considerations regarding the legal and civic status of female members within the state.

In 1600, Modesta Pozzo's work entitled *The Worth of Women* was published, eight years after her death, and dedicated to her daughter.[1] It was published under the pseudonym "Moderata Fonte". She wrote:

> When [a woman] takes a husband, especially if he's poor, as is often the case, what exactly does she gain from it, except that instead of being her own mistress and the mistress of her own money, she becomes a slave, and loses her liberty and, along with her liberty, her control over her own property, surrendering all she has to the man whom she has bought.[2]

Obviously, Fonte considered marriage – at least in Venice – to be of no advantage for the women of her time. Following Venetian law, married women lost their liberty in "a city as free as the sea itself", as she writes elsewhere, addressing the remarkable civic liberties the inhabitants of Venice enjoyed in the late sixteenth century. In addition to losing their liberty, once a Venetian woman married, her husband became the rightful owner of her property. As Fonte writes, "[I]f she were alone, without a husband, she *could* live like a queen on her dowry (more or less so, of course, according to her social position)."[3] The English translation is misleading here, as the verb "could" is in the irrealis mood in Italian. Fonte speaks here of the impossible: Marriage was a condition for dowry. There was no such thing as women living independently from their families on their own dowry.

This quote raises the two issues I will discuss in my chapter: First, the theoretical justification for private property within early modern property theories and, second, the reasons that were given for assuming that the relevant subjects within these theories were mostly adult, white, male persons. I will start by outlining some basic arguments of early modern property theories, and I will introduce two of their most prominent examples: The theories of John Locke (1632–1704) and Jean-Jacques Rousseau (1712–1778), respectively. Even though these property theories were developed in the early modern age, they have remained very influential to the present day in several ways. Not only are Locke's and Rousseau's property theories considered canonical as such, but they also shape and influence contemporary property theories. It is therefore worthwhile to look closely at some of their main assumptions and address their ambivalences and gender biases.

In the following, I will first address the terminological distinction between property and possessions because it is closely connected to the issue of rights to ownership. I will then introduce some main assumptions of normative theories concerning legitimate ways of acquiring property. I will do so by examining two dimensions of legitimate ownership: First, how private property can be legitimately acquired according to early modern theories in political philosophy and, second, how the right to private property is normatively justified according to these theories. Finally, I will turn to the question of who the relevant subjects in these theories actually are, with a special focus on the status of women. For my answer, I will draw on the theories of property by John Locke and Jean-Jacques Rousseau.

I. Private property and ownership

When we reflect on the right to ownership in political philosophy, two distinctions are helpful: The distinction between common and private property on the one hand and the distinction between possession and property on the other. The first is relevant for theories of acquisition since they are based on this distinction by assuming that any object owned by an individual was first common property, e.g. farming land. The second distinction is necessary when looking at the legal status of an object: Whether something is only in my possession or is actually my property has important consequences with regard to my rights and obligations concerning this object.

The right of individuals within the state to own private property (as opposed to collective property) has been debated by philosophers for centuries. Two main lines of argument can be distinguished here, going as far back as the writings of Plato and Aristotle. First, it is beneficial for an individual to own private property since it would, among other things, enable her to develop her virtues, thus rendering her capable of leading a happy life. This view can be traced to Aristotle.[4] Second, it is overall harmful for most individuals to own private property since it would foster the individual's vices, such as envy or greed. This would be a position brought forward in many of Plato's dialogues.[5] In addition, by creating a socioeconomic hierarchy, private property would increase power inequalities within a society, which would lead to conflicts within society.

These two differing perspectives on private property and its merits and dangers can also be found in the arguments of most thinkers in early modern political thought. Arguments concerning the legitimate ways of acquiring private property in particular were often shaped depending on which of these two views was favoured. For instance, in John Locke's well-known theory of property in his *Two Treatises of Government* (1689), we can find a number of arguments that strongly support the first concept of private property – namely, that it is overall beneficial for individuals to own property. According to Locke, private property is necessary for an individual's well-being, public safety, and stability.[6] By contrast, Rousseau's writings on property – for example his *Discourse on the Origin of Inequality* (1755) – emphasise the negative consequences owning private property might entail: The dependence on material goods, the loss of an individual's autonomy, and the development of and increase in power inequalities.

I would like to address the second distinction, that between property and possession, at more length, as it stands in close relation to the possibility of assuming a right to private property. Even though we can possess all kinds of material objects, not all of them, strictly speaking, are our property. The necessary conditions for a material object to be my property are as follows:

> An external object is my property, if I can exclude other people from the use of this object with their assumed consent, in case I can use it, perhaps under certain conditions, at will or consume it, and if I can sell it and/or at least bequeath it.[7]

While the condition of using an external object at will may not need further explanation, the first stipulation, that of excluding other people from the use of it, certainly has to be spelled out in more detail. On which grounds, we could ask, is a person allowed to exclude others?

To give a general definition of property, it is not enough to determine the legal relation of a person and an object. Additionally, an agreement on the claims of the owner against the non-owner and vice versa is needed. This is also (at least in part) the case with the claims of the present owner and the potential future owners (heirs). A specific agreement and the procedures that constitute it lie at the heart of (normative) claims to private property. Part of this agreement involves mutually binding rules. The reason for this is that social coexistence calls for procedures to regulate and permanently define claims on certain objects. Related to this is a codification of these rules and procedures for the acquisition and keeping of property. This codification is accompanied by the creation of an independent body, a jurisdiction. These generally accepted rules are binding for members, and non-compliance with these rules is punishable. The decision as to how ownership is defined may be rejected or redefined by the members of any given society. In sum, the distinction between possession and property relies on the idea of a (hypothetical) contract between the members of society, a contract that normatively grounds their right to claim an object as their own and to exclude others from using it. This normative claim can again be codified in terms of positive right. Thus, it is the legal title to a particular good that makes it the property of someone and not only her possession. Since this is of course only a very rough sketch of some background concepts concerning property, I will now introduce two exemplary positions on private property.

In §5 of his *Second Treatise of Government* John Locke states,

> Though men as a whole own the earth and all inferior creatures, every individual man has a property in his own person; this is something that nobody else has any right to. The labour of his body and the work of his hands, we may say, are strictly *his*. So when he takes something from the state that nature has provided and left it in, he mixes his labour with it, thus joining to it something that is his own; and in that way he makes it his property.[8]

Appropriation by labour thus causes the acquisition of something from common property and its transition into the private property of a person. But to be actually able to cultivate land, for instance, a person has to acquire it first and exclude others from its use. In other words, we can understand the idea of private property only when we add the idea of common ownership as its "other". Rousseau introduces the following criteria for determining the legitimacy of the right of the first occupier:

> [T]he following conditions are necessary: first, the land must not yet be inhabited; secondly, a man must occupy only the amount he needs for his subsistence; and, in the third place, possession must be taken, not by an empty ceremony, but by labour and cultivation, the only sign of proprietorship that should be respected by others, in default of a legal title.[9]

We here see clearly the precondition of all theories of property: Society. There have to be "others" who make boundaries such as "mine" and "yours" necessary.[10] The realities of living together and of possible conflicts with each other require laws and mutually binding contracts. One function of these contracts is to define legitimate ways through which private property can be acquired. Locke's "labour theory of property", as quoted above, introduces labour as a criterion for the legitimate acquisition of property, that is, separating an object from common property and turning this object into private property.

But why is it necessary at all for individuals to own property? There are two main reasons according to theorists such as Locke: An instrumental one and a moral one. Private property is of instrumental worth because it secures an individual's subsistence. Property is acquired through labour and serves to help an individual survive. But, of course, every individual is part of a family, and it would be wrong to neglect this when reading early modern philosophy. As Natalie Zemon Davis points out, the dimension of the future and the notions of strategy and planning became very important factors in early modern times.[11] One important aim of each family was to secure the existence of the next generation and, if possible, to provide for them in the best way possible. The same sentiment can also be found in Locke's work – for example when he emphasises the importance of defending the family's property for the sake of the next generation.[12]

"[I]t is impossible to conceive how property can come from anything but manual labour: for what else can a man add to things which he does not originally create, so as to make them his own property?" Rousseau writes in his *Discourse on the Origin of Inequality*.[13] At first glance, this seems to suggest a similarity between the position of both Locke and Rousseau. However, while Locke emphasises the positive aspects of private property, one could say that hardly any thinker of the time pointed as clairvoyantly and sharply to the negative aspects of private property as Rousseau did in his writings. It is not at all the case that Rousseau rejects private property altogether. Unlike Locke, however, Rousseau emphasises that the legitimate possession of private property should always be oriented towards the common good. In relation to the negative consequences of a political order that disregards the limitation of private property and does not strictly control the ways in which property is acquired, Rousseau criticises the social order of his time. Rousseau's criticism of the intensification of social inequalities and dependencies in his time is of a particular interest due to their continuation and intensification to the present day.

Against this background, Rousseau also argues that the state should protect the private property of its citizens and provide the framework for a legally legitimised property system. But according to him, every owner of private property is only a "trustee of the public good".[14] This is the basis for the legitimate right to property of the individual. Ownership of private property is only legitimate because it promotes the common good – for example because the concern for private property promotes a certain attachment to the home country. Therefore, private property enjoys an ambivalent status in Rousseau's political theory. It has a negative side because it enables and reinforces the inequalities and dependencies between human beings, and this leads to conflicts and war, according to Rousseau. But private property also has a functional side since the common good – and ultimately the state – can benefit from private property.

In short, one can say that in these theories the public sphere within the state is a place where individual rights of all kinds are exercised. We have also seen that the legitimisation of the modern state attributes a central role to the right to private property and its protection by the state. The state is rationally legitimised by two normative factors: First, it allows its citizens to live under conditions of permanent and stable ownership and, second, this property of the citizens is legally legitimised and protected by the institutional order. In short, the state is both a normative precondition of and the framework for legitimate private property. But since women are for the most part not considered able to become public agents, the subjects relevant to these theories are solely male persons.[15]

Having completed this examination of Locke's and Rousseau's positions regarding the right of ownership and the normative value they place on private property, I will now continue to look at the status of women in these two theories with regard to property rights. John Locke and, later, Jean-Jacques Rousseau presented a number of influential hypotheses concerning the status of women and their place in society and in the household. In the writings of both we can find arguments denying women straightforwardly the right to own private property (as in Rousseau) or granting them only limited rights to do so (as in Locke). In the remainder of the chapter, I will critically assess both lines of argument, especially regarding the legal and civic status of female members within the state.

II. The status of women within early modern theories of property

Within early modern normative political thought, reflections on the legitimacy of political rule were of particular importance, as the idea of divine right became increasingly precarious. Through a three-step contractarian argument, thinkers like Thomas Hobbes (1588–1679) and John Locke tried to explain the importance and function of the nation-state. Their main interest was the normative justification of political authority and the assessment of the legitimate limits of this rule. By developing arguments for political rule and certain restrictions on the autonomy of all members of the state, these theories make universal claims and yet are implicitly quite particular. As Jacqueline Broad and Karen Green, for instance, point out, "Though 'the citizen' is intended to be a universal concept, applicable to both men and women, on closer inspection it turns out to be reflective of male experience alone."[16] This means that within most of the respective theories it is (implicitly) assumed that the citizen of the envisioned nation-state is male, and all other members of the state are confined to the sphere of the household. This results in a tension between the universal claim all these theories seem to be making and the fact that, in most of them, women, together with other groups, such as slaves, servants, and unpropertied men, are regarded as unfit or unable to achieve morally good lives or participate in the public sphere.[17] Since the status of women is thus located outside the public sphere, these political theories do not consider them relevant subjects. Additionally, women are not considered to stand to the same degree as male inhabitants of the nation-state under the laws of reason and will, but mainly under the laws of nature.[18]

As Jean Elshtain points out, Locke's political theory and his assumption of separate spheres can best be understood when we take into account his empiricist epistemology:

> The split in Lockean epistemology between reason as formal rationality and passion as scarcely contained desire, and the notions of human personality erected upon it, *require* a public-private split of a particular kind, one that allows human beings to exist in two divergent spheres.[19]

These spheres, i.e. the state and the household, are necessary since they enable each person to lead a life according to his or her disposition. Regarding a person's position in a particular sphere, the notion of the contract is crucial. One reason for this is that both spheres are hierarchically structured. Under the assumption that all human beings are free and equal and have a desire for security,[20] political rule is based on free and mutual consent, and this is equally true for the patriarchal structure of the private sphere (in the family), as this order is also based on the consent of both parties, husband and wife. This assumption of basic equality, in combination with the marital contract, subsequently results in the limitation of the powers of the husband and father as the head of the family: He has no absolute power over the members of the family.[21]

Keeping this in mind, it is interesting to see that Locke is ambivalent within his property theory in relation to the gender dimension. In his *Two Treatises of Government*, he explicitly extends his property theory to women as well.[22] His basic assumption that each person owns the fruits of their labour and their own body also extends to women. But it is important to note that a woman's right to own property is only mentioned in the context of the family: She enjoys certain rights as a member of the family but not as an individual. In the sphere of the household, which is under the rule of "a Master of the Family",[23] women can have possessions and, of course, contribute to the overall household income, but since they do not have the status of a citizen, they cannot claim a legal right to private property in the public sphere. So even though Locke does not assume that in the private sphere women are subordinate to men, they are still not autonomous since they cannot be head of the family and cannot be part of the public sphere in order to claim property rights.

Thus, one could say that there is a tension in Locke's position on women's rights to ownership: The exercise of property rights is limited to cases in which the property of the family is threatened by outsiders. In these cases, and if the paterfamilias is absent, Locke mentions the possibility that his wife could replace him and fight (legally) for the property interests of the family and its heirs. However, within the family, especially in marriage, things are more complex. Locke states that in marriage sometimes husband and wife will have different opinions ("wills"). It seems therefore necessary that the "[r]ule should be placed somewhere, [and] it naturally falls to the Man's share, as the abler and the stronger".[24] And yet, according to Locke, the wife is still in "free and full possession of what by Contract is her peculiar Right, and gives the Husband no more power over her Life, than she has over his".[25] This seems to imply that although Locke assumes a natural inequality of men and women in some sense, at the same time they seem to have an equally strong claim to their individual property, meaning here "life, liberty and estate".[26] As Susan Moller Okin rightly states in this regard,

> When it does not suit his case or the prejudices of his time to promote women's equality, Locke appeals to "nature" to legitimize their subordination to men. With the patriarchal family thus reinstated, the exclusion of women from political rights is implicitly justified by the assumption that, as the head of his family, the father alone can represent its interests in the wider society.[27]

Locke's assumptions about gender equality regarding ownership rights are in stark contrast to Rousseau's conception of women regarding their education and position within society. Rousseau's statements about the inequality of men and women relate both to anatomy, i.e. the "natural" differences, and mental faculties. According to him, women cannot be considered citizens at all because it is in their nature to be inferior to men, and therefore the appropriate place for women is the patriarchally structured family.[28] Rousseau states in a way that is very similar to (and in fact almost identical with) Locke that

> [f]or various reasons derived from the nature of the matter, the father ought to command in the family. In the first place, the authority of the father and of the mother ought not to be equal; rather, there has to be a single government, and when opinions are divided there has to be one predominant voice that decides.[29]

Apart from this, Rousseau emphasises that when it comes to the education of their children, each of the parents has their own responsibility, and it is important that mother and father complement one another in raising a family. But Rousseau is far from granting the female members of the family any rights to private property, a fact that results from his understanding of the nature of women.

The concept of nature has a double meaning for Rousseau. On the one hand, nature is

> that which has been overcome, but on the other hand, also what has to be imitated. . . . It is chronologically set *before* the civil society . . .; but at the same time it is more original than civil society and forms the norm for social relations.[30]

Hence, there is a tension in Rousseau's thought between an equality of the sexes, in the sense that both belong to the species "human being", and the fact that all differences between man and woman are gender differences for him. For Rousseau, gender roles are synonymous with gender differences: "[A]nd by doing so, not only does he endorse traditional gender roles, but he also justifies those roles on the basis of anatomical-physiological gender differences."[31] Not only does Rousseau accept the assumption of a distinct separation between the public and private sphere, but he also buys into its underlying justification and thus adopts a traditional conception of the well-ordered, patriarchal hierarchy within the private household. Rousseau's rationale for this hierarchy also corresponds to the traditional explanatory patterns in which the natural order sets and normatively legitimates human laws. By assuming that everything in nature has a function and an aim, the political and private spheres play a crucial role in the realisation of these individual aims. Their respective structures are seen as essential for the well-being of each individual, the community, and the family as a whole.

III. Conclusion

The following conclusions can be drawn for theories of ownership in early modern political theory, especially with regard to their gender dimensions. First, the normative premises of property theories in relation to their arguments in favour of or against private property can be traced back to antiquity. Second, there are certain ambivalences within and between these theories with regard to female ownership.

It is important to note here that my point of criticism lies not with these negative or flawed conceptions of women in general but with the particular weaknesses in the arguments of these theories. Rousseau's assumptions concerning the nature of women have especially proven to be a weakness in his argument for the reasons mentioned earlier. It is important to address the inconsistencies and ambivalences of these theories for an important reason: Locke's theory of property and Rousseau's political thought remain very influential today. Their arguments are still studied and used in contemporary political thought, and they belong to the canonical texts of political philosophy.[32] And yet, especially with regard to the (im-)possibility of women owning private property, they have hardly been discussed.

Additionally, these thinkers are omnipresent in discussions today even if they are often used as a foil for refutation. Yet they do not fully represent the discourse on property rights of their time. So, one strategy as a feminist researcher can be to criticise the canonical theories themselves and point out their gender biases, inconsistencies, and ambivalences, as I have done. But this can be problematic, at least for the reason that this strategy is continuing a patrilineal tradition by focussing only on the positions and works of male philosophers.[33] This might even make us, the researchers and scholars, complicit in ignoring or silencing the voices of female thinkers within the early modern discourse. For this reason, and to escape a patrilineal approach, it seems necessary to reconstruct at least in part the early modern discourse on private property by adding a selection of voices to it. At the beginning of my chapter I mentioned one very early voice in the discourse: Modesta Pozzo/Moderata Fonte. Her work was written and published long before John Locke's *Two Treatises of Government*, which was published in 1689, and, of course, long before Jean-Jacques Rousseau's major political writings, which were published between 1755 (*Discourse on Inequality*) and 1762 (*The Social Contract*). Neither Locke nor Rousseau mentions Pozzo, and it is not known if they had read her writings. What we know for a fact is that after the publication of these very influential texts, female thinkers began to respond critically to them.[34] It is important to add these female voices to this discourse to reconstruct the early modern theories of property and hopefully receive a broader account of property rights.

Notes

1 Moderata Fonte (pseudonym of Modesta di Pozzo di Forzi): 1555–1592, cf. Jacqueline Broad and Karen Green (eds.), *A History of Women's Political Thought in Europe 1400–1700*, Cambridge 2009 [Cambridge University Press], p. 117.
2 Moderata Fonte, *The Worth of Women. Wherein Is Clearly Revealed Their Nobility and Their Superiority to Men,* ed. and trans. Virginia Cox, Chicago 1997 [University of Chicago Press], p. 113.
3 Ibid., p. 113 (emphasis A.S.).
4 cf. Aristotle: Politics 1263a, in: *The Complete Works of Aristotle*, ed. Jonathan Barnes, Princeton 1984 [Princeton University Press]. Aristotle's works are cited according to Bekker pagination.
5 cf. Plato: Republic 462b-c, in: *The Collected Dialogues of Plato*, ed. Edith Hamilton and Huntington Cairns, Princeton 1961 [Princeton University Press]. Plato's works are cited according to Stephanus pagination.
6 It is important to note, however, that this functional relation between an individual's (basic) needs and her property also implies a limitation on private property. According to Locke, owning more than one needs results in a violation of other people's rights to property.
7 Reinhard Brandt, "Vorwort", in: Andreas Eckl and Bernd Ludwig (eds.), *Was ist Eigentum? Philosophische Eigentumstheorien von Platon bis Habermas*, Munich 2005 [C.H. Beck], pp. 7–11, p. 8f., translation AS.
8 John Locke, *Two Treatises of Government*, ed. Peter Laslett, Cambridge 1988 [Cambridge University Press], p. 270.
9 Jean-Jacques Rousseau, *Discourse on the Origin of Inequality*, London and Toronto 1923 [J.M. Dent and Sons], p. 20.
10 Which could translate into material boundaries such as fences; see Janine Maegraith's contribution on fences in this volume.
11 cf. Natalie Zemon Davis: *Frauen und Gesellschaft am Beginn der Neuzeit. Studien über Familie, Religion und die Wandlungsfähigkeit des sozialen Körpers*, Berlin 1986 [Verlag Klaus Wagenbach], pp. 19–26.
12 cf. Locke, *Two Treatises of Government*, pp. 390ff.
13 Jean-Jacques, *Discourse on the Origin of Inequality*, p. 189.
14 Jean-Jacques Rousseau, *The Social Contract and Other Later Political Writings*, ed. Victor Gourevitch, Cambridge 1997 [Cambridge University Press], p. 56.
15 cf. Jean Bethke Elshtain, *Public Man, Private Woman. Women in Social and Political Thought*, Princeton 1987 [Princeton University Press].
16 Jacqueline Broad and Karen Green (eds.), *A History of Women's Political Thought in Europe 1400–1700*, Cambridge 2009 [Cambridge University Press], p. 3.
17 cf. Seyla Benhabib and Linda Nicholson, "Politische Philosophie und die Frauenfrage", in: Herfried Münkler and Iring Fetscher (eds.), *Pipers Handbuch der politischen Ideen. Vol. 5: Neuzeit. Vom Zeitalter des Imperialismus zu den neuen sozialen Bewegungen*, Munich and Zurich 1987 [Piper], pp. 513–562, p. 514.
18 cf. Ellen Kennedy and Susan Mendus (eds.), *Women in Western Political Philosophy. Kant to Nietzsche*, St. Martin's and New York 1987 [Palgrave Macmillan], pp. 6ff.

19 Elshtain, *Public Man, Private Woman*, p. 117.
20 cf. Locke, *Two Treatises of Government*, pp. 330f.
21 cf. Ibid., p. 323.
22 cf. Ibid., p. 321.
23 Ibid., p. 323.
24 Ibid., p. 321.
25 Ibid.
26 Ibid., p. 323.
27 Susan Moller Okin, *Women in Western Political Thought*, Princeton 1979 [Princeton University Press], pp. 200f.
28 Rousseau mentions this several times – for example at the beginning of his writings on political economy and in his social contract.
29 Rousseau, *The Social Contract and Other Later Political Writings*, p. 4.
30 Benhabib and Nicholson, "Politische Philosophie", p. 535, translation AS.
31 Ibid., p. 536.
32 Numerous recent publications on the works of these thinkers as well as the curricula of philosophy departments around the world show and sometimes even address this, cf. for example Michaela Rehm and Bernd Ludwig (eds.), *John Locke. Zwei Abhandlungen über die Regierung. Klassiker Auslegen vol. 43*, ed. Otfried Höffe, Berlin 2012 [Akademie Verlag], p. IX. For a deeper discussion please see: Lisa Shapiro, "Revisiting the Early Modern Philosophical Canon", in: *Journal of the American Philosophical Association* 2, 3 (2016), pp. 365–383.
33 cf. Jim Jose, "No More Like Pallas Athena. Displacing Patrilineal Accounts of Modern Feminist Political Theory", in: *Hypatia. A Journal of Feminist Philosophy* 19, 4 (2004), pp. 1–22.
34 One of these female thinkers would be Priscilla Wakefield (1751–1832). As some of her writings show, she criticises in detail traditional and influential assumptions about women in political philosophy. In her book *Reflections on the Present Condition of the Female Sex; With Suggestions for its Improvement*, first published in 1798, she argues for radical reforms that are based on her negative assessment of the mostly male and dominating political thought of her time. Wakefield's work is therefore an important voice within the early modern discourse, and her demands seem strikingly familiar even today, cf. Priscilla Wakefield, *Reflections on the Present Condition of the Female Sex; With Suggestions for its Improvement*, Cambridge University Press 2015.

Bibliography

Aristotle, "Politics", in: Jonathan Barnes (ed.), *The Complete Works of Aristotle*, Princeton 1984 [Princeton University Press], pp. 1986–2129.

Benhabib, Seyla and Linda Nicholson, "Politische Philosophie und die Frauenfrage", in: Herfried Münkler and Iring Fetscher (eds.), *Pipers Handbuch der politischen Ideen. Vol. 5: Neuzeit. Vom Zeitalter des Imperialismus zu den neuen sozialen Bewegungen*, Munich and Zurich 1987 [Piper], pp. 513–562.

Brandt, Reinhard, "Vorwort", in: Andreas Eckl and Bernd Ludwig (eds.), *Was ist Eigentum? Philosophische Eigentumstheorien von Platon bis Habermas*, Munich 2005 [C.H. Beck], pp. 7–11.

Broad, Jacqueline and Karen Green (ed.), *A History of Women's Political Thought in Europe 1400–1700*, Cambridge 2009 [Cambridge University Press].

Davis, Natalie Zemon, *Frauen und Gesellschaft am Beginn der Neuzeit. Studien über Familie, Religion und die Wandlungsfähigkeit des sozialen Körpers*, Berlin 1986 [Verlag Klaus Wagenbach].

Elshtain, Jean Bethke, *Public Man, Private Woman. Women in Social and Political Thought*, Princeton 1987 [Princeton University Press].

Fonte, Moderata, *The Worth of Women. Wherein Is Clearly Revealed Their Nobility and Their Superiority to Men*, ed. and trans. Virginia Cox, Chicago 1997 [University of Chicago Press].

Jose, Jim, "No More Like Pallas Athena. Displacing Patrilineal Accounts of Modern Feminist Political Theory", in: *Hypatia. A Journal of Feminist Philosophy* 19, 4 (2004), pp. 1–22.

Kennedy, Ellen and Susan Mendus (ed.), *Women in Western Political Philosophy. Kant to Nietzsche*, St. Martin's and New York 1987 [Palgrave Macmillan].

Locke, John, *Two Treatises of Government*, ed. Peter Laslett, Cambridge 1988 [Cambridge University Press].

Okin, Susan Moller, *Women in Western Political Thought*, Princeton 1979 [Princeton University Press].

Plato, "Republic", in: Edith Hamilton and Huntington Cairns (eds.), *The Collected Dialogues of Plato*, Princeton 1961 [Princeton University Press], pp. 575–844.

Rehm, Michaela and Bernd Ludwig (eds.), *John Locke. Zwei Abhandlungen über die Regierung. Klassiker Auslegen*, vol. 43, ed. Otfried Höffe, Berlin 2012 [Akademie Verlag].

Rousseau, Jean-Jacques, *Discourse on the Origin of Inequality*, London and Toronto 1923 [J.M. Dent and Sons].

———, *The Social Contract and Other Later Political Writings*, ed Victor Gourevitch, Cambridge 1997 [Cambridge University Press].

Shapiro, Lisa, "Revisiting the Early Modern Philosophical Canon", in: *Journal of the American Philosophical Association* 2, 3 (2016), pp. 365–383.

Wakefield, Priscilla, *Reflections on the Present Condition of the Female Sex; With Suggestions for its Improvement*, Cambridge 2015 [Cambridge University Press].

PART II

Gifts, symbolic values, and strategies

FIGURE 3.1 Map of Norway, indicating the approximate location of the Giske estate, Frederico de Wit, *Nova et accurata totius Europae descriptio*, *c.* 1700 (detail).

Source: Library of Congress Geography and Map Division, Washington, D.C., U.S.A., public domain, G5700 1700. W5 TIL, http://hdl.loc.gov/loc3.gmd/g5700.ct000125 (15.02.2020, 12:30 CET).

3

LANDED PROPERTY AS MARITAL GIFTS

Women and landownership in fifteenth-century Norway

Susann Anett Pedersen

ABSTRACT

While law first and foremost favoured the family line in transmission of property in late mediaeval Norway, it simultaneously presented men and women with the opportunity to distribute parts of their property as they wished in the shape of gifts. The exchange of marital gifts between husband and wife thus became an important part of married couples' property arrangements and allowed them to develop strategies that benefited the longest living spouse, sometimes at the cost of their respective kin groups. Property could pass from one kin group to another permanently or temporarily through the gift institution, and among the landowning elite the property changing hands could be of immense value. This chapter discusses how married couples of the landowning elite organised their landed property and the role marital gift exchange played in these arrangements. In particular, it explores widows' access to their marital gifts in the wake of their husbands' deaths and the challenges and opportunities they faced in retaining these gifts in varying contexts. As such, this chapter contributes to the discussion of what role gender and social status played as women pursued securing their economic interests in the late Middle Ages.

I. Retaining marital gifts in practice

During the years 1407–1425, Sigrid Erlendsdotter controlled one of the richest estates in late mediaeval Norway. According to Sigrid, her husband Håkon Sigurdsson had given her the Giske estate as a gift to keep if she outlived him. After Håkon's death in 1407, Sigrid kept collecting the revenue from the estate. There were, however, those who opposed her claim to Giske. Håkon Sigurdsson's heirs – his sister's children – continually challenged the validity of the gift. The two parties met in court immediately following Håkon's death as well as on several occasions in the mid-1420s. By 1425, Sigrid Erlendsdotter's opponents had gained ground, and during the summer of that year, one of her husband's heirs seized the Giske estate.

The fact that Sigrid retained one of the richest estates in late mediaeval Norway as a marital gift for almost twenty years following her husband's death calls for attention. It is interesting both because of the size and value of the gift and because of the long-lasting court case and its consequences for Sigrid and her late husband's heirs. Marital gifts were often exchanged between spouses in the Middle Ages to secure the economic future of the spouse who lived the longest. As Sigrid's case demonstrates, such gift exchange did not always go uncontested. The objective of the following chapter is to explore gift exchange between husband and wife in late mediaeval Norway and to investigate how women sought to retain these gifts following the death of a husband. Some widows did not experience any difficulties in retaining gifts they had been promised by their spouses, while others had to fight their late husbands' relatives over control of the property and its revenue. Although scholars have already noted some of the challenges a widow in the Nordic countries faced economically following her husband's death, the situation for women of the landowning elite in late mediaeval Norway has not yet been the subject of a detailed study.[1] As this chapter explores the gendered aspects of marital gift exchange, it also demonstrates how women's economic situation and scope of action changed as they moved from one marital status to another.

From the end of the fourteenth century and throughout the late Middle Ages, Norway was in a union with Denmark and governed by the Crown in Copenhagen.[2] Yet Norway had its own law, the National Law Code of Magnus the Lawmender from 1274, and legal system.[3] Property disputes were usually settled on a local level, but large conflicts between members of the landowning elite could be brought to the Norwegian Council of the Realm.[4] Inheritance law strictly regulated the transmission of property from one generation to another, but it is not possible to read from law alone how different and often complex inheritance cases were settled. To understand property devolution in practice, it is therefore necessary to study how law was interpreted through analysing sources of actual cases from the late Middle Ages, such as contracts, donation letters, and court proceedings.[5] Only then is it possible to grasp the complexity of property transmission and widows' opportunities and challenges in retaining gifts in different contexts.

II. Married couples' property arrangements

The devolution of marital property following the death of a spouse was closely connected to property regulation within marriage. Property ownership within marriage could legally be arranged in different ways, and the chosen arrangement affected the devolution of the marital property. A wife and husband could either own their respective property separately, or they could own their property jointly in part or in total. If the married couple held their property separately, each of their properties would pass directly to their respective heirs when they died. If, however, they held their property jointly, law prescribed how this property should be distributed between the remaining spouse and the deceased spouse's heirs. Husband and wife could enter a *helmingsfélag* (joint property of halves). If they made such an agreement, the longer-lived of the two was entitled to half the marital property at the death of their spouse, while the heirs of the deceased spouse were entitled to the other half.[6] Another option was for a couple to own parts of their property jointly and other parts separately.[7] The husband and wife both contributed to the marital economy, no matter how they chose to organise the marital property. The woman could bring a *heimanfylgja*, her dowry, and her husband then gave her a *tilgjǫf*, an indirect dowry, in return.[8] The *heimanfylgja* became the woman's separate property, if the couple chose to keep their property separate in marriage, and would be inherited by her heirs when she passed away. The husband also brought his own separate property, sometimes called his *heimanfylgja*, which would later pass to his heirs.[9] If the husband outlived his wife, he would keep the *tilgjǫf*, but if she outlived him, the wife would keep it and her heirs after her.[10] Husband and wife could bring both movable and immovable property into the marriage, as law did not to any significant degree determine exactly what the *heimanfylgja* and *tilgjǫf* should consist of. Nonetheless, the tendency among the landowning elite was that both women and men brought landed property into the marriage.[11]

When one of the spouses passed away, the arrangements made before their death decided how much and what parts of the marital property the remaining spouse and the deceased spouse's heirs were entitled to. Sometimes the arrangements would favour the deceased's heirs, while at other times they would favour the remaining spouse. If, then, a couple also had exchanged marital gifts, it could be that the remaining spouse was entitled to far more than the deceased spouse's heirs. If, for instance, a married couple had agreed to a *helmingsfélag* (joint property) and had also promised each other gifts of additional property, then the remaining spouse would be entitled to half of the total marital property as well as the gift (see Figure 3.2).[12]

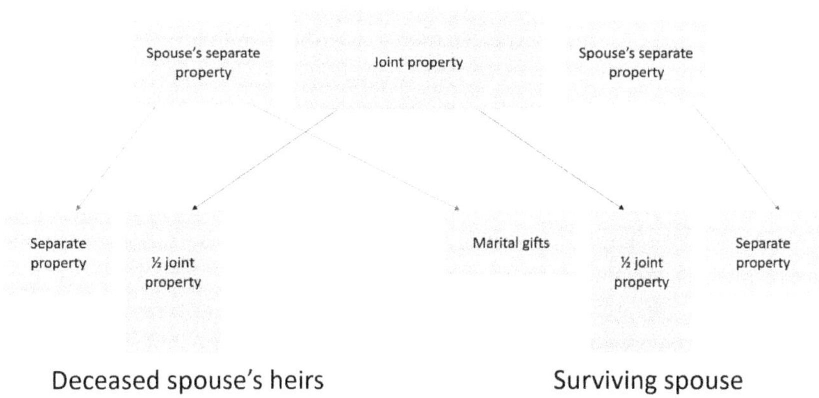

FIGURE 3.2 Married couples' property arrangements in late mediaeval Norway.

Source: © Susann Anett Pedersen.

III. Strategic gift exchange between spouses

Husband and wife could exchange a variety of gifts either at the time of their wedding or at a later point in their life together. In some cases, these gifts were of a practical and economical nature, with the purpose of strengthening the receiver's economic situation. At other times, spouses exchanged gifts of a more sentimental character. Unfortunately, preserved documents are scarce as far as gifts of movable goods as well as the exchange of objects of sentimental value are concerned. Still, the few sources we do have concerning movables provide valuable and interesting insights into the gift exchange between married couples in late mediaeval Norway.

A document compiled by Sigrid Erlendsdotter's husband in Bergen in 1391 or 1392 is possibly our best source of information about sentimental gifts exchanged between spouses. In this particular and one-of-a-kind document, Håkon Sigurdsson listed the various gifts he had bestowed upon Sigrid Erlendsdotter over a period of several years as well as the gifts he had received from her.[13] This document not only gives information concerning the content and value of gifts exchanged, but it also provides us with information about the different occasions when they were given. The first gift Håkon gave his wife was a Christmas gift of a golden diadem decorated with large pearls. Another year, Sigrid received a golden brooch. Following the birth of their daughter, Ingeborg, Håkon gave Sigrid several gifts: A second golden diadem, a psalter that his mother had owned, and a belt with four buckles. Additionally, when Håkon and Sigrid celebrated Christmas with her father at Losna, Håkon gave her a gilded buckle. All of these valuable objects were Sigrid's to keep as her private property and for her to do with as she pleased. The gifts Håkon in turn received from his wife were a large silver bowl that Sigrid's father had given her and a silver cup. When and where he received these gifts is not specified in the document. While this particular married couple could have been exceptionally generous towards each other, it is likely that similar gifts were exchanged between other couples of the Norwegian landowning elite, if not for affection, then at least to demonstrate wealth and power.

More important for the spouses' economic well-being in marriage and after was the exchange of immovable goods – landed property – in the shape of marital gifts. The National Law Code regulated the transfer of property between generations, ruling that the bulk of an individual's property should pass to his or her heirs as inheritance. As such, law made sure that property was kept within the kin group, leaving men and women with few opportunities to pass property out of the family. Nevertheless, law allowed individuals to distribute parts of their property as they pleased through the institution of gifts. The practice of giving gifts was an opening in the law, however small, allowing married couples to develop common strategies and to secure the economic future of the spouse who lived the longest.

Women of the landowning elite received a variety of gifts from their husbands in connexion with marriage. When marriage was first agreed to, the woman who was to be married often received a *festargjǫf* (betrothal gift) from her future husband. Then, on the day of their wedding, or the following day, he gave her a *bekkjargjǫf* (bench gift) and a *morgingjǫf* (morning gift).[14] As the National Law Code did not regulate these gifts, each couple and family's needs, in combination with custom, dictated their content. Most often, the gifts consisted of landed property. Margareta Jensdotter, for instance, received two farms in Jämtland as her morning gift when she married Jørgen Karlsson, which she sold in 1477.[15]

Gift-giving was a mutual tradition. Women not only received gifts from their husbands, but they also bestowed gifts upon their husbands in return. Most often, rather than wives being the sole giver, they appear as givers when husband and wife exchanged gifts. Law allowed mediaeval men and women to distribute as they wished up to one-tenth of their inherited property and one-fourth of property they had obtained by other means. Such gifts were called the *tíundargjǫf* (gift of one-tenth) and the *fjórðungsgjǫf* (gift of one-fourth).[16] Together with gifts given by and to the king himself, these gifts were what the National Law Code termed "legal gifts".[17] While it was perfectly possible for men and women to give gifts to whom they pleased, it was quite common in late mediaeval Norway for these gifts to be exchanged between husband and wife.[18] Gyrid Hallbjørnsdotter and Jørund Arnesson promised each other gifts of one-fourth and one-tenth of all of their respective property in 1374.[19] When Magnhild Oddsdotter married Benkt Harniktsson in the 1430s, she received both a betrothal gift and a morning gift and was promised gifts of one-tenth and one-fourth of all of her husband's immovable and movable property.[20] It is likely that Magnhild also promised her husband gifts of one-tenth and one-fourth of her property, but since it was she who outlived him, it was her claim to the marital gifts that was put into force after his death and thus put into the written record. As such, spouses often had reciprocal claims to part of each other's property. When the marriage between Hans Sigurdsson and Ingeborg Åkesdotter was arranged in 1464, it was stated in their marriage contract that if she outlived him and they had no children, "then she should have her morning gift, her clothing, her silver and her gold, gifts of one-fourth and one-tenth of the undivided property. Thereafter, what was left of their estate should be divided in halves with his heirs."[21] By contrast, if Hans Sigurdsson outlived his wife and they were childless, he was to have "his horses, his armour, his golden rings and the best things at the estate" before the marital property was divided in half.[22]

When a married couple exchanged gifts, the ownership of the land in question was not transferred at the conclusion of the contract. Rather, the gifts were a mutual *promise* exchanged between the married couple that the longest living spouse would keep the property in question.[23] The institution of giving gifts can thus be compared to the tradition of writing last wills – a tradition that gained a foothold in neither Norway nor Denmark in the Middle Ages.[24] Through the few last wills preserved, it is evident that the compiler was often concerned about their loved ones' spiritual rather than economic well-being.[25] The institution of spousal gift exchange was thus the most important channel through which spouses gave each other economic support. All forms of marital gifts need to be considered an economic security for the widow or widower and were an addition to the portion of the marital property they were entitled to.

The practice of spousal gift exchange was also common in Sweden and Iceland. Swedish spouses most often exchanged gifts consisting of self-obtained land but in some instances promised each other a tenth of their inherited property as well.[26] In Iceland, the gift of one-fourth was most commonly used to transfer property between spouses.[27] Agnes S. Arnórsdóttir argues that in Iceland, gift exchange between husband and wife was especially related to the need to protect a widow.[28] Johanna A. Raeder, who has studied the Swedish context, argues that married couples with no children promised parts of their respective property to the longest living spouse particularly as a result of their mutual economic commitment.[29] Mutual gift exchange between husband and wife as an economic security net was thus a practice common in the Nordic countries that favoured the longest living spouse and the continuation of the household.

IV. Property devolution

When one of the spouses passed away, it was time for the widow or widower and the deceased spouse's heirs to divide the marital property between themselves according to agreements made while both spouses were alive. If a widow's late husband's heirs contested her hold on the marital gifts her husband had promised her, it could lead to severe economic consequences for her. To many widows, it was important to obtain their marital gifts not only to keep living in accordance with their rank but also to enable a new marriage.

To late mediaeval men and women death was an omnipresent threat. Individuals thoroughly planned the redistribution of their property in the case of their own deaths, usually in accordance with their family's wishes, and updated these plans continuously throughout their lifetimes as their situation changed.[30] As a rule, we should assume that the deceased's wishes were respected in the process of property devolution, as demonstrated in a variety of sources. When her betrothed died before they married, Ingeborg Åkesdotter received the landed property she had been promised as her morning gift from his mother, Philippa Hansdotter.[31] Another example is Elene Jonsdotter, who received several gifts from her first husband, Henrik Skakt, in 1452.[32] In addition to pawning to Elene and promising her the revenue from a farm that his relatives were not allowed to cash out until after her death, Henrik gave her a farm as her betrothal or morning gift (he was not quite sure of the terminology). By 1459, Henrik Skakt had passed away and Elene remarried. She had obtained the property Henrik had promised her, but his relatives sought to retrieve the farm she received as her betrothal or morning gift, to which they had allodial rights.[33] To sort this out, Henrik Skakt's relatives simply bought the land from his widow. As a consequence, his kin recovered the property and Elene did not suffer economically. In fact, it might have been favourable for her to convert her morning gift to ready money, which she could bring into her new marriage. As such, arrangements could be made peacefully between a widow and her deceased husband's family to the satisfaction of both sides, and the widow recovered what law and the couple's own arrangements entitled her to.[34]

Devolution of marital property did not always occur peacefully. When disputes occurred, it was seldom the division of the marital property in total the two parties disagreed on, but rather the ownership to certain parts of it. Marital gifts were often the subject of these disputes. Gyrid Hallbjørnsdotter and Jørund Arnesson exchanged promises of marital gifts in 1374, but when he passed away sometime around 1400, Gyrid had trouble obtaining her marital gifts.[35] In 1403, she received a sum equivalent to her dowry, but it was not until 1410 that she recovered the gifts Jørund had promised her while they were married.[36] This is a good example of how property devolution could continue for years if the parties involved disagreed as well as an indication that some parts of the marital property were easier to recover than others. In this case, it was the marital gifts that presented difficulties. This was also the case in 1485, when the widowed Ingerd Erlendsdotter met her late husband's heir in court to divide his "gifts and debts" between them.[37] In this case, we must assume that the rest of the marital property had been divided between the two as prescribed by law and property arrangements made before her husband's death. The fact that law did not regulate marital gifts was likely one of the reasons why widows' rights to them were regularly contested.

While there could be several reasons for a widow to fall out with her husband's heirs, some specific contexts seem to have provoked conflict more often than others, and the lack of mutual children was the most prominent trigger. When a couple did have children together, the process of property devolution became a family matter settled between parties with corresponding interests. The main goal was to ensure each family member's economic security and the continuation of the household. Details of settlements between a widow and her children are seldom given in surviving documents, indicating that the devolution of the marital property was carried out as planned.[38] If the children were minors at the time of their father's death, their mother managed their property as well as her own until they came of age. As a widow, Philippa Hansdotter tended to both her own and her son's property and arranged her son's betrothal to Ingeborg Åkesdotter in 1464.[39] Åsa Håvardsdotter managed both her own property and the land belonging to her two minor sons as a widow.[40] In cases where a marriage had not produced any children, however, husband and wife had different heirs in each of their respective kin groups. In these cases, a deceased man's property had to be divided between his widow and his siblings, parents, or more distant relatives. It was often in such instances, when an inheritance was to be settled between a kin group from which a gift had originated and a kin group who had recently obtained the property in question, that conflicts occurred. Court records demonstrate that a number of gift letters became the subject of discussion and dispute between widows and their late husbands' heirs. Unfortunately, only a few cases provide us with details concerning these discussions. One of the best documented conflicts between a childless widow and her late husband's heirs is that of Sigrid Erlendsdotter and the Giske estate from the beginning of the fifteenth century, mentioned in the introduction.

V. A widow and her claim to immobile property: Sigrid Erlendsdotter and the Giske estate

The dispute between Sigrid Erlendsdotter and her late husband's heirs was probably the largest dispute concerning marital gifts in the fifteenth century. Not only did the dispute concern the richest estate in Norway at the time, but it also dragged on for several decades following Håkon Sigurdsson's death in 1407.[41] The marriage between Sigrid and Håkon had produced a daughter, but she died at a young age.[42] As such, the married couple had no mutual heirs when the head of the household passed away. In the years that followed, Sigrid claimed her right to the estate on the grounds that Håkon had bestowed it upon her, and his relatives challenged her claim. No documentation exists, other than the court proceedings that followed Håkon's death, regarding how the married couple had chosen to organise their landed marital property. Therefore, it is only the remnants from the dispute itself that provide insight into the organisation and devolution of Sigrid and Håkon's marital property.

The court records never specify exactly what kind of gift Sigrid received the Giske estate as. In the sources, it is referred to as a testament and unspecified gifts.[43] As this was neither the first nor the last time the estate's owner promised the Giske estate to someone else as a gift, it is possible to establish as probable what kind of marital gift Håkon gave his wife. One option is that Sigrid received the estate to keep, as precedence of such a gift is found in 1354. At this time, Håkon Sigurdsson's own mother received the entire estate as a gift from her father.[44] As the value of Giske exceeded the upper limit of one-tenth of inherited property a person was legally allowed to bestow upon another as a gift, Håkon's grandfather gathered his other heirs' consent, thus making the gift legal. He also included some precautions in the gift letter in case they opposed him later. While it is a possibility that Sigrid Erlendsdotter received the estate in total, this is not very likely. Håkon Sigurdsson's heirs clearly opposed Sigrid's claim to the Giske estate, and nothing indicates that the estate was meant to pass over to Sigrid's kin group. Another and more likely option exists – namely, that she was given Giske to keep as usufructus for a certain period of time, just like a woman named Ingeborg Åkesdotter was meant to do half a century later. When the marriage between Hans Sigurdsson, a later owner of the estate, and Ingeborg Åkesdotter was arranged in 1464, she was promised a large sum of money as part of her morning gift. To ensure her this money, he pawned her the Giske estate.[45] Most likely, a similar agreement had been made between Sigrid Erlendsdotter and Håkon Sigurdsson, entitling her to collect revenue from the estate until she had obtained the sum of money agreed to.

In the course of the twenty years following Håkon's death, Sigrid had to defend her claim to the estate in court on several occasions as she was challenged by her late husband's heirs. Håkon's heirs were his sister's three children, Katarina Jonsdotter, Ingeborg Jonsdotter, and Sigurd Jonsson. Already in 1409, Sigrid met with their representative, Katarina's husband Alv Haraldsson, in court.[46] While the only preserved document from this specific occasion is scarce as to information concerning why exactly the two parties met in court, the judges concluded that Sigurd, Katarina, and Ingeborg were Håkon's legal heirs. Nothing is said, however, about Sigrid passing over the property at this point. It might be that the document was meant to establish the heirs' legal right to the estate, but that Sigrid was entitled to keep Giske according to her arrangements with Håkon for a given period of time. Sigrid kept the estate until the mid-1420s, but then Sigurd Jonsson made claim to Giske.[47] Since it is likely that Sigrid had been promised the revenue from the estate up to a certain sum, it is possible that the core of the dispute at this point was whether she had obtained the sum she had been promised or if she was entitled to collect the revenue from Giske for some time yet. While Sigurd Jonsson wanted to settle the case and retrieve the estate once and for all, his opponent repeatedly prolonged the case by failing to present proof of Sigrid's right to Giske. In the years between 1424 and 1426, the two parties met frequently in court, but at no point did their judges find themselves able to pass a sentence.[48] Instead, the opposing parties were sent back and forth between courts. In the end, Sigurd Jonsson seized the estate by force in 1425, leaving it up to Sigrid and her new husband to take their case to the king and the Norwegian Council of the Realm if they still wanted to challenge his hold on it. Even though the court case continued the following year, no final settlement is preserved. The estate did remain, however, within Sigurd Jonsson's family, and from 1426 onwards, Sigrid Erlendsdotter completely disappears from the sources.

This particular case sheds light on both the widow's scope of action and how marital gifts were treated in court. One such aspect is the widow's use of representatives or the lack thereof. As she fought to keep her hold on Giske, Sigrid Erlendsdotter faced powerful men who had experience dealing with property issues in court. Alv Haraldsson, who represented Håkon Sigurdsson's three young heirs in court in 1409, owned quite an amount of land himself and was hired by men and women alike to represent their economic interests in court.[49] Sigurd Jonsson was still a relatively young man when he faced Sigrid Erlendsdotter in court in the 1420s, but he was building up a political career and would later become one of the most powerful men in the country.[50] Against Alv Haraldsson, Sigrid appeared in court herself. As it is uncertain what exactly was at stake when they met in 1409, it is difficult to ascertain what she did or did not achieve. Interestingly, Sigrid's brother, Eindride Erlendsson, who was among the leading men in Norway during the reigns of the union monarchs Queen Margaret (1388–1389) and King Erik of Pomerania (1389–1442), did not partake in this case to support his sister.[51] As he was successive governor of two of the most important royal residences in Norway, his duties may have kept him occupied elsewhere.[52] It is possible that the need for a male representative was one of the reasons why Sigrid chose to marry the Swede Magnus Magnusson in 1410.[53] As demonstrated by Johanna A. Raeder, remarriage was a strategy Swedish widows used to obtain someone to protect their economic interests.[54] This is also applicable in a Norwegian context. As long as they were married, Magnus represented his wife in court. Yet there is one interesting exception. When Magnus did not appear in court on 23 June 1425 and failed to send a legal representative, the court dissolved even though Sigrid was present. She was not considered a legal representative of her husband.[55] As a married woman, Sigrid had to count on her husband to secure her marital gift for her.

Another interesting aspect of the case of Sigrid and the Giske estate is how the opposing parties and their judges discussed the marital gift in court and the accusations Sigrid met. Even though the first court record from the case dates back to 1409, a gift letter or last will is not mentioned in any preserved material until 1424. At this point, Sigurd Jonsson claimed the testamentary letter to be a forgery and proclaimed that "I do not believe that his last will is genuine and I will not uphold it unless the law proves it to me, because it is suspicious."[56] Unfortunately, the document does not reveal exactly why he did not find the last will trustworthy. Even though accusations of forgery and lies appeared in late mediaeval court cases at irregular intervals and therefore cannot always be taken at face value, there are other details in these records that indicate that something was not as it should be. Sigrid's opponent and the judges in the case frequently asked her husband to bring more proof to court.[57] Proof used in court could be either written documents or witnesses.[58] Even though Sigrid's husband promised to do so, no further proof from their side is documented in the source material, and the accusations seem to have stood uncontested.

Finally, it is worth considering that the judges in the case, consisting of prominent men who were well versed in the law, had a hard time delivering a verdict. The difficulties in determining the validity of the documents as well as passing a sentence in the case indicate that the practice of marital gift exchange could be tricky. Since the National Law Code only to a limited extent treated the institution of marital gifts, it was up to the judges to pass a sentence according to arrangements made between husband and wife – arrangements that varied from marriage to marriage. As such, it was vital for the outcome of a case that all relevant documentation was presented. In this particular case, the court requested more documentation, but Magnus Magnusson failed to present further proof of his wife's right to the estate.[59] When documentation of the marital arrangements was difficult to procure, the judges lacked information on which to base their sentence. Where and by whom a sentence should be passed was also a matter of discussion. When Magnus Magnusson and Sigurd Jonsson met before the archbishop of Nidaros and several leading political figures in 1424, they were sent to the Norwegian Council of the Realm in Bergen to have the case settled there.[60] The reasons given for doing so were many. Bergen was the law district in which most of the Giske estate was located and where Håkon Sigurdsson had lived. It was where Håkon had given his wife gifts and written his last will, and it was also where the inheritance had been divided. When the two parties met in Bergen a year and a half later, however, the court found it difficult to rule on such a large and difficult case and did not want to announce a verdict without consulting the archbishop on the matters of testamentary and marital gifts.[61] Instead, the councillors tried to reconcile the two parties by suggesting they reach a friendly settlement, as this was the preferred way to solve disputes, but none of the involved were interested in such a solution.[62] This last and perhaps desperate attempt to try to solve the case by compromise demonstrates the complexity of the case and the judges' perplexity regarding the situation. The case seems to have ended with Sigurd Jonsson's seizure of the estate, as the courts failed to intercede.

VI. Conclusion: Preferring couple to kin

While inheritance law protected the family line's interests, openings existed for married couples to dispose of parts of their property as they wished and to develop economic strategies for their mutual benefit. This was by no means particular to either Norway or the other Nordic countries in the late Middle Ages, as a range of legal acts that supplemented law and custom concerning marital property arrangements existed throughout Europe.[63] In Norway, it was first and foremost through the institution of gift exchange that married couples could dispose of property as they wished. The gift could contain mobile valuables, but it usually consisted of immobile property. It was either to become part of the remaining spouse's private property or was handed over with the entitlement of usufruct during the remaining spouse's lifetime. While it was a possibility to give gifts to others, married couples often chose to give such gifts to each other in the form of the *festargjǫf* (betrothal gift), *bekkjargjǫf* (bench gift), and *morgingjǫf* (morning gift) as well as the *tíundargjǫf* (gift of one-tenth) and *fjórðungsgjǫf* (gift of one-fourth). Presumably, most women had no trouble recovering the gifts promised to them by their husbands. However, as law only to a limited extent regulated marital gifts, widows' rights to them were regularly contested.

As the case of Sigrid Erlendsdotter demonstrates, disputes concerning marital gifts could be both long-lasting and difficult to solve. Since marital property arrangements varied from couple to couple and the role played by gifts differed, it could be tricky to solve cases where the opposing parties presented different stories. As such, women could find themselves in an exposed position as they entered widowhood, a new state that could alter women's economic situation as well as their scope of action.[64] Sigrid Erlendsdotter's case also demonstrates, however, that elite women could thrive even in challenging situations. There is no reason to assume that Sigrid's economic situation changed after Håkon's death in 1407. Despite the challenges presented by some of the most powerful men in the country, Sigrid did in fact control the Giske estate – the richest secular estate in the country – until 1425. Marital gift exchange was a strategy used by married couples to benefit the longest living spouse economically, sometimes at the cost of the deceased's own kin.

Notes

1 For Sweden, see Mia Korpiola and Elsa Trolle Önnerfors, "Inheritance Law, Wills, and Strategies of Heirship in Medieval Sweden", in: Mia Korpiola and Anu Lahtinen (eds.), *Planning for Death. Wills and Death-Related Property Arrangements in Europe, 1200–1600*, Leiden and Boston 2018 [Brill], pp. 29–65, pp. 45–53; Johanna Andersson Raeder, *Hellre hustru än änka. Äktenskapets ekonomiska betydelse för frälsekvinnor i senmedeltidens Sverige [The economic meaning of marriage for noble women in late medieval Sweden]*, Stockholm 2011 (PhD thesis, University of Stockholm); Gabriela Bjarne Larsson, "Wives or Widows and Their Representatives", in: *Scandinavian Journal of History* 37, 1 (2012), pp. 49–68; *Laga fång för medeltidens kvinnor och män. Skriftbruk, jordmarknader och monetarisering i Finnveden och Jämtland 1300–1500*, Stockholm 2010, pp. 97–101. For Iceland, see Agnes S. Arnórsdóttir, *Property and Virginity: The Christianization of Marriage in Medieval Iceland 1200–1600*, Århus 2010 [Aarhus University Press], p. 366. Arnórsdóttir has also treated legal gifts in "Death and Donation. Different Channels of Property Transfer in Late Medieval Iceland", in: Maria Ågren and Amy Louise Erickson (eds.), *The Marital Economy in Scandinavia and Britain 1400–1900*, Aldershot and Burlington 2005 [Ashgate], pp. 207–219. In a Norwegian context, Ragnhild Ormøy has briefly treated marital gift exchange in the high Middle Ages (Ragnhild Ormøy, *Kvinner og eiendom i vestnorske bygder ca. 1270–1350*, Bergen 1984 (Unpublished hovudoppgåve, University of Bergen), pp. 32–34, 52–56).

2 For an English presentation of Norwegian and Scandinavian history in the period, see e.g. Knut Helle (ed.), *The Cambridge History of Scandinavia. Volume I: Prehistory to 1520*, Cambridge 2003 [Cambridge University Press].

3 The National Law Code of Magnus the Lawmender was introduced in 1274 and stayed valid until the Law of Christian IV replaced it in 1604. In this chapter, I have used Absalon Taranger's translation of The National Law Code, hereafter referred to as MLl (*Magnus Lagabøters landslov*, trans. Absalon Taranger, Oslo 1962).

4 To a large extent, the Norwegian Council of the Realm ruled the country on behalf of the king and consisted of the most powerful lay and ecclesiastical men in Norway.

5 Norwegian mediaeval documents are collected and published in the series *Diplomatarium Norvegicum* I-XXIII (DN), eds. C. C. A. Lunge et al., Christiania and Oslo 1849–2011. The published documents can be found both in print and through an online database at www.dokpro.uio.no (accessed 10 December 2019).

6 Another form of joining property existed, the *þriðjungsfélag* (through which the husband was entitled to two-thirds of the joint property, while the wife was entitled to one-third), but this form of organising property was to large extent replaced by the *helmingarfélag* in the late Middle Ages. Kathrine Græsdal, . . . *Legge i felaget alt det som de da eier og kommer til å eie . . . Om kvinner, eiendom og ekteskap i norsk middelalder*, Tromsø 2002 (Unpublished master thesis, University of Tromsø), p. 76; Lars Ivar Hansen, "The Field of Property Devolution in Norway During the Late Middle Ages: Inheritance Settlements, Marriage Contracts and Legal Disputes", in: Kim Esmark et al. (eds.), *Disputing Strategies in Medieval Scandinavia*, Leiden 2013 [Brill], pp. 247–277, p. 257.

7 For more on the different forms of marital property, see Græsdal, "Legge i felaget alt det som de da eier og kommer til å eie"; in English: Idem, "Joint Ownership in Medieval Norway", in: Lars Ivar Hansen (ed.), *Family, Marriage and Property Devolution in the Middle Ages*, Tromsø 2000 [University of Tromsø], pp. 81–97; Hansen, *The Field of Property Devolution*; "Inheritance, Property and Marriage in Medieval Norway", in: Cordelia Beattie and Matthew Frank Stevens (eds.), *Married Women and the Law in Premodern Northwest Europe*, Woodbridge, Suffolk and Rochester, NY 2013 [Boydell & Brewer], pp. 11–30.

8 MLl, Inheritance section, 1 § 2. Agnes Arnórsdóttir has demonstrated that the terms *tilgjǫf* and *heimanfylgja* usually appeared when spouses entered a contract of separate property in Iceland. In fact, a contract of separate property was often referred to as "a contract of *tilgjǫf*". When the married couple entered a contract of *félag*, it was not that important to name its different components since each of them was entitled to half of the marital property anyway (Arnórsdóttir, *Property and Virginity*, pp. 304–305). This might apply to the Norwegian context as well, but further research on the topic is needed before any conclusions can be made.

9 MLl, Inheritance section, 7 § 9.

10 MLl, Inheritance section, 3 § 3.

11 E.g. DN 1, 463. It was not unheard of, however, for women to bring money into the marriage if it was more practical for the newlywed couple – for instance if the bride moved far away from her family's land when she married (e.g. DN 3, 834).

12 A similar practice is also known from late mediaeval Iceland (Arnórsdóttir, *Death and Donation*, p. 210.).

13 DN 1, 537. The document also listed the gifts' value and was probably kept by Håkon and Sigrid at Giske.

14 The bench gift was a gift the groom gave his wife at their wedding feast and was related to the woman's chastity (Arnórsdóttir, *Property and Virginity*, pp. 364–365). The bench and morning gifts were to a large extent exclusive to the elite (Rigmor Frimannslund, "Morgongåva, Norge", in: *Kulturhistorisk leksikon for nordisk middelalder fra vikingetid til reformationstid*, vol. XI, Kopenhagen 1966, col. 699).

15 DN 3, 917.

16 MLl, Inheritance section, 21§1.

17 Norwegian law was slightly more strict than Swedish law (The National Law of King Magnus Eriksson), which ruled that an individual could give away only one-tenth of inherited property as legal gifts, but no restrictions existed concerning land a person had obtained herself (Larsson, *Laga fång för medeltidens kvinnor och män*, p. 82.).

18 It was also fairly common that gifts of one-tenth and one-fourth were given to someone close to the original landowner, most often a younger relative. In such cases, gifts were given to secure the young relative a good marriage. Margareta Eilivsdotter did, for

instance, give her relative Katarina Jonsdotter and her new husband gifts of one-tenth and one-fourth (DN 1, 671). Also, Katarina Jonsdotter favoured one of her heirs, Alv Knutsson, in giving him a gift of one-tenth a short time prior to his marriage to Magnhild Oddsdotter (DN 2, 810).

19 DN 1, 426.

20 DN 2, 843.

21 "Tha scal hwn haffwa først sine morgengaffwor, siin klæde, sit sølff oc sit gul, fierdingx gioff oc tinde gioff aff vskiffto, Oc sidan skifftæ til hælffninge med hans arffwa, bade løst oc fast, hwat som effter ær" (DN 16, 219, transl. author).

22 "Sinæ hæstæ, Sit harnisk, sine gulringe, oc thet bezste tingh j gardin ær" (DN 16, 219, transl. author).

23 E.g. DN 16, 219, DN 9, 317.

24 Helle Vogt, "Protecting the Individual, the Kin and the Soul. Donation Regulations in Danish and Norwegian Medieval Legislation", in: Ole-Albert Rønning, Helle Møller Sigh and Helle Vogt (eds.), *Donations, Inheritance and Property in the Nordic and Western World from Late Antiquity until Today*, Abingdon and New York 2017 [Routledge], pp. 130–145, pp. 135–137.

25 Through a study of all wills compiled in Norway in the period between 1225 and 1520, Aud Strømme has found that twenty-eight testators favoured their spouse in their last will. Twenty-five of these testators did this by giving gifts to the church for their spouse's soul. Strømme argues that the small amount of last wills in which one spouse donated property to the other indicates that aristocrats did not find it necessary to help the remaining spouse economically for the longest living spouse to maintain their standard of living (Aud Strømme, *Norske testamenter og sjelegavebrev fra middelalderen: en undersøkelse av omfang og bruk*, Trondheim 1995 [Unpublished hovudoppgåve, University of Trondheim], pp. 91–92). It is important, however, not to underestimate the importance of securing the afterlife for one's family through the purchase of prayers for their souls. Catharina Andersson argues that it is anachronistic to separate religious motives from other motives for making donations (Catharina Andersson, *Kloster och aristokrati. Nunnor, munkar och gåvor i det svenska samhället till 1300-talets mitt*, Göteborg 2006 [PhD thesis, University of Göteborg], p. 73). Furthermore, as married couples could make economic arrangements by means other than last wills, we cannot conclude from last wills alone that mediaeval men and women did not see the need to secure each other's economic future.

26 Andersson Raeder, *Hellre hustru än änka,* p. 117.

27 Arnórsdóttir, *Property and Virginity*, p. 366.

28 Ibid., p. 368.

29 Andersson Raeder, *Hellre hustru än änka*, pp. 107–108.

30 For instance, Alv Knutsson and his siblings determined how to divide the future inheritance between them years before they actually obtained the property in question (DN 2, 903).

31 DN 18, 87.

32 DN 9, 317.

33 DN 9, 335.

34 Ragnhild Ormøy's research on women and property in western Norway *c.* 1270–1350 supports the view that widows usually recovered a large part of the marital property when they and their late husband's heirs split it following his death (Ormøy, *Kvinner og eiendom*, p. 46).

35 DN 1, 426.

36 DN 2, 576 and 611.

37 DN 1, 945.

38 E.g. Katarina Jonsdotter and her son Eiliv divided property between them that Katarina and Eiliv's father had owned together in marriage (it had been a gift from a relative of hers) (DN 2, 781).

39 DN 2, 810, DN 16, 219.

40 E.g. DN 1, 563.

41 *Islandske Annaler indtil 1578*, ed. Gustav Storm, Christiania 1888 (hereafter referred to as IA), VII 1407.

42 DN 1, 537.
43 "Um Gizsko ok alt Gizsko gooz testamentum ok giofuer" DN 1, 699.
44 DN 2, 323.
45 DN 16, 219.
46 DN 1, 621.
47 Sigurd and his sisters' kin owned several of the large estates in Norway. Likely, an agreement was made that Sigurd would inherit the Giske estate, while his sisters inherited landed property elsewhere. Division of their maternal and paternal inheritance is mentioned in 1409, but it does not specify how the division of property should be made (DN 1, 621). We do know, however, that Katarina received, among other property, the Manvik estate as a gift from a relative (DN 1, 671). While the sources are silent concerning Ingeborg's share, we can only assume that she, too, received landed property.
48 DN 1, 699, 700, 705, 706, 713.
49 E.g. DN 2, 566, 584.
50 Erik Opsahl, "Art Sigurd Jonsson", in: *Norsk biografisk leksikon* (published online 2009, last update 2015), https://nbl.snl.no/Sigurd_Jonsson (accessed 10 December 2019).
51 Lars Hamre, *Norsk historie frå omlag år 1400. Førelesningar*, Oslo 1968 [Universitetsforlaget], pp. 53, 83.
52 Eindride Erlendsson was governor at Akershus (mentioned in the sources with this title *c.* 1405–1408) and Tønsberghus (mentioned *c.* 1411–1438), in addition to holding several royal offices simultaneously throughout his lifetime (Halvard Bjørkvik, Art. "Eindride Erlendsson", in: *Norsk biografisk leksikon* (published online 2009), https://nbl.snl.no/Eindride_Erlendsson (accessed 10 December 2019).
53 IA VII 1410.
54 Andersson Raeder, *Hellre hustru än änka*, p. 68.
55 DN 1, 705.
56 "mik tykker hans testamenti bref ekke skælikt væra ok ekke vil iak halda thet vttan laghen visa mik thet. thy at thet ær grunsamlikt" (DN 1, 699, transl. author).
57 DN 1, 699.
58 Tine Berg Floater, *Med nøkler i beltet og loven i ryggen. Kvinners stilling i rettssystemet i Norge i hundreåret etter Landslovens innføring*, Oslo 1997 (Unpublished hovudoppgåve, University of Oslo), p. 106.
59 DN 1, 699.
60 Ibid.
61 DN 1, 713.
62 Ibid. On the preference for compromise as a solution to disputes, see e.g. Berg Floater, *Med nøkler i beltet og loven i ryggen*, pp. 13–16.
63 See e.g. Korpiola and Lahtinen (eds.), *Planning for Death*.
64 The exposed position of late mediaeval women in the Nordic countries is discussed in e.g. Andersson Raeder, *Hellre hustru än änka*.

Sources

Diplomatarium Norvegicum I-XXIII (DN), eds. C. C. A. Lunge et al., Christiania and Oslo 1849–2011.

Islandske Annaler indtil 1578 (IA), ed. Gustav Storm, Christiania 1888.

Magnus Lagabøters landslov (MLl), trans. Absalon Taranger, Oslo 1962.

Bibliography

Andersson, Catharina, *Kloster och aristokrati. Nunnor, munkar och gåvor i det svenska samhället till 1300-talets mitt*, Göteborg 2007 [Phd thesis, University of Göteborg].

Andersson Raeder, Johanna, *Hellre hustru än änka. Äktenskapets ekonomiska betydelse för frälsekvinnor i senmedeltidens Sverige [The economic meaning of marriage for noble women in late medieval Sweden]*, Stockholm 2011 [Phd thesis, University of Stockholm].

Arnórsdóttir, Agnes S., "Death and Donation. Different Channels of Property Transfer in Late Medieval Iceland", in: Maria Ågren and Amy Louise Erickson (eds.), *The Marital Economy in Scandinavia and Britain 1400–1900*, Aldershot and Burlington 2005 [Ashgate], pp. 207–219.

———, *Property and Virginity: The Christianization of Marriage in Medieval Iceland 1200–1600*, Århus 2010 [Aarhus University Press].

Berg Floater, Tine, *Med nøkler i beltet og loven i ryggen. Kvinners stilling i rettssystemet i Norge i hundreåret etter Landslovens innføring*, Oslo 1997 [Unpublished hovudoppgåve, University of Oslo].

Bjørkvik, Halvard, "Art Eindride Erlendsson", in: *Norsk biografisk leksikon* (published online 2009), https://nbl.snl.no/Eindride_Erlendsson (accessed 10 December 2019).

Frimannslund, Rigmor, "Art Morgongåva, Norge", in: *Kulturhistorisk leksikon for nordisk middelalder fra vikingetid til reformationstid*, vol. XI, Kopenhagen 1966 [Rosenkilde & Bagger], col. 699.

Græsdal, Kathrine, "Joint Ownership in Medieval Norway", in: Lars Ivar Hansen (ed.), *Family, Marriage and Property Devolution in the Middle Ages*, Tromsø 2000 [University of Tromsø], pp. 81–97.

———*Legge i felaget alt det som de da eier og kommer til å eie. . . . Om kvinner, eiendom og ekteskap i norsk middelalder*, Tromsø 2002 [Unpublished master's thesis, University of Tromsø].

Hamre, Lars, *Norsk historie frå omlag år 1400. Førelesningar*, Oslo 1968 [Universitetsforlaget].

Hansen, Lars Ivar, "The Field of Property Devolution in Norway During the Late Middle Ages: Inheritance Settlements, Marriage Contracts and Legal Disputes", in: Kim Esmark, Hans Jacob Orning, Gerd Althoff and Helle Vogt (eds.), *Disputing Strategies in Medieval Scandinavia*, Leiden 2013 [Brill], pp. 247–277.

———, "Inheritance, Property and Marriage in Medieval Norway", in: Cordelia Beattie and Matthew Frank Stevens (eds.), *Married Women and the Law in Premodern Northwest Europe (Gender in the Middle Ages 11)*, Woodbridge, Suffolk and Rochester, NY 2013 [Boydell & Brewer], pp. 11–30.

Helle, Knut (ed.), *The Cambridge History of Scandinavia. Volume I: Prehistory to 1520*, Cambridge 2003 [Cambridge University Press].

Korpiola, Mia and Anu Lahtinen (eds.), *Planning for Death. Wills and Death-Related Property Arrangements in Europe, 1200–1600* (Medieval Law and Its Practice 23), Leiden and Boston 2018 [Brill].

Korpiola, Mia and Elsa Trolle Önnerfors, "Inheritance Law, Wills, and Strategies of Heirship in Medieval Sweden", in: Mia Korpiola and Anu Lahtinen (eds.), *Planning for Death. Wills and Death-Related Property Arrangements in Europe, 1200–1600*, Leiden and Boston 2018 [Brill], pp. 29–65.

Larsson, Gabriela Bjarne, *Laga fång för medeltidens kvinnor och män. Skriftbruk, jordmarknader och monetarisering i Finnveden och Jämtland 1300–1500* (Rättshistoriskt bibliotek 66), Stockholm 2010 [Institutet för rättshistorisk forskning].

———, "Wives or Widows and their Representatives", in: *Scandinavian Journal of History* 37, 1 (2012), pp. 49–68.

Opsahl, Erik, "Art Sigurd Jonsson", in: *Norsk biografisk leksikon* (published online 2009, last update 2015), https://nbl.snl.no/Sigurd_Jonsson (accessed 10 December 2019).

Ormøy, Ragnhild, *Kvinner og eiendom i vestnorske bygder ca. 1270–1350*, Bergen 1984 [Unpublished hovudoppgåve, University of Bergen].

Strømme, Aud, *Norske testamenter og sjelegavebrev fra middelalderen: en undersøkelse av omfang og bruk*, Trondheim 1995 [Unpublished hovudoppgåve, University of Trondheim].

Vogt, Helle, "Protecting the Individual, the Kin and the Soul. Donation Regulations in Danish and Norwegian Medieval Legislation", in: Ole-Albert Rønning, Helle Møller Sigh and Helle Vogt (eds.), *Donations, Inheritance and Property in the Nordic and Western World from Late Antiquity until Today (Routledge Studies in Cultural History)*, Abingdon and New York 2017 [Routledge], pp. 130–145.

FIGURE 4.1 Map of Scotland, indicating the location of Glasgow, Frederico de Wit, *Nova et accurata totius Europae descriptio*, *c.* 1700 (detail).

Source: Library of Congress Geography and Map Division, Washington, D.C., U.S.A., public domain, G5700 1700. W5 TIL, http://hdl.loc.gov/loc.gmd/g5700.ct000125 (15.02.2020, 12:15 CET).

4

MARRIED WOMEN'S TESTAMENTS

Division and distribution of movable property in seventeenth-century Glasgow

Rebecca Mason

ABSTRACT

The death of a married woman in early modern Scotland sparked the division of her and her husband's movable estate, with her husband, children, and kinship network all staking a claim to her share of marital goods. Marital property arrangements and testamentary practices in Scotland were closely aligned with procedures found in other civil legal traditions on the Continent. Unlike women under the English common law doctrine of coverture, married women in Scotland were entitled to bequeath a customary share of marital property before death. The amount depended on whether they had any children with their husbands. Even when a married woman died without leaving a written testament, her husband was not automatically granted the right to retain control and ownership of all marital goods and assets. This chapter will show how married women of middling to lower status in seventeenth-century Glasgow asserted ownership of particular movable goods and assets when faced with the prospect of death and will investigate the kinds of goods married women bequeathed in testaments in Glasgow's commissary (reformed church) court across the seventeenth century. It will also investigate the effects of intestacy on the marital household and will explain why husbands and wives often treated household goods as jointly owned in their testaments. In doing so, this chapter adds a valuable contribution to our understanding of gender relations, household strategies, and marital property arrangements in an urban settlement in early modern Scotland.

I. Introduction: Wives and movable property in Scots law

In the spring of 1607, Elspeth Braidwood, the wife of Robert Horner, a burgess of Glasgow, professed her dying wishes in her dwelling place[1]. Faced with her own mortality (and indeed passing away three days later), Elspeth appointed her husband, Robert, as the only executor to her movable estate, entitling him to settle outstanding credit arrangements made in her name. In her testament, Elspeth noted that she and her "poor tailor" husband, Robert, collectively owned household furniture and three old boats worth a total of £38 14s 4d Scots (£2 19s 10d sterling), and that her husband was to retain her share of free goods. Elspeth also declared before her friends and neighbours that she left her daughter from her previous marriage, Margaret Snodger, "hir part of all [th]e goods and geir [th]at pertains to hir", which included various items of women's clothing.[2] Elspeth had contracted a "testament testamentar" before her death, which included a latter will and legacy, the appointment of an executor, and an inventory of her goods and any outstanding debt. If a Scottish wife died without bequeathing her goods in a testament, however, her husband would often register a "testament dative" with the court, which included a detailed list of her goods, any unresolved household debt, and the transmission of property in accordance with intestate succession.

The documentation of married women's goods in testaments, written either before or after death, is peculiar, as during marriage their movable property rights were severely restricted in legal handbooks. In his 1579 *Practicks*, Scottish legal writer Sir James Balfour placed restrictions upon what kind of movable property was shared within marriage and remained separate.[3] Balfour stated that under the doctrine of *jus mariti*, much of a wife's movable property transferred to her husband upon marriage, including the rents of her heritable property.[4] If a woman brought household furniture, livestock, or kitchen utensils to her marriage household, she relinquished all ownership of such goods unless she specifically safeguarded these assets within her marriage contract. An exception to this rule was the wife's paraphernalia. These particular assets were made up of her clothing, jewellery, and chests and remained her own separate property throughout her marriage. Her husband retained considerable administrative rights to these assets, yet the contents of the wife's paraphernalia were entirely hers to bequeath prior to her death.[5]

Testaments have received a considerable amount of attention by Scottish historians. They provide a rich source with which to explore the lives of women and men in early modern Scotland. Elizabeth Ewan, in her study of testaments registered in the pre-Reformation Commissariot of St Andrews, argued that it was "not uncommon" for married women to make testaments prior to death.[6] Ewan also discovered that wives with living husbands constituted at least twenty-five percent (sixty-three of 253) of all married people's testaments between 1549 and 1551.[7] Winifred Coutts has asserted that most Scottish women who wrote testaments were, or had been, married.[8] Coutts has found that as many as one-third of testaments registered in Dumfries commissary court between 1600 and 1665 were contracted by women.[9] Cathryn Spence has used women's testaments to explore their business activities and debt networks in sixteenth-century Edinburgh.[10] Historians agree that Scottish women, especially those who were married, formed a considerable number of female testators in mediaeval and early modern Scotland. What is often missing from this debate, however, is an explanation as to why so many Scottish wives left testaments before death. A close analysis of married women's testaments raises some pertinent questions with regard to the division and distribution of movable property following the dissolution of the marital economy in early modern Scotland. First of all, if married women supposedly retained limited movable property rights within marriage, why would they formally bequeath household goods to their husbands in a testament? Second, if movable property simply defaulted to husbands within marriage, why would husbands decide to register a testament when their wives had already died?

Building on current debates surrounding women's testamentary practices in early modern Scotland, this chapter will explain why so many married women left testaments in seventeenth-century Glasgow and will uncover what these legal documents can tell us about the formation of marital property arrangements and testamentary practices in urban Scottish households. It begins by contextualising the choice of legal sources and explains how marital property was divided and distributed in Scottish legal handbooks following the death of a spouse. It will then go on to explore the extent of married women's testamentary practices in seventeenth-century Glasgow and will investigate what assets they bequeathed in their testaments prior to death.

II. Evidence and method

Marital property arrangements and testamentary practices in Scotland were closely aligned with procedures found in other civil legal traditions on the Continent.[11] Scots law during the early modern period was a "mixed" legal system (and indeed is to the present day). Scots law was an "amalgam of many different elements" by the start of the seventeenth century and consisted of a mix of Roman, civil, canon, and custom law that was codified in legal handbooks and statutes across the late mediaeval and early modern period.[12] Married women's legal status and rights to property consisted of a mix of rules and regulations found within these legal traditions. Even though married women had limited rights to movable goods within marriage, husbands were liable for their wives' debts, including those they had incurred before marriage.[13] Husbands were also expected to provide their wives with food and "necessaries" relative to their social worth during marriage.[14] Married women were entitled to express administrative authority over household objects by assuming the office of *praepositura*.[15] This allowed married women to contract household debts and purchase household "necessaries" without receiving the consent of their husbands. Husbands, however, remained liable for the incurred debt. One physical demarcation that distinguished Scottish wives from their English counterparts was that married women in Scotland retained their own natal surname throughout their married life.[16] This practice stemmed from other civil legal traditions. Julie Hardwick found that married women in early modern France similarly retained their natal surname upon marriage, and that the practice in itself reinforced bilateral kinship ties.[17]

Only certain kinds of property could be transmitted in testaments. Scots law made a distinction between immovable heritable and movable property that had a "very important bearing" on rights of succession and on matrimonial property during the early modern period.[18] Heritable property, such as land or rights attached to land, could not be transmitted in a testament, as it was bound by primogeniture (the preference for the firstborn male).[19] Land purchased during the marriage, however, could be freely given by husbands and wives during marriage, with parents often choosing to provide their daughters or younger sons with rights to purchased land in their marriage contracts.[20] The legal differentiation between "old" inherited property and "self-made" estates touches upon the importance of kinship and the retention of immovable property within the kin network. Husbands were prevented from disposing of their wives' inherited estate during marriage without seeking their prior consent and the consent of their wives' heirs (i.e. children or her natal kin).[21] Ownership of married women's inherited land was transferred to either their children or, if they died childless, their next of kin.[22]

Early modern Glasgow provides a suitable framework for a study on married women's testaments for several reasons. The city was continually expanding across the seventeenth century, with its population increasing from 7,000 inhabitants at the beginning of the period to 15,000 inhabitants by 1700.[23] Glasgow was an ever-growing mercantile city, with the River Clyde providing the passageway for ships importing sugar from Barbados, claret wine from France, and tobacco from Virginia.[24] It had an established university, founded in 1451, that educated the sons of nobles, gentry, merchants, and craftsmen, and multiple bustling marketplaces attracted traders and dealers from near and afar.[25] Glasgow's commissary court, a Reformed church court, served not only the men and women of the city but also those who lived in neighbouring settlements on the west coast of Scotland. Located in the southwest tower of Glasgow's cathedral, just a short distance from the city's main marketplaces, the commissary court was headed by a commissar judge and his deputy. The jurisdiction of the commissary court was complex, with the commissar judge employing a mixture of civil and canon law in his judgments after the Scottish Reformation of 1560. Thomas Green has shown how canon law continued to be followed in the commissary court as long as it did not contradict the reformed religion.[26] The commissary court held exclusive jurisdiction over the proving of testaments and received much of its revenue from "quots". This was a proportion of the deceased person's movable estate payable for confirmation of the testament in accordance with its material worth.[27]

The testaments analysed in this chapter fit neatly into two categories: testament dative and testament testamentar. Testament datives were registered intestate, meaning that the deceased wife did not formally assign her share of property to another person or persons before her death.[28] The deceased wife's "voice" is entirely absent from a testament dative. Testament datives were registered by the commissary court on behalf of the deceased wife, with the commissar judge also confirming the appointment of an executor dative to the estate. They also detailed the deceased wife's list of outstanding credit arrangements and provided an inventory of any goods she owned before her death. Testament datives are often sidelined by historians because they do not contain a latter will and legacy, yet they can provide important details regarding the customary division of property following a wife's death. By contrast, testament testamentars were written up by a married woman prior to death. These contained a latter will and legacy in which she formally bestowed her customary share of property to her husband, children, extended family members, and friends.[29] In a testament testamentar, a wife would also appoint an executor to settle her movable estate after her death, which entitled the executor to pursue debtors and divide the estate in accordance with her wishes. Considered alongside one another, testament datives and testament testamentars can reveal a great deal about married women's rights to certain kinds of movable property, both within marriage and upon death, in early modern Scotland.

A quantitative analysis of approximately 6,000 testaments registered in Glasgow's commissary court in six-year samples provides statistical evidence of the extent of married women's involvement in testamentary practices across the seventeenth century.[30] A qualitative analysis of one hundred married women's testaments in Glasgow's commissary court provides a glimpse into the kind of goods they owned and transmitted, including how they conceptualised their movable property rights before death. Despite the fact that married women were granted limited movable property rights within marriage in comparison to their husbands, this chapter will show that they assumed ownership of a significant proportion of their marital goods and assets in their testaments. Even though the majority of movable goods, such as livestock, household furnishings, kitchen utensils, and money, were normatively owned by husbands during marriage, this chapter will show that married women frequently bequeathed, or assumed ownership of, assets that were legally viewed as belonging to their husbands during marriage. In doing so, this chapter adds a valuable contribution to our understanding of gender relations, household strategies, and marital property arrangements in an urban settlement in early modern Scotland.

III. Dividing and distributing the marital estate

Scottish legal writers focussed their attention on what happened to the marital estate following the death of the husband. Household goods and assets were automatically divided into three parts upon the husband's death. These were recorded as the relict's (widow's) part, the bairn's (child's) part, and the dead's part (see Figure 4.2).[31] The bairn's part was split between all children (excluding the principal heir) regardless of gender and consisted of one-third of the father's movable assets.

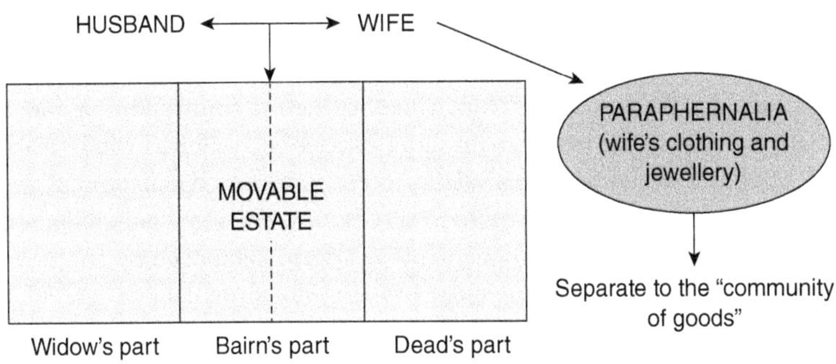

FIGURE 4.2 The customary division of movable goods following the death of a spouse in Scots law (after the heir claimed "heirship-moveables", outstanding debts had been recalled, and creditors had been paid).

Source: © Rebecca Mason.

While forbidden from claiming a bairn's part, the heir (often the eldest son) was entitled to "heirship-moveables", which consisted of one of each of the "best" goods in the house.[32] These items were removed before the father's movable estate was split into thirds. If the husband left only a widow behind and no children, movable property was divided in half, with the surviving wife claiming half of the movable estate as her share. Likewise, if a father died leaving no widow, the children were entitled to claim half of his movable estate as their bairn's part.

It is difficult, however, to reconstruct how widows and children divided up household goods and assets. If a husband died without leaving a testament, it is unclear how the widow and children decided who received a particular item. For instance, if the heir claimed the "best" bed, did they automatically receive accompanying bed linens and cushions? Did daughters always receive items that were gendered as female, such as women's clothing and jewellery? How did the children of a shoemaker divide up their father's clothing and work tools? How did two quarrelling sons decide who received their father's embroidered waistcoat? While these questions are difficult to answer, it is clear that individual negotiations within families would take place following the drawing up of the testament. Widows and children were expected to liaise with one another when deciding how household goods were claimed and distributed following the death of the head of the household. When family disputes surrounding the division of the marital estate were not resolved through extra-judicial avenues, the commissary court heard complaints from aggrieved litigants who sought to claim, or defend, their rightful share of household property.

Scottish legal writers asserted that a widow's right to her share of household goods was "not simply a right of property but a debt".[33] A widow was only entitled to claim these assets as soon as the husband's estate had been settled and outstanding creditors had been paid. Accordingly, if the husband died insolvent, the widow would receive no share of his estate, with the rights of creditors preferred in this instance. After creditors had been paid and the widow and children had claimed their relative shares, the remaining proportion of the husband's goods was recorded as the dead's part; this comprised of assets that were considered freely bequeathable by the husband prior to his death. If he did not assign his dead's part in a testament testamentar, his heirs (either his children or his next of kin) were entitled to claim ownership of these assets before the commissary court. The only goods that were not subject to the distribution of assets following the death of a husband were the wife's paraphernalia. All other goods brought into marriage and acquired within marriage by both the husband and wife were subject to the customary distribution of assets.

Husbands in Scotland were unable to disinherit their wives and children from their share of movable goods in testaments and were compelled by law to assign equal proportions of their movable estate to their immediate family circle.[34] Under English common law, husbands in early modern England were free to leave their goods to whomever they wished and were not compelled to leave a proportion of their movable estate to their wives and children upon death.[35] However, ecclesiastical courts within England, including courts in the cities of York and London, practiced the tradition of dividing the movable estate into thirds following the husband's death, with the practice commonly referred to as "reasonable parts" in

England. Amy Erickson has observed that by the end of the seventeenth century in England the freemen of the city of York asked and were granted relief from the "onerous duty" of providing their widows and children with reasonable parts.[36] Lindsay R. Moore has noted that at the turn of the eighteenth century in England a series of statutes made it legal for a husband to bequeath all of his goods to an heir of his choice.[37] The widow's right to an automatic share of her husband's assets upon his death in England had substantially deteriorated by the eighteenth century, while the practice seemingly flourished in Scotland.

The "tripartition" of marital goods upon death in Scotland was based on the concept of the "community of goods" between husbands and wives during marriage.[38] However, if the marriage was dissolved by death before a year and a day or before the birth of a child "who was heard cry", the surviving spouse was entitled to retrieve the movable assets they had brought into the marriage.[39] This exception reveals how the community of goods only took hold following the birth of children or the perceived longevity of marriage. The community of goods was also found within other civil legal systems across Europe, with Hardwick noting that marital community property was divided in a similar manner after the death of either spouse in customary law areas of northern France.[40] Jutta Sperling has found that Portuguese husbands and wives were considered joint owners of their marital estate, and that strict succession rules meant two-thirds of each parent's property was to be divided equally among all children, with only one-third to be freely willed away.[41]

The idea of the community of goods in Scotland coexisted alongside the husband's right of *jus mariti* even though the two legal concepts might seem directly opposed. This is because the community of goods did not necessarily grant Scottish wives concrete rights to their movable property within marriage. Instead, the community of goods reaffirmed a widow's automatic interest in a proportion of household goods following the death of her husband. As Katie Barclay argues, "[J]oint ownership did not imply equal right to administration."[42] Even though the community of goods recognised a wife's interest in a proportion of goods upon her husband's death, it was the husband who was considered the actual owner of these assets during marriage. As the Scottish legal writer Sir James Dalrymple (Lord Stair) noted in his 1681 *Institutions* (revised in 1693), the husband retained the sole privilege of distributing and governing movable property within marriage, excluding only the paraphernalia.[43] Yet while the husband was entitled to sell and dispose of movable property during their marriage, he was forbidden from submitting a deed that came into effect on his death. The widow's right to an automatic share of her husband's goods could not be defeated by a testament, a legal rule that stands true to this day. A husband was prevented from defrauding his wife of her rightful share of movable goods when he was deemed to be on his deathbed.[44] Logically, the husband's right to *jus mariti* was automatically voided when he appeared on the cusp of death.

Scottish legal writers also debated and disagreed over whether a married woman could leave a testament without her husband's consent. In his 1579 *Practicks*, Sir James Balfour asserted that a wife could not make a testament without receiving her husband's consent but noted that the husband did "ane honest and godlie thing if not he permitts and grantis to his wife licence and powar" to do so.[45] Writing in his *Major Practicks* (*c.*1608–1633), Sir Thomas Hope reiterated Balfour's assertions by stating that "ane womane being frie [i.e. unmarried], and not subject to no man, may make ane testament", but that a married woman always required her husband's consent.[46] However, by the end of the seventeenth century, Dalrymple in his 1681 *Institutions* and Sir George Mackenzie in his 1694 *Institutions* were of the opinion that a married woman could, in fact, make a testament without her husband's consent, noting that she was entitled to transmit goods that she would have ordinarily received upon her husband's death.[47] Anne Ashley in a 1953 article was the first to argue that there is no evidence to suggest that consent was necessary when married women were bequeathing their share of assets in Scotland.[48] Ilya Kotlyar has since argued that there is indeed "no sign" that the husband's authorisation was required in Scottish practice, stating that the restriction outlined in Balfour was an "anachronism" by the late sixteenth century.[49] According to Ashley and Kotlyar, married women were entitled to freely leave their share of the common goods to whomever they wished in a testament – a third if there were children, a half if there were none.[50]

Scottish legal writers tended to focus heavily on the division of the movable estate following the death of the husband, which has led to the belief that the movable estate was not similarly divided following the death of the wife. Coutts and Spence have asserted that only the husband's movable estate was subject to the customary division of assets, and that a wife was not required to make provisions for her children in her testament.[51] Even though a married woman was not expected to leave her children a bairn's part upon her death, it is important to note that the children's inheritance portions were only calculated from the marital estate following the death of the father. If a married woman died before her husband, however, she was still entitled to assign her share of marital goods in a testament, amounting to one-third if she had children or one-half if she had none. If she died intestate, her closest heirs (children or kin) were entitled to claim her free share – not her husband. Balfour in his 1579 *Practicks* suggested that if a burgess had lawful children with his wife, her death would similarly prompt the division of the marital estate into thirds, noting that this customary practice was observed "past [the] memorie of man".[52] Dalrymple in his 1681 *Institutions* also pondered the division of assets following the death of a married woman, noting that if a wife died before her husband, "her Executors, Legators, and nearest of kin have a share of the free moveables the Husband hath the time of her death."[53] If a husband was not entered as the executor to his wife, he faced losing ownership of a significant proportion of his movable goods, depending, of course, on the presence of children. A close look at married women's testamentary practices in Glasgow's commissary court across the seventeenth century reveals how husbands and wives negotiated the division and distribution of household assets in a legal context, with married women exerting considerable authority over their share of the common goods in their testaments.

IV. Married women's testaments: The transfer of movable property

Women and men living in and around Glasgow registered their testaments in the city's commissary court. A quantitative analysis of approximately 6,000 testaments recorded in Glasgow's commissary court between 1610 and 1695 reveals that around twenty-eight percent of all those registered by men and women across the entire period belonged to married women (see Table 4.1). More notably, the testaments of married women constituted around seventy-five percent of all women's testaments, while widow's testaments formed only thirteen percent of women's testaments. This is highly significant when compared with the testamentary practices of women in early modern England. Erickson has shown how women's wills form approximately twenty percent of the two million English wills that survive from the 1550s to the 1750s, with approximately eighty percent of women's wills belonging to widows in the late seventeenth century.[54] In addition, in her study of women's wills in Hull across the fifteenth and sixteenth centuries, Elisabeth Salter asserted that the majority of female will makers in her sample were widows, primarily because "a married woman's property defaulted to her husband" under English common law.[55]

Of the married women's testaments registered across the period in Glasgow's commissary court, 420 out of 1,262 (twenty-five percent) were testament testamentars and contained a latter will and legacy (see Table 4.2). Turning once again to early modern England, Erickson has argued that married women in England were less likely to make a will and testament prior to their death than widows, with wives in Lancashire and Cheshire forming only between 0.3 and 5.6 percent of female will makers between 1660 and 1837. The English common law doctrine of coverture, which stripped women of all movable property rights upon marriage,

TABLE 4.1 The total number of men's and women's testaments registered in Glasgow commissary court in six-year samples (1610–1695). The top number in each column represents the total number and the bottom number represents the percentage.

Year	*Man* *i = % of A*	*Single woman* *i = % of A*	*Married woman* *i = % of A*	*Widow* *i = % of A*	*Married couple* *i = % of A*	*Total no. of wills (A)*
1610–1615	726 *55.9*	77 *5.9*	438 *33.7*	52 *4.0*	6 *0.5*	1,299
1625–1630	698 *56*	65 *5.2*	418 *33.5*	58 *4.7*	8 *0.6*	1,247
1645–1650	427 *73.1*	31 *5.3*	90 *15.6*	29 *5.0*	6 *1*	583
1660–1665	633 *56.7*	35 *3.1*	372 *33.3*	64 *5.7*	13 *1.2*	1,117
1670–1675	884 *62.8*	72 *5.1*	352 *25.1*	75 *5.3*	24 *1.7*	1,407
1690–1695	228 *82.6*	10 *3.6*	12 *4.4*	14 *5.1*	12 *4.3*	276
Total	3,596 *60.6*	290 *4.9*	1,682 *28.4*	292 *4.9*	69 *1.2*	5,929 *100*

Source: NRS, Glasgow commissary court, Register of Testaments, CC9/7/vols. 6–11, 20–24, 29–35, 37–42, 47–49 © Rebecca Mason.[56]

TABLE 4.2 Percentage of men's and women's testaments registered intestate (testament dative) and prior to death (testament testamentar) across the seventeenth century (further tabulated from Table 4.1). The top number in each column represents the total number and the bottom represents the percentage.

Sex and marital status of deceased	*Testament dative i = % of A*	*Testament testamentar i = % of A*	*Total (A)*	*% of total*
Man	2,211 *61.5*	1,385 *38.5*	3,596	*60.6*
Single woman	197 *67.9*	93 *32.1*	290	*4.9*
Married woman	1,262 *75*	420 *25*	1,682	*28.4*
Widow	181 *62*	111 *38*	292	*4.9*
Married couple	63 *91.3*	6 *8.7*	69	*1.2*
Total	3,914 *66*	2,015 *34*	5,929	*100*

Source: NRS, Glasgow commissary court, Register of Testaments, CC9/7/vols. 6–11, 20–24, 29–35, 37–42, 47–49 © Rebecca Mason.[57]

seems to have hindered the majority of married women in England from disposing of their goods prior to death. Rather than reflecting the property interests of a small number of elite wives, the married women who contracted testament testamentars in Glasgow were largely of middling to lower status; they were married to indwellers, craftsmen, merchants, and burgesses of the city and neighbouring settlements. Their husband's occupational standing within the community, as well as the household's economic status, enabled a substantial minority of married women to claim and distribute a share of their marital estate prior to death in Glasgow's commissary court.

The majority of testaments in Glasgow's commissary court were registered intestate as "testament datives" (see Table 4.2). Testament datives conformed to the customary division of assets (in thirds or halves) as detailed in legal handbooks, depending on the presence of spouses, children, and kin. Testament datives formed the largest percentage of testaments registered in Glasgow's commissary court across the period. Very few Scotsmen and women formally bequeathed their movable property before their death, with testament datives shedding further light on those people who often died in possession of considerable to limited movable assets. Despite the unlimited testamentary rights granted to men, over sixty percent of men's testaments were registered intestate across the seventeenth century.[58] By comparison, seventy-five percent of married women's testaments were written intestate and registered following death. When married women died without leaving a written testament, their husbands often treated their goods and debt as "literal co-ownership", extending to every single item.[59] Turning briefly to England, a direct consequence of coverture meant that a married couple's movable estate was not subject to a customary division following the death of the wife. Erickson has asserted that a married woman's death in early modern England "bore no legal or financial implications" for her widower, as he was automatically entitled to retain control of all movable goods.[60] Contrary to the experience of English wives, it seems that Scottish wives were treated as one of a pair upon death, with their share of assets passing on to their heirs, even when they died intestate. Married women's contribution to the marital economy in Scotland was recognised upon death, as their children or kin group could request the transfer of property that was normatively owned by husbands during marriage.

Married women were expected to formally assign their dead's part to their husbands in a testament in order for them to retain full control of the marital estate as widowers. In February 1609, Mareoun Law left her entire dead's part, worth £59 8s 4d Scots (£4 11s 5d sterling), to her husband, William.[61] Bessie Campbell left her dead's part to her husband, John Roger, in February 1604, with the customary division of goods in half revealing that they had no children.[62] Before her death in October 1607, Margaret Inglis, the wife of John Asloane, formally left her dead's part worth £58 4d Scots (£4 9s 3d sterling) to her husband in her testament.[63] Property arrangements forged in marriage contracts also prevented married women from bequeathing their dead's part to anyone else apart from their husband. In March 1587, Margaret Mortoun, noting that she was "seik in bodie but weill in mynd", left her dead's part to her husband, James Reid, stating that she had promised him in their contract of marriage that "quhatsumever gudis and geir s[h]all happin to be acqyired or gottin be him *and me* during our lyftymes [th]e samin s[h]all pertene to [th]e said James" following her death.[64] Instances of married women assigning all goods to their husbands, either in marriage contracts or testaments, offer unique insights into ideas about male attitudes to property ownership within marriage.[65] It seems that many husbands expected their wives to assign ownership of all goods over to them prior to death, a decision that suggests a level of coercion within marriage. It is difficult, however, to know how far intimidation underlay these statements, but the very fact that husbands legally depended on their wives assigning movable property rights to them before death further confirms that ownership of marital goods did not simply default to them as widowers and that the community of goods was dissolved following the death of either spouse.

When married women died intestate without assigning their dead's part to their husbands, the wives' heirs (children or next of kin) were entitled to retrieve the property before the commissary court. If married women died leaving children behind, it seems that their husbands were entitled to administer these assets until their own death, or at least until the children had reached the age of majority. Daughters came out of their age of minority at the age of twelve (reflecting the age they could marry) and could be free of legal guardians at the age of twenty-one (or upon marriage), whereas sons came out of their age of minority at the age of fourteen.[66] Jonet Drew confirmed her share of inheritance before the burgh (town) court of Glasgow in October 1629, after the recent death of her father, John Drew. Alongside claiming £100 Scots (£7 13s 10d sterling) as her bairn's part, she noted that she had also received an additional 400 merks (£21 10s 9d sterling) as her "mothers pairt of geir".[67] Her mother, Margaret Bunteine, had died fifteen years previously, and her father had since remarried.[68] While John was permitted to manage his previous wife's free share of goods during his lifetime, it was his daughter Jonet who was entitled to claim ownership of the property following his own death.

Widowers often became embroiled in executory disputes with their wives' kin regarding the control and ownership of marital goods when their wives died intestate. In January 1645, Jonet and Christian Paterson (Jonet with her husband's consent) initiated legal proceedings in Glasgow's commissary court against their deceased sister's widower, William Scheills, a maltman burgess of Glasgow. Their sister, Margaret Paterson, had died intestate in April 1644, and William had subsequently registered a testament dative on her behalf in December of the same year.[69] Producing the testament dative, Jonet and Christian argued before the commissar judge that William owed them Margaret's dead's part, which included various items of women's clothing, brewing equipment, and household debt amounting to a total of £174 15s 6d Scots (£13 8s 11d sterling). The commissar judge ruled that Jonet and Christian, as the deceased wife's closest heirs, were to receive Margaret's share of marital goods.[70] It greatly benefited husbands to permit their wives to formally assign their goods to them in a testament testamentar, as it prevented the wives' kin from demanding their share of the property.

Questions remain over the extent to which married women leaving testaments indicates relatively generous or comparatively restricted property rights within marriage. As noted previously, the scarcity of married women's testaments in early modern England seems to reflect that these women had little to no movable property rights within marriage and that intestate succession simply confirmed their husbands' continued ownership of household goods. In seventeenth-century Glasgow, however, one-quarter of all testaments written before death belonged to married women. On the one hand, it could be argued that married women in Scotland were granted individual property rights to a proportion of their marital goods and that many exercised their right to bequeath their free share of the marital estate before death. On the other hand, it could be argued that wives contracted testaments so frequently because their husbands wanted them to transfer favourable property rights to them before death. When husbands were not specifically named in their wives' testaments, they potentially lost control of a significant share of their marital property, with the wives' kin groups staking a claim to a proportion of assets, depending on the presence of children. However, given that three-quarters of married women's testaments were registered intestate in Glasgow's commissary court, it seems that many husbands simply accepted, rather than rejected, the division of the community of goods into customary shares. Husbands assigned inheritance shares to children and confirmed the settlement of outstanding household debt, a practice that shows that the community of goods was dissolved following the death of either spouse in Glasgow. Turning to look at the kinds of goods married women bequeathed in their testaments, the following section will investigate how wives conceptualised their movable property rights before death and will assess whether there was a hierarchical ordering or gendering of objects in their testaments.

V. What wives bequeathed

Details contained within the testaments of married women indicate gendered patterns of property-holding within marriage and the management of movable property following the death of a wife. A married woman's testament included a detailed inventory of the debts due to and owed by her as well as the value of her share of free goods following the customary division of the estate into halves or thirds, even when she predeceased her husband.[71] A testament also appointed the executor, who was entitled to take control of the entire movable estate. The executor was able to sue the deceased wife's debtors and was also considered liable for settling the wife's debts. After the settlement of outstanding credit arrangements, the remainder of the movable estate was distributed amongst the widower, children, and extended kin.[72]

Married women often disposed of specific items within their testaments as if these goods belonged to them individually. When Jonet Dickie, the wife of John Gottray, contracted a testament before her death in December 1592, she noted that the goods and debts belonged to her alone "at the tyme of her departing".[73] At times, husbands described certain assets as belonging to their wives alone, despite women's limited movable property rights within marriage. When Bessie Drew, the wife of John Drew, died intestate in January 1613, her husband confirmed in her testament dative that she owned livestock, clothing, and spinning yarn "as her awin proper gudis" and also confirmed the customary division of their marital estate into thirds.[74] By contrast, in many testament datives husbands treated their household goods as jointly owned with their wives. When Francis Stewart, the wife of Robert Wilson, died intestate in July 1670, her testament dative noted that Francis "and hir said husband" had "noe goods [or] geir" apart from a cow, a calf, and some household furnishings collectively worth £26 Scots (£2 sterling).[75] When Jean Maine, the wife of John Weir, a maltman burgess of Glasgow, died intestate in October 1646, her husband noted in her testament dative that they "baith owned" brewing equipment, foodstuffs, silver coins, and household furnishings at the time of her death.[76] In her 1604 testament, Margaret Gilmour, the wife of Gavin Allan, noted that she was "infectit with the pest", and that she and her husband left "thair haill gudis & geir" to their two sons, John and Archibald. If their sons were to pass away as a result of the plague, however, Margaret noted that their marital goods were to be divided equally between their respective kin groups.[77] Deborah Simonton has argued that married couples in Scotland "shaped their own marital economies" by altering, or reinforcing, their property rights in their marriage contracts and testaments.[78] The choice of whether husbands and wives treated certain goods as separately or jointly owned seems to have been a private one that was reflected in their testaments.

Testament testamentars reveal the kind of goods that married women claimed ownership of before death, including how they described their material worth. Catherine Richardson has suggested that the ways in which women described their assets help draw out particular questions about early modern attitudes towards material objects.[79] Testaments also help determine whether married women's goods were specifically gendered, with the expectation that most, if not all, of their personal assets consisted of items of paraphernalia. Before her death in February 1648, Agnes Bell, the wife of Robert Paterson, contracted her testament testamentar "be hir awin mouth" in her dwelling place in the parish of Cambuslang, just outside of Glasgow. Agnes and her husband treated their goods as jointly owned, with the clerk recording that they both owned livestock, foodstuffs, and household furniture worth £320 Scots (£24 12s 4d sterling).[80] Agnes then bequeathed specific items of clothing to her children. After calculating the inventory and any outstanding household debts, Agnes declared her latter will and legacy:

> Followes [th]e deids l[att]re will & legacies . . . At davidsdykes [th]e xiiii day of Februarie 1648 yeirs The quhilk day I Agnes Bell spous to Ro[ber]t Petirsone in davidsdykes Leave my soull to god hoiping the same to be saved throw the death & passione of Jesus Chryst my redeamer Nixt I nominat & appoint the s[ai]d Ro[ber]t Patersone my spous my onlie exe[cuto]r & universall intro[mette]r w[i]t[h] my haill gudis & geir to be uset & disponet upone at his pleaso[u]r for [th]e weill proffeit & utilitie & behove of [th]e bairnes procreat betwixt him & me To [the]m I lieve the same & debts being payit except onlie these my Legacies Following Viz I lieve to Jonet Kedder my dochter my meikle cloathe kist and scho to give to Katherine Kedder my uther daughter so meikle of worth [th]erof as Thomas Russell in davidsdyke sall ordaine I lieve to [th]e s[ai]d Bernet Kedder my sone the maist of my frie kist I lieve my grein coat to Agnes Patersone my dochter.

> Follows the deceased's latter will and legacy . . . At Daviesdykes the 14 day of February 1648 years The which day I Agnes Bell spouse to Robert Paterson in Davidsdykes Leave my soul to God hoping the same to be saved through the death and passion of Jesus Christ my redeemer Next I nominate and appoint the said Robert Paterson my spouse my only executor and universal intromitter with my whole goods to be used and disponed upon at his pleasure for the well-being profit and utility of the children procreated between him and me To them I leave my goods and debts being paid except the following legacies Following first I leave to Jonet Kedder my daughter my best clothes chest and she to give to Katherine Kedder my other daughter much of the worth of the clothes chest as Thomas Russell in Davidsdyke shall ordain I leave to Bernet Kedder my son the most of my free chest I leave my green coat to Agnes Paterson my daughter.[81]

As can be gleaned from this particular testament testamentar, Agnes left most of her free share of marital goods to her husband Robert, while bequeathing specific items of clothing and chests to her daughters and sons. Agnes was married twice during her lifetime, as her children had different surnames (Kedder and Paterson). She differentiated between her material assets, yet remained ambiguous with regard to how much they were worth. Her daughter from her previous marriage, Jonet Kedder, received her best clothes chest, while her daughter from her current marriage, Agnes Paterson, was given a green coat. Agnes also instructed her daughter Jonet to give her sister Katherine assets worth a similar amount, while her son, Bernet Kedder, was promised most of the free goods in her chest.

Married women tended to record specific details when bequeathing their paraphernalia by including comprehensive descriptions of their items of clothing. In July 1601, Margaret Kyle, the wife of William Kyle, left her niece a "black kirtill [gown]", a "reid coat", and her "twa best petticoats".[82] In February 1610, Margaret Greg, the wife of Patrick Morrand, left "hir best kirtill" to her sister Mareoun and "ane pair of bodyces" to her eldest sister, Jonet.[83] Jonet Fleming, the wife of James Arnat, left her "weiring claithes", including an "auld kirtill", to her mother, Jonet Walker, before her death in July 1606, with her husband entitled to the rest of her free goods.[84] Elizabeth Locheid, the wife of Gilbert Adam, left her "best plydes with hir worsit [woollen] skirt" to her daughter Margaret and her "best cloak" to her granddaughter Jonet in 1607.[85] Helen Craig, the wife of William Greinleis, a burgess of Paisley, left her sister and her mother various items of clothing in her 1607 testament, with her sister Isobel receiving her "best kirtill" and her mother, Margaret, receiving her "best plydes".[86] Aside from gifting clothing to her kin, Helen also noted that her daughter Margaret was to receive her entire dead's part. Details on the condition, colour, and worth of their clothing show that married women were aware of the material value of such assets when calculating their inventories. Some married women remained ambiguous when gifting their paraphernalia, however. For instance, Katherine Gray, the wife of Edward McLagert, simply left her son Patrick "a cloik [cloak]", while leaving the remainder of "her cloathes" to her daughter Jonet, without providing further details on their accumulated worth.[87]

Married women also asserted ownership of goods in their testaments that would have been considered as belonging to their husbands under their right of *jus mariti*. Many wives clearly considered themselves the owners of various kinds of marital goods, including household furniture, kitchen utensils, brewing equipment, foodstuffs, livestock, and money. Lena Cowen Orlin has suggested that while English wives retained no movable property rights as a result of coverture, there was an "active compensatory ethic at work in common culture" that acknowledged women's former claims to their material possessions.[88] Orlin has shown that goods that English wives brought into marriage were often regifted back to them by their husbands in their wills.[89] Likewise, assets that wives actively used or managed during marriage were often configured as belonging to them alone in their testaments in Scotland, a practice that somewhat indicates acknowledgement of the true owner in spite of the law. In January 1607, Marie Kynloch, the wife of William Pettigrew, left a brewing cauldron to her sister Isobel in her testament.[90] In February 1610, Margaret Greg, the wife of Patrick Morrand, left Jonet Madie, the daughter of David Madie, a "stark" – a tool commonly used for working leather – in her testament.[91] Before her death in July 1597, Bessie Kennedy, the wife of Gilbert McMartein, left her son 40s Scots (3s 1d sterling), her daughter various items of clothing, and her two granddaughters a hogget (adolescent ewe).[92] As Alexandra Shepard has noted, accounting processes during the early modern period involved "highly sophisticated forms of numeracy that drew on a set of qualitative as well as quantitative principles that transcended local boundaries, and that moderated the tenor of social relations".[93] How married women itemised and accounted for their share of marital goods before death in their testaments reflects how these assets were conceptualised and figured within their respective marital households during marriage.

Many wives also stated conditions in their testaments compelling their husbands to care for children. In February 1606, Margaret Cunningham, the wife of William Galbraith, left her dead's part worth £17 2d Scots (£1 6s 4d sterling) equally to her husband and her son John Galbraith on the condition that they were both "agrit and thankfull to the rest of hir bairnes", possibly from a previous marriage.[94] In January 1600, Jonet Gemmill, the wife of Daniel Broun, urged her husband to bring up their daughter Jonet in "godis feir" and to use her share of goods to continue to provide for her until she came of age.[95] After dividing the marital estate into thirds, Marie Fleming compelled her husband John Stark to transfer her share, worth £357 11s 1s Scots (£27 10s 1d sterling), to their second son, James Stark, noting that he would not receive any heritable property through the custom of primogeniture and should be well provided for with movable property.[96]

Married women would also choose to divide their share of goods between their surviving husbands and their children to ensure they were similarly provided for. In September 1606, Margaret Huid, the wife of John Smyth, left her dead's part, worth £107 3d Scots (£8 4s 8d sterling), equally to her husband and her children.[97] In June 1610, Margaret Hunter, wife of David Cochrane, also left her dead's part equally to her husband and her son Robert Cochrane.[98] Moreover, Margaret stipulated that her brother William Hunter and her sister Christine Hunter were to receive the goods if her husband and her son were to die soon after, perhaps alluding to the fact that they were both in ill health. In May 1605, Malie Boyd, the wife of James Montford, left her dead's part to her four sons, noting that her husband could make use of the goods until the children "be of perfyte age".[99] Agnes Dempster, the wife of John Harbert, left her dead's part, worth £8 11s 1d Scots (13s 2d sterling), equally to her three sons, with her husband retaining administrative rights until they had reached fourteen years of age.[100]

Although less frequent, some married women did choose to bequeath their goods and assets to other members of their family aside from their husbands. Marioun Craig, the wife of John Towris, left her dead's part to her daughter Catherine Towris and various members of her kin in January 1604, meaning that her husband lost ownership of one-third of their marital goods.[101] Before her death in December 1592, Jonet Dickie, the wife of John Gottray, left her two sisters, Christian and Margaret, "hir best claithis" and ordered the rest of her goods to be divided equally between her three children.[102] Married women also asked members of their kin to manage their children's property and care for them upon receipt of such goods. Before her death in October 1605, Margaret Mathie, the wife of John Johnstone, asked her brother William to look after her young daughter Jonet following her death.[103] Isobel

Lauchland, a remarried widow, asked her kin to manage her children's inheritance portions and compelled her second husband, John Hunter, to deliver her children into the care of members of her kin, a decision that suggests the children were born of a previous marriage.[104] Mareoun Montgomerie, the wife of John Broun, stipulated in her 1602 testament that her brother Marshall Montgomerie was to assist her husband in raising her two-year-old daughter, Jonet, and that they should both use her share of goods to provide the child with care maintenance.[105]

Husbands and wives frequently imagined their marital goods and debt as jointly owned in testaments. For husbands to retain full control of their marital estate, their wives were expected to confer ownership of household goods on them before death, despite maintaining limited rights to movable goods within marriage. Wives were found gifting a variety of objects to their husbands, children, and kinship network, with detailed accounts of their assets offering insight into their material, emotional, and economic value. Married women who contracted testaments before death regularly bequeathed their paraphernalia, a finding that somewhat confirms the gendered ordering of household goods within marriage. Mothers left daughters (and sometimes sons) their dresses, skirts, and chests, while childless wives left female members of their kin group their wearing apparel. There is, however, some evidence to show that married women bequeathed specific assets that would have belonged to their husbands during marriage. Discussions behind closed doors clearly enabled some women to exert considerable authority over specific marital goods in their testaments, including brewing equipment, livestock, cash, and household furniture.

VI. Conclusion

An in-depth analysis of married women's testaments in Glasgow's commissary court reveals that the division of the community of goods took effect not only on the husband's death but also on the wife's death. Wives could and did bequeath household goods in testaments, with many women in Glasgow exercising their right to do so. What ownership of goods meant to women within marriage, however, is less clear. Husbands and wives often interpreted their movable assets, and debts related to their marital estate, as jointly owned and administered in testaments, which suggests that some wives may have considered themselves joint owners of goods within marriage despite the fact that their ability to exercise authority over these objects within a legal framework was severely limited. At face value, the normative transfer of certain "things" to husbands and wives within marriage enforced a hierarchical ordering of objects and proprietary rights in the household. Household furniture, foodstuffs, and livestock were considered as belonging to husbands. Dresses, jewellery, and chests were understood as primarily belonging to married women, with husbands possessing administrative rights as patriarchal heads of household.[106] Yet married women's testaments reveal that they asserted ownership over a wide range of household goods and assets prior to death, and that their husbands were not automatically entitled to retain ownership of all marital goods as widowers either.

Married women's testamentary practices in Glasgow largely conformed to the transmission of goods within the family network, as husbands, children, and kin were overwhelmingly named as the recipients of their assets. The fact that immovable property, such as land, was strictly protected within the family network could also explain why a significant number of married women left testaments in seventeenth-century Glasgow's commissary court. Married women's movable property rights upon death were embedded in a concept of joint ownership, with the law of succession dictating who received particular household property and why. The eldest son was guaranteed to inherit his parents' heritable estate, while younger children were entitled to an equal proportion of their parents' movable goods. The customary division of marital goods into thirds or halves following the death of a wife reflects the importance of providing the widower, children, and kin with distinctive movable property rights following the dissolution of the marital economy. Married women's property, both heritable and movable, ultimately remained within the kin network, with the presence of children directing its immediate transmission.

Married women formed the majority of women contracting testaments in Glasgow's commissary court across the seventeenth century, with their testamentary practices surpassing the testaments of single women and widows. Investigating married women's testaments enhances historical understanding of not only the lives and experiences of these women but also the influence of inheritance and marital property law regimes and the sometimes contradictory custom involved in directing a married woman's movable property upon her death. Testament testamentars provide a wealth of details into how married women thought about, conceptualised, and distributed their movable goods prior to death. Despite being much overlooked, testament datives provide important information concerning the distribution of marital goods when married women died without leaving a written testament. Married women's testaments in seventeenth-century Glasgow demonstrate the division of objects via family status and gender, the distribution pattern, and the private negotiations to be found within specific households.

Notes

1 NRS, Glasgow commissary court, Register of Testaments, The TT of Elspeth Braidwood, CC9/7/5/fols. 21–22. By 1600, £12 Scots was worth £1 sterling; £1 Scots was worth 1s 6d sterling; 1 Scottish merk was worth 1s 1d sterling. English monetary values have been included in parentheses throughout for ease of reference. See A. J. S. Gibson and T. C. Smout, *Prices, Food, and Wages in Scotland, 1550–1780*, Cambridge 1995 [Cambridge University Press].

2 Ibid.

3 Katie Barclay, *Love, Intimacy and Power. Marriage and Patriarchy in Scotland, 1650–1850*, Manchester 2011 [Manchester University Press], p. 49.

4 James Balfour, *Practicks*, ed. P. G. B. McNeill, Edinburgh 1962 [The Stair Society], p. 93; James Dalrymple, *1st Viscount Stair, The Institutions of the Law of Scotland*, 1st ed., Edinburgh 1693, I. IV. ix, pp. 27–28.

5 Balfour, *Practicks*, p. 93; Thomas Hope, *Major Practicks 1608–1633, 1–2*, ed. J. A. Clyde, Edinburgh 1937–1938 [The Stair Society], I, Part II, Title 17, paragraph 15 and 21, pp. 136–137; For a discussion of paraphernalia see Rebecca Mason, "Married Women, Property and Paraphernalia in Early Modern Scotland", in: Anna Bellavitis and Beatrice

Zucca (eds.), *Gender, Law and Economic Well-Being in Europe from the Fifteenth to the Nineteenth Century. North Versus South?* Abington 2018 [Routledge], pp. 200–214.

6 Elizabeth Ewan, "'To the Longest Livar'. Provisions for the Dissolution of the Marital Economy in Scotland, 1470–1550", in: Amy L. Erickson and Maria Ågren (eds.), *The Marital Economy in Scandinavia and Britain 1400–1900*, Aldershot 2005 [Routledge], pp. 191–206, p. 198.

7 Ibid.

8 Winifred Coutts, "Wife and Widow. The Evidence of Testaments and Marriage Contracts c. 1600", in: Elizabeth Ewan and Maureen M. Meikle (eds.), *Women in Scotland, 1100–1750*, East Linton 1999 [Tuckwell Press], p. 181.

9 Winifred Coutts, "Women, Children and Domestic Servants in Dumfries in the Seventeenth Century. Their Economic Status as Seen through the Registers of Testaments and Grants of Confirmation from 1600 to 1655", in: *Transactions of the Dumfriesshire and Galloway Natural History and Antiquarian Society* 3, 61 (1986), pp. 73–83; Coutts, "Wife and Widow", pp. 176–186.

10 Cathryn Spence, "Women and Business in Sixteenth-Century Edinburgh. Evidence from Their Testaments", in: *Journal of Scottish Historical Studies* 28, 1 (2008), pp. 1–19.

11 Christine Hagen, Margareth Lanzinger and Janine Maegraith, "Competing Interests in Death-Related Stipulations in South Tirol, c. 1350–1600", in: Mia Korpiola and Anu Lahtinen (eds.), *Planning for Death. Wills and Death-Related Property Arrangements in Europe, 1200–1600, Vol. 23, Medieval Law and Its Practice*, Leiden 2018 [Brill], pp. 88–118, p. 88.

12 R. A. Houston, "Custom in Context: Medieval and Early Modern Scotland and England", in: *Past & Present* 211 (2011), pp. 35–76; Brian P. Levack, "Law, Sovereignty and the Union", in: Roger A. Mason (ed.), *Scots and Britons: Scottish Political Thought and the Union of 1603*, Cambridge 1994 [Cambridge University Press], pp. 213–237, p. 217.

13 Balfour, *Practicks*, p. 95.

14 Ibid.

15 Stair, *Institutions*, I, IV, X, XVI, pp. 29–30.

16 Gordon Des Brisay and Karen Sander Thomson, "Crediting Wives. Married Women and Debt Litigation in the Seventeenth Century", in: Elizabeth Ewan and Janay Nugent (eds.), *Finding the Family in Medieval and Early Modern Scotland*, Aldershot 2008 [Ashgate], pp. 85–98, p. 90; Cathryn Spence, *Women, Credit and Debt in Early Modern Scotland*, Manchester 2016 [Manchester University Press], p. 48.

17 Julie Hardwick, *The Practice of Patriarchy: Gender and Politics of Household Authority in Early Modern France*, Pennsylvania 1998 [Pennsylvania State University Press], p. 73.

18 William M. Gordon, "Property and Succession Rights", in: William M. Gordon (ed.), *Roman Law, Scots Law and Legal History*, Edinburgh 2007 [Edinburgh Studies in Law], pp. 194–210, p. 195; See also Katie Barclay, "Natural Affection, Children, and Family Inheritance Practices in the Long Eighteenth Century", in: Janay Nugent and Elizabeth Ewan (eds.), *Children and Youth in Premodern Scotland*, Rochester 2015 [Boydell & Brewer], pp. 136–152, pp. 142–143.

19 Amy L. Erickson and Maria Ågren, "The Marital Economy in Comparative Perspective", in: Amy L. Erickson and Maria Ågren (eds.), *The Marital Economy in Scandinavia and Britain 1400–1900*, Aldershot 2005 [Routledge], pp. 3–20, pp. 8–9.

20 Thomas Craig, *The Jus Feudale*, 1–2, trans. J A Clyde, Edinburgh and London 1934 [Hodge], II, pp. 692–694.

21 Balfour, *Practicks*, p. 95, 104, 163.

22 Ibid., p. 163.

23 George Smith Pryde, "The City and Burgh of Glasgow, 1100–1750", in: Robert Miller and Joy Tivy (eds.), *The Glasgow Region: A General Survey*, Glasgow 1958 [T. & A. Constable], pp. 134–149, p. 144; E. P. Dennison, "Glasgow: To 1700", in: Michael Lynch, Stana Nenadic and I. Maver (eds.), *The Oxford Companion to Scottish History*, Oxford 2001 [Oxford University Press], pp. 266–267.

24 T. C. Smout, "The Glasgow Merchant Community in the Seventeenth Century", in: *The Scottish Historical Review* 47, 143 (1968), pp. 53–71.

25 Dennison, "Glasgow: To 1700", pp. 266–267.
26 Thomas Green, "Romano-Canonical Procedure in Reformation Scotland. The Example of the Court of the Commissaries of Edinburgh", in: *The Journal of Legal History* 36, 3 (2015), pp. 217–235.
27 Quots were set as costing 12 d in the pound of the testator's free goods in 1420. See Balfour, *Practicks*, p. 217.
28 The equivalent of English letters of administration. See Amy L. Erickson, *Women and Property in Early Modern England*, London 1993 [Routledge], pp. 34–39, 206–207.
29 The equivalent of English probate. See Lloyd Davis, "Women's Wills in Early Modern England", in: Nancy E. Wright, Margaret W. Ferguson and A. R. Buck (eds.), *Women, Property, and the Letters of the Law in Early Modern England*, Toronto 2004 [University of Toronto Press], pp. 219–236; Lloyd Bonfield, *Devising, Dying, and Dispute in Early Modern England*, Farnham 2012 [Ashgate], pp. 225–241; Cordelia Beattie, "Married Women's Wills: Probate, Property, and Piety in Later Medieval England", in: *Law and History Review* (2019), pp. 1–32.
30 This data was collected using the official government resource Scotland's People, www.scotlandspeople.gov.uk/ (accessed 12 February 2020).
31 Balfour, *Practicks*, p. 217; Stair, *Institutions*, III. VIII. xxx, lii, pp. 502, 510.
32 Balfour, *Practicks*, p. 234; Craig, *Jus feudale*, II, pp. 719–721. The "heirship-moveables" were not included in the will and testament, as they were considered heritable property (despite the fact that they were movable assets). See Ilya Kotlyar, "The Evolution of the Scots Law and Practice of Succession, 1300–2000", in: Maria Gigliola Di Renzo Villata (ed.), *Succession Law, Practice and Society in Europe Across the Centuries*, Cham 2018 [Springer], pp. 167–206, p. 176.
33 Frederick Parker Walton, *Handbook of Husband and Wife According to the Law of Scotland*, 2nd ed., Edinburgh 1922 [W. Green], p. 206.
34 Coutts, "Wife and Widow", p. 179.
35 Amy L. Erickson, "Property and Widowhood in England 1660–1840", in: Sandra Cavallo and Lyndan Warner (eds.), *Widowhood in Medieval and Early Modern Europe*, 2nd ed., Abington 1999 [Routledge], pp. 145–163; Janet S. Loengard, "'Which May Be Said to Be Her Own'. Widows and Goods in Late-Medieval England", in: Maryanne Kowaleski and P. J. P. Goldberg (eds.), *Medieval Domesticity. Home, Housing and Household in Medieval England*, Cambridge 2008 [Cambridge University Press], pp. 162–176.
36 Erickson, "Property and Widowhood in England 1660–1840", p. 153.
37 Lindsay R. Moore, *Women Before the Court: Law and Patriarchy in the Anglo-American World, 1600–1800*, Manchester 2019 [Manchester University Press], p. 24.
38 Kotlyar, "The Evolution of the Scots Law and Practice of Succession: 1300–2000", p. 177.
39 George Mackenzie, *Institutions of the Law of Scotland*, London 1694, I. VI, p. 37.
40 Julie Hardwick, "Widowhood and Patriarchy in Seventeenth Century France", in: *Journal of Social History* 26 (1992), pp. 133–148, p. 134.
41 Jutta Sperling, "Marriage, Kinship and Property in Portuguese Testaments (1649–1650)", in: Shona Kelly Wray and Jutta Gisela Sperling (eds.), *Across the Religious Divide: Women, Property, and Law in the Wider Mediterranean (ca. 1300–1800)*, New York 2010 [Routledge], pp. 158–174, p. 160.
42 Barclay, *Love, Intimacy and Power*, p. 49.
43 Stair, *Institutions*, I. IV. ix, pp. 27–28.
44 Kotlyar, "The Evolution of the Scots Law and Practice of Succession: 1300–2000", pp. 193–194.
45 Balfour, *Practicks*, p. 216.
46 Hope, *Major Practicks*, I, Part IV, Title I, paragraph 2, p. 285.
47 Stair, *Institutions*, III. VIII. xxxvii, p. 504; Mackenzie, *Institutions*, III. IX, p. 214.
48 Anne Ashley, "Property in Relation to Marriage and Family", in: *Juridical Review* 65 (1953), pp. 37–68.
49 Kotlyar, "The Evolution of the Scots Law and Practice of Succession: 1300–2000", p. 178.
50 Ibid., pp. 178–179.

51 Coutts, "Wife and Widow", p. 177; Spence, "Women and Business in Sixteenth-Century Edinburgh", p. 4.
52 Balfour, *Practicks*, p. 217.
53 Stair, *Institutions*, III. VIII. Xliii, p. 506.
54 Erickson, *Women and Property in Early Modern England*, p. 204.
55 Elisabeth Salter, "Women's Last Wills and Testaments in Hull, England (c.1450–1555)", in: *Early Modern Women* 12, 2 (Spring 2018), pp. 33–53, p. 36.
56 NRS, Glasgow commissary court, Register of Testaments, CC9/7/vols. 6–11, 20–24, 29–35, 37–42, 47–49.
57 Ibid.
58 Men who were deaf and dumb or declared insane were forbidden from contracting a written testament. See Balfour, *Practicks*, pp. 216–217.
59 Kotlyar, "The Evolution of the Scots Law and Practice of Succession: 1300–20000", p. 194.
60 Erickson, "Property and Widowhood in England 1660–1840", p. 145.
61 NRS, Glasgow commissary court, Register of Testaments, The TT of Mareoun Law, CC9/7/5/fols. 393–394.
62 NRS, Glasgow commissary court, Register of Testaments, The TT of Bessie Campbell, CC9/7/3/fols. 183–184.
63 NRS, Glasgow commissary court, Register of Testaments, The TT of Margaret Inglis, CC9/7/5/fols. 123–124.
64 NRS, Glasgow commissary court, Register of Testaments, The TT of Margaret Mortoun, CC9/7/4/fols. 99–101. My emphasis. Loose translation: "[W]hatever goods and gear shall happen to be acquired or obtained by him and me during our lifetimes, the same shall belong to the said James."
65 Joanne Bailey, *Unquiet Lives: Marriage and Marriage Difficulties in England, 1660–1800*, Cambridge 2003 [Cambridge University Press], pp. 104–105.
66 Balfour, *Practicks*, pp. 114, 121.
67 Glasgow City Archives, Glasgow burgh court, book of bonds, B10/10/1/fol. 97.
68 NRS, Glasgow commissary court, Register of Testaments, The TD of Margaret Bunteine, CC9/7/12/ fols 118–121.
69 NRS, Glasgow commissary court, Register of Testaments, The TD of Margaret Paterson, CC9/7/29/fols. 376–378.
70 NRS, Glasgow commissary court, Register of Decreets and Decrees Dative, CC9/3/14/ fols. 131–132.
71 J. Irvine Smith, "Succession Part II: The History of Particular Branches of Scots Law and Practice: The Law of Property", in: *Introduction to Scottish Legal History*, Edinburgh 1958 [Stair Society], pp. 208–221, pp. 212–215.
72 Kotlyar, "The Evolution of the Scots Law and Practice of Succession: 1300–2000", p. 179.
73 NRS, Glasgow commissary court, Register of Testaments, The TT of Jonet Dickie, CC9/7/3/fols. 60–61.
74 NRS, Glasgow commissary court, Register of Testaments, The TD of Bessie Drew, CC9/7/9/fols. 217–220. The word "proper" is defined in the Dictionary of the Scots Language as "belonging, pertaining or appropriate to one as a property, quality or part". See "Proper *adj.*", Dictionary of the Scots Language. 2004. Scottish Language Dictionaries Ltd., www.dsl.ac.uk/entry/dost/proper (accessed 27 March 2019).
75 NRS, Glasgow commissary court, Register of Testaments, The TD of Francis Stewart, CC9/7/38/fols. 275–276.
76 NRS, Glasgow commissary court, Register of Testaments, The TD of Jean Maine, CC9/7/30/fol. 80.
77 NRS, Glasgow commissary court, Register of Testaments, The TT of Margaret Gilmour, CC9/7/4/fols. 34–36.
78 Deborah Simonton, "Community of Goods, Coverture and Capability in Britain: Scotland Versus England", in: Anna Bellavitis and Beatrice Zucca (eds.), *Gender, Law and Economic Well-Being in Europe from the Fifteenth to the Nineteenth Century*, Abington 2018 [Routledge], pp. 31–46, p. 37.

79 Catherine Richardson, "'A Very Fit Hat': Personal Objects and Early Modern Affection", in: Tara Hamling and Catherine Richardson (eds.), *Everyday Objects: Medieval and Early Modern Material Culture and Its Meanings*, Farnham 2010 [Ashgate], pp. 289–298, p. 289.
80 NRS, Glasgow commissary court, Register of Testaments, The TT of Agnes Bell, CC9/7/30/fols. 388–390.
81 Opening excerpt from Agnes Bell's 1648 latter will and legacy in her testament testamentar (with modern English translation). NRS, Glasgow commissary court, Register of Testaments, CC9/7/30/fols. 388–390.
82 NRS, Glasgow commissary court, Register of Testaments, The TT of Margaret Kyle, CC9/7/3/fols. 63–64.
83 NRS, Glasgow commissary court, Register of Testaments, The TT of Margaret Greg, CC9/7/6/fols. 250–251.
84 NRS, Glasgow commissary court, Register of Testaments, The TT of Jonet Fleming, CC9/7/4/fols. 264–265.
85 NRS, Glasgow commissary court, Register of Testaments, The TT of Elizabeth Locheid, CC9/7/5/fols. 71–73.
86 NRS, Glasgow commissary court, Register of Testaments, The TT of Helen Craig, CC9/7/5/fols. 57–58.
87 NRS, Glasgow commissary court, Register of Testaments, The TT of Katherine Gray, CC9/7/4/fols. 114–115.
88 Lena Cowen Orlin, "Empty Vessels", in: Tara Hamling and Catherine Richardson (eds.), *Everyday Objects: Medieval and Early Modern Material Culture and Its Meanings*, Farnham 2010 [Ashgate], pp. 299–308, p. 304.
89 Ibid., p. 304.
90 NRS, Glasgow commissary court, Register of Testaments, The TT of Marie Kynloch, CC9/7/4/fols. 420–422.
91 NRS, Glasgow commissary court, Register of Testaments, The TT of Margaret Greg, CC9/7/6/fols. 250–251.
92 NRS, Glasgow commissary court, Register of Testaments, The TT of Bessie Kennedy, CC9/7/5/fols. 199–200.
93 Alexandra Shepard, *Accounting for Oneself: Worth, Status, and the Social Order in Early Modern England*, Oxford 2015 [Oxford University Press], p. 2.
94 NRS, Glasgow commissary court, Register of Testaments, The TT of Margaret Cunningham, CC9/7/5/fols. 222–223.
95 NRS, Glasgow commissary court, Register of Testaments, The TT of Jonet Gemmill, CC9/7/6/fols. 326–327.
96 NRS, Glasgow commissary court, Register of Testaments, The TT of Marie Fleming, CC9/7/6/fols. 322–323.
97 NRS, Glasgow commissary court, Register of Testaments, The TT of Margaret Huid, CC9/7/5/fols. 108–109.
98 NRS, Glasgow commissary court, Register of Testaments, The TT of Margaret Hunter, CC9/7/6/fols. 396–397.
99 NRS, Glasgow commissary court, Register of Testaments, The TT of Malie Boyd, CC9/7/3/fols. 103–105.
100 NRS, Glasgow commissary court, Register of Testaments, The TT of Agnes Dempster, CC9/7/4/fols. 270–271.
101 NRS, Glasgow commissary court, Register of Testaments, The TT of Jonet Gilmour, CC9/7/4/fols. 144–145.
102 NRS, Glasgow commissary court, Register of Testaments, The TT of Jonet Dickie, CC9/7/3/fols. 60–61.
103 NRS, Glasgow commissary court, Register of Testaments, The TT of Margaret Mathie, CC9/7/4/fols. 75–76.
104 NRS, Glasgow commissary court, Register of Testaments, The TT of Isobel Lauchland, CC9/7/4/fols. 107–108.

105 NRS, Glasgow commissary court, Register of Testaments, The TT of Mareoun Montgomerie, CC9/7/4/fols. 207–208.
106 For a discussion on the gendering of household goods see Karin Gottschalk, "Does Property Have a Gender? Household Goods and Conceptions of Law and Justice in Late Medieval and Early Modern Saxony", in: *The Medieval History Journal* 8, 1 (2005), pp. 7–24, p. 7.

Sources

Archives

Glasgow City Archives (GCA)

Glasgow burgh court

- Book of bonds:
    - B10/10/1

National Records of Scotland (NRS)

Glasgow commissary court

- Register of Testaments:
    - CC9/7/3; CC9/7/4; CC9/7/5; CC9/7/6; CC9/7/9; CC9/7/12; CC9/3/14; CC9/7/30; CC9/7/38
- Register of Decreets and Decrees Dative
    - CC9/3/14; CC9/3/7

Printed sources

Balfour, James, *Practicks*, vol. 1–2, ed. P. G. B. McNeill, Edinburgh 1962 [The Stair Society].

Craig, Thomas, *The Jus Feudale*, vol. 1–2, trans. J. A. Clyde, Edinburgh and London 1934 [Hodge], II, pp. 692–694.

Hope, Thomas, *Major Practicks 1608–1633*, vol. 1–2, ed. J. A. Clyde, Edinburgh 1937–1938 [The Stair Society].

Mackenzie, George, *Institutions of the Law of Scotland*, London 1694, I. VI.

Stair, James Dalrymple, *1st Viscount, The Institutions of the Law of Scotland*, 1st ed., Edinburgh 1681 (revised in 1693), I. IV. ix, pp. 27–28.

Bibliography

Ashley, Anne, "Property in Relation to Marriage and Family", in: *Juridical Review* 65 (1953), pp. 37–68.

Bailey, Joanne, *Unquiet Lives: Marriage and Marriage Difficulties in England, 1660–1800*, Cambridge 2003 [Cambridge University Press].

Barclay, Katie, *Love, Intimacy and Power. Marriage and Patriarchy in Scotland, 1650–1850*, Manchester 2011 [Manchester University Press] (Gender in History).

———, "Natural Affection, Children, and Family Inheritance Practices in the Long Eighteenth Century", in: Janay Nugent and Elizabeth Ewan (eds.), *Children and Youth in Premodern Scotland*, Rochester 2015 [Boydell & Brewer], pp. 136–152.

Beattie, Cordelia, "Married Women's Wills: Probate, Property, and Piety in Later Medieval England", in: *Law and History Review* (2019), pp. 1–32.

Bonfield, Lloyd, *Devising, Dying, and Dispute in Early Modern England*, Farnham 2012 [Ashgate], pp. 225–241.

Coutts, Winifred, "Wife and Widow. The Evidence of Testaments and Marriage Contracts *c.* 1600", in: Elizabeth Ewan and Maureen M. Meikle (eds.), *Women in Scotland, 1100–1750*, East Linton 1999 [Tuckwell Press], pp. 176–186.

———, "Women, Children and Domestic Servants in Dumfries in the Seventeenth Century. Their Economic Status as Seen through the Registers of Testaments and Grants of Confirmation from 1600 to 1655", in: *Transactions of the Dumfriesshire and Galloway Natural History and Antiquarian Society* 3, 61 (1986), pp. 73–83.

Davis, Lloyd, "Women's Wills in Early Modern England", in: Nancy E. Wright, Margaret W. Ferguson and A. R. Buck (eds.), *Women, Property, and the Letters of the Law in Early Modern England*, Toronto 2004 [University of Toronto Press], pp. 219–236.

Dennison, E. P., "Glasgow: To 1700", in: Michael Lynch, Stana Nenadic and I. Maver (eds.), *The Oxford Companion to Scottish History*, Oxford 2001 [Oxford University Press], pp. 266–267.

DesBrisay, Gordon and Karen Sander Thomson, "Crediting Wives. Married Women and Debt Litigation in the Seventeenth Century", in: Elizabeth Ewan and Janay Nugent (eds.), *Finding the Family in Medieval and Early Modern Scotland*, Aldershot 2008 [Ashgate] (Women and Gender in the Early Modern World), pp. 85–98.

Erickson, Amy L., *Women and Property in Early Modern England*, London 1993 [Routledge].

———, "Property and Widowhood in England 1660–1840", in: Sandra Cavallo and Lyndan Warner (eds.), *Widowhood in Medieval and Early Modern Europe*, 2nd ed., Abington 1999 [Routledge], pp. 145–163.

Erickson, Amy L. and Maria Ågren, "The Marital Economy in Comparative Perspective", in: Amy L. Erickson and Maria Ågren (ed.), *The Marital Economy in Scandinavia and Britain 1400–1900*, Aldershot 2005 [Routledge], pp. 3–20.

Ewan, Elizabeth, "'To the Longest Livar'. Provisions for the Dissolution of the Marital Economy in Scotland, 1470–1550", in: Amy L. Erickson and Maria Ågren (eds.), *The Marital Economy in Scandinavia and Britain, 1400–1900*, Aldershot 2005 [Routledge], pp. 191–206.

Gibson, A. J. S. and T. C. Smout, *Prices, Food, and Wages in Scotland, 1550–1780*, Cambridge 1995 [Cambridge University Press].

Gordon, William M., "Property and Succession Rights" in: *Idem, Roman Law, Scots Law and Legal History*, Edinburgh 2007 [Edinburgh Studies in Law], pp. 194–210.

Gottschalk, Karin, "Does Property Have a Gender? Household Goods and Conceptions of Law and Justice in Late Medieval and Early Modern Saxony", in: *The Medieval History Journal* 8, 1 (2005), pp. 7–24.

Green, Thomas, "Romano-Canonical Procedure in Reformation Scotland. The Example of the Court of the Commissaries of Edinburgh", in: *The Journal of Legal History* 36, 3 (2015), pp. 217–235.

Hagen, Christine, Margareth Lanzinger and Janine Maegraith, "Competing Interests in Death-Related Stipulations in South Tirol, *c.* 1350–1600", in: Mia Korpiola and Anu Lahtinen (eds.), *Planning for Death. Wills and Death-Related Property Arrangements in Europe, 1200–1600*, Leiden 2018 [Brill] (Medieval Law and Its Practice 23), pp. 88–118.

Hardwick, Julie, "Widowhood and Patriarchy in Seventeenth Century France", in: *Journal of Social History* 26 (1992), pp. 133–148.

———, *The Practice of Patriarchy: Gender and Politics of Household Authority in Early Modern France*, Pennsylvania 1998 [Pennsylvania State University Press].

Houston, R. A., "Custom in Context: Medieval and Early Modern Scotland and England", in: *Past & Present* 211 (2011), pp. 35–76.

Kotlyar, Ilya, "The Evolution of the Scots Law and Practice of Succession, 1300–2000", in: Maria Gigliola Di Renzo Villata (ed.), *Succession Law, Practice and Society in Europe Across the Centuries*, Cham 2018 [Springer], pp. 167–206.

Levack, Brian P., "Law, Sovereignty and the Union", in: Roger A. Mason (ed.), *Scots and Britons: Scottish Political Thought and the Union of 1603*, Cambridge 1994 [Cambridge University Press], pp. 213–237.

Loengard, Janet S. "'Which May Be Said to Be Her Own. Widows and Goods in Late-Medieval England", in: Maryanne Kowaleski and P. J. P. Goldberg (eds.), *Medieval Domesticity. Home, Housing and Household in Medieval England*, Cambridge 2008 [Cambridge University Press], pp. 162–176.

Mason, Rebecca, "Married Women, Property and Paraphernalia in Early Modern Scotland", in: Anna Bellavitis and Beatrice Zucca (eds.), *Gender, Law and Economic Well-Being in Europe from the Fifteenth to the Nineteenth Century. North versus South?* Abington 2018 [Routledge] (Gender and Well-Being), pp. 200–214.

Moore, Lindsay R., *Women Before the Court: Law and Patriarchy in the Anglo-American World, 1600–1800*, Manchester 2019 [Manchester University Press] (Gender in History).

Orlin, Lena Cowen, "Empty Vessels", in: Tara Hamling and Catherine Richardson (eds.), *Everyday Objects. Medieval and Early Modern Material Culture and its Meanings*, Farnham 2010 [Ashgate], pp. 299–308.

Paton, G. Campbell H., "Husband and Wife. Property Rights and Relationships", in: *An Introduction to Scottish Legal History*, Edinburgh 1958 [Stair Society], pp. 99–115.

Pryde, George Smith, "The City and Burgh of Glasgow, 1100–1750", in: Robert Miller and Joy Tivy (eds.), *The Glasgow Region. A General Survey*, Glasgow 1958 [T. & A. Constable], pp. 134–149.

Richardson, Catherine, "'A Very Fit Hat': Personal Objects and Early Modern Affection", in: Tara Hamling and Catherine Richardson (eds.), *Everyday Objects: Medieval and Early Modern Material Culture and its Meanings*, Farnham 2010 [Ashgate], pp. 289–298.

Salter, Elisabeth, "Women's Last Wills and Testaments in Hull, England (c.1450–1555)", in: *Early Modern Women* 12, 2 (Spring 2018), pp. 33–53.

Sanderson, Margaret H. B., *A Kindly Place? Living in Sixteenth-Century Scotland*, East Linton 2002 [Tuckwell Press].

Shepard, Alexandra, *Accounting for Oneself: Worth, Status, and the Social Order in Early Modern England*, Oxford 2015 [Oxford University Press].

Simonton, Deborah, "Community of Goods, Coverture and Capability in Britain. Scotland versus England", in: Anna Bellavitis and Beatrice Zucca (eds.), *Gender, Law and Economic Well-Being in Europe from the Fifteenth to the Nineteenth Century. North versus South?* Abington 2018 [Routledge] (Gender and Well-Being), pp. 31–46.

Smith, Irvine, "Succession Part II: The History of Particular Branches of Scots Law and Practice: The Law of Property", in: *An Introduction to Scottish Legal History*, Edinburgh 1958 [Stair Society], pp. 208–221.

Smout, T. C., "The Glasgow Merchant Community in the Seventeenth Century", in: *The Scottish Historical Review* 47, 143 (April 1968), pp. 53–71.

Spence, Cathryn, "Women and Business in Sixteenth-Century Edinburgh. Evidence from their Testaments", in: *Journal of Scottish Historical Studies* 28, 1 (2008), pp. 1–19.
———, *Women, Credit and Debt in Early Modern Scotland*, Manchester 2016 [Manchester University Press].
Sperling, Jutta, "Marriage, Kinship and Property in Portuguese Testaments (1649–1650)", in: Shona Kelly Wray and Jutta Gisela Sperling (eds.), *Across the Religious Divide: Women, Property, and Law in the Wider Mediterranean (ca. 1300–1800)*, New York 2010 [Routledge], pp. 158–174.
Walton, Frederick Parker, *Handbook of Husband and Wife According to the Law of Scotland*, 2nd ed., Edinburgh 1922 [W. Green].

Dictionaries

"Proper *adj*", in: *Dictionary of the Scots Language*, 2004 [Scottish Language Dictionaries], www.dsl.ac.uk/entry/dost/proper (accessed 27 Mar 2019).

Websites

Scotland's People, www.scotlandspeople.gov.uk/ (accessed 12 February 2020).

FIGURE 5.1 Map of Tyrol, Guillaume de L'Isle, Philippe Buache, *Carte d' Europe*, 1769 (detail).

Source: Library of Congress Geography and Map Division, Washington, D.C., U.S.A., public domain, G5700 1724. L5 TIL, http://hdl.loc.gov/loc.gmd/g5700.ct000045 (15.02.2020, 13:00 CET).

5

HYBRID LEGAL CULTURES AMONG THE EARLY MODERN TYROLEAN NOBILITY

Marriage contracts and the symbolic value of assets

Siglinde Clementi

ABSTRACT

In this chapter, the idea of the ideational in the material developed by ethnologist Ulrike Langbein for analysing inheritance practices in the late twentieth century will be applied as a fundamental cultural idea to the property arrangements that were made upon marriages between nobles during the early modern period. Marriage contracts prove to be extremely interesting sources when they are analysed with this double approach of material basis and ideational meaning. They accompanied and structured a highly significant juncture in families' management of their assets. At first glance, marriage contracts appear to focus on specifying the relevant assets and modalities of their exchange. But when interpreted against the backdrop of the living environment and the cultural ideas of the people involved, such agreements reveal themselves to have been the basis for complex and conflict-prone negotiations that aimed to maintain social continuity even as new familial entities were formed and built. The safeguarding and enhancement of the honour of all participants – including, or perhaps especially, that of women – were, despite the patrilineal orientation and alongside the priority of material protection, the most important concern. This "negotiated honour" is manifested in the marriage contracts on the basis of the nobility's own set of values, including its specific ideas of justice and family strategies structured along gender and generational lines.[1]

I. Introduction

The following considerations are accompanied by two premises that are simultaneously open research questions: The issue of the status of marital goods and the discussion as to their symbolic significance. Regarding how dowries or marriage portions are viewed, there exist two contrasting standpoints that have been formulated by Jack Goody and Diane Owen Hughes. Goody defines the transfer of property via marriage and inheritance as bilateral "diverging devolution".[2] Family assets, he writes, were passed on via marriage practices and inheritance to heirs of both genders – to sons and daughters. Owen Hughes, by contrast, views dowries as the practical consequence of the choice to exclude daughters from succession.[3] Many voices have since joined this discussion, most recently those of Simona Feci and Isabelle Chabot.[4] At its core, the issue here is the status of marital property in intra-family wealth transfer processes and the gender-specific implications of this status. And in my own protagonist-centred, microhistorical approach, I start from the assumption that marriage represented a first step in the complex process of inheritance both for an affected daughter and from the perspective of her family of origin.

The second premise has to do with the theory of intangible inheritance and picks up on several theses that the anthropologist Ulrike Langbein formulated recently in her analysis of inheritance processes. "The sober-seeming principle of agnatic seniority," writes Langbein, "is highly symbolic. It serves the yearning for social continuity that symbolically overcomes mortality and transcends social time."[5] Therefore, to understand the process of inheritance, we need to ask about the ideational component of that which is material. Since marriage can be considered a first step in the process of inheritance, one that constituted both the basis of women's personal property and a fundamental social ritual that gave rise to new kinship ties via the negotiation of asset values, we can and must inquire as to the ideational in the material in this regard as well.

The present chapter approaches this complex of questions by way of two steps. The first will be to analyse the assets and ownership rights negotiated over in the marriage contracts of Tyrolean aristocrats, and the second will be to discuss their symbolic, ideational significance.

II. Political and legal contexts

The studied families were members of the Tyrolean nobility; these were landed nobles, kin groups not immediate to the empire that situated and oriented themselves within the heterogeneous territory of Tyrol.[6] Three centres of rule overlapped in the territory of early modern Tyrol: The Habsburg-dominated county of Tyrol with its seat of government in Innsbruck, the prince-bishopric of Brixen, and the prince-bishopric of Trento. In a legal sense, both bishoprics were immediate to the empire but simultaneously bound to the Tyrolean counts by individual treaties. And throughout the entire early modern period, it was the counts who embodied Tyrol's pre-eminent authority in terms of taxation and military matters.[7] The Tyrolean landowning noble families administrated fiefs and occupied offices both of the county of Tyrol and of the prince-bishoprics of Brixen and Trento, but the prevailing power constellation and their landownership entailed their fundamental orientation toward Innsbruck. That city was the seat of the Habsburg court in Tyrol, it was simultaneously the seat of the Upper Austrian government, and it was thus also the place where the Tyrolean estates (*Landstände*) met for the State Diet (*Landtag*);[8] furthermore, numerous male and several female representatives of these families occupied political offices there. Some members of these families also aimed beyond Innsbruck and assumed offices at the court in Graz or, as occurred above all with the Trautson family, in Vienna. Additionally, all three ruling entities present in Tyrol's territory conferred honorary offices that were significant to the noble families as social capital and were also typically handed down from fathers to their male heirs.[9] Furthermore, members of these families also occupied clerical sinecures in prince-bishoprics and assumed important functions at monasteries in the region and occasionally farther afield (such as in Gurk, Seckau, or Passau).[10]

Despite the existence of other legal codices within the same geographic space (like the Statute of Trento that was valid within the prince-bishopric of Trento as well as various more specific statutes), the legal frame of reference for these noble families was the Tyrolean Law Code (*Tiroler Landesordnung*), which had entered force in 1526 and was amended in 1532 and again in 1573. The legal orientation in Tyrol thus corresponded to the political and cultural orientation in Tyrol's Habsburg-dominated territory, for the Tyrolean Law Code – which had been decreed by Tyrol's Habsburg rulers – was the principal legal foundation during the early modern period even if the area represented a space of transition, not just culturally and politically but also legally, between northern and southern legal cultures.[11] Fundamental orientation towards the Tyrolean Law Code and additional vague referral to customs among nobles – according to noble custom and territorial laws, say the sources – have proven valid for the families studied so far, who were centred in the county of Tyrol, with individual lines in the territory's southern region, as was the case with the Wolkenstein-Trostburgs, the Welspergs, and the Spaurs. While it is thinkable that families oriented more towards the south – such as the Thuns, the Arcos, the Lodrons, and the Madruzzos – were differently oriented, this cannot be evaluated on the basis of the analysis conducted thus far. The marriage contracts examined so far that involve marriages between members of the studied families with members of more southern-oriented families such as the Madruzzos or the Arcos likewise refer to the Tyrolean Law Code and noble customs in Tyrol.[12]

During the early modern period, Tyrolean territory was a place where two different legal systems – the system of marriage portions, which predominated in German-speaking lands, and the Italian dowry system – that determined the legal practice regarding marital property regimes came together.[13] While the "Germanic" system of marriage portions was characterised by greater reciprocity in the exchanges that took place when a couple married (the marriage portion from the bride's side and the morning gift and counter-dowry from that of the groom), the Italian dowry system was more one-sided. It featured a dowry from the bride's side without a counter-gift from the groom and daughters' systematic renunciation of their inheritances in return.[14] The ways in which these differing systems came together in early modern Tyrol and influenced the legal practice of the Tyrolean nobility will be the object of analysis in the following. First, the legal foundations and types of wealth negotiated over in marriage contracts will be looked at, after which a second step will discuss the associated symbolic valency of marriage portions and the interrelationship of material values and symbolic capital.

The sources used for the present analysis are marriage contracts as well as documents that have come down to us in parallel therewith: Receipts, letters of renunciation, widows' endowments, and private correspondence of Tyrolean noble families whose family archives are extant and accessible.[15] Difficult-to-reconstruct genealogies form the basis upon which to understand generational dynamics as well as marriage and inheritance practices.[16]

III. The marital property regime

The central type of wedding gift detailed in early modern Tyrolean marriage contracts was the marriage portion (*Heiratsgut/Heimsteuer*). It was quite often comprised of a monetary sum from a woman's paternal inheritance plus a sum from her maternal inheritance. It was thus that Anna von Wolkenstein – upon marrying Anton von Spaur in 1566 – received a marriage portion from her paternal inheritance in the amount of 3,000 guilders as well as an additional 1,000 guilders from her maternal inheritance, with the latter being one-quarter of the marriage portion that her mother had brought into the marriage to her father, Wilhelm von Wolkenstein; the remaining 3,000 guilders went to Anna's three siblings.[17] In the lion's share of cases, the marriage portion was a sum of money. Only the few inheriting daughters also contributed real estate to their marriages. In 1550, for example, Elisabeth Lang von Wellenburg augmented the wealth brought to the marriage by her groom, Kaspar von Wolkenstein-Trostburg, with a marriage portion that included not only 11,000 guilders in the form of lease proceeds but also her future inheritance of half the domain of Kitzbühel, which took place several years later and made a very important contribution to the consolidation of the Wolkenstein-Trostburg family's Trento line.[18] While inheriting daughters from neighbouring areas in the north – the Archbishopric of Salzburg, Bavaria, and Augsburg – were also accorded fiefdoms as marriage portions, marriage arrangements where both prospective spouses were from Tyrol drew clear distinctions between allodia (freehold estates) and fiefdoms. The latter could only be inherited by women if they were designated "women's fiefdoms", which was possible only with the consent of the respective overlords.[19] Otherwise, a woman could inherit only the allodial property of her father, with any fiefdoms going to the male heir who was next in line. Anna von Wolkenstein – explicitly identified as an "inheriting daughter" in her marriage contract – brought to her 1521 marriage to Michael von Neuhaus "any and all possessions left by him [her late father, Anton], with no exceptions, . . . excepting the men's fiefdoms as listed".[20]

In numerous marriage contracts, only part of the marriage portion was specified as a sum of money to be paid out, with the rest consisting of lease proceeds. Of the 3,000 guilder marriage portion that Maria Klara Ingram contributed to her 1677 marriage to Vinciguerra d'Arco, the family of the bride promised a payout of only 2,000 guilders following the wedding, with the rest consisting of interest on capital investments, the provenance, amounts, and yields of which were all noted in the marriage contract.[21]

During the period under study, marriage portions increased considerably in size, from the 1,000 or 1,500 guilders that was common at the outset of the sixteenth century to average marriage portion values of between 3,000 and 6,000 guilders in the seventeenth century. Numerous marriage arrangements, above all for transregional marriages, saw far higher sums pledged, with the marriage portions of the Fugger daughters being among the highest. In 1582, Adalberta Fugger brought 15,000 guilders to her marriage to Christoph von Wesperg. In the 1542 marriage of Veronika Fugger and Daniel Felix Spaur, it was 26,770 guilders, while the marriage of Susanna Fugger and Balthasar Trautson in 1555 featured a marriage portion of 30,000 guilders.[22] Marriages within Tyrol could also sometimes feature high-value marriage portions: Johanna Madruzzo contributed 15,000 guilders to her 1609 marriage to Albrecht von Wolkenstein and was pledged a morning gift of 6,000 guilders.[23]

Payout modalities were part of the marriage arrangements; they were either tacitly assumed or specified in the marriage contracts. These dispositions ranged from a lapidary "on the wedding day",[24] "following renunciation, the wedding, and consummation",[25] or "within one year of consummation"[26] to more complicated arrangements, such as half within one year and the second half within the marriage's second year,[27] to be paid over five years at the rate of 200 guilders annually[28] or 100 guilders annually until the entire amount of 6,000 guilders had been paid out.[29]

In addition to the marriage portion, brides brought a trousseau (*Ausfertigung*) into their marriages. The trousseau was a standard component of every aristocratic marriage contract and encompassed the material goods that a woman brought into married life; in the aristocratic context, these were her clothing, jewellery, and ribbons. Such marriage contracts make only cursory reference to the contents of such trousseaus and typically indicate just their overall value, with 1,000 guilders quite often being stated as a minimum. There did, however, exist more valuable trousseaus worth up to 2,500 guilders. The significance of the trousseau in the aristocratic context has to do with the representative duties of a noble wife and lady of the house. Together with her husband – albeit subject to a higher degree of public attention – she had the responsibility of representing their "house" on various occasions (such as acts of hereditary homage, festive events at court, and religious celebrations), and even in everyday life she had to help project the splendour of the house to the outside world and represent the honour of their estate in a way that was evident for all to see. For this reason, the importance of the trousseau as a part of every noblewoman's wealth should not be underestimated, and marriage contracts lend clear expression to this importance. The bride's family would thereby emphasise the significance of the material contribution they were making to the marriage in addition to the marriage portion.

The great significance of marriage arrangements from the viewpoint of the women affected by them also arose from the fact that this exchange of assets was an important first step – and often the only step – in their succession to inherited wealth, thus forming the basis for their financial means as wives and (even more centrally) for their sustenance as widows. While daughters who had received dowries automatically did without their inheritance portions in the Italian dowry system,[30] the implementation of this legally mandated measure among the Tyrolean nobility occasioned great difficulty.[31] In the Tyrolean Law Code, in contrast to the Statute of Trento, renunciation of one's inheritance from the family in return for a marriage portion befitting one's status applied only to noble daughters and not to daughters belonging to town and rural jurisdictions (*städtische und ländliche Gerichte*). It contradicted the otherwise applicable principle of dividing family inheritance equally among all children. On this, the Tyrolean Law Code of 1573 stated that all children were to inherit equal portions, although the sons were to be accorded "a considerable advantage [. . .] in the interest of upholding the family lineage and name".[32] An exception in this respect is represented by noble daughters, who – insofar as they were not inheriting daughters – renounced their paternal and maternal inheritances in return for their marriage portions, which typically consisted of paternal and maternal bequests. The Tyrolean Law Code refers to this practice of renunciation among noble daughters and sisters as an "old custom" but does not clearly regulate it in a legal sense. While the Tyrolean Law Code of 1532 stipulated noble daughters' renunciation simply of their paternal and maternal inheritances, while retaining all further inheritances, the Tyrolean Law Codes of 1573 and 1606 stipulated more severe versions of this provision in cases where the groom was from outside the borders of the county of Tyrol.[33] In such cases, families had the option to expand their daughters' renunciations to also cover inheritances from their brothers, sisters, and cousins, probably as a preventive measure to preclude any possible transfers of property outside the territory via inheriting daughters. This legal ambivalence and vagueness paved the way for great inconsistency in actual legal practice, especially considering how the associated processes of negotiation had to reconcile the contrasting interests of two different families.[34]

The vast majority of marriage contracts, both purely Tyrolean and "trans-Tyrolean", make reference to an obligation on the part of the bride to renounce her inheritance. Tyrol's noble families paid extremely careful attention to the practical implementation of daughters' legally defined renunciation of their inheritance claims, for rescinded renunciations were capable of seriously disturbing the painstakingly achieved balance of inheritances among siblings. Primogeniture was not practiced by the Tyrolean nobility during the sixteenth and seventeenth centuries.[35] In most cases, several of a family's sons would marry, and upon their father's death the family's assets would usually continue being administrated as a whole (an arrangement referred to as an *Auszeigung*) for a certain period, after which they were distributed equally among the brothers, while the daughters, in turn, renounced their inheritance claims more or less entirely upon receipt of their marriage portions.[36] The standard formulation used in marriage contracts and letters of renunciation indicated that daughters renounced all inheritance from their fathers, mothers, and brothers even though the Tyrolean Law Code stipulated only renouncement of the inheritance that a daughter would receive from her mother and her father. Daughters did, however, retain their rights to all further inheritances as well as the right to inherit in the event of their brothers' premature deaths.

Upon a daughter's marriage, the maternal inheritance frequently had yet to be distributed; in such cases, a daughter renounced only her paternal inheritance following her marriage, providing her renouncement of her maternal inheritance only after her mother's death. The two daughters of Susanna Trautson née Fugger, who had herself brought 30,000 guilders into her marriage to Balthasar Trautson, were accorded relatively low marriage portions of 2,000 guilders each upon marrying (supplemented by 2,000 guilder counter-dowries [*Widerlagen*] and morning gifts [*Morgengaben*] of 1,000 and 1,500 guilders, respectively), but both marriage contracts make reference to the 4,000 guilders from their maternal inheritance (*Muttergut*) that they could expect upon their mother's and father's deaths.[37] So, in this case, maternal inheritance was not part of the marriage portions, but rather paid out later; it did, however, still represent an important component of the daughters' assets. In such cases, daughters thus renounced only their paternal inheritances at first, renouncing their maternal inheritances only after the specified bequests from their mothers had been paid out. It was only inheriting daughters whose assets flowed into the assets of the families into which they married, though their "standard women's assets" – which were documented separately – did not. And in Tyrol, in contrast to the Italian practice in which mothers' assets became part of the family's assets, maternal inheritances were distributed in strictly equal shares among all children from all of the mothers' marriages.[38] In this way, and within this legal framework, Tyrolean noblewomen enjoyed relative freedom in the management of their assets.

III.a The husband's counter-gifts

With regard to the marital property regime in Tyrol, one can observe a striking difference between "intra-Tyrolean" and "trans-Tyrolean" marriages in terms of reciprocation of the marriage portion contributed by the bride's family via a typically equal sum of money from the groom's family as a commitment to the bride's financial support in the event of her widowhood. The counter-dowry was customary among the nobility throughout the German-speaking lands[39] but not typical in Tyrol, as is mentioned in the marriage contract of Johann Trautson and Sidonia von Wolkenstein (1593).[40] The Tyrolean Law Code contains no mention of this asset category. For the most part, a counter-dowry – being a future-oriented patrimonial right that only took effect upon a woman's being widowed – distributed the financial burden of a marriage and the widow's support equally between the families of the bride and the groom. Anton Trautson, for example, countered the 2,000 guilder dowry that Maria Villinger contributed to their 1587 marriage with an equal sum of 2,000 guilders and also provided her with 1,000 guilders as a morning gift.[41] Probably as a result of their orientation towards the North, the Trautsons always included counter-dowries in their marriage contracts; they were especially prone to marrying women from noble houses elsewhere in Austria and southern Germany, where counter-dowries were expected.[42] In the marriage arrangements made between Marx Sittich von Wolkenstein and Anna Maria Trautson, it was explicitly mentioned that though counter-dowries were not standard practice in Tyrol, the Trautson family insisted upon them anyway.[43] And in reverse cases, when the groom was a Trautson, the family always provided a counter-dowry that was equal in value to the bride's marriage portion. In only one case did the counter-dowry exceed the value of the marriage portion. In 1630, Johann Franz Trautson countered the 3,000 guilder marriage portion contributed by Maximiliana zu Hohenzollern with 6,000 guilders and added a morning gift in the amount of 2,000 guilders. This was presumably a marriage of quite some prestige, a fact that was done justice with a large counter-dowry.[44]

The morning gift was a standard component of noble marriage contracts in early modern Tyrol, contrasting with what was customary in the Italian dowry system as well as with the practices of other social milieus present in Tyrol during the eighteenth century.[45] The morning gift – alongside the counter-dowry, when present – was the husband's central contribution within the marital property regime. In the case of Tyrol, it was unthinkable for an aristocratic marriage contract not to stipulate a morning gift, for which reason the morning gift was an asset of the utmost importance as a standard component both of "women's assets" and of the Tyrolean marital property regime as a whole.

In both marriages between Tyrolean nobles and transregional noble unions, the groom always presented the bride with a morning gift.[46] Within the studied sample, a morning gift was absent from only one marriage contract, that of Paul Sixtus Trautson and Anna Gräfin von Monfort, whereby the bride was a widow whose previous marriage portion in the amount of 4,000 guilders had been matched by a counter-dowry of equal value and her widow's dower was quite generous.[47] The value of the morning gift was usually a certain ratio of the value of the marriage portion, often being half or one-third. In 1615, for example, Maximilian Trautson made Anna Katherina von Wolkenstein a morning gift of 2,000 guilders for her contributed marriage portion of 4,000 guilders, while Elisabeth von Wolkenstein was able to expect "the third penny" (*den dritten Pfennig*) as a morning gift from Christoph von Spaur – i.e. one-third of her contributed marriage portion of 8,000 guilders.[48]

In several cases, the morning gift was of a value equal to that of the marriage portion; this happened above all when a counter-dowry was included, often according to the scheme of a 2,000 guilder marriage portion, a 2,000 guilder counter-dowry, and a 2,000 guilder morning gift.[49] In two cases, the morning gift was actually of greater value than the marriage portion. In 1589, Balthasar Trautson presented his second wife, Maria von Welsperg, with a morning gift of 3,000 guilders, although she had contributed a marriage portion of "only" 2,000 guilders. In this case, the counter-dowry – which was otherwise always present in Trautson marriage contracts – was omitted; instead, the groom made the bride a gift of 2,000 guilders in addition to his large morning gift "because he is already of considerable age and blessed with several children".[50] When marriage portions were very high, the morning gift was typically also very high. The inheriting daughter, Elisabeth Lang von Wellenburg, was provided with a morning gift of

5,000 guilders by Kaspar von Wolkenstein, and Albrecht von Wolkenstein made Johanna Madruzzo, whose marriage portion was 15,000 guilders, a morning gift of 6,000 guilders.[51] In the case of the Fugger daughters, the morning gift was based not on their very high marriage portions but on the grooms' significantly lower counter-dowries. Susanna Fugger's 30,000 guilder marriage portion was countered by Balthasar Trautson's 2,000 guilders, and his morning gift was half that amount; Adalberta Fugger, whose marriage portion was worth 15,000 guilders, had to make do – according to the "custom of the land in Bavaria" – with the "third penny" of her husband's 2,000 guilder counter-dowry, which came to 666.40 guilders.[52]

Theoretically, a wife was already able to freely dispose of her morning gift during her marriage. Apart from a woman's movable goods – her clothing, jewellery, and ribbons; typically also tableware (in particular valuable silver items); and sometimes furniture, such as chests and beds – the morning gift was the only "women's asset" with this feature. A great many marriage contracts make reference – occasionally even emphatic reference – to these "freedoms" of the wife and widow. "As for the morning gift, the wife Adalberta is to have full freedom to dispose of this as she pleases during her lifetime," reads the 1582 marriage contract between Christoph von Welsperg and Adalberta Fugger.[53] The morning gift's status as a free gift with which the wife could do as she pleased is affirmed in the marriage contract between Paul Sixtus Trautson and Maria Katherina von Königsegg, and the contract entered into by Brigitta Trautson and Maximilian Hendl zu Goldrain explicitly states that the wife was permitted to use her morning gift freely during the marriage.[54] In practice, however, this freedom was contradicted by a social expectation that a wife would give the morning gift back to her husband. This possibility was mentioned in the Tyrolean Law Code and seems to have been something of an "optional obligation": A good wife left her morning gift to her husband in her will. And many wives did indeed conform to these expectations in their last wills and testaments.[55] A central point in the wills of numerous young noble wives was their gifting of (i.e. returning) their morning gifts to their husbands in the event that they should pass away first – and indeed only then, as many wills explicitly stated. The husband was thereby absolved of the obligation to relinquish the morning gift to his wife's heirs, as he was indeed obligated to do with her other marital goods (the marriage portion and her trousseau or movable goods). So while the morning gift was an integral component of women's assets, it was the husband's contribution – together with the counter-dowry and the widow's dower – that provided for his wife as a widow; and if his wife ended up passing away before he did, the logic entailed by separation of property dictated that this gift by the husband was not to pass on to the family of the wife.

IV. Characteristics of marital goods and their securement

Upon having been contributed by the bride's family, the marriage portion was entrusted to the husband's administration, as the marriage contracts clearly state. The husband (or his father, or sometimes his widowed mother) was obligated to secure it with all of his property, both with the property he held at the point at which the marriage took place and with all property he might acquire subsequent to marrying. He likewise agreed to secure any counter-dowry as well as the morning gift with his own property, although these monies – in contrast to the marriage portion – were classified as future patrimonial rights of a widow. The marriage portion was therefore an asset that passed from the bride's family into the husband's administration upon marriage or according to the modalities and timeframes that had been negotiated. In a legal sense, the marriage portion assumed a peculiar intermediate status, belonging to two legal persons in different ways: The wife was the legal owner but did not have usufruct of it, while her husband was entrusted with the marriage portion's administration but was not permitted to dispose of or otherwise alter it without her agreement (and that of her gender guardian [*Anweiser*]).[56] The counter-dowry and morning gift were assets that the husband pledged his wife as future rights. They were therefore not paid out during the marriage, but rather promised to the bride should she be widowed.

In the vast majority of cases, it was a strict requirement for all marital goods to be secured with the allodial property, fiefs, and pledged property of the husband or his father, although in the case of fiefs and pledged property, permission had to be obtained from the overlord or pledgor. While the language that mandates such securement is typically brief and lapidary – "with all of his property" (*auf allen seinen Gütern*) – with the only other mention typically being of the fiefs and the obligation to obtain their overlord's permission, Hans von Seiboltsdorff promised his bride Elisabeth Khuen-Belasi in their 1536 marriage contract that he would secure her entire property, her marriage portion, her morning gift, her future maternal inheritance, and everything that she was still to inherit "on any and all of his titular property, be it fief, allodial, leased, tithed, or pledged land, immovable or movable, held currently or in the future, even if it is undivided and owned jointly with his Seiboltsdorff brothers". Where her property was secured with fiefs, he promised to obtain permission from their overlord, and should the property he held jointly with his brothers be divided, he agreed to affirm the securement of her property with his portion.[57] Securing a woman's assets safeguarded her sustenance as a widow, as this embodied a guarantee that her rights to these assets from her husband's property would actually be granted should he pass away before she did. But the fact that this was not only about the individual rights of the woman but also about securing the rights of her heirs is clearly expressed in the 1630 marriage contract between Johann Franz Trautson and Maximiliana von Hohenzollern in which a separate "letter of assurance" (*Vergewissbrief*) is demanded that seems not to have been otherwise typical among the nobility.[58]

In cases where future husbands were not yet emancipated (*emanzipiert*) – i.e. were not yet economically independent[59] – at the point at which their marriages were arranged, their fathers secured the marital goods of their sons' future wives on the family estates;[60] widowed and ruling mothers, by contrast, secured this property with their family estates and sometimes also with their own.[61] As widows, mothers also appeared as representatives of their daughters. For example, the widowed mother of Maria Gräfin Gondola provided her daughter with a marriage portion of

24,000 guilders for her 1702 marriage to Veit Dominicus Wolkenstein-Trostburg as inheritance (*als erblich*), with 16,000 guilders being paid out within one year and 8,000 guilders that would remain in the possession of the "Countess Widow" and accrue interest of five percent annually.[62]

A marriage contract served to render a transfer of wealth from the bride's family to the family of the groom a legally sanctioned transaction; the husband could use the woman's assets during the marriage but was not permitted to divest or otherwise alter them, meaning that despite the husband's usufruct, the wife remained the legal owner of the marriage portion.[63] This "proprietary in-between" inhabited by wives and husbands in connexion with marriage portions is expressed with particular clarity in the 1555 marriage contract between Balthasar Trautson and Susanna Fugger: "[T]he well-named spouses, during their marriage, shall enjoy and use to their mutual benefit the aforementioned marriage portion, morning gift, and counter-dowry in a manner that is trustworthy and prudent".[64] Marriage contracts sought first and foremost to secure both the wife's in-between proprietary position – as the legal owner without usufruct – and her rights as a widow. Marriage contracts attempted to ensure the disbursement of the marital goods, and above all of the marriage portion, in a legal sense, as the actual payout or its delay or failure to occur frequently gave rise to conflicts between families. They also served to stipulate the daughters' renunciation of their inheritance in return for disbursement of the marriage portion, for their non-compliance in this regard could likewise lead to conflicts. Finally, marriage contracts were meant to guarantee that widows would actually be accorded both the monetary rights and the social rights to which they were entitled, for the widow's endowment was a particularly precarious matter in the financial management of the family.

V. Arrangements for widowhood

In stark contrast to the Italian dowry system's *patti dotali* (dowry contracts), which did not take widowhood into account, provisions regarding widowhood and the widow's dower take up the greatest amount of space in Tyrolean marriage contracts. While contracts from the first half of the sixteenth century still frequently employed blanket references to the provisions of the Tyrolean Law Code, arrangements pertaining to possible widowhood and the widow's dower began to receive far more detailed attention from the mid-sixteenth century onwards, particularly in transregional marriage contracts. As a general rule, the Tyrolean Law Code stipulated separation of goods between husband and wife, with inheritance practices in cases of childlessness being based on their respective families of origin. If children were present, the inheritance went to them or to the next generation in a descending line.[65] The Tyrolean Law Code accorded the husband the right to administer his wife's wealth, meaning all of her assets, regardless of whether they had been brought into the marriage as her marriage portion or inherited later on.[66] In most marriage contracts, this provision was taken as a given, though reference was always made, as described earlier, to the husband's obligation to secure these "women's assets" along with his own. Following the husband's death, the "women's assets" were to pass to the widow via either the payout of interest on them[67] or disbursement in full.[68] And in contrast to how things stood with the morning gift, the widow's marriage portion and other assets had to be returned to her before the claims of any other creditors were resolved.[69] Following the widow's death, her property was either to go to her children as maternal inheritance or to be returned to her family of origin in cases of childlessness. An exception here was the counter-dowry, which could be used by the woman for the rest of her life but was to be returned to the husband's family upon her death.[70]

In numerous marriage contracts, and above all for "Tyrolean" marriages during the first half of the sixteenth century, the rules for the eventuality of widowhood were treated in brief with either a statement that the provisions of the Tyrolean Law Code were to be adhered to or a more general statement that the widow was to be "appropriately endowed" or both.[71] In the later marriage contracts, and above all the contracts with brides from outside of Tyrol, however, the provisions for widowhood tended to be highly refined. One example of this is the final and most detailed section of the 1587 marriage contract between Anton Trautson and Maria Villinger. Following the husband's death, his widow was to be endowed with 5,000 guilders – i.e. with the marriage portion, the counter-dowry, and the morning gift – regardless of whether children were present unless Maria had already employed the morning gift otherwise during her lifetime, which was something that she had explicitly been given the right to do. Additionally, the widow was to be entitled to everything "that belongs to her body", meaning everything she brought into the marriage and received personally during the marriage. Of the table silver that had been gifted at the wedding, she was to receive half, and if she was without children, all of it. If the marriage had produced children, Maria was to have the right "to remain on his estate" – i.e. to administer the family assets and assume guardianship of the children, albeit with help from two curators "from the inner circle of friends" (*aus den negsten befreundeten*). Maria's "free goods" (*Freigut*) were to be divided equally among all of her children, including any from a possible remarriage. But if she were to remarry, Maria was only to be permitted to contribute 1,000 guilders. If she were to pass away before her husband, he was to be permitted to use her assets until his death, after which her wealth would go to the children as maternal inheritance. If she were to die childless, he was to receive unimpeded ownership of all her goods unless she stipulated otherwise in her will, which it was her right to do. This provision does not conform to the Tyrolean Law Code, which established limited freedom of testation: Half of the wealth accrued during a marriage and a third of one's inherited assets could be willed to one's spouse.[72] In the marriage contracts, frequent blanket reference is made to freedom of testation, especially with regard to the women. Several contracts contain wording to the effect that the husband may use the woman's assets for the rest of his life should she not state otherwise in her will,[73] or it is written that the provisions of the Tyrolean Law Code shall apply should the wife die without having written a will.[74]

The marriage contract of Anton Trautson and Maria Villinger is one of the few sets of arrangements that also contain a provision regarding the common household's movable goods, in contrast to the woman's movable goods, to which she was in any case entitled. This provision stated that if Anton died with the marriage having been childless, Maria was to receive 1,600 guilders from his movable goods; if children were present, it would be 800 guilders. The Tyrolean Law Code addresses this question in detail, giving separate mention to noble widows and widows belonging to municipalities. A noble widow had a right to the best horse, the best bed with its accessories, a maiden's bed (*Jungfrauenbett*) and three pillows, and "mourning clothes" (*Clagegewandt*) for the maiden and one manservant. Additionally, she was to receive food for one year (*Jahrspeyse*) insofar as she did not remarry during this initial year of her widowhood. And, finally, she also had a right to part of the table silver; other kitchenware was subject to the other heirs' decision.[75] Marriage contracts often, like in the agreement between Anton Trautson and Maria Villinger, determined a lump sum of money for a man's movable goods – Johann Franz Trautson and Maximiliana zu Hohenzollern agreed upon 3,000 guilders; Maximilian Hendl zu Goldrain and Brigitte Trautson agreed upon 1,000 guilders; and Paul Sixtus Trautson and Anna Monfort agreed upon 4,000 guilders[76] – but the table silver was treated separately, with the widow being accorded half of it in the lion's share of cases. In exceptional cases, there is simply a guarantee of a certain share of the movable goods, such as in the marriage contract of Paul Sixtus Trautson and Susanna Veronica von Meggau, where either spouse was to be accorded half of the movable goods regardless of whether children were present.[77]

Movable goods were an important basis of sustenance, especially for widows, although noble widows could increasingly count on a separate widow's dower in addition to their widows' endowments. And from the second half of the sixteenth century onwards, marriage contracts always specified a widow's dower that was sometimes defined in considerable detail. The standard sum for a "widows' allowance" (*wittibliches Deputat*) lay between 400 and 600 guilders annually, and this was supplemented by the promise of "housing befitting of her rank" in the form of a widow's residence or an additional monetary annuity in its place. While marriage contracts that stipulated very high marriage portions (as well as those of inheriting daughters) do not contain their own widow's dower provisions – as these women could live well as widows from the yields produced by their marriage portions – the widow's dower, as an additional allowance for women with modest or small marriage portions, provided a decisive boost to standards of living, as widows pledged by the families into which they had married. For the aforementioned Maria Villinger, the use of her marital goods was supplemented by a widow's residence and 400 guilders annually; for Maria Christina Paumgarten, who married Maximilian Karl von Wolkenstein in 1648, the yield on her marital goods was supplemented by the pledge of a widow's residence of her choice and 600 guilders annually as well as hay and straw for two horses or 100 guilders annually for this purpose plus as much wine as she required.[78] In marriage contracts involving women from outside of Tyrol, great importance was also placed on the individual provisions for the widow's dower. Maria Christina Paumgarten was to be able to choose a widow's residence (*wittiblicher Beisitz*) from among the buildings owned by Maximilian Karl von Wolkenstein should she wish to remain in Tyrol, or "if she prefers to once again live in her homeland of Bavaria", she was to receive an additional 900 guilders annually.[79] As a rule, however, it was assumed that widows would remain where they had lived during their marriages, and they would have to be appropriately provided for there – something for which the families into which they had married bore increasing responsibility over the course of the sixteenth century.

The widow had usufruct of her marital goods – the marriage portion, the counter-dowry, and the morning gift – with the counter-dowry resulting in a burden for the husband's side that was even higher than that seen with a simple marriage contract stipulating a marriage portion and morning gift. While usufruct of marital goods persisted up to full disbursement of the widow's endowment, or even for the rest of the widow's life (with some marriage contracts according the widow the right to use the assets of her deceased husband up to the endowment's complete disbursement), a woman's rights to live in her widow's residence and to receive payment of her widow's dower were typically limited to her period of widowhood, meaning that these rights expired if she remarried.

In the Tyrolean Law Code, the logic of separation of marital goods meant that the husband, if his wife died first, had to return the wealth that she had brought into the marriage to her heirs, children, or other relatives.[80] While a few marriage contracts referred just generally to the provisions of the Tyrolean Law Code or "the law of the land" (*Landrecht*) in this regard,[81] or simply stipulated that everything go to her heirs upon her death,[82] numerous marriage contracts did not keep to this rule and instead accorded the husband the right to use the assets of his wife for the rest of his life, with them only going to her heirs after his death.[83] The case was usually different with the morning gift and the counter-dowry. As mentioned earlier, wives often willed their morning gifts back to their husbands; but if they did not, the husbands still had the right to use them until their own deaths, after which they passed to their wives' heirs.[84] And the counter-dowry, as an asset of which the woman had usufruct, by definition went back to the husband and his heirs. The husband's usufruct in the event of his wife's death was usually limited to the marriage portion; her movable goods went immediately to her heirs.[85] Sometimes the husband's usufruct was limited strictly to the time he spent as a widower, expiring if he remarried.[86] Only a few marriage contracts accorded the husband freedom to choose between lifelong usufruct and receiving a third as his own.[87] And in cases where the marriage portion's value was very high, the degree to which the husband enjoyed usufruct was also sometimes limited. Albrecht von Wolkenstein was granted usufruct of half of his wife's 15,000 guilder marriage portion, while Balthasar Trautson enjoyed usufruct of half of the 30,000 guilder marriage portion contributed by his wife, Susanna Fugger.[88]

From the wives' perspective (but also from the husbands', where usufruct was concerned), marriage contracts quite frequently functioned as a corrective to the Tyrolean Law Code, which in most respects stipulated separation of goods.[89] In this context, it was primarily widows who were accorded additional rights – sometimes higher rates of interest on their marriage portions, more favourable rules on the division of movable goods, a widow's allowance, or a widow's residence (*Witwensitz*). As a rule, the more valuable the marital goods and the more prestigious the marriage, the more favourable the conditions negotiated for the widow. Women from neighbouring territories who married Tyroleans were frequently granted particularly detailed arrangements for their widowhoods. Such favourable conditions included the widow's right to maintain her position, assume guardianship of the children, and administer the family property.[90] Among the Tyrolean nobility, these rights of the widow did not go without saying (though the widower's rights most certainly did); the widow's rights had to be specifically granted and indeed were in a great number of marriage contracts, usually until the children reached the age of majority and with the assistance of two aristocratic "friends" as co-guardians. Finally, the widow was often given usufruct of her husband's assets until her widow's endowment had been fully disbursed.[91]

V. Material value and symbolic valence

At first glance, marriage contracts – as shown in the foregoing – prominently featured stipulations of material asset values and the modalities by which they were to be exchanged, with property, possession, administration, usufruct, rates of interest, and future rights being points of negotiation. But if one interprets these agreements before the backdrop of the protagonists' social environment and cultural notions, they appear to have formed a basis for complex, ideational, and conflict-prone processes of exchange aimed at ensuring social continuity despite the constitution of new family units and new ties associated with both kinship and friendship. In this, three objectives of aristocratic familial policy enjoyed priority: (i) The formation of kinship bonds and friendly relations between noble families and preventive measures by which to avoid conflicts; (ii) gains in prestige and material goods for sons and husbands and their respective houses; and (iii) providing for daughters – as wives and especially as widows – as well as ensuring their future rights. These objectives were pursued before the backdrop of a fundamentally patrilineal orientation that had its sights set on generational continuity of the family in the male line and the preservation – and, if possible, growth – of wealth in the form of allodia, fiefdoms, pledged property, and special rights (*Gerechtigkeiten*) as the economic basis of a noble house. From the perspective of daughters and their families, marriage agreements could be considered acts of early inheritance; as compensation for renouncing her claim to an inheritance, a daughter was to be well provided for as a widow, with her rights – for example as a guardian and regent – preventatively defined. All this was additionally meant to ensure her acceptance of this arrangement, which was quite unfavourable to her in a material sense due to both the renunciation of her own inheritance and the principle of separate goods. Revoked renunciations of inheritance by daughters could severely disrupt the balance between the inheritances of a family's various inheriting brothers and were frequently the cause of vigorous and prolonged conflicts, in particular because notions of justice collided and more than just individual interests were at stake, as this involved two families and houses with (possibly) opposed concerns and demands.

Determining the value of marriage portions was done according to a specific set of criteria. First, they had to be appropriate to their recipients' rank. The Tyrolean Law Code speaks here of a "considerable marriage portion in accordance with origins and wealth".[92] The trousseau was defined as befitting the woman's rank in every marriage contract, and it went without saying that the morning gift – as a value set in relation to the marriage portion – was likewise to be of similarly appropriate value. Second, all sisters had to be provided for in a way that was strictly equal.[93] Finally, marriage portions had to make possible appropriate provision for the daughters as widows. Were they someday to find themselves widowed, they were in no case to burden their families of origin. From the perspective of the sons and their families, by contrast, this was about obtaining a marriage befitting one's rank that was maximally advantageous both materially and symbolically, a marriage that would contribute to augmenting the family's wealth and honour without incurring excessively high costs in return.

The significance of marital goods went far beyond their purely material value, but even so, their material value for the establishment of a noble house and their economic use as part of the family economy should not be underestimated. Oftentimes the husbands were not yet of age;[94] in other words, they were not yet economically independent and had yet to inherit. For this reason, the marriage portion represented an important financial basis upon which to found a new household, in addition to income from official positions and paternal allowances.[95] Alongside this monetary gain, a high-value marriage portion also boosted the status of the husband's family as "symbolic capital" consisting of honour and social prestige even if the material value of marriage portions was usually small compared with the value of the family's assets.[96] And from the perspective of the bride's family, the honour conveyed via marriage was tied to the suitable provision for their daughter as a wife and above all as a widow.

My fundamental thesis asserts that in early modern noble marriage arrangements, wealth and honour, material value and symbolic capital went hand in hand in a specific way, with not only the value of the marital goods but also the successful balancing of family and individual gains, burdens, and obligations entailing higher status. Every marriage represented processes of negotiation that revolved around achieving balance between the three central objectives of noble family policy portrayed here (preservation and growth of assets, continuity between generations, and social safeguarding of daughters/widows), though the immediate goal of individual marriages – apart from material gains and provision for the daughters – was the establishment of friendly relations between families. The material value of the marriage portions was not a secondary matter: The daughters had to be well provided for, and the sons were to be afforded the most advantageous marriages possible. In both cases, this was about negotiated material conditions and honour as social capital. So fundamentally, and despite generally patrilineal orientation and differing priorities, the negotiation of marriage agreements aimed to establish new social relationships while preserving and increasing the prestige of all those involved, including, or even especially, that of the wives, in sharp contrast to the glaringly unequal treatment they experienced in a material sense. This "negotiated honour" becomes quite vividly apparent in the marriage contracts when one examines the assets and future rights subject to negotiation as well as the aristocratic canon of values with its specific notions of justice and the attendant gender-specific and generationally derived strategies.

VI. Conclusion

A brief return here to the initial question as to the relationship between marriage portions/dowries and family inheritances is warranted: Did marriage portions serve to exclude daughters from family inheritances, or was marriage part of the process of "diverging devolution", with a part of family inheritance, as Goody felt, in any case running via cognatic lines of descent? The research on Italian territories and their dowry system based on Roman law clearly tends to support the first hypothesis. But the transitional space between the Italian legal tradition and German-speaking territories analysed here points in a different direction, highlighting how the impression made by the very well researched Italian dowry system is by no means sufficient to answer this question. A more detailed look at the system of marital goods gives rise to conclusions that differ in certain respects. The marriage portions of Tyrolean noble daughters (with the exception of the few inheriting daughters) were modest compared with the inheritance portions of their brothers, and in return daughters were required to more or less comprehensively renounce their inheritance rights. But this renunciation of inheritance was not clearly defined by law, and daughters typically reserved the right to inherit assets beyond their patrilineal inheritances. Oftentimes the maternal inheritance was not transferred as part of the marriage portion, and women were for the most part also accorded all other possible future inheritances – sometimes even those of the brothers and in all cases those of their sisters and other relatives. Additionally, the renunciation of inheritance rights in Tyrol was required only of noble daughters and not of wives from the urban bourgeoisie and rural communities. Daughters in Tyrol were thus by no means fundamentally excluded from family inheritances. And a look at actual practice in neighbouring Graubünden shows that in its marital property regime, there existed a specific ratio between the value of the marriage portion and the inheritance portions of all a family's children. As Jon Mathieu has recently shown, noble marriage contracts there specified daughters' marriage portions' corresponding shares of the family inheritances along with the "man's advantage" (*Mannsvorteil*).[97] As much as the tendency was indeed to limit female inheritance, with an eye to preventing women from inheriting real estate to the greatest possible extent, it is equally clear that the significance of women's assets nonetheless stands out in the aristocratic context. Accordingly, women's assets in Tyrol – consisting of the marriage portion and often a counter-dowry, the morning gift, later inheritances, and movable goods – differed from women's assets in the Italian dowry system, where it was usual for them to tacitly become part of the family assets and thus the sons' inheritance portions upon the death of the wife;

instead, they were divided in strictly equal portions among all of the woman's children even if these children were from multiple marriages. The foundation of such women's assets was laid upon marriage and anchored in the corresponding marriage contracts; and the significance of these assets as well as the associated honour with regard to the constitution and maintenance of friendly and kin relations, subject as they were to continual renegotiation, was beyond dispute within the networks of relationships among the nobility.

Notes

1 This contribution was judiciously translated from the original German into English by Christopher Roth.

2 Jack Goody, "Bridewealth and Dowry in Africa and Eurasia", in: Jack Goody and S. J. Tambiah (eds.), *Bridewealth and Dowry*, Cambridge 1973 [Cambridge University Press], pp. 1–58; Jack Goody, "Inheritance, Property and Women. Some Comparative Considerations", in: Jack Goody, J. Thirsk and E. P. Thompson (eds.), *Family and Inheritance. Rural Society in Western Europe. 1200–1800*, Cambridge 2011 [Cambridge University Press], pp. 10–36.

3 Diana Owen Hughes, "From Brideprice to Dowry in Mediterranean Europe", in: *Journal of Family History* 3 (1978), pp. 262–296 (also in Marion Kaplan (ed.), *The Marriage Bargain. Women and Dowries in European History*, New York 1985 [Routledge], pp. 13–57).

4 Simona Feci, "The Exclusion of Women from Inheritance Rights: An Unresolved Issue?" in: Margareth Lanzinger et al. (eds.), *Stipulating – Litigating – Mediating. Negotiations of Gender and Property*, Leiden forthcoming [Brill]; Isabelle Chabot, "Family Justice and Public Justice in Dowry and Inheritance Conflicts Between Florentine Families (Forteenth to Fifteenth Centuries)", in: Margareth Lanzinger et al. (eds.), *Stipulating – Litigating – Mediating. Negotiations of Gender and Property*, Leiden forthcoming [Brill].

5 Ulrike Langbein, "Vom Ideellen im Materiellen: Plädoyer für einen mikroskopischen Blick auf das Erbe", in: Stefan Brakensiek, Michael Stolleis and Heide Wunder (eds.), *Generationengerechtigkeit? Normen und Praxis im Erb- und Ehegüterrecht 1500–1850* (Zeitschrift für Historische Forschung, Beiheft 37), Berlin 2006 [Dunker und Humblot], pp. 283–300; Ulrike Langbein, *Geerbte Dinge. Soziale Praxis und symbolische Bedeutung des Erbens*, Köln 2002 [Böhlau]. On the term "intangible inheritance", see works including the pioneering study by Giovanni Levi, *Das immaterielle Erbe. Eine bäuerliche Welt an der Schwelle zur Moderne*, Berlin 1986 [Wagenbach]; original version: L'eredità immateriale. *Carriera di un esorcista nel Piemonte del Seicento*, Torino 1985 [Einaudi].

6 For a general impression of the history of Tyrol's nobility, see Hans Hochenegg, *Der Adel im Leben Tirols. Eine soziologische Studie* (Veröffentlichungen der Universität Innsbruck 70), Innsbruck 1971 [Österr. Komm.-Buchh].

7 Klaus Brandstätter, "Tyrol, die herrliche, gefirstete Grafschaft ist von uralten zeiten gehaissen und auch so geschrieben . . . 'Zur Geschichte des Begriffs' Tirol", in: *Geschichte und Region / Storia e regione* 9 (2000), pp. 11–30; Heinz Noflatscher, "Tirol, Brixen, Trient", in: Anton Schindling and Walter Ziegler (eds.), *Die Territorien des Reiches im Zeitalter der Reformation und Konfessionalisierung. Land und Konfession 1500–1650. Bd. 1: Der Südosten* (Katholisches Leben und Kirchenreform im Zeitalter der Glaubensspaltung 49), Münster 1989 [Aschendorff], pp. 86–101; Friedolin Dörrer, "Die limitierte Landeshoheit der Bischöfe von Trient und Brixen in Beziehung zur gefürsteten Grafschaft Tirol", in: Erwin Riedenauer (ed.), *Landeshoheit. Beiträge zur Entstehung, Ausformung und Typologie eines Verfassungselements der römisch-deutschen Reiches* (Studien zur Bayrischen Verfassungs- und Sozialgeschichte Band XVI), Munich 1994 [Komm. für Bayrische Landesgeschichte], pp. 135–144; Joseph Kögl, *La sovranità dei vescovi di Trento e di Bressanone. Diritti derivanti al clero diocesano dalla sua sopressione*, Trento 1964 [Tipografia Arcivescovile Artiginelli].

8 Werner Köfler, *Land, Landschaft, Landtag: Geschichte der Tiroler Landtage von den Anfängen bis zur Aufhebung der landständischen Verfassung 1808*, Innsbruck 1998 [Wagner].

9 Anton Emmert, *Geschichtliche Darstellung der Erblandämter in der gefürsteten Grafschaft Tirol*, Innsbruck 1838 [Rauch].

10 Klaus Brandstätter, "Kirchliche Karrieren der Wolkensteiner in der Frühen Neuzeit", in: Gustav Pfeifer and Kurt Andermann (eds.), *Die Wolkensteiner*. Facetten des Tiroler Adels in Spätmittelalter und Neuzeit (Veröffentlichungen des Südtiroler Landesarchivs 30), Innsbruck 2009 [Wagner], pp. 149–194; Heinz Noflatscher, "Frömmigkeit und Patronage. Zum Adelsklerus um 1700", in: Josef Nössing and Helmut Stampfer (eds.), *Kunst und Kirche in Tirol. Festschrift zum 70. Geburtstag von Karl Wolfgruber*, Bozen 1987 [Athesia], pp. 131–151.

11 Siglinde Clementi, Ellinor Forster, Christian Hagen, Margareth Lanzinger and Janine Christina Maegraith, "Rechtsräume und Geschlechterordnungen als soziale Prozesse – transregional. Vereinbaren und Verfügen in städtischen und ländlichen Kontexten im südlichen Tirol vom 15. bis zum frühen 19. Jahrhundert – ein erster Projektbericht", in: *Geschichte und Region / Storia e regione* 22, 2 (2013), pp. 165–172; On the legal history of Tyrol, see Martin Schennach, *Gesetz und Herrschaft. Die Entstehung des Gesetzgebungsstaates am Beispiel Tirols*, Cologne and Vienna 2010 [Böhlau]; Marco Bellabarba, *La giustizia ai confini. Il principato vescovile di Trento agli inizi dell'età moderna*, Bologna 1996 [Il Mulino], and on early modern administration in southern Tyrol, see Marcello Bonazza, *Il fisco in una statalità divisa. Impero, principi e ceti in area trentino-tirolese nella prima età moderna* (Annali dell'Istituto storico italo-germanico. Monografie 35), Bologna 2001 [Il Mulino]. For a comparison of various marital regimes, see Margareth Lanzinger, "Variationen des Themas: Mitgiftsysteme", in: Margareth Lanzinger, Gunda Barth-Scalmani, Ellinor Forster and Gertrude Langer-Ostrawsky (eds.), *Aushandeln von Ehe. Heiratsverträge der Neuzeit im europäischen Vergleich*, Cologne, Weimar and Vienna 2010 [Böhlau], pp. 469–492; Margareth Lanzinger, "Mitgift, Heiratsgut und Ehegüterregime: Variationen und Übergänge", in: *Geschichte und Region / Storia e regione* 19, 1 (2010), pp. 123–143; Siglinde Clementi, "Heiraten in Grenzräumen. Vermögensarrangements adeliger Ehefrauen und -männer im frühneuzeitlichen Tirol", in: *Geschichte und Region / Storia e regione* 28, 2 (2018), pp. 44–69.

12 Marriage contract of Albrecht von Wolkenstein and Johanna Madruzzo, 1609: Südtiroler Landesarchiv (SLA), Wolkenstein-Trostburg 676; marriage contract of Sigmund von Spaur and Barbara von Arco, 1535: SLA, Welsperg-Spaur 481. Here and in the following the references to individual marriage contracts are by no means exhaustive, instead being intended merely as examples.

13 Lanzinger, "Variationen des Themas: Mitgiftsysteme"; Lanzinger, "Mitgift, Heiratsgut und Ehegüterregime"; Clementi, "Heiraten in Grenzräumen".

14 Wilhelm Brauneder, *Die Entwicklung des Ehegüterrechts in Österreich. Ein Beitrag zur Dogmengeschichte und Rechtstatsachenforschung des Spätmittelalters und der Neuzeit*, Salzburg and Munich 1973 [Fink]; Anke Hufschmid, *Adlige Frauen im Weserraum zwischen 1570 und 1700. Status – Rollen – Lebenspraxis*, Münster 2001 [Aschendorff]; Karl-Heinz Spieß, *Familie und Verwandtschaft im deutschen Hochadel des Spätmittelalters 13. bis Anfang des 16. Jahrhunderts*, Stuttgart 1993 [Steiner]; Lanzinger/Barth-Scalmani/Forster/Langer-Ostrawsky, Aushandeln von Ehe; on the Italian dowry system, see Giulia Calvi and Isabelle Chabot (eds.), *Le ricchezze delle donne. Diritti patrimoniali e poteri familiari in Italia* (XIII – XIX secc.), Turin 1998 [Rosenberg & Sellier]; Renata Ago and Benedetta Borello (eds.), *Famiglie, circolazione di beni, circuiti di affetti in età moderna*, Rom 2009 [Viella]; Thomas Kuehn, *Law, Family, and Women: Toward a Legal Anthropology of Renaissance Italy*, Chicago 1991 [University of Chicago Press]; Stanley Chojnacki, *Women and Men in Renaissance Venice. Twelve Essays on Patrician Society*, Baltimore and London 2000 [The John Hopkins University Press]; Anna Bellavitis, *Identitè, mariage, mobilité social. Citoyennes et citoyens à Venise au XVIe siècle*, Rome 2001 [École Francaise de Rome]; Anna Bellavitis, *Famille, genre, trasmission à Venise au XVIe siècle*, Rome 2008 [École Francaise de Rome].

15 This contribution draws on material from an ongoing research project on wealth arrangements, gender relations, and kin among the Tyrolean nobility between 1500 and

1700. Up to now, research has been devoted to the houses of Wolkenstein-Trostburg, Trautson, Spaur, Trapp, Welsperg, Kuhen-Belasi, and Arco.

16 A large collection of genealogies of Tyrolean noble houses in various degrees of completion: SLA, Bibliothek, Stephan von Mayerhofen, Genealogien des Tyroler Adels, um 1800, transcription by Kurt Staffler, ca. 1937. This goes all the more for the genealogical tables published in the *Biographisches Lexikon des Kaiserthums Oesterreich* (Constant von Wurzbach). On the problems associated with incomplete genealogical tables and family trees, see Hufschmid, *Adlige Frauen*, p. 237; Spieß, *Familie und Verwandtschaft*, pp. 428–437; Siglinde Clementi, "Deren von Wolkenstein. Familienstrategien, Heirat und Geschlechterbeziehungen bei den Wolkenstein-Trostburg (um 1500 bis 1650)", in: Gustav Pfeifer and Kurt Andermann (eds.), *Die Wolkensteiner. Facetten des Tiroler Adels in Spätmittelalter und Neuzeit* (Veröffentlichungen des Südtiroler Landesarchivs 30), Innsbruck 2009 [Wagner], p. 114.

17 Her mother, Anna Botsch von Zwingenberg, left her estate to her husband Wilhelm for his lifelong use; following his death, it was to be divided among their four children, Kaspar, Melchior Hannibal, Maria, and Anna, although the father acted "out of no special fairness" (*aus keiner sonderen Gerechtigkeit*) and already made the money available to the daughters when they married: Marriage contract of Anton von Spaur and Anna von Wolkenstein, 1566: SLA, Archiv Wolkenstein-Trostburg 772 and Urk. 1233. The sons received their shares from their maternal inheritance somewhat later: TLMF Bibliothek, Hs. 2647, fol. 749v – 750r.

18 Marriage contract of Kaspar von Wolkenstein and Elisabeth Lang von Wellenburg, 1550: SLA, Wolkenstein-Trostburg 678; see also Siglinde Clementi, "Deren von Wolkenstein. Familienstrategien, Heirat und Geschlechterbeziehungen bei den Wolkenstein-Trostburg (um 1500 bis 1650)", in: Gustav Pfeifer and Kurt Andermann (eds.), *Die Wolkensteiner. Facetten des Tiroler Adels in Spätmittelalter und Neuzeit* (Veröffentlichungen des Südtiroler Landesarchivs 30), Innsbruck 2009 [Wagner], pp. 111–147.

19 Wilfried Beimrohr, "Das landesfürstliche Lehnwesen in Tirol", in: *Tiroler Heimat* 79 (2015), pp. 33–61; Art. Weiberlehen, in: Handwörterbuch der deutschen Rechtsgeschichte, Bd. V, Berlin 1998, Sp. 1206–1209.

20 "*aller vnd yeder seiner (ihres Vaters Anton) verlassen hab vnd gueter kaine ausgenommen, [. . .] ausgenommen vnd hindan gesetzte die manslehen*". Marriage contract of Michael von Neuhaus and Anna von Wolkenstein, 1521: SLA, Wolkenstein-Trostburg 1770 and 1886.

21 Costituzione di dote Vinciguerra d'Arco e Maria Klara Ingram von Liebenrain und Frasburg, Biblioteca Comunale di Trento (BCTN), Fondo Segala, BCT1–2548 22.

22 Marriage contract of Christoph von Welsperg and Adalberta Fugger, 1582: SLA, Wolkenstein-Trostburg 802; marriage contract of Daniel Felix von Spaur and Veronika Fugger, 1542: SLA, Welsperg-Spaur 528; marriage contract of Balthasar Trautson and Susanna Fugger, 1555: TLA, Trautson Pos. 104,2, as well as Urk. 297.

23 Marriage contract of Albrecht von Wolkenstein and Johanna Madruzzo, 1609: SLA, Wolkenstein-Trostburg 676.

24 Marriage contract of Anton von Spaur and Anna von Wolkenstein, 1566: Südtiroler Landesarchiv (SLA), Archiv Wolkenstein-Trostburg 772 and Urk. 1233.

25 Marriage contract of Christoph von Welsperg/Primör and Adalberta Fugger, 1582: SLA, Archiv Wesperg 802.

26 Marriage contract of Balthasar Trautson and Maria Sidonia Welsperg, 1589: TLA, Trautson, Pos. 104,8.

27 Marriage contract of Johann Trautson and Sidonia von Wolkenstein, 1593: SLA, Wolkenstein-Trostburg 678.

28 Marriage contract of Georg von Greifensee and Barbara Khuen-Belasi, 1536: TLA, Archiv Khuen-Belasi, Karton 3.

29 Marriage contract of Wilhelm von Arz and Maria Christina von Wolkenstein, 1616: SLA, Wolkenstein-Trostburg 464.

30 Feci, "The Exclusion of Women from Inheritance Rights".

31 Siglinde Clementi, "Undivided Brothers – Renouncing Sisters. Family Strategies of Low Nobility in Sixteenth- and Seventeenth-Century Tyrol", in: Anna Bellavitis and Beatrice Zucca Micheletto (eds.), *Gender, Law and Economic Well-Being in Europe from the Fifteenth to the Nineteenth Century*, London and New York 2019 [Routledge], pp. 149–164.

32 "*ain zimlicher Vorthail / zu erhaltung stammens vnd Namens*". TLO 1532, 1573 and 1606 (III), 9 stipulates that "every child, respectively" is to inherit "an equal share" (*yedes Kind für sein haupt ain gleich Tail*), but the daughters "modestly" (*mit beschaidenhait*). In III, 34, noble daughters' renunciation of their inheritances is established.

33 TLO 1532, 1573 und 1606, III, 34.

34 Clementi, "Undivided Brothers – Renouncing Sisters".

35 This conclusion was drawn from looking through several genealogies of noble families in Tyrol but is of a preliminary character and needs to be verified by an analysis of the inheritance practices of these families – an undertaking I seek to realise as part of my current research project. For an overview of the Italian situation, see: Gérard Delille, "Strategie di alleanza e demografia del matrimonio", in: Michela De Giorgio and Christiane Klapisch-Zuber (eds.), *Storia delle donne in Italia: Storia del matrimonio*, Roma and Bari 1996 [Laterza], pp. 283–303; Gianna Pomata, "La storia moderna", in: Anna Rossi-Doria (ed.), *A che punto è la storia delle donne*, Roma 2003 [Viella], pp. 43–61. Among the German high nobility, Karl-Heinz Spieß observed the rise of primogeniture at the end of the seventeenth century: "Lordship, Kinship, and Inheritance among the German High Nobility in the Middle Ages and Early Modern Period", in: David Warren Sabean u.a. (eds.), *Kinship in Europe. Approaches to Long-Term Development (1300–1900)*, New York and Oxford 2007 [Berghahn], pp. 57–75.

36 See Clementi, "Deren von Wolkenstein"; Siglinde Clementi, *Körper, Selbst und Melancholie. Die Selbstzeugnisse des Landadeligen Osvaldo Ercole Trapp (1634–1710)* (Selbstzeugnisse der Neuzeit 26), Vienna, Cologne and Weimar 2017 [Böhlau]; Clementi, "Undivided Brothers – Renouncing Sisters".

37 Marriage contract of Balthasar Trautson and Susanna Fugger, 1555: TLA, Archiv Trautson, Pos. 104, 2 Urk 297; marriage contract of Ludwig Freiherr von Hoyos and Susanna Trautson, 1580: TLA, Archiv Trautson, Pos. 104,5; marriage contract of Maximilian Hendl zu Goldrain and Brigitta Benigna Trautson, 1595: TLA, Archiv Trautson Urk. 305.

38 See Giulia Calvi and Isabelle Chabot (eds.), *Le ricchezze delle donne. Diritti patrimoniali e poteri familiari in Italia* (XIII – XIX secc.), Turin 1998 [Rosenberg & Sellier].

39 Hufschmid, *Adlige Frauen*. On Austrian lands, see Brauneder, *Die Entwicklung des Ehegüterrechts*.

40 Marriage contract of Johann Trautson and Sidonia von Wolkenstein, 1593: SLA, Wolkenstein-Trostburg 678.

41 Marriage contract of Anton Trautson and Maria Villinger, 1587: TLA, Trautson Urk. 300.

42 Brauneder, *Die Entwicklung des Ehegüterrechts*.

43 Marriage contract of Marx Sittich von Wolkenstein and Anna Maria Trautson, 1588: SLA, Wolkenstein-Trostburg Urkunden 1138; as well as TLA, Trautson Urk. 301.

44 Marriage contract of Johann Franz Trautson and Maximiliana zu Hohenzollern, 1630: TLA, Trautson Pos. 104,11.

45 Margareth Lanzinger, "Von der Macht der Linie zur Gegenseitigkeit. Heiratskontrakte in den Südtiroler Gerichten Welsberg und Innichen 1750–1850", in: Margareth Lanzinger, Gunda Barth-Scalmani, Ellinor Forster and Gertrude Langer-Ostrawsky (eds.), *Aushandeln von Ehe. Heiratsverträge der Neuzeit im europäischen Vergleich*, Cologne, Weimar and Vienna 2010 [Böhlau], pp. 205–367.

46 On the practice in other social milieus, see Lanzinger/Maegraith, Konkurrenz um Vermögen; Lanzinger, Von der Macht der Linie.

47 Marriage contract of Paul Sixtus Trautson and Anna Gräfin von Monfort, 1591: TLA, Archiv Trautson, Urk. 303.

48 Marriage contract of Elisabeth von Wolkenstein and Christoph von Spaur, 1613: SLA, Wolkenstein-Trostburg-Toblino 417/3. See the provisions on the morning gift in the Tyrolean Law Code: TLO, III, 7 and 38.

49 For example in the marriage contract of Paul Sixtus Trautson and Maria Katharina von Königsegg, 1664: TLA, Trautson Pos. 104, 20.

50 "*weil er mit ainem zimlichen Alter beladen, vnd alberait mit etlichen kindern begabt*". Marriage contract of Balthasar Trautson and Maria Sidonia von Welsperg, 1589: TLA, Trautson, Pos. 104,8.

51 Marriage contract of Kaspar von Wolkenstein and Elisabeth Lang von Wellenburg, 1550: SLA, Wolkenstein-Trostburg 678; marriage contract of Albrecht von Wolkenstein and Johanna Madruzzo, 1609: SLA, Wolkenstein-Trostburg 676.

52 Marriage contract of Balthasar Trautson and Susanna Fugger, 1555: TLA, Trautson Pos. 104,2, as well as Urk. 297; marriage contract of Christoph von Welsperg and Adalberta Fugger, 1582: SLA, Wolkenstein-Trostburg 802. In return for her 26,770 guilders, Veronika Fugger was provided with a morning gift worth a mere 1,500 guilders. Marriage contract of Daniel Felix von Spaur and Veronika Fugger, 1542: SLA, Welsperg-Spaur 528.

53 "*Der morgengabe halber soll sy die frau Adalberta dieselbe in irem leben ihres gefallens zuvergeben, zuverschaffen oder zuverschenken frey macht vnd gewalt haben*". Marriage contract of Christoph von Welsperg and Adalberta Fugger, 1582: SLA, Wolkenstein-Trostburg 802.

54 Marriage contract of Paul Sixtus Trautson and Maria Katherina von Königsegg, 1664: TLA, Trautson Pos. 104,20; marriage contract of Brigitta Trautson and Maximilian Hendl zu Goldrain, 1595: TLA, Trautson Urk. 305.

55 TLO 1573, III, 7, and on testamentary dispositions, see Clementi, *Deren von Wolkenstein*, pp. 140.

56 TLO 1573, III, 1.

57 "*auf all vnd jedes sein hab vnd guet urbar, aigen, zins, zehent, pfandtgultn ligendes varende gegenwärtige vnd kunftige hab vnd guetter was alles vnd sovil er des allesamt vnd bei seinen gebruedern deren von Seiboltsdorff ungetailt hat*". Marriage contract of Hans von Seiboltsdorf and Elisabeth Khuen-Belasi, TLA, Archiv Khuen-Belasi, Urk. 4.12.1536, Karton 3.

58 Marriage contract of Johann Franz Trautson and Maximiliana zu Hohenzollern, 1630: TLA, Archiv Trautson, Pos. 104,11.

59 On emancipation, see Sandra Cavallo, "Le emancipazioni. Una fonte per lo studio dei rapporti famigliari intra- e inter-generazionali", in: Anna Bellavitis and Isabelle Chabot (eds.), *Famiglia e poteri in Italia tra medioevo ed età moderna*, Roma 2009 [Viella], pp. 347–370; Thomas Kuehn, *Emancipation in late medieval Florence*, New Brunswick, NJ 1982 [Rutgers University Press]; Sandra Cavallo, *Artisans of the Body in Early Modern Italy. Identities, Families and Masculinities*, Manchester and New York 2007 [Manchester University Press], pp. 202–208.

60 Marriage contract of Albrecht von Wolkenstein and Johanna von Madruzzo 1609, SLA, Wolkenstein-Trostburg 676; marriage contract of Ferdinand von Wolkenstein and Anna Maria Waldburg 1596, SLA; Wolkenstein-Trostburg 678; marriage contract of Kaspar von Wolkenstein and Elisabeth Lang von Wellenburg 1550, SLA; Wolkenstein-Trosburg 678.

61 Marriage contract of Maria Margareta Trautson and Hans Joachim Graf Slavata, 1663: TLA, Archiv Trautson, Pos. 104, 19.

62 Marriage contract of Veit Dominicus Wolkenstein-Trostburg and Maria Gräfin Gondola, 1702: SLA, Archiv Wolkenstein-Trostburg 3259.

63 TLO, 1573, III, 1.

64 "*sy de wolernannte eeleut sollen in werender ehe, sollich ir vorbenanndt heüradtguet, morgengab vnd widerlag treulich vnd one geverde, mit einander genüßen vnd zu baider nuz geprauchen*". Marriage contract of Balthasar Trautson and Susanna Fugger, 1555: TLA, Archiv Trautson, Pos. 104, 2 Urk. 297.

65 TLO 1573, III, 38.

66 TLO 1573, III, 1.

67 TLO 1573, III, 39.

68 TLO 1573, III, 40 and 41.

69 TLO 1573, III, 1.

70 One example is the marriage contract of Balthasar Trautson und Susanna Fugger, 1555: TLA, Trautson, Pos. 104,2, as well as Urk. 297.

71 Marriage contract of Marx Oswald von Wolkenstein and Magdalena Khuen, 1607: SLA, Wolkenstein-Trostburg 464; Hans Trautson und Brigitta Maria Susanna Madruzzo, 1531: TLA, Trautson Urk 286; marriage contract of Wilhelm Wolkenstein und Anna von Annenberg, 1505: SLA, Wolkenstein-Trostburg 756; marriage contract of Peter von Spaur und Dorothea Ainichen, 1491: SLA, Welsperg-Spaur 323.

72 TLO 1573, III, 34 and 35.

73 Marriage contract of Wilhelm von Arz and Maria Christina von Wolkenstein, 1616: SLA, Wolkenstein-Trostburg 464; marriage contract of Veit Dominicus von Wolkenstein and Maria Gondola, 1702: SLA, Wolkenstein-Trostburg 3259; marriage contract of Johann Jakob Waldburg-Zeil and Johanna von Wolkenstein, 1621: SLA, Wolkenstein-Trostburg 3259; marriage contract of Marx Sittich von Wolkenstein and Anna Maria Trautson, 1588: SLA, Wolkenstein-Trostburg-Urkunden 1138 and TLA, Trautson, Urk. 301.

74 Marriage contract of Albrecht von Wolkenstein and Johanna Madruzzo, 1609: SLA, Wolkenstein-Trostburg 676.

75 TLO 1573, III, 40.

76 Marriage contract of Johann Franz Trautson and Maximiliana zu Hohenzollern, 1630: TLA, Trautson Pos. 104,11; Maximilian Hendl zu Goldrain and Brigitte Trautson, 1595: TLA, Trautson Urk. 305; Paul Sixtus Trautson and Anna Monfort, 1591: TLA, Trautson Urk. 303.

77 Marriage contract of Paul Sixtus Trautson and Susanna Veronica von Meggau, 1604: TLA, Trautson Urk. 307.

78 Marriage contract of Maximilian Karl von Wolkenstein and Maria Christina Paumgarten, 1648: SLA, Wolkenstein-Trostburg 874.

79 "*Da sye lieber widerumb in Bayrn als irhem Vatterlandt wohnen wollte*", ibid.

80 TLO 1573, III, 42.

81 Marriage contract of Kaspar von Wolkenstein and Elisabeth Lang von Wellenburg, 1550: SLA, Wolkenstein-Trostburg 678; marriage contract of Marx Oswald von Wolkenstein and Magdalena Khuen, 1607: SLA, Wolkenstein-Trostburg 464; Hans Trautson and Brigitta Maria Susanna Madruzzo, 1531: TLA, Trautson Urk 286; Maximilian Trautson and Anna Katherina von Wolkenstein, 1615: SLA, Wolkenstein-Trostburg 1081.

82 Marriage contract of Anton von Spaur and Anna von Wolkenstein, 1566: SLA, Wolkenstein-Trostburg 772 and 1233.

83 Marriage contract of Christoph von Welsperg and Adalberta Fugger, 1582: SLA, Wolkenstein-Trostburg 802; marriage contract of Albrecht von Wolkenstein and Johanna Madruzzo, 1609: SLA, Wolkenstein-Trostburg 676; Herrand Wolkenstein and Barbara von Schernberg und Goldegg, 1580: SLA, Wolkenstein-Trostburg 1177; Johann Jakob von Waldburg-Zeil and Johanna von Wolkenstein, 1621: SLA, Wolkenstein-Trostburg 3259; marriage contract of Balthasar Trautson and Susanna Fugger, 1555: TLA, Trautson Pos. 104,2. The Tyrolean Law Code provided for the possibility of lifelong usufruct only in cases of marriage portions worth less than 25 guilders: TLO 1573, III, 20.

84 TLO 1573, III, 42.

85 Marriage contract of Johann Trautson and Sidonia von Wolkenstein, 1593: SLA, Wolkenstein-Trostburg 678; Marriage contract of Maximilian Karl von Wolkenstein and Maria Christina Paumgarten, 1648: SLA, Wolkenstein-Trostburg 874.

86 Marriage contract of Johann Sigmund Thun and Anna Margaret von Wolkenstein, 1628: SLA, Wolkenstein-Trostburg 464.

87 Marriage contract of Wilhelm von Arz and Maria Christina von Wolkenstein, 1616: SLA, Wolkenstein-Trostburg 464.

88 Marriage contract of Albrecht von Wolkenstein and Johanna Madruzzo, 1609: SLA, Wolkenstein-Trotburg 676; marriage contract of Balthasar Trautson and Susanna Fugger, 1555: TLA, Trautson, Pos. 104,2 and Urk. 297.

89 Similar findings in Hagen/Lanzinger/Maegraith, Verträge als Instrumente der Vermögensabsicherung.

90 Marriage contract of Veit Dominicus von Wolkenstein and Maria Gondola, 1702: SLA, Wolkenstein-Trostburg 3259; marriage contract of Johann Jakob Waldburg-Zeil and

Johanna von Wolkenstein, 1621: SLA, Wolkenstein-Trostburg 3259; marriage contract of Albrecht von Wolkenstein and Johanna Madruzzo, 1609: SLA, Wolkenstein-Trostburg 676; Pauls Sixtus and Susanna Veronica von Meggau, 1604: TLA, Trautson Urk. 307; marriage contract of Christoph von Welsperg and Adalberta Fugger, 1582: SLA, Wolkenstein-Trostburg 802.

91 Marriage contract of Daniel Felix von Spaur and Veronika Fugger, 1542: SLA, Welsperg-Spaur 528; marriage contract of Kaspar von Wolkenstein and Elisabeth Lang von Wellenburg, 1550: SLA, Wolkenstein-Trostburg 678; marriage contract of Ferdinand Karl von Wolkenstein and Kunigunde Felicitas Bissingen, 1674: SLA, Wollkenstein-Trostburg 545; marriage contract of Johann Franz Trautson and Christina von Mansfeld, 1640: TLA, Trautson Pos. 104,13; one year long: marriage contract of Pauls Sixtus Trautson and Susanna Veronica von Meggau, 1604: TLA, Trautson Urk. 307. The widow's usufruct up to the widow's endowment's complete disbursement is also stipulated by the Tyrolean Law Code: TLO 1573, III, 38.

92 "*zimlich heyratsguet nach gelegenhait des herkumens vnd vermögens*", TLO 1573, III, 34.

93 Clementi, "Heiraten in Grenzräumen".

94 On emancipation, see Cavallo, "Le emancipazioni"; Kuehn, *Emancipation*; Cavallo, *Artisans of the Body*, pp. 202–208.

95 Clementi, *Deren von Wolkenstein*.

96 See Ibid., p. 143 ff.; Hufschmid, *Adlige Frauen*, p. 275; Spieß, *Familie und Verwandtschaft*, p. 344. For a fundamental discussion of honour as symbolic capital, see Pierre Bourdieu, *Entwurf einer Theorie der Praxis auf der Grundlage der kabylischen Gesellschaft*, Frankfurt am Main 1979 [Suhrkamp], especially pp. 335–377; on the term "social capital" and its interaction with cultural and economic capital, see ibid., "Ökonomisches Kapital, kulturelles Kapital, soziales Kapital", in: Reinhard Kreckel (ed.), *Soziale Ungleichheiten* (Soziale Welt, Sonderband 2), Göttingen 1983 [Schwartz], pp. 183–198; and on honour as a historical category, see Martin Dinges, "Die Ehre als Thema der historischen Anthropologie. Bemerkungen zur Wissenschaftsgeschichte und zur Konzeptualisierung", in: Klaus Schreiner and Gerd Scherhoff (eds.), *Verletzte Ehre. Ehrkonflikte in Gesellschaften des Mittelalters und der frühen Neuzeit* (Norm und Struktur 5), Cologne, Weimar and Vienna 1995 [Böhlau], pp. 29–62, as well as Sibylle Backmann u.a. (eds.), *Ehrkonzepte in der Frühen Neuzeit. Identitäten und Abgrenzungen*, Berlin 1998 [Akademie Verlag]. On noble honour, see Otto Gerhard Oexle, "Aspekte der Geschichte des Adels im Mittelalter und in der Frühen Neuzeit", in: Hans-Ulrich Wehler (ed.), *Europäischer Adel 1750–1950*, Göttingen 1990 [Vandenhoeck & Ruprecht], pp. 19–56; Frank Dierkes, *Streitbar und ehrenfest. Zur Konfliktführung im münsterländischen Adel des 16. und 17. Jahrhunderts*, Münster 2007 [Aschendorff], p. 23 ff.; Clementi, *Körper, Selbst und Melancholie*, pp. 61 ff. and 143; Clementi, "Heiraten in Grenzräumen"; Heinz Reif, *Westfälischer Adel 1770–1860. Vom Herrenstand zur regionalen Elite*, Göttingen 1979 [Vandenhoeck & Ruprecht], pp. 41–49.

97 Jon Mathieu, "Vermögensarrangements und Verwandtschaft im frühneuzeitlichen Graubünden: Grundmuster, schichtspezifischer Wandel, Einordnung", in: *Geschichte und Region* 28, 2 (2018), pp. 149–168.

Bibliography

Sources

Austria, Tiroler Landesarchiv, Trautson.

Austria, Tiroler Landesarchiv, Khuen-Belasi.

Italy, Biblioteca Comunale di Trento, Fondo Segala.

Italy, Bolzano, Südtiroler Landesarchiv, Wolkenstein-Trostburg.

Italy, Bolzano, Südtiroler Landesarchiv, Welsperg.

Italy, Bolzano, Südtiroler Landesarchiv, Welsperg-Spaur.

Italy, Bolzano, Südtiroler Landesarchiv, Bibliothek, Stephan von Mayerhofen, Genealogien des Tyroler Adels, um 1800, transcription by Kurt Staffler, ca. 1937.

Encyclopaedias

Art. Weiberlehen, *Handwörterbuch der deutschen Rechtsgeschichte*, Bd. V, Berlin 1998, Sp. 1206–1209.

Research bibliography

Ago, Renata and Benedetta Borello (eds.), *Famiglie, circolazione di beni, circuiti di affetti in età moderna*, Rom 2009 [Viella].

Backmann, Sibylle et al. (eds.), *Ehrkonzepte in der Frühen Neuzeit. Identitäten und Abgrenzungen*, Berlin 1998 [Akademie-Verlag].

Beimrohr, Wilfried, Das landesfürstliche Lehnwesen in Tirol, in: *Tiroler Heimat* 79 (2015), pp. 33–61.

Bellabarba, Marco, *La giustizia ai confini. Il principato vescovile di Trento agli inizi dell'età moderna*, Bologna 1996 [Il Mulino].

Bellavitis, Anna, *Identitè, mariage, mobilité social. Citoyennes et citoyens à Venise au XVIe siècle*, Rome 2001 [École Francaise de Rome].

———*Famille, genre, trasmission à Venise au XVIe siècle*, Rome 2008 [École Francaise de Rome].

Bonazza, Marcello, *Il fisco in una statalità divisa. Impero, principi e ceti in area trentino-tirolese nella prima età moderna (Annali dell'Istituto storico italo-germanico. Monografie 35)*, Bologna 2001 [Il Mulino].

Bourdieu, Pierre, *Entwurf einer Theorie der Praxis auf der Grundlage der kabylischen Gesellschaft*, Frankfurt a.M. 1979 [Suhrkamp].

———"Ökonomisches Kapital, kulturelles Kapital, soziales Kapital", in: Reinhard Kreckel (ed.), *Soziale Ungleichheit (Soziale Welt, Sonderband 2)*, Göttingen 1983 [Schwartz], pp. 183–198.

Brandstätter, Klaus, "Tyrol, die herrliche, gefirstete Grafschaft ist von uralten zeiten gehaissen und auch so geschrieben . . . 'Zur Geschichte des Begriffs' Tirol", in: *Geschichte und Region/Storia e regione* 9 (2000), pp. 11–30.

———"Kirchliche Karrieren der Wolkensteiner in der Frühen Neuzeit", in: Gustav Pfeifer and Kurt Andermann (eds.), *Die Wolkensteiner. Facetten des Tiroler Adels in Spätmittelalter und Neuzeit (Veröffentlichungen des Südtiroler Landesarchivs 30)*, Innsbruck 2009 [Wagner], pp. 149–194.

Brauneder, Wilhelm, *Die Entwicklung des Ehegüterrechts in Österreich. Ein Beitrag zur Dogmengeschichte und Rechtstatsachenforschung des Spätmittelalters und der Neuzeit*, Salzburg and Munich 1973 [Fink].

Calvi, Giulia and Isabelle Chabot (eds.), *Le ricchezze delle donne. Diritti patrimoniali e poteri familiari in Italia* (XIII–XIX secc.), Turin 1998 [Rosenberg & Sellier].

Cavallo, Sandra, *Artisans of the Body in Early Modern Italy. Identities, Families and Masculinities*, Manchester and New York 2007 [Manchester University Press], pp. 202–208.

———"Le emancipazioni. Una fonte per lo studio dei rapporti famigliari intra- e intergenerazionali", in: Anna Bellavitis and Isabelle Chabot (eds.), *Famiglia e poteri in Italia tra medioevo ed età moderna*, Roma 2009 [Viella], pp. 347–370.

Chabot, Isabelle, "Family Justice and Public Justice in Dowry and Inheritance Conflicts Between Florentine Families (Forteenth to Fifteenth Centuries)", in: Margareth Lanzinger et al. (eds.), *Stipulating – Litigating – Mediating. Negotiations of Gender and Property*, Leiden forthcoming [Brill].

Chojnacki, Stanley, *Women and Men in Renaissance Venice. Twelve Essays on Patrician Society*, Baltimore and London 2000 [The John Hopkins University Press].

Clementi, Siglinde, "Deren von Wolkenstein. Familienstrategien, Heirat und Geschlechterbeziehungen bei den Wolkenstein-Trostburg (um 1500 bis 1650)", in: Gustav Pfeifer and Kurt Andermann (eds.), *Die Wolkensteiner. Facetten des Tiroler Adels in Spätmittelalter und Neuzeit (Veröffentlichungen des Südtiroler Landesarchivs 30)*, Innsbruck 2009 [Wagner], pp. 111–147.

———*Körper, Selbst und Melancholie. Die Selbstzeugnisse des Landadeligen Osvaldo Ercole Trapp (1634–1710) (Selbstzeugnisse der Neuzeit 26)*, Vienna, Cologne and Weimar 2017 [Böhlau].

———“Undivided Brothers – Renouncing Sisters. Family Strategies of Low Nobility in Sixteenth- and Seventeenth-Century Tyrol”, in: Anna Bellavitis and Beatrice Zucca Micheletto (eds.), *Gender, Law and Economic Well-being in Europe from the Fifteenth to the Nineteenth Century*, London and New York 2019 [Routledge], pp. 149–164.

———“Heiraten in Grenzräumen. Vermögensarrangements adeliger Ehefrauen und -männer im frühneuzeitlichen Tirol”, in: *Geschichte und Region/Storia e regione* 28, 2 (2018), pp. 44–69.

Clementi, Siglinde, Ellinor Forster, Christian Hagen, Margareth Lanzinger and Janine Christina Maegraith, “Rechtsräume und Geschlechterordnungen als soziale Prozesse – transregional. Vereinbaren und Verfügen in städtischen und ländlichen Kontexten im südlichen Tirol vom 15. bis zum frühen 19. Jahrhundert – ein erster Projektbericht”, in: *Geschichte und Region/Storia e regione* 22, 2 (2013), pp. 165–172.

Delille, Gérard, “Strategie di alleanza e demografia del matrimonio”, in: Michela De Giorgio and Christiane Klapisch-Zuber (eds.), *Storia delle donne in Italia: Storia del matrimonio*, Roma and Bari 1996 [Laterza], pp. 283–303.

Dierkes, Frank, *Streitbar und ehrenfest. Zur Konfliktführung im münsterländischen Adel des 16. und 17. Jahrhunderts*, Münster 2007 [Aschendorff].

Dinges, Martin, “Die Ehre als Thema der historischen Anthropologie. Bemerkungen zur Wissenschaftsgeschichte und zur Konzeptualisierung”, in: Klaus Schreiner and Gerd Scherhoff (eds.), *Verletzte Ehre. Ehrkonflikte in Gesellschaften des Mittelalters und der frühen Neuzeit (Norm und Struktur 5)*, Cologne, Weimar and Vienna 1995 [Böhlau], pp. 29–62.

Dörrer, Friedolin, “Die limitierte Landeshoheit der Bischöfe von Trient und Brixen in Beziehung zur gefürsteten Grafschaft Tirol”, in: Erwin Riedenauer (ed.), *Landeshoheit. Beiträge zur Entstehung, Ausformung und Typologie eines Verfassungselements der römisch-deutschen Reiches (Studien zur Bayrischen Verfassungs- und Sozialgeschichte Band XVI)*, Munich 1994 [Komm. für Bayrische Landesgeschichte], pp. 135–144.

Emmert, Anton, *Geschichtliche Darstellung der Erblandämter in der gefürsteten Grafschaft Tirol*, Innsbruck 1838 [Rauch].

Feci, Simona, “The Exclusion of Women from Inheritance Rights: An Unresolved Issue?” in: Margareth Lanzinger et al. (eds.), *Stipulating – Litigating – Mediating. Negotiations of Gender and Property*, Leiden forthcoming [Brill].

Goody, Jack, “Bridewealth and Dowry in Africa and Eurasia”, in: Jack Goody and S.J. Tambiah (eds.), *Bridewealth and Dowry*, Cambridge 1973 [Cambridge University Press], pp. 1–58.

———“Inheritance, Property and Women. Some Comparative Considerations”, in: Jack Goody, J. Thirsk and E. P. Thompson (eds.), *Family and Inheritance. Rural Society in Western Europe. 1200–1800*, Cambridge 2011 [Cambridge University Press], pp. 10–36.

Hochenegg, Hans, *Der Adel im Leben Tirols. Eine soziologische Studie (Veröffentlichungen der Universität Innsbruck 70)*, Innsbruck 1971 [Österr. Komm.-Buchh.].

Hufschmid, Anke, *Adlige Frauen im Weserraum zwischen 1570 und 1700. Status – Rollen – Lebenspraxis*, Münster 2001 [Aschendorff].

Hughes, Diana Owen, “From Brideprice to Dowry in Mediterranean Europe”, in: *Journal of Family History* 3 (1978), pp. 262–296 (also in Marion Kaplan (ed.), *The Marriage Bargain. Women and Dowries in European History*, New York 1985 [Routledge], pp. 13–57).

Köfler, Werner, *Land, Landschaft, Landtag: Geschichte der Tiroler Landtage von den Anfängen bis zur Aufhebung der landständischen Verfassung 1808*, Innsbruck 1998 [Wagner].

Kögl, Joseph, *La sovranità dei vescovi di Trento e di Bressanone. Diritti derivanti al clero diocesano dalla sua sopressione*, Trento 1964 [Tipografia Arcivescovile Artiginelli].

Kuehn, Thomas, *Emancipation in Late Medieval Florence*, New Brunswick, NJ 1982 [Rutgers University Press].

———*Law, Family, and Women: Toward a Legal Anthropology of Renaissance Italy*, Chicago 1991 [University of Chicago Press].

Langbein, Ulrike, *Geerbte Dinge. Soziale Praxis und symbolische Bedeutung des Erbens*, Köln 2002 [Böhlau].

———"Vom Ideellen im Materiellen: Plädoyer für einen mikroskopischen Blick auf das Erbe", in: Stefan Brakensiek, Michael Stolleis and Heide Wunder (eds.), *Generationengerechtigkeit? Normen und Praxis im Erb- und Ehegüterrecht 1500–1850 (Zeitschrift für Historische Forschung, Beiheft 37)*, Berlin 2006 [Dunker und Humblot], pp. 283–300.

Lanzinger, Margareth, "Mitgift, Heiratsgut und Ehegüterregime: Variationen und Übergänge", in: *Geschichte und Region/Storia e regione* 19, 1 (2010), pp. 123–143.

———Variationen des Themas: Mitgiftsysteme, in: Margareth Lanzinger/Gunda Barth-Scalmani/Ellinor Forster/Gertrude Langer-Ostrawsky, *Aushandeln von Ehe. Heiratsverträge der Neuzeit im europäischen Vergleich*, Cologne, Weimar and Vienna 2010 [Böhlau], pp. 469–492.

Levi, Giovanni, *Das immaterielle Erbe. Eine bäuerliche Welt an der Schwelle zur Moderne*, Berlin 1986 [Wagenbach]; original version: L'eredità immateriale. *Carriera di un esorcista nel Piemonte del Seicento*, Torino 1985 [Einaudi].

Mathieu, Jon, "Vermögensarrangements und Verwandtschaft im frühneuzeitlichen Graubünden: Grundmuster, schichtspezifischer Wandel, Einordnung", in: *Geschichte und Region* 28, 2 (2018), pp. 149–168.

Noflatscher, Heinz, "Frömmigkeit und Patronage. Zum Adelsklerus um 1700", in: Josef Nössing and Helmut Stampfer (eds.), *Kunst und Kirche in Tirol. Festschrift zum 70. Geburtstag von Karl Wolfgruber*, Bozen 1987 [Athesia], pp. 131–151.

———"Tirol, Brixen, Trient", in: Anton Schindling and Walter Ziegler (eds.), *Die Territorien des Reiches im Zeitalter der Reformation und Konfessionalisierung. Land und Konfession 1500–1650. Bd. 1: Der Südosten (Katholisches Leben und Kirchenreform im Zeitalter der Glaubensspaltung 49)*, Münster 1989 [Aschendorff], pp. 86–101.

Oexle, Otto Gerhard, "Aspekte der Geschichte des Adels im Mittelalter und in der Frühen Neuzeit", in: Hans-Ulrich Wehler (ed.), *Europäischer Adel 1750–1950*, Göttingen 1990 [Vandenhoeck & Ruprecht], pp. 19–56.

Pomata, Gianna, "La storia moderna", in: Anna Rossi-Doria (ed.), *A che punto è la storia delle donne*, Roma 2003 [Viella], pp. 43–61.

Reif, Heinz, *Westfälischer Adel 1770–1860. Vom Herrenstand zur regionalen Elite*, Göttingen 1979 [Vandenhoeck & Ruprecht].

Schennach, Martin, *Gesetz und Herrschaft. Die Entstehung des Gesetzgebungsstaates am Beispiel Tirols*, Cologne and Vienna 2010 [Böhlau].

Spieß, Karl-Heinz, *Familie und Verwandtschaft im deutschen Hochadel des Spätmittelalters. 13. bis Anfang des 16. Jahrhunderts*, Stuttgart 1993 [Steiner].

Spieß, Karl-Heinz, "Lordship, Kinship, and Inheritance among the German High Nobility in the Middle Ages and Early Modern Period", in: David Warren Sabean u.a. (eds.), *Kinship in Europe. Approaches to Long-Term Development (1300–1900)*, New York and Oxford 2007 [Berghahn], pp. 57–75.

PART III

Women's access to immobile property

FIGURE 6.1 Map of Tyrol, displaying the area near Brixen and Sonnenburg, Guillaume de L'Isle, Philippe Buache, *Carte d' Europe*, 1769 (detail).

Source: Library of Congress Geography and Map Division, Washington, D.C., U.S.A., public domain, G5700 1724. L5 TIL, http://hdl.loc.gov/loc.gmd/g5700.ct000045 (15.02.2020, 13:15 CET).

6

FENCED IN OR OUT?

Women and landownership in early modern southern Tyrol

Janine Maegraith

ABSTRACT

Fences are omnipresent in today's environment. They visualise property borders and range from ornamental to insurmountable elements of control. When looking at fences one does not necessarily think of gender. They convey property demarcations, but they are not connected with either female or male possessions. On the other hand, movable goods and smaller things are often associated with women, and work has been done analysing contemporary consumption habits in view of gender.[1] The fence, although being an object, is associated with landed property, which in turn is often thought to have been in predominantly male possession. The question is whether the object "fence" signifies differences in access to property, whether landed property was more in male possession, why this might have been the case, and in how far the law facilitated this or left some scope for wider access. In a metaphorical sense, in this paper the fence visualises the legal, social, institutional, and political conditions for women's access to landed property. By looking at sixteenth and seventeenth century court records of the town of Brixen and the rural court district of Sonnenburg, this paper investigates women and landownership comparing all social strata of town and countryside with the exception of the nobility.

I. Introduction: The function and meaning of fences

What do fences convey historically? According to Christina Kotchemidova, fences establish cultural values and can perpetuate cultural ideas. They are also visual establishments of property rights, although fences might have predated the law.[2] John Streamas, focussing on American history, discusses how the fence mediates social relations and how fences can fence in as well as out, obstructing equal opportunities.[3] With this he points to the wider historical concept of inclusion and exclusion, of common land and private ownership of land. These double meanings of fences are also reflected in their definitions in historical dictionaries, such as Zedler's

Universal Lexicon and the Grimms's dictionary. These focus on the material, functional, and legal meaning of fences. The distinction between dead fences made of wood or wicker and live fences consisting of hedges, for example, raises questions of resources as well as functionality. The main role of fences is defined as protection against wild and domesticated animals and mischievous people (*muthwilliger und böser Leute*). But fences also serve as protection for livestock. Fences defined property rights and asserted the right to demarcate a garden (*Gartenrecht*) and to delimit the boundaries between neighbours preventing or reacting to conflicts. However, nobody was allowed to build a fence that would reduce common land. This was regulated by the district courts.[4] The manipulation of fences was sanctioned heavily. Late mediaeval Tyrolean *Weistümer*, or local statutes, contain numerous references to fences. For example, in the sixteenth century statutes of the court district of Enneberg, which belonged to the court district of Sonnenburg, the alteration of landmarks or poles (*marchstain oder stecken*) resulted in a fine of 50 *Pfund Berner*, equivalent to 10 gulden. Similarly, if somebody built a fence on neighbouring ground, every fence post resulted in a fine of 5 *Pfund Berner*, and both parties were to be reconciled with the help of the magistracy.[5] The fines amounted to significant sums; a weaver's loom and tools were appraised in an inventory in 1580 at 10 gulden, for example.[6] This shows the importance given to the physical demarcation of property rights. The fence offers a useful means to look at the law and practice of property rights. In addition, it adopts the border between movable and immovable property: It demarcates real estate boundaries but remains an object.

II. Fences and property in early modern Tyrol

Fences were omnipresent in early modern Europe. They can be seen in many illustrations, drawings, maps, and frescoes of surrounding fields, areas around houses, and gardens in Tyrol (see Figures 6.2. and 6.3).[7]

In Tyrol, fences are not listed in inventories, but they are mentioned in other legal documents, such as lease contracts or real estate descriptions in purchase deeds. Some documents contain conditions for the upkeep of the fence; others describe pieces of land as being fenced. Purchase, leasehold, and exchange contracts generally describe the borders of the sold real estate combined with the demand to respect its boundaries. In 1591, for example, the chaplain in Sonnenburg drew up a leasehold contract with the local weaver, Veit Prunner. He leased him a piece of land that had been previously untilled and was situated between Veit's other fields. Veit was supposed to cultivate and manure it and fence it, as was expected of a good tenant. He also had to provide the material for the fence. For the lease, he was to pay an annual rent in kind (rye, peas, two chickens, ten eggs, and a basket of cherries) to the chaplain.[8] In the absence of cadastres, land registers, and exact measurements, such (material) boundaries were defined by descriptions of borders and neighbouring pieces of land and customary rights. Thus, they were prone to negotiations and legal disputes. But the boundaries were not always visible. Forests or alpine meadows were not necessarily fenced; instead, landmarks – for example stones – indicated their boundaries.

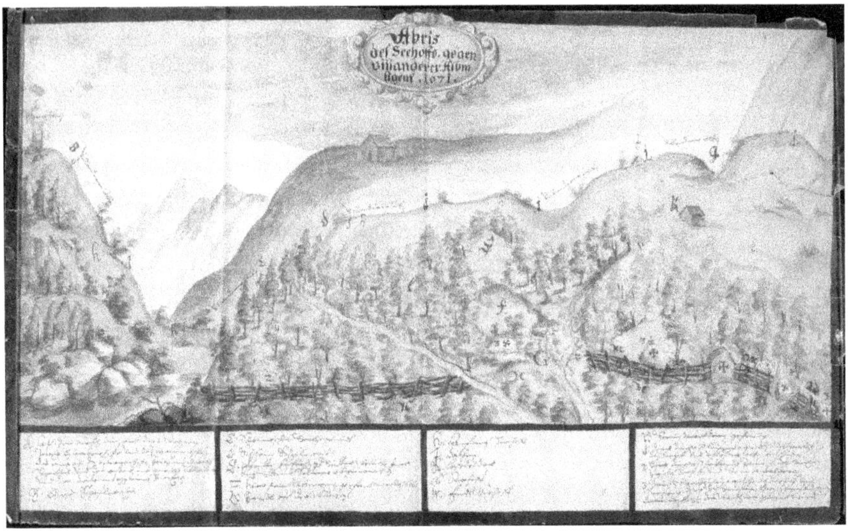

FIGURE 6.2 *Plan zum Seehof auf der Villanderer Alm*, 1671. This outline ("Abris") shows the demarcation of the Seehof using "Marksteine", boundary stones or landmarks, and a fence. The legend specifies the traversing fence to be the boundary between "Seehof" and "Seinßwaldern".

Source: Südtiroler Landesarchiv, Akten des Landeshauptmannschaftlichen Gerichts Bozen, Nr. 3547.

FIGURE 6.3 *Pergsmappa zur Gaider Alpe auf Nördersberg im Vinschgau*, 1784. The map shows a dispersed settlement with farmsteads spread across the area. The farms are characterised by a residential building and a farm building surrounded by a fence.

Source: Südtiroler Landesarchiv, Akten der Servitutenregulierungskommission, Nr. 466.

If fences visualise property borders, then they also point to the local law and practice of property rights. What were the forms of landownership, their appertained legal rights, and gender distribution in early modern Tyrol that led to a landscape traversed by fences? Did they also visualise legal practices of property transfer, such as inheritance, marital property, and commercial transactions? As mentioned, fences are material signifiers of properties; they establish ownership and exclude common rights. This already suggests unequal access to land use and land markets.[9] For mediaeval and early modern Central Europe, the existence of land markets has been affirmed, although much more research is needed on the varying property structures, rights, transmissions, and dynamics of the land market(s).[10] Markus Cerman, for example, stressed the importance of analysing characteristics of more dynamic land markets visible in flexible approaches such as leasehold systems, urban investments into the countryside, the emergence of smallholders, and commercialisation of agriculture. Likewise, Bas van Basel and Hermann Zeitlhofer, amongst others, showed the significance of studying land markets in their social and economic contexts, of unearthing the social distribution of landownership.[11] Zeitlhofer, for example, investigated property transfers, social changes, gender ratios, and hereditary serfdom in his study of a rural district in southern Bohemia between 1640 and 1840. His aim was to look at links between property transmission and demographic, economic, and social developments in rural societies. In terms of gender he found, for example, that while a preference for sons in successorship was always verifiable, the gender ratio changed significantly over time, especially in the nineteenth century, in favour of sons (from one in four to one in twelve).[12] With a higher proportion of male successorship, which I could also find in my research areas in Tyrol, access to landownership for women would necessarily be restricted as well, especially if one keeps in mind that a large portion of property was transferred through inheritance and marriage in the early modern period, as Amy Erickson has pointed out.[13]

It is, therefore, important to study women's access to property. Women constitute half of the population, and their access to the land markets could make a huge difference. Establishing their market participation can be an additional indicator of how dynamic those markets were. The law established the legal framework of the markets, but the legal practice was decisive and could create restrictions, such as limitations on wealth distribution through inheritance practice. How inheritance and succession were practiced mattered since this determined transfer of land and inheritance compensation payments constituted vital funds for the livelihoods of the ceding heirs. I argue that in Tyrol the law left sufficient scope for women to participate in the market and that separation of marital property enabled them to act individually, but that social practices confined their full involvement, and thus an otherwise fairly flexible land market became markedly gendered. The fence, then, on an abstract level would represent restricted access to landed property for women.

In my research project, I am focussing on two court districts: The town court of Brixen and the manorial court district of Sonnenburg.[14] Brixen was an independent bishopric with large holdings both surrounding the town and farther afield. The town court comprised the town itself, Albeins, and the rural court of Pfeffersberg with farmsteads and vineyards.[15] Sonnenburg was a Benedictine nunnery in the Puster Valley with a considerable, albeit not coherent, rural territory consisting of two parts: The large holdings of the court district of Enneberg and the *Hofgericht* Sonnenburg, the jurisdiction of the abbey. I focus on the latter, which encompassed the villages of Sonnenburg, Pflaurenz, and Fassing and various holdings in the Ladin Gader Valley (Val Badia, with Untermoi, Welschellen, and Weitental), Mühlwald Tal (Valle dei Molini), and Ahrntal (Valle Aurina, with Michelreis and Weißenbach).[16]

The choice of Brixen and Sonnenburg allows for comparisons between different practices in town and countryside. The main sources are the court records (*Verfachbücher*) that contain all legal documents and proceedings connected with changes in landownership, such as purchase, lease, and exchange contracts, but also inheritance proceedings and inventories, marriage contracts, securities on marriage portions, wills, and many others. These court records are not, however, equivalent to land registers and do not show property distribution.[17] All relevant cases for certain time periods are extracted and compiled in a case database.[18] The chapter focusses on the second half of the sixteenth century and sample years in the beginning of the seventeenth century. The sixteenth century is particularly interesting, as this was the period when the *Tioler Landesordnung*, or Tyrol law code, was implemented (in 1526) and revised (in 1532 and 1573).[19] The Tyrol law code regulated property rights comprehensively, and its third book determined marital property law, inheritance law, and bequests. A heightened awareness of the law and an increase in written records as opposed to oral agreements can be identified during this transition time from the late Middle Ages to the early modern period.[20]

Although people's well-being was not solely dependent on landownership, it is important to study its social and gender distribution. House and landownership secured in many cases the main means of income in the early modern period.[21] It could facilitate access to means of production, common rights, and income in rural and urban contexts. Subsistence farming was still widespread in sixteenth-century Tyrol. Cole and Wolf stressed in their study published in the book *The Hidden Frontier*, for example, that landownership was the basis of economic security. The division of peasant holdings, therefore, either through inheritance or sale, was viewed as a danger to economic viability.[22] In such an agrarian economy – predominantly alpine, with very high altitudes – it can be assumed that landownership as well as access to use of land was seen as vital, and the analysis of this is important to understand the social structure of this society.[23] In urban as well as rural contexts, ownership of real estate was important and linked not only with economic viability but also with social status. One important aspect thereby is inheritance practice and martial property law: Who was destined to become successor to the landed property and how was property defined within a marriage?

The Tyrol law code specified separation of marital property. According to this, the surviving spouse had, in principle, no entitlement to the property of the deceased spouse.[24] Husband and wife could not inherit from each other unless they made a testamentary bequest. But even bequests in wills were subject to restrictions: Only a third of inherited or half of gained wealth was allowed to be bequeathed. The remaining two-thirds or half was reserved for the next of kin.[25] Inheritance, by contrast, was not as strictly predefined. The Tyrol law code stated that all legitimate children were the sole heirs to their parents' estate. It did not specify a gender hierarchy other than that the sons should receive a fitting advantage.[26] Also, the law did not specify whether or how the estate should be divided, and thus different inheritance practices developed in the county of Tyrol.[27] If no legitimate children existed, then the estate would go to the next of kin of the deceased, including female next of kin, such as daughters, sisters, and nieces. Regarding the movables or personal belongings of the parents, though, the law stipulated a gendered pattern: The daughters should receive their mother's movables, such as her trousseau, clothing, fabrics, and ornaments, and the sons should get their father's clothing, ornaments, weapons, books, and seal.[28] These personal items thus gained a specific legal meaning and were not freely transferable.[29]

In the manorial court district of Sonnenburg and in Brixen, a form of impartible inheritance prevailed. The landed property would go to one or in some cases two or three sons (undivided fraternal property), and the siblings or ceding heirs were compensated in money and goods. If there was no real estate, the money or investments were distributed among the siblings evenly, if it was the mother's estate, or almost evenly in the case of fathers' estates, with a son receiving a "fitting advantage". In most cases where siblings were compensated, daughters received less money but more movables than their brothers.[30] In a previous study, I was able to show that during the sixteenth century a predominantly male successorship was practised in the rural court district of Sonnenburg and also in the town court of

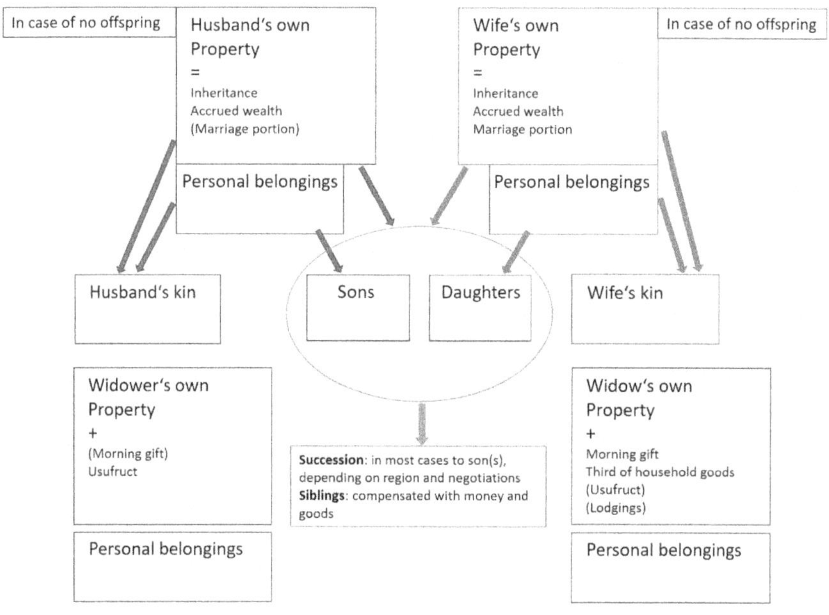

FIGURE 6.4 Practice of transfer in the court districts of Brixen and Sonnenburg, sixteenth century.

Source: © Janine Maegraith.

Brixen (albeit to a lesser extent).[31] With such an inheritance practice, and the surviving spouse having no entitlement to the estate of the deceased, most holdings were kept undivided.[32] This practice could suggest a lesser involvement of women in the land markets.

III. Land purchase contracts and gender distribution of property

In November 1600, Christina Urbanin, widow of Melchior Goldtwurm, former district magistrate in Sonnenburg, sold a cottage situated in the village of Sonnenburg. She was advised by her gender guardian. This was not the first time she was selling real estate; Christina had been obliged to sell several pieces of land to be able to pay off debts and make ends meet. This particular house, called "Salpach", came with a kitchen garden and entitlements to commons and firewood attached to it. She had inherited it from her father. The buyer was Christina Priesthoferin, maid servant of Anthon Grawbart, chaplain in the convent of Sonnenburg. She was also advised by her gender guardian, who was her son-in-law, Kastl Scheiterer, burger in the neighbouring community of Sankt Lorenz. Christina Priesthoferin gave a reason for her purchase: The house was solely in the interest of her grandchildren, the children of said Kastl Scheiterer. The house and garden were sold for 160 gulden and paid off in three instalments over three years.[33] A case study like this shows that women were active in the land markets. In this case, the female seller and buyer were probably both widows, and they were legally obliged to have a gender guardian present.[34] As was specified in all purchase deeds, the buyer was obligated to respect the described boundaries of the property to prevent any trespassing on neighbouring properties – even if no fence was mentioned. What is significant in this deed is that the buyer gave the reason for her purchase as an investment for her grandchildren. But how representative is this case?

The general form of landownership in early modern Tyrol was hereditary land tenure, which gave tenure holders far-reaching rights to dispose of their property. But the land remained under the authority of the landlord. Thus, landowners were subject to dues and obligations, and land transfers needed formal seigneurial consent. On this condition, hereditary land tenure granted the holders the rights to freely bequeath, sell, transfer, or lease their property.[35] Consequently, the court records contain contracts sealing succession, leaseholds, inter vivos transfers, exchanges, or sales. Here, land purchase contracts will serve as an indicator for participation in the land markets, whether farms, pieces of land, houses, or gardens were bought and sold. I look at gender distribution of sellers and buyers and the influence of the transmission of different property forms on the gender distribution. This analysis can help us understand the causes behind unequal landownership and gender distribution whether or not inheritance practice, marital property law, or economic means were determining factors. The data could also indicate if there were opportunities for ceding heirs or wives and widows to buy and sell land on the market with their compensation money or marriage portion.

TABLE 6.1 Sellers and buyers of real estate by gender, manorial court district of Sonnenburg (1568–1600, 1610–1612).

	Type 1	*Type 2*	*Type 3*	*Total*
Total	49 (27%)	98 (55%)	32 (18%)	**179 (100%)**
seller (f)	7 (14%)	3 (3%)	6 (19%)	**16 (9%)**
seller (m)	35 (71%)	86 (88%)	24 (75%)	**145 (81%)**
seller (couple)	4 (8%)	4 (4%)	2 (6%)	**10 (6%)**
seller (group)	3 (6%)	5 (5%)	0	**8 (4%)**
buyer (f)	6 (12%)	0	0	**6 (3%)**
buyer (m)	37 (76%)	87 (89%)	31 (97%)	**155 (87%)**
buyer (couple)	6 (12%)	11 (11%)	1 (3%)	**18 (10%)**
buyer (group)	0	0	0	**0**
buyers and sellers (f)	13 (13%)	3 (2%)	6 (9%)	**22 (6%)**
buyers and sellers (m)	72 (73%)	173 (87%)	55 (86%)	**300 (84%)**
buyers and sellers (couple)	10 (10%)	15 (8%)	3 (5%)	**28 (8%)**
buyers and sellers (group)	3 (3%)	5 (3%)	0	**8 (2%)**
District SB	25 (51%)	5 (5%)	18 (56%)	**48 (27%)**
Gadertal	3 (6%)	43 (44%)	4 (13%)	**50 (28%)**
Mühlwaldtal	20 (41%)	39 (40%)	9 (28%)	**68 (38%)**
Ahrntal	1 (2%)	7 (7%)	0	**8 (4%)**
Outside	0	4 (4%)	1 (3%)	**5 (3%)**

Type 1: House, house and garden, or field; cottage with/without garden; barn; mill; fuller
Type 2: Farms
Type 3: Field, meadow, plot, vineyard with/without press
District SB: District of Sonnenburg (villages Sonnenburg, Pflaurenz, Fassing)

TABLE 6.2 Sellers and buyers of real estate by gender, town court of Brixen (1574, 1600).

	Type 1	*Type 2*	*Type 3*	*Total*
Total	33 (49%)	10 (15%)	24 (36%)	**67 (100%)**
seller (f)	5 (15%)	0	5 (21%)	**10 (15%)**
seller (m)	20 (61%)	9 (90%)	18 (75%)	**47 (70%)**
seller (couple)	7 (21%)	0	0	**7 (10%)**
seller (group)	1 (3%)	1 (10%)	1 (4%)	**3 (4%)**
buyer (f)	1 (3%)	2 (20%)	1 (4%)	**4 (6%)**
buyer (m)	31 (94%)	7 (70%)	23 (96%)	**61 (91%)**
buyer (couple)	1 (3%)	1 (10%)	0	**2 (3%)**
buyer (group)	0	0	0	**0**
buyers and sellers (f)	6 (9%)	2 (10%)	6 (13%)	**14 (10%)**
buyers and sellers (m)	51 (77%)	16 (80%)	41 (85%)	**108 (81%)**
buyers and sellers (couple)	8 (12%)	1 (5%)	0	**9 (7%)**
buyers and sellers (group)	1 (2%)	1 (5%)	1 (2%)	**3 (2%)**
Brixen town	29 (88%)	0	8 (33%)	**37 (55%)**
Pfeffersberg	1 (3%)	8 (80%)	4 (17%)	**13 (19%)**
Albeins	3 (9%)	2 (20%)	9 (38%)	**14 (21%)**
Outside	0	0	3 (12%)	**3 (4%)**

Type 1: House, house and garden, or field; barn; mill; fuller
Type 2: Farms
Type 3: Field, meadow, plot, vineyard with/without press

The purchase deeds contain the date of the purchase; information on the seigneurial consent; the names, occupations (sometimes), and place of residence of seller and buyer; the property and a brief description of its type and location; any dues and obligations on the land; the boundaries; the negotiated price; and the payment terms. Sometimes the contracts describe the context of the sale, such as inheritance cases or insolvency. And for a few it is possible to determine whether the property was inherited – as was the case with Christina Urbanin's house – or whether it stemmed from an earlier purchase or exchange. The contracts offer valuable information, but they do not indicate the size of the property. For the court district of Sonnenburg, the years 1568–1600 and 1610–1612 were used, of which 179 purchase deeds were extracted from the court books. For Brixen, sixty-seven purchase contracts for the years 1574 and 1600 were found.[36] The purchase deeds were analysed by gender of sellers and buyers, whether they appeared as couples or as groups. The latter represented mostly groups of inheriting children, where their guardians sold their property to generate cash for their further upbringing and sustenance or to pay off debts on their inheritance.

III.a Gender of sellers and buyers

The analysis shows a distinct gender imbalance with predominantly male participation. Overall, women represented six percent of the buyers or sellers in Sonnenburg and ten percent of the buyers or sellers in Brixen. This apparent difference between rural and urban contexts is accentuated in the proportion of sellers and buyers. In Brixen, women represented fifteen percent of the sellers and four percent of the buyers. In Sonnenburg, women sold houses, farms, or pieces of land in nine percent of cases and bought real estate in three percent. While women were more present in the land markets in the town of Brixen than in rural Sonnenburg, both localities show that women were participating more as sellers than as buyers. But the conclusive result is that they participated in the land market in the town more so than in the countryside. The fact that women were more active as sellers could be explained by women selling inherited land but would not explain why they did not buy much.

Wives were allowed to sell or buy property but only with the prior knowledge and consent of their husbands; similarly, unmarried women (and widows) had to have a gender guardian.[37] This is why women, who acted individually, nevertheless appeared in the presence of their husbands or their gender guardians at the signing of the purchase contracts. And they did this as wives, widows, and unmarried women alike: In Sonnenburg, thirty-seven percent of women involved in transactions were married, forty-two percent were widowed, and twenty-one percent were unmarried. In Brixen, fifty percent of female buyers and sellers were married and fifty percent were widowed, whilst no unmarried women participated.[38] How much these proportions represent the actual distribution of married, widowed, and unmarried women can unfortunately not be reconstructed. In all likelihood, unmarried women in Brixen, for example, are underrepresented. The high proportion of married women in the land market is striking, especially compared to their near absence in the land markets in other areas, such as Neckarhausen in southwest Germany, where partible inheritance and community of accrued gain could have offered more favourable conditions for women.[39] The result here shows that wives acted independently – in agreement with their husbands – and utilised their money or their inheritance. The strong participation of widows is not surprising and can be found in other areas as well. Widows often had to sell property to generate funds and overcome cash shortages, for example. But all in all, marital status was only a defining factor to the extent that unmarried women were underrepresented, whereas married and widowed women participated almost evenly. One reason for the underrepresentation of unmarried women could be age and the fact that they had not inherited and not received a marriage portion yet.[40]

Wives also appeared in conjunction with their husbands and bought or sold property jointly as a married couple. Significantly, couples appeared as buyers and sellers in Brixen in seven percent of cases and in Sonnenburg in eight percent. Couples as sellers or buyers in an area with separation of marital property does not imply that the purchased property was held in community. Instead, one spouse was usually contributing to the purchase power that would be separated out at the time of death of a spouse; or one spouse owned the land on sale, but both appeared as sellers for another reason. In cases of sales, it could imply that the wife was the owner of the property, which was possibly inherited.

But couples as buyers, where both bought together, resulted in the husband keeping the land title. This originated from the Tyrol law code, which stipulated that property bought by a husband in his and his wife's name should revert to him or his heirs after death unless his wife or widow could prove that half was paid with her own money. Even then, the title to the purchased property was to remain with the husband or his heirs, and his wife or widow was entitled to a compensation payment.[41] This can be illustrated with a case from Sonnenburg in 1588, where a husband used his wife's marriage portion to pay for half the purchase price. This led to a dispute between her and his kin. It was negotiated that after his death she would be compensated with her share and the land would go to his next of kin, and that her husband would keep the land title after her death.[42] Couples as buyers appeared in Sonnenburg more often than in Brixen. In Brixen, more couples sold property, which could reflect, similar to women as sellers, a slightly higher ratio of women's succession to property or a legal and financial need to appear as a couple.

This points to differences in marital property systems. Separation of marital property meant that spouses could make land transactions independently. Therefore, women appear as participants in the land market, but the proportion of couples is comparatively small. In an area with community marital property, the participation of couples was much higher and the combined resources made land acquisitions easier. For the Styrian estates Aflenz and Veitsch, for example, Birgit Heinzle showed a participation rate of couples as buyers of 68.4% and as sellers of 34.1%. She affirmed that the combined marital resources made land acquisitions easier. Strikingly, she also found a very low participation rate of women as sole actors: Women bought hardly any real estate (only 1.6%) but sold it at a rate of 10.9%.[43] This corresponds to the findings for late mediaeval and early modern northeast Norfolk, where Jane Whittle found that only one in twelve tenants, or 8.4%, were female. The court rolls allowed Whittle to calculate the acreage, and she found that women held 12.4% of the area studied. But most of the female tenants received land as wives jointly with their husbands, and women were more likely than men to get land from relatives. Marital status seemed to have been a determining factor since Whittle could also show that the women who did act on their own were mostly widows.[44] Whether marital status was a defining factor depended on the local legal contexts. In Sonnenburg and Brixen, as just shown, marital status or marital status as proxy for age was important insofar as unmarried (possibly younger) women appeared less frequently, but married and widowed women acted almost equally often.

Dana Štefanová offers a different angle on the question of women and landownership and investigates how long female sellers had been in possession of their holdings before they sold it. For the north Bohemian estate of Frýdlant, in the sixteenth to eighteenth centuries, she found that widows were involved in selling real estate in sixteen percent of her 943 cases. With the help of record linkage, she could indeed show that some of the widows managed their farms for many years prior to selling it and that there were no obvious attempts of the sovereignty to curtail this.[45] All these case studies confirm that the legal and social context, such as marital property regimes, inheritance practice, legal rights for women, community and sovereignty control, and differences according to marital status, shaped the land markets and affected the participation rates of women and men.[46] Accordingly, the lower rate of women buying real estate in Styria (1.6%) compared with the two Tyrolean regions investigated (max. four percent) poses the question of which aspects were more determining and whether separation of marital property might have given women even more opportunity to act individually as wives, widows, and unmarried women. This was the case with Dorothea Baumgartnerin, for example, who bought the farm Unterweg in Pinzagen/Pfeffersberg in the town district of Brixen for 700 gulden in May 1574. The boundaries and dues of the buildings, stable, fields, and meadows she had to observe were specified in the former deeds. Dorothea Baumgartnerin appeared at court accompanied by her gender guardian. She might have been married, but her husband was not named and took no part in this transaction.[47]

III.b Transfer of landownership by type of property

Dorothea's case is quite particular, in that she bought an entire farmstead. This points to the question of what types of properties women bought and sold and whether the ratios show further gender-specific aspects. The purchase deeds reveal a variety of different types of landed property being sold. For this study, I grouped

TABLE 6.3 Types of property sold in Sonnenburg (1568–1600, 1610–1612) and Brixen (1574, 1600).

	Type 1	*Type 2*	*Type 3*
Sonnenburg	27%	55%	18%
Price range in gulden	13–510	150–1,866 (4,000)	0–640
Median in gulden	77	530	145
Brixen	49%	15%	36%
Price range in gulden	63–1,600	170–2,340	7–415
Median in gulden	210	709	173

Type 1 = Buildings
Type 2 = Farms
Type 1 = Fields
Source: © Janine Maegraith.

the landed property into three different types: Type 1 for buildings (houses and cottages with and without gardens, barns, mills), Type 2 for farms (including divided farms), and Type 3 for pieces of land (fields, meadows, gardens, vineyards). Analysing the ratio of the different types sold and bought can shed some light on whether more affordable land or buildings were traded that could have been accessible to a wider population, including women.

Unsurprisingly, farms were traded most frequently (fifty-five percent) in the rural district of Sonnenburg. Significantly, though, buildings comprised twenty-seven percent of trades, and pieces of land made up less than a fifth of all transactions (eighteen percent). Even when looking at the geographic distribution, houses and pieces of land such as gardens were mostly traded in the villages, whereas cottages were bought and sold in the agricultural areas, notably in the Mühlwald Valley. This distribution gives the impression of a fairly flexible land market, especially when considering the purchase prices. Buildings were traded at a very wide range of prices, between 13 and 510 gulden, with a median of 77 gulden.[48] The median price of farms and parts of farms, by contrast, was a more substantial 530 gulden. Individual pieces of land had a median price of 145 gulden. Buildings, especially the cheaper cottages, and pieces of land could have been possible alternative purchases for less wealthy people, especially ceding heirs and women, who held less capital than property-owning men. Indeed, women in the court district of Sonnenburg constituted fourteen percent of sellers and twelve percent of buyers of buildings. Women bought buildings valued between 20 and 160 gulden, with a median of 84 gulden, slightly above the overall median purchase price for buildings. This indicates that women invested in buildings for their livelihood. After all, the possession of a house or cottage involved access to some common rights.[49] In Sonnenburg, women also appeared as sellers of pieces of land in nineteen percent of cases, but no women bought a field. Neither did they buy a farm, although in three percent of cases women appeared as sellers of farms. Women possibly inherited land, held it in ownership for some time, and then sold it on the market, but they did not actively buy any land in Sonnenburg. Instead, they bought and sold houses and cottages, which were much more affordable.

In the town of Brixen, buildings made up the largest category (forty-nine percent), and the majority of the traded buildings were situated in the town itself. Pieces of land, including vineyards, were sold in thirty-six percent of cases, and even here a third were traded in the town of Brixen and the rest in Pfeffersberg and Albeins, or even outside the court district. In the agricultural areas, farms were traded in fifteen percent of cases. This appears to have been a flexible market, especially with such a strong ratio of individual pieces of land such as vineyards.[50] In a wine-growing area this is not surprising. But the price range of the buildings, farms, and land qualifies the assumed flexibility. Prices for buildings fluctuated between 63 and 1600 gulden, and the median was 210 gulden – much higher than buildings in the district of Sonnenburg. Farms and pieces of land were traded for a wide range of prices as well, and all three types show higher median values than in the district of Sonnenburg. This might explain why fewer women bought buildings in Brixen (only three percent of cases), whereas they sold them in fifteen percent of cases (see Table 6.2). Even the ratio of couples buying houses is much lower (three percent) than in Sonnenburg (twelve percent). Similarly, while twenty-one percent of sellers of pieces of land were female, only four percent of buyers were women.

The difference in market behaviour, the prevailing of selling over buying, is significant. Why did women in Brixen sell buildings or land more often than those in the countryside? Why did women in the countryside hardly ever buy a farm? As mentioned earlier, this might point to the fact that they had slightly better chances to inherit houses in Brixen. However, selling off their inheritance would mean reducing it to a certain extent. What could the reasons for shedding landed property have been? Women might have needed the capital, preferred other forms of property, or felt social pressure to sell. To trace their reasons needs more research. Still, buying a house in Brixen or a farm in the countryside seemed to have been a predominantly male undertaking. The sample of farms in Brixen is too small to be significant and concerns mainly the rural district outside the town. Nevertheless, it is worth considering that in the two cases in which women bought a farm, one of them was the aforementioned Dorothea Baumgartnerin.

Higher prices for farms could have been one reason why women were mostly excluded as sole buyers and appeared only with their husbands. In both court districts, couples made up about a tenth of buyers of farms, indicating that women were involved in trading farms in conjunction with their husbands. But, as mentioned before, while a wife could contribute to the purchase price, the husband and his kin usually retained the land title. However, price cannot be the sole explanation for women's absence as buyers of pieces of land; although more affordable, women appear mostly as sellers of gardens and vineyards but are absent as buyers of these types of properties in Sonnenburg and are underrepresented in Brixen. In both areas, men decidedly dominated the property market. However, women's participation was not insignificant.

III.c Financing purchases

One possible explanation for female underrepresentation in the property market could be a lower purchasing power of women. The deeds show that purchases were mostly financed through a combination of down payment and instalments over several years, and in some cases by transferring existing debts of the seller to the buyer, who promised to settle those debts. Often, all three options were part of the negotiations. Buying a farm, therefore, could be a complex financial transaction that required a down payment in cash and participation in the credit market.[51] Legally, women were able to do so even as wives, and they did participate in the housing market. In 1588, for example, Christan Hauser, weaver in the village of Pflaurenz, and his wife Elspeth Pliderein sold a house with a garden, bathhouse, and baking house for 100 gulden. The house and its appurtenances were all adjoined and probably surrounded by a fence, and the property's boundaries and rights of way were clearly defined. The buyer was Ellena Lienspergerin, wife of Michael Zisa, carpenter in Pflaurenz. Elspeth Pliderein had gained ownership of the house and its appurtenances after the death of her former husband under the condition that she raise their two children and compensate them with their paternal inheritance share. Such an arrangement could occur when a widow's marriage portion exceeded the value of her late husband's estate and her payout would have thus overallocated the deceased husband's estate. The ensuing payment negotiation was based on the condition of the children's compensation: The buyer, Ellena Lienspergerin, was instructed to pay the compensation of 20 gulden directly to the guardians of the children and to pay the remaining purchase price in two instalments to the seller.[52] In this case, although the seller appears in conjunction with her husband, the house was the property of the wife, stemming from her former husband. The buyer was also married but bought the property with her own money and in her own name. Ellena, the buyer, took up the obligation of the seller and paid with the purchase price the outstanding inheritance debts of Elspeth. Ellena financed this transaction using her own, probably inherited, funds; this can be seen in her will and security for her husband, who partook in her transactions only with his labour, not with his money.[53] Entitlement to inheritance shares, marriage portions, or other credit, even if this was not in cash but as financial assets, enabled a person to take part in such transactions.

Consequently, one could assume that women holding financial assets and credit in the form of marriage portions and inheritance shares would have had the means to partake in the property market as buyers more than was recorded. So why did they not participate more? Did women have less economic means than men? Separation of marital property and preference for male successors contributed to a perpetuation of the property structure, and it was harder for women to accumulate more wealth if they were not a daughter-heir. One reason was that the monetary inheritance compensation shares for daughters were often lower than those for sons.[54] Another was that a wife's marriage portion was invested in the husband's property, but she did not receive interest on it, and as a widow she did not have a claim on any gain in value. Instead, she received back what she had brought into the marriage and inherited, supplemented by the morning gift and a third of the household goods.[55] The analysis of the purchase deeds shows that the overall median purchase price paid by women in the district of Sonnenburg, for example, is about four times lower (84 gulden) than what men paid. This could point to economic means as an excluding factor. However, in Brixen women's purchasing power was about the same as men's and their median purchase price was even slightly higher. But the property market remained male-dominated. It could be that if a wife's property remained invested in her husband's farm, workshop, or business, she could not freely dispose of her money, as it was bound up with her husband's property. In addition, husbands had the legal entitlement to manage their wife's property during marriage. The Tyrol law code prescribes that the husband shall be the "owner, enjoyer and guardian" of all the property his wife shall bring in and receive during their marriage.[56] Wives needed the agreement of their husbands, and the results show that they had it in some cases. In theory, unmarried and widowed women would have had more freedom if they had the means. It seems, therefore, that although women's property was constrained by the law, it left some leeway. But how much depended on the legal practice and gender relations?

III.d Change over time?

What remains an important question is how this changed over time. With regard to the eighteenth century, it was shown that the property structure as a whole changed significantly in this area, with a rise of cottagers and smallholders.[57] But how this affected the gender distribution in landownership still has to be analysed. Preliminary results for Sonnenburg and Brixen for the sample year 1670 indicate some changes during the seventeenth century, although the numbers of purchase deeds are very low and thus statistically not robust. The beginning of the seventeenth century shows for both localities a considerable participation rate of women of around ten percent, which, in the case of Sonnenburg, is a significant rise. But in 1670, this fell to eight percent in Brixen, and no women were selling or buying property in Sonnenburg at all.[58] Table 6.4 also shows stark fluctuations regarding the types of properties sold. In Sonnenburg in 1610–1612, and in Brixen in

TABLE 6.4 Types of property sold in Sonnenburg and Brixen by percent (rounded).

	Type 1	*Type 2*	*Type 3*	*Female*	*N*
Sonnenburg 1568–1600	25	55	20	6	158
Sonnenburg 1610–1612	43	43	14	10	21
Sonnenburg 1670	22	50	28	0	18
Brixen 1574	40	18	42	11	38
Brixen 1600	62	10	28	10	29
Brixen 1670	17	33	50	8	6

Type 1 = Buildings
Type 2 = Farms
Type 1 = Land
Source: © Janine Maegraith.

1600, the ratio of buildings peaked, whereas pieces of land were traded the least in Sonnenburg. A strong link between female buyers and buildings was already established earlier. This is strengthened by the fact that mainly farms were traded in the 1670s in Sonnenburg, and at the same time female buyers and sellers disappeared from the market. In Brixen, the link can be seen in the decline of houses being sold in 1670.

Without question, this needs further research to substantiate changes over time. But this early analysis confirms that the land market in the two southern Tyrol districts was predominantly male and stayed male in the seventeenth century. Although it showed flexibility in types of property and also in the range of values, women participated less than men – even if we take couples into account. The values given in the contracts were negotiated based on the price of the last sale, often dating back several years. Property values are not necessarily equivalent to market values, and the early modern Tyrolean land market has to be seen in its legal context, with its preconditioned restrictions, such as access to economic means due to inheritance and marital property structures, and in the context of kinship relations and entitlements.[59] This did not exclude women as economic actors per se, but the unequal distribution of economic means through inheritance and marital property seemed to have limited women's independent economic practice in the property market.

IV. Conclusion: The fence as a signpost for inequality

Why does this matter? Involvement of women in the property market had repercussions for the status of women in the household, in their marriage and family, but also in the community. With access to common rights through a house or cottage, for example, women could improve their community status and their livelihoods. Utilising property rights could also strengthen women's decision-making regarding their livelihoods or enable them to participate in the credit market. All this women did to some extent, as we have seen, but the question remains as to what limited the scope of their economic practice. The law created some obstacles, but it was more the legal and social practice that produced an imbalance in the property market. Amy Erickson has emphasised, for example, the remaining economic disparity between men and women that continues today, although the laws have changed, and this indicates that other factors have to be considered.[60]

In Tyrol, hereditary land tenure provided fairly secure property rights by the late Middle Ages, and these were codified in the Tyrol law code at the beginning of the sixteenth century. At the same time, a relatively dynamic land market evolved in which not only farms but also fields, meadows, plots, houses, gardens, cottages, and vineyards were bought and sold frequently between kin as well as non-kin members.[61] Complex payment terms reveal an existing credit network and sophisticated financial market, and some urban investments in the countryside can be traced as well.[62] But in spite of such flexible preconditions, women remained underrepresented in the property market. The reasons for this are linked to a complex mix of legal and social norms and practices. Separation of marital property contributed to a perpetuation of existing property structures in which women were in most cases not able to grow their financial means. At the same time, it enabled women to buy and sell property independently. Women were less likely to inherit the main estate than men and would, with a few exceptions, only do so if no brothers were present or the brothers decided to pursue a different career. Daughters received lower inheritance compensation payments. Therefore, women had less landed property and fewer financial means than men. This, in turn, is reflected in the lower participation rate of women in the property market, especially as buyers. However, they were not completely absent, and in the town of Brixen women made up a tenth of all sellers and buyers. Women showed legal resourcefulness and made use of their rights and funds.

However, by restricting wealth for women, the legal structure preconditioned a gendered property structure for both women and ceding heirs in general, including men. Therefore, women's purchasing power was not the only thing affected. Ceding male heirs faced similar consequences in which compensation money and in some cases training in a craft had to suffice. In some cases, they were able to buy a cottage or small house and stay in the region, or they married into property; in other cases, emigration was a common option.[63] Therefore, although the land market did offer opportunities, local labour markets were also needed to secure people's livelihoods. This points to the need to take all kinds of wealth into account, not just landownership but also training, money and investments, credit, and especially material goods, as they all formed the basis for people's daily livelihoods. The houses that were bought and sold on the market needed to be furnished with mobile household goods and tools, and the adjacent gardens or farm meadows needed to be equipped with fences.

So, what did the fence represent in early modern Tyrol? In 1578, for example, Urban Niderweg exchanged his farm for the farm belonging to Balthas Schweingras and Margreth Scherlehnerin, a married couple living in the Mühlwald Valley, in the court district of Sonnenburg. Urban's farm "Holzlehen" is described as having a fence around it and bordering on the grasslands of Balthas's farm holdings. With the farm comes the entitlement to graze five cattle and fifteen goats on the grassland. Urban adds an accurate description of the borders because they extended beyond the fence and were marked with border stones and crosses. The fence and the extending "invisible" borders become even more important with the entitlements to graze livestock on adjacent fields.[64] Here the fence materialised not only property rights but also entitlements to land use; it excluded others from grazing rights and demarcated the boundaries of the farm. The fence also materialised unequal opportunities in the property market and a gendered property structure. But it also signposts the importance of objects as part of a complex composition of wealth. Just as material objects could obtain gendered meanings in the context of inheritance and marriage – if considering the trousseau and the passing on of the mother's personal goods to her daughters, for example – so, too, could the fence be viewed as a signifier of gendered distribution of real estate.

Notes

1 For example, Amanda Vickery, "His and Hers: Gender, Consumption and Household Accounting in Eighteenth-Century England", in: *Past & Present, Supplement* 1 (2006), pp. 12–38; Renata Ago, *Gusto for Things. A History of Objects in Seventeenth-Century Rome*, Chicago 2013 [University of Chicago Press].

2 Christina Kotchemidova, "The Culture of the Fence: Artifacts and Meanings", in: *Counterblast* 2 (2008), pp. 1–4, here p. 4.

3 John Streamas, "Looking Between Fences in American History", in: *Radical History Review* 108 (2010), pp. 161–174, here pp. 168, 173.

4 Art. "Zaun", in: Johann Heinrich Zedlers Universal-Lexicon aller Wissenschaften und Künste, 1731–1754, col. 184–188; Art. "Zaun", in: Deutsches Wörterbuch von Jacob Grimm und Wilhelm Grimm, 16 Bände in 32 Teilbänden, vol. 31, Leipzig 1961, col. 406–410, www.woerterbuchnetz.de/DWB?lemma=zaun (accessed 08 December 2019); Deutsches Rechtswörterbuch drw, Online, https://drw-www.adw.uni-heidelberg.de/drw/info/ search: "Zaun" (12 January 2020).

5 "Statutenbuch Enneberg", in: Ignaz V. Zingerle (ed.), *Die tirolischen Weisthümer. 4, im Auftr. der Kaiserlichen Akad. der Wiss., part 2: Burggrafenamt, Etschland, Eisackthal und Pusterthal*, Wien 1891 [Braumüller], pp. 708–733, here p. 729.

6 Südtiroler Landesarchiv (SLA) Sonnenburg Verfachbuch (VfB) 4, 1580–1581, no fol., 26 November 1581.

7 See, for example, the fifteenth-century frescoes in the cathedral cloister, Bressanone/Brixen. The holdings of the Südtiroler Landesarchiv in Bolzano (SLA) contain sixteenth- and seventeenth-century maps showing boundaries of pastureland and alpine pastures, for instance, with fences. For example, map with the boundaries of the pasturelands of Tartsch and Mals, c. 1580, SLA, Gemeindearchiv Tartsch, Akten, IV d.

8 SLA, Sonnenburg VfB 9, 1590–1591, no fol., 11 March 1591.

9 The contribution is based on the research project The Role of Wealth in Defining and Constituting Kinship Spaces from the Sixteenth to the Eighteenth Century, financed by the Austrian Science Fund (FWF project number P29394), https://kinshipspaces.univie.ac.at/ (accessed 8 December 2019); see also Margareth Lanzinger and Janine Maegraith, "Vermögen als Medium der Herstellung von Verwandtschaftsräumen vom 16. bis zum 18. Jahrhundert – ein Projektbericht mit Objektperspektive", in: *Frühneuzeit-Info* 28 (2017), pp. 14–34.

10 See, amongst others, Markus Cerman, "Bodenmärkte und ländliche Wirtschaft in vergleichender Sicht: England und das östliche Mitteleuropa im Spätmittelalter", in: *Jahrbuch für Wirtschaftsgeschichte* 2 (2004), pp. 125–148; Markus Cerman, "Ansätze und Bedeutung von Bodenmärkten für untertäniges Land im spätmittelalterlichen östlichen Mitteleuropa", in: Michael Pammer, Herta Neiß and Michael John (eds.), *Erfahrung der Moderne: Festschrift für Roman Sandgruber zum 60. Geburtstag*, Stuttgart 2007 [Steiner], pp. 19–41, here p. 16; Hermann Zeitlhofer, *Besitzwechsel und sozialer Wandel. Lebensläufe und sozioökonomische Entwicklungen im südlichen Böhmerwald, 1640–1840*, Wien, Köln and Weimar 2014 [Böhlau], pp. 18–19; Bas van Bavel, "The Organization and Rise of Land and Lease Markets in Northwestern Europe and Italy, c. 1000–1800", in: *Continuity and Change* 23, 1 (2008), pp. 13–53.

11 Zeitlhofer, *Besitzwechsel*; van Bavel, *Organization*, p. 53.

12 Zeitlhofer, *Besitzwechsel*, esp. ch. 7.6.3.

13 Amy Louise Erickson, "Coverture and Capitalism", in: *History Workshop Journal* 59 (2005), pp. 1–16, here 2; Amy Louise Erickson, *Women and Property in Early Modern England*, London and New York 1993 [Routledge], Introduction.

14 In the context of our FWF research project The Role of Wealth in Defining and Constituting Kinship Spaces from the Sixteenth to the Eighteenth Century, we address questions around property markets by looking at today's southern Tyrol. We analyse wealth transfers in context with the prevailing legal constraints, such as inheritance, marital property, gender, and kinship entitlements, and in view of a more comprehensive understanding of wealth that includes not only real estate but also objects, money and investments, rights and entitlements, and training. People's well-being was thus not solely

dependent on landownership. Margareth Lanzinger and Janine Maegraith, "Landownership or Landlessness: The Complex Meaning of Property in Southern Tyrol (Sixteenth to Nineteenth Centuries)" (paper presented at the Rural History Conference 2017, KU Leuven, 11–13 September 2017); Janine Maegraith, "Landlessness. Reviewing the Early Modern Property Structure in Southern Tyrol", in: *Zeitschrift für Agrargeschichte und Agrarsoziologie ZAA* 68 (2020), pp. 19–37.

15 On Brixen see Erika Kustatscher, *Die Städte des Hochstifts Brixen im Spätmittelalter: Verfassungs- und Sozialgeschichte von Brixen, Bruneck und Klausen im Spiegel der Personengeschichte (1200–1550)*, Innsbruck and Wien 2007 [StudienVerlag]; Philipp Tolloi, *Das Bürger- und Inwohnerbuch der Stadt Brixen von 1500–1593. Edition und Kommentar*, Wien 2012 [Magisterarbeit].

16 Wilhelm Baum, "Sonnenburg", in: Ulrich Faust and Waltraud Krassnig (eds.), *Germania Sacra III/3: Die benediktinischen Mönchs- und Nonnenklöster in Österreich und Südtirol*, St. Ottilien 2000 [EOS-Verlag], pp. 604–702, here pp. 685–690; Rainer Loose, "Zur Siedlungsentwicklung in Enneberg", in: *Veröffentlichungen des Tiroler Landesmuseums Ferdinandeum* 66 (1986), pp. 51–70.

17 Wilfried Beimrohr, *Mit Brief und Siegel: Die Gerichte Tirols und ihr älteres Schriftgut im Tiroler Landesarchiv*, Innsbruck 1994 [Tiroler Landesarchiv], pp. 97–101. All "civil law" cases were copied into a court district's court book. The court books for this area are in the Südtiroler Landesarchiv (SLA), Bolzano/Bozen.

18 For Brixen, cases of sample years of the sixteenth century, 1670, and 1780 are compiled, and for Sonnenburg, cases of all surviving books of the sixteenth century, 1610–1612, 1670, and 1780s. This is work in progress, and all results are tentative.

19 Martin Paul Schennach, *Gesetz und Herrschaft: Die Entstehung des Gesetzgebungsstaates am Beispiel Tirols*, Cologne 2010 [Forschungen zur deutschen Rechtsgeschichte 28], pp. 481–585; Josef Pauser and Martin Schennach (eds.), *Die Tiroler Landesordnungen von 1526, 1532 und 1573: historische Einführung und Edition. In collaboration with Verena Schumacher*, Wien, Köln and Weimar 2018 [Boehlau].

20 Christian Hagen, Margareth Lanzinger and Janine Maegraith, "Competing Interests in Death-related Stipulations in South Tirol ca. 1350–1600", in: Mia Korpiola and Anu Lahtinen (eds.), *Planning for Death: Wills, Inheritance and Property Strategies in Medieval and Reformation Europe*, Leiden and Boston 2018 [Brill], pp. 88–118.

21 Margareth Lanzinger and Janine Maegraith, "Houses and the Range of Wealth in Early Modern Gender- and Intergenerational Relationships", in: *Jahrbuch für Europäische Geschichte / European History Yearbook* 18 (2017), pp. 14–34.

22 John W. Cole and Eric R. Wolf, *The Hidden Frontier. Ecology and Ethnicity in an Alpine Valley*, New York and London 1974 [Academic Press], pp. 79–81.

23 On the geography and environment of the Alps and their implications for the economy, see Jon Mathieu, *History of the Alps 1500–1900: Environment, Development*, trans. Matthew Vester, Morgantown 2009 [West Virginia University Press].

24 Tiroler Landesordnung (TLO), 1573, book III (III), 20.

25 TLO, 1573, III, 3. However, in our research area this option was not very common in wills, and even less so in rural areas.

26 TLO, 1573, III, 8 and 9.

27 On the development and existence of different inheritance practices in early modern Tyrol, see Paul Rösch, "Lebensläufe und Schicksale. Auswirkungen von zwei unterschiedlichen Erbsitten in Tirol", in: Paul Rösch (ed.), *Südtiroler Erbhöfe. Menschen und Geschichten*, Bozen 1994 [Edition Raetia], pp. 61–70; Rudolf Palme, "Die Entwicklung des Erbrechtes im ländlichen Bereich", in: Paul Rösch (ed.), *Südtiroler Erbhöfe: Menschen und Geschichten*, Bozen 1994 [Edition Raetia], pp. 25–37.

28 TLO, 1573, III, 9.

29 See, for example, Karin Gottschalk, *Eigentum, Geschlecht, Gerechtigkeit. Haushalten und Erben im frühneuzeitlichen Leipzig*, Frankfurt am Main and New York 2003 [Campus].

30 Margareth Lanzinger and Janine Maegraith, "Konkurrenz um Vermögen im südlichen Tirol des 16. Jahrhunderts", in: *L'Homme. Z.F.G.* 27, 1 (2016), pp. 15–31; Lanzinger and Maegraith, *Vermögen*, pp. 204–206.

31 Changes in the seventeenth and eighteenth centuries still have to be researched. Janine Maegraith, "Gender Imbalance in the Use, Ownership, and Transmission of Property in

Early Modern Southern Tyrolean Urban and Rural Contexts", in: Margareth Lanzinger, Janine Maegraith, Siglinde Clementi, Ellinor Forster and Christian Hagen (eds.), *Negotiations of Gender and Property Through Legal Regimes; Litigating – Mediating – Stipulating, Conference Proceedings*, Leiden and Boston 2020 (submitted) [Brill].

32 In exceptions, the Tyrol law code did allow for a division to be made, provided the holdings could secure a living for more than one child. TLO, 1573, V, 3.

33 SLA, Sonnenburg VfB 15, 1599–1600, no fol., 11 November 1600.

34 TLO, 1573, III, 53, which states that all women who "do not have a man" should have an "Anweiser" or gender guardian. The court records show that in almost all cases widows appeared in the presence of a gender guardian. Ernst Holthöfer, "Die Geschlechtsvormundschaft. Ein Überblick von der Antike bis ins 19. Jahrhundert", in: Ute Gerhard (ed.), *Frauen in der Geschichte des Rechts. Von der Frühen Neuzeit bis zur Gegenwart*, München 1997 [Beck], pp. 390–451.

35 Palme, "Entwicklung", p. 29; Martin P. Schennach, "Geschichte des bäuerlichen Besitz- und Erbrechts in Tirol – ein Überblick", in: *Hofgeschichten der 2002 und 2004 verliehenen Erbhöfe*, Innsbruck 2003 [Tiroler Erbhöfe Nr. 21], pp. 9–30. However, restrictions remained regarding testamentary bequests.

36 SLA, Sonnenburg, VfB A 742, 1568–1573, VfB 1–15, 1573–1600, VfB 18, 1608–1612; Brixen (Stadtgericht), VfB 61–62, 1574, VfB 110–113, 1600.

37 The local statute of Enneberg, for example, specifies this in context of inter vivos transfers, Zinergle, *Weisthümer*, p. 731.

38 In Sonnenburg, one widow appeared four times; this has been considered.

39 David Warren Sabean, *Property, Production, and Family in Neckarhausen, 1700–1870*, Cambridge 1990 [Cambridge University Press], pp. 358–360. This could also be seen in the context of a relatively high ratio of women remaining unmarried in this area.

40 Unfortunately, ages cannot be reconstructed on the basis of the existing evidence. This assumption is qualified by a not insignificant number of presumably young widows who just gave birth to their first child at the time their husband died or are recorded as being pregnant.

41 TLO, 1573, III, 42.

42 SLA, Sonnenburg VfB 7, 1588, fol. 226–230, 5 July 1588.

43 Birgit Heinzle, "Gemeinsam oder getrennt? Vermögensregelungen in den Heiratsbriefen der Herrschaft Aflenz (Steiermark), 1494–1550", in: *Geschichte und Region / Storia e regione* 27, 2 (2018), pp. 23–44, here p. 33.

44 Jane Whittle, "Inheritance, Marriage, Widowhood and Remarriage: A Comparative Perspective on Women and Landholding in North-East Norfolk, 1440–1580", in: *Continuity and Change* 13, 1 (1998), pp. 33–72, here pp. 35–39.

45 Dana Štefanová, *Erbschaftspraxis, Besitztransfer und Handlungsspielräume von Untertanen in der Gutsherrschaft: die Herrschaft Frýdlant in Nordböhmen, 1558–1750*, Wien and München 2009 [Oldenburg], pp. 156–160.

46 See also Whittle's conclusion, Whittle, "Inheritance", p. 66.

47 SLA, Brixen Stadtgericht VfB 62, 1574, fol. 97v-98v, 1 May 1574.

48 SLA, Sonnenburg, VfB A 742, 1568–1573, VfB 1–15, 1573–1600, VfB 18, 1608–1612.

49 On common rights see, for example, Niels Grüne, Jonas Hübner and Gerhard Siegl (eds.), *Ländliche Gemeingüter: kollektive Ressourcennutzung in der europäischen Agrarwirtschaft = Rural Commons: Collective Use of Resources in the European Agrarian Economy*, Innsbruck, Wien and Bozen 2015 [StudienVerlag].

50 Significantly, gardens were hardly ever sold independently, but rather were attached to houses.

51 Similar financing models of short- and long-term payment terms can be found in Frýdlant, Štefanová, *Erbschaftspraxis*, pp. 101–105.

52 SLA, Sonnenburg VfB 7, 1588, pp. 311–315, 3 October 1588. In Tyrol, children of a deceased parent were usually allocated two guardians. Either the parents named their preferred guardians in their will or the court made the decision. See TLO, 1573, III, 46.

53 SLA, Sonnenburg VfB 13, 1595–1596, no fol., 19 July 1595.

54 Maegraith, "Gender Imbalance".

55 Lanzinger and Maegraith, "Konkurrenz"; Maegraith, "Gender Imbalance".

56 TLO, 1573, III, 1.
57 Maegraith, "Landlessness".
58 SLA, Sonnenburg VfB 39, 1669–1670; Brixen VfB 244, 1670.
59 See also Giovanni Levi, *Das immaterielle Erbe. Eine Bäuerliche Welt an der Schwelle zur Moderne*, Berlin 1986 [Wagenbach Klaus], pp. 75–106.
60 Erickson, *Women and Property*, Introduction.
61 See Janine Maegraith, "Selling, Buying and Exchanging Peasant Land in Early Modern Southern Tyrol" (Paper presented at the workshop "Trading Peasant Land. Patterns and Strategies of Land Transactions in Late Medieval Central Europe and Northern Italy", 22 November 2018, 23 November 2018, Pavia), forthcoming publication in: Ertl Thomas, Thomas Frank and Samuel Nussbaum (eds.), *Busy Tenants. Peasant Land Markets in Central Europe (15th to 16th Century)*, Stuttgart 2020 [Franz Steiner] (submitted).
62 Thomas Ertl, "Small Landlords: Land Transactions in and Around Bozen (South Tirol) in the Mid-thirteenth Century", in: *Vierteljahresschrift für Sozial- und Wirtschaftsgeschichte* 104, 1 (2017), pp. 7–28.
63 On cottagers and smallholders in this region, see Georg Jäger, *Kleinhäusler und Schellenschmiede, Früchtehändler und Pfarrwirte. Zur Tradition ländlicher Gewerbe in Tirol*, Innsbruck 2005 [Wagner]; Maegraith, "Landlessness".
64 SLA, Sonnenburg VfB 3, 1578–1579, pp. 183–187, 12 June 1578.

Archives

Südtiroler Landesarchiv (SLA), Bozen, Italien.
Sonnenburg Verfachbuch (VfB).
A 742, 1568–1573.
1–15, 1573–1600.
3, 1578–1579, pp. 183–187, 12. June 1578.
4, 1580–1581, no fol., 26. November 1581.
7, 1588, fol. 226–230, 5. July 1588.
7, 1588, pp. 311–315, 3. October 1588.
9, 1590–1591, no fol., 11. March 1591.
13, 1595–1596, no fol., 19. July 1595.
18, 1608–1612.
39, 1669–1670.
Brixen Verfachbuch (VfB) (Stadtgericht).
61–62, 1574, fol. 97v-98v, 1. May 1574.
110–113, 1600.
244, 1670.

Published sources

Art. "Zaun", in: *Deutsches Wörterbuch von Jacob Grimm und Wilhelm Grimm, 16 Bände in 32 Teilbänden*, vol. 31, Leipzig 1961, col. 406–410, www.woerterbuchnetz.de/DWB?lemma=zaun (accessed 8 December 2019).

Art. "Zaun", in: *Johann Heinrich Zedlers Universal-Lexicon aller Wissenschaften und Künste*, 1731–1754, col. 184–188.

"Statutenbuch Enneberg", in: Ignaz V. Zingerle (ed.), *Die tirolischen Weisthümer. 4, im Auftr. der Kaiserlichen Akad. der Wiss., part 2: Burggrafenamt, Etschland, Eisackthal und Pusterthal*, Wien 1891 [Braumüller], pp. 708–733.

Tiroler Landesordnung (TLO), Book III, 1573, in: Pauser, Josef and Martin Schennach (eds.), *Die Tiroler Landesordnungen von 1526, 1532 und 1573: historische Einführung und Edition. In collaboration with Verena Schumacher*, Wien, Köln and Weimar 2018 [Boehlau].

Bibliography

Ago, Renata, *Gusto for Things. A History of Objects in Seventeenth-Century Rome*, Chicago 2013 [University of Chicago Press].

Baum, Wilhelm, "Sonnenburg", in: Ulrich Faust and Waltraud Krassnig (eds.), *Germania Sacra III/3: Die benediktinischen Mönchs- und Nonnenklöster in Österreich und Südtirol*, St. Ottilien 2000 [EOS-Verlag], pp. 604–702.

Beimrohr, Wilfried, *Mit Brief und Siegel: Die Gerichte Tirols und ihr älteres Schriftgut im Tiroler Landesarchiv*, Innsbruck 1994 [Tiroler Landesarchiv].

Cerman, Markus, "Bodenmärkte und ländliche Wirtschaft in vergleichender Sicht: England und das östliche Mitteleuropa im Spätmittelalter", in: *Jahrbuch für Wirtschaftsgeschichte* 2 (2004), pp. 125–148.

———"Ansätze und Bedeutung von Bodenmärkten für untertäniges Land im spätmittelalterlichen östlichen Mitteleuropa", in: Michael Pammer, Herta Neiß and Michael John (eds.), *Erfahrung der Moderne: Festschrift für Roman Sandgruber zum 60. Geburtstag*, Stuttgart 2007 [Steiner], pp. 19–41.

Cole, John W. and Eric R. Wolf, *The Hidden Frontier. Ecology and Ethnicity in an Alpine Valley*, New York and London 1974 [Academic Press].

Erickson, Amy Louise, *Women and Property in Early Modern England*, London and New York 1993 [Routledge].

———"Coverture and Capitalism", in: *History Workshop Journal* 59 (2005), pp. 1–16.

Ertl, Thomas, "Small Landlords: Land Transactions in and around Bozen (South Tirol) in the Mid-Thirteenth Century", in: *Vierteljahresschrift für Sozial- und Wirtschaftsgeschichte* 104, 1 (2017), pp. 7–28.

Gottschalk, Karin, *Eigentum, Geschlecht, Gerechtigkeit. Haushalten und Erben im frühneuzeitlichen Leipzig*, Frankfurt a. M. and New York 2003 [Campus].

Grüne, Niels, Jonas Hübner and Gerhard Siegl (eds.), *Ländliche Gemeingüter: kollektive Ressourcennutzung in der europäischen Agrarwirtschaft = Rural Commons: Collective use of Resources in the European Agrarian Economy*, Innsbruck, Wien and Bozen 2015 [StudienVerlag].

Hagen, Christian, Margareth Lanzinger and Janine Maegraith, "Competing Interests in Death-related Stipulations in South Tirol ca. 1350–1600", in: Mia Korpiola and Anu Lahtinen (eds.), *Planning for Death: Wills, Inheritance and Property Strategies in Medieval and Reformation Europe*, Leiden and Boston 2018 [Brill], pp. 88–118.

Heinzle, Birgit, "Gemeinsam oder getrennt? Vermögensregelungen in den Heiratsbriefen der Herrschaft Aflenz (Steiermark), 1494–1550", in: *Geschichte und Region/Storia e regione* 27, 2 (2018), pp. 23–44.

Holthöfer, Ernst, "Die Geschlechtsvormundschaft. Ein Überblick von der Antike bis ins 19. Jahrhundert", in: Ute Gerhard (ed.), *Frauen in der Geschichte des Rechts. Von der Frühen Neuzeit bis zur Gegenwart*, München 1997 [Beck], 390–451.

Jäger, Georg, *Kleinhäusler und Schellenschmiede, Früchtehändler und Pfarrwirte. Zur Tradition ländlicher Gewerbe in Tirol*, Innsbruck 2005 [Wagner].

Kotchemidova, Christina, "The Culture of the Fence: Artifacts and Meanings", in: *Counterblast* 2 (2008), pp. 1–4.

Kustatscher, Erika, *Die Städte des Hochstifts Brixen im Spätmittelalter: Verfassungs- und Sozialgeschichte von Brixen, Bruneck und Klausen im Spiegel der Personengeschichte (1200–1550)*, Innsbruck and Wien 2007 [StudienVerlag].

Lanzinger, Margareth and Janine Maegraith, "Konkurrenz um Vermögen im südlichen Tirol des 16. Jahrhunderts", in: *L'Homme. Z.F.G.* 27, 1 (2016), pp. 15–31.

———"Landownership or Landlessness: The Complex Meaning of Property in Southern Tyrol (Sixteenth to Nineteenth Centuries)", (paper presented at the Rural History Conference 2017, KU Leuven, September 11–13, 2017).

———"Houses and the Range of Wealth in Early Modern Gender- and Intergenerational Relationships", in: *Jahrbuch für Europäische Geschichte/European History Yearbook* 18 (2017), pp. 14–34.

———"Vermögen als Medium der Herstellung von Verwandtschaftsräumen vom 16. bis zum 18. Jahrhundert – ein Projektbericht mit Objektperspektive", in: *Frühneuzeit-Info* 28 (2017), pp. 14–34.

Levi, Giovanni, *Das immaterielle Erbe. Eine Bäuerliche Welt an der Schwelle zur Moderne*, Berlin 1986 [Wagenbach Klaus].

Loose, Rainer, "Zur Siedlungsentwicklung in Enneberg", in: *Veröffentlichungen des Tiroler Landesmuseums Ferdinandeum* 66 (1986), pp. 51–70.

Maegraith, Janine, "Gender Imbalance in the Use, Ownership, and Transmission of Property in Early Modern Southern Tyrolean Urban and Rural Contexts", in: Margareth Lanzinger, Janine Maegraith, Siglinde Clementi, Ellinor Forster and Christian Hagen (eds.), *Negotiations of Gender and Property through Legal Regimes. Litigating – Mediating – Stipulating, Conference proceedings*, Leiden and Boston 2020 (submitted) [Brill].

———"Landlessness. Reviewing the Early Modern Property Structure in Southern Tyrol", in: *Zeitschrift für Agrargeschichte und Agrarsoziologie ZAA* 68 (2020), pp. 19–37.

———"Selling, Buying and Exchanging Peasant Land in Early Modern Southern Tyrol", in: Thomas Ertl, Thomas Frank and Samuel Nussbaum (eds.), *Busy Tenants. Peasant Land Markets in Central Europe (15th to 16th Century)*, Stuttgart 2020 [Franz Steiner].

Mathieu, Jon, *History of the Alps 1500–1900: Environment, Development*, trans. Matthew Vester, Morgantown 2009 [West Virginia University Press].

Rudolf Palme, "Die Entwicklung des Erbrechtes im ländlichen Bereich", in: Paul Rösch (ed.), *Südtiroler Erbhöfe: Menschen und Geschichten*, Bozen 1994 [Edition Raetia], pp. 25–37.

Rösch, Paul, "Lebensläufe und Schicksale. Auswirkungen von zwei unterschiedlichen Erbsitten in Tirol", in: Paul Rösch (ed.), *Südtiroler Erbhöfe. Menschen und Geschichten*, Bozen 1994 [Edition Raetia], pp. 61–70.

Sabean, David Warren, *Property, Production, and Family in Neckarhausen, 1700–1870*, Cambridge 1990 [Cambridge University Press].

Schennach, Martin Paul, *Gesetz und Herrschaft: Die Entstehung des Gesetzgebungsstaates am Beispiel Tirols*, Cologne 2010 [Forschungen zur deutschen Rechtsgeschichte 28].

Štefanová, Dana, *Erbschaftspraxis, Besitztransfer und Handlungsspielräume von Untertanen in der Gutsherrschaft: die Herrschaft Frýdlant in Nordböhmen, 1558–1750*, Wien and München 2009 [Oldenburg].

Streamas, John, "Looking Between Fences in American History", in: *Radical History Review* 108 (2010), pp. 161–174.

Tolloi, Philipp, *Das Bürger- und Inwohnerbuch der Stadt Brixen von 1500–1593. Edition und Kommentar*, Wien 2012 [Magisterarbeit].

van Bavel, Bas, "The Organization and Rise of Land and Lease Markets in Northwestern Europe and Italy, *c.* 1000–1800", in: *Continuity and Change* 23, 1 (2008), pp. 13–53.

Vickery, Amanda, "His and Hers: Gender, Consumption and Household Accounting in Eighteenth-Century England", in: *Past & Present, Supplement* 1 (2006), pp. 12–38.

Whittle, Jane, "Inheritance, Marriage, Widowhood and Remarriage: A Comparative Perspective on Women and Landholding in North-East Norfolk, 1440–1580", in: *Continuity and Change* 13, 1 (1998), pp. 33–72.

Zeitlhofer, Hermann, *Besitzwechsel und sozialer Wandel. Lebensläufe und sozioökonomische Entwicklungen im südlichen Böhmerwald, 1640–1840*, Wien, Köln and Weimar 2014 [Böhlau].

FIGURE 7.1 Map of the Ottoman Empire, indicating the areas of Vidin and Antakya, Johann Baptist Homann, *Imperium Turcicum in Europa, Asia et Africa Regiones Proprias Tributarias, Clientelares sicut et omnes eusdem Beglirbegatus seu Praefecturas Generales exhibens*, 1737 (detail).

Source: Bibliothèque nationale de France, département Cartes et plans, CPL GE DD-2987 (5839 BIS), public domain, https://gallica.bnf.fr/ark:/12148/btv1b59622189?rk=407727;2 (15.02.2020, 13:45 CET).

7

WOMEN, LAND, AND USUFRUCT IN THE EIGHTEENTH-CENTURY OTTOMAN EMPIRE

A case study of Vidin and Antakya[1]

Fatma Gül Karagöz

ABSTRACT

Like many other societies in the early modern period, agricultural production was the major economic activity in the Ottoman Empire. Ottoman rulers secured the continuity of production by legal norms that limited the rights of access for the peasants. The Ottoman peasant was not the owner of the land, as the property right belonged to the state, which allowed the appointed administrators (*sipahi*) of a district the right to collect taxes upon agricultural production. The peasants could use the land as long as they kept the production intact and paid the taxes. Legally, female peasants in the Ottoman Empire had less opportunity to obtain usufruct rights, but under certain circumstances they could enjoy them as men did. The aim of this chapter is to analyse the number of women as usufruct owners and proprietors in agricultural production as reflected in the court record books (*sidjil*) in the first half of the eighteenth century. This period came after a long period of political and economic crisis in the seventeenth century and led to improved chances for women. The court records of two cities, Vidin and Antakya, are chosen as a case study to investigate women' s arguments to gain or maintain the right of usufruct of agricultural land or privately owned gardens and vineyards.

I. An introduction to the land law in the Ottoman Empire

The early modern Ottoman Empire had an economy based mostly on agriculture and livestock production. The continuity of this economic system was protected by restrictions on private property. While Ottoman law recognised private property on land, an important percentage of agricultural land was categorised as *mîrî*, which could be basically defined as state property or property of the treasury.[2] The most specific differentiation of *mîrî* land from private land was explained by the judge Ebussuud (1490–1574), the mufti of Istanbul (*şeyhülislam*) of Suleyman I.[3] Ebussuud made a distinction between private immovable things and *mîrî* immovable things in many of his legal opinions.[4] He used Islamic legal terminology to explain the peculiarities of the land law.[5] Movable goods, houses, shops, buildings located in villages or towns, vineyards, and gardens could be subject to private property. They could be sold or donated or be subject to any kind of alienation. When a landowner died, vineyards and gardens could be transferred to the heirs as private property. However, agricultural lands were seen as *mîrî*. While private property could be transferred by sale, *mîrî* land could only be transferred with the permission of the "landlord" (*sâhib-i arz*, *sâhib-i timar*, or *sipahi*)[6] and by the payment of a title deed duty.

The rights of peasants (*raiyyet*) to *mîrî* land were defined as usufruct right (*tasarruf*) rather than private property (*mülk*). In this system, only the state as such was entitled to have ownership of agricultural land. The right to collect taxes on agricultural production was left to the "landlord", who also had to provide soldiers in times of war. Ottoman land law was based on the protection of the small- and middle-scale production units. Land usufruct was left to peasants in exchange for a lease, but the amount paid by the peasant was not considered rent. The situation of peasants was therefore similar to lifelong tenancy, but legally the payment was not a form of rent – it was taxation.[7] The agricultural production in the *mîrî* system was based mainly on family labour, especially in the Balkans and Anatolia.[8] The land tax (*resm-i çift*) collected from every unit that could be cultivated by a plough and a pair of oxen was determined on the basis of households. Men were considered the primary beneficiaries of usufruct.[9] Since agricultural land was not part of the private property of the peasant, he could not enter contracts, such as sales or mortgages. He could leave the usufruct to his son, but the usufruct was not a part of inheritance in the strict sense of the term.[10]

The regulations on usufruct and taxation changed progressively, first by a decree issued in 1567, which allowed daughters of deceased peasants to claim the usufruct of their fathers' land, in case they did not have any male siblings, by payment of a title deed duty (*resm-i tapu*).[11] Before the decree of 1567, local custom already had a significant influence on land law and taxation, which enabled childless widows (*bive*) to obtain land usufruct in some provinces as long as there were no male relatives, who could claim the land.[12] By the beginning of the seventeenth century, the regulations about the transfer of usufruct became more flexible to handle the population pressure caused by a series of rebellions that began in the late sixteenth century, followed by a wave of migration. The change in climate known as the Little Ice Age, which led to the failure of harvests, was another factor in the crisis. Many peasants left their land, searching for other, more fertile places to settle down. In consequence, the land, now sparsely populated, produced less income for the sultan. Thus, in this situation where fewer subjects were available and more were needed to render the land productive and to generate tax, the number of relatives who could gain usufruct rights after the death of a peasant was legally expanded, and women also profited from this expansion. A typical example was the transfer of usufruct rights from a male peasant to his father, mother, brother, or sister after his death.

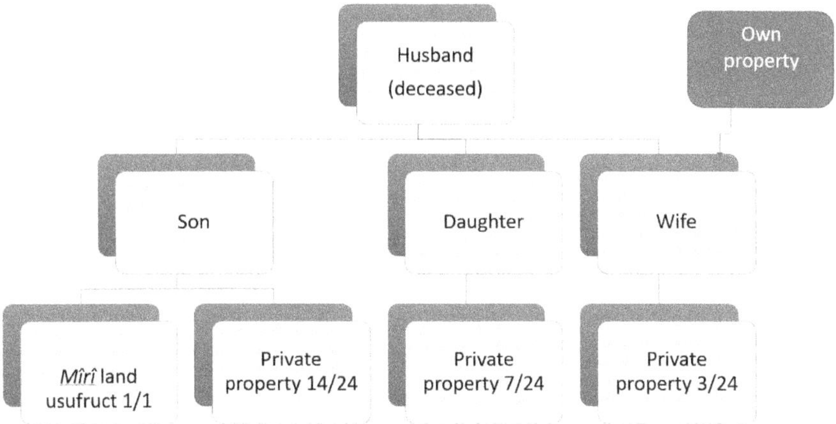

FIGURE 7.2 Visualisation of the inheritance pattern defined in the Quran: The wife (*Ashabü'l-feraiz*) receives one-eighth, the son, as male relative (*Asabe*), receives a double share, while daughters receive a single share (in this case also considered *Asabe*).

Source: © Fatma Gül Karagöz.

The principles of land inheritance were also based on the duality between private property and usufruct. The transfer of *mîrî* land's usufruct to relatives was accepted as "ordinary transfer" (*adi intikal*), and the inheritance of any private property was classified as "transfer by sharia" (*şer'i intikal*) or simply "inheritance". The inheritance of private property was shaped by the sharia and developed by religious scholars. Since most principles of inheritance were precisely defined in the Quran, it was the field less open to interpretation. There were three groups of heirs. The first group mainly consists of closer relatives (*ashabü'l-feraiz*, owners of a fixed share), who also took priority.[13] The second group of beneficiaries (*asabe*) was comprised in principle of male relatives, excluding those with a connexion through women. If there was such a group of relatives, and if the estate of the deceased person was large enough, *asabe* would get a share of the inheritance after *ashabü'l-feraiz*. If there were no persons qualified to be part of these two groups, the inheritance was given to the rest of the relatives (*zevi'l-erham*).[14] Although these principles secured the share of women, their position was not equal to male relatives. A son received a double share, while a daughter got only a single share, from the deceased father's estate (Figure 7.2).

Unlike private property, *mîrî* land could not be divided between heirs. After the death of the usufruct owner, in the case of *mîrî* land, if the father had one son, he had to obtain the usufruct of the land as a whole. If he had more than one son, they obtained the usufruct collectively. If there was a son and a daughter, the daughter could not acquire any share of the usufruct. The daughter (or daughters) could obtain the usufruct if there was no living son only at the time of the death of the father (Figure 7.3). Basically, the idea was to keep the *mîrî* land undivided. The second difference between *mîrî* land and private property was the payment of a title deed duty (*resm-i tapu*) for *mîrî* land. While the son (or sons) could obtain the usufruct right without the payment, the daughter like other relatives had to pay the title deed.

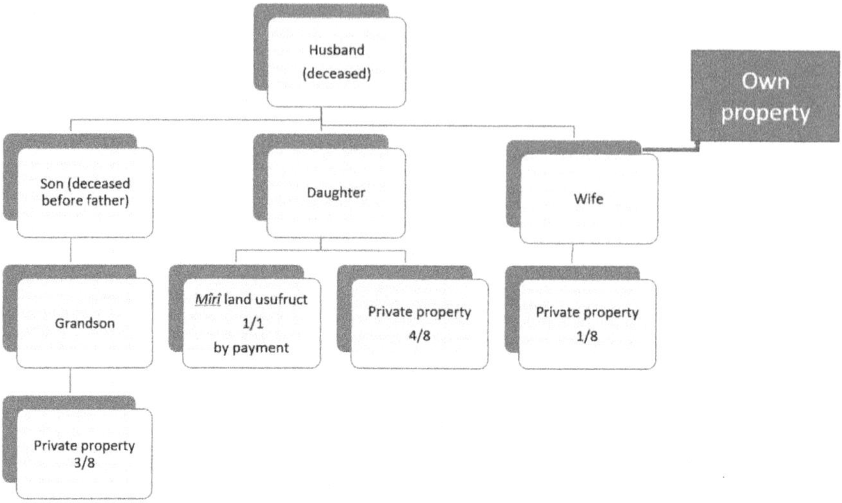

FIGURE 7.3 Inheritance pattern in the absence of sons after the law: The wife (*Ashabü'l-feraiz*) receives a share of one-eighth of the private property, the daughter (also *Ashabü'l-feraiz*) receives half, and the grandson (*Asabe*) receives the rest of the deceased's private property. The daughter obtains access to the usufruct of the *mîrî* land by payment.

Source: © Fatma Gül Karagöz.

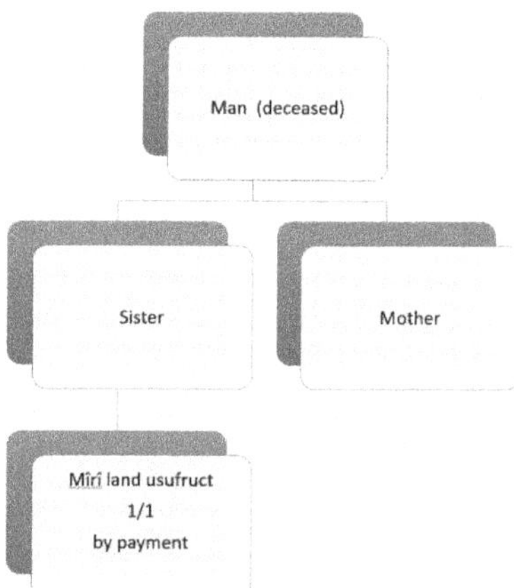

FIGURE 7.4 The transfer of land usufruct from an unmarried or widowed man.

Source: © Fatma Gül Karagöz.

The status and role of women in the Ottoman Empire have been reconsidered since the 1970s using court records.[15] Ronald C. Jennings's pioneering work on the sharia court of the town Kayseri was followed by the works of many others, challenging the traditional image and role of women in the early modern Ottoman Empire.

These works described Ottoman women as self-confident agents who came to court to buy and sell property and who could manage commercial investments.[16] The property law within marriage in Islamic and Ottoman law was based on the separation of goods. A husband had no right to control his wife's property (Figures 7.2 to 7.6).[17]

Women, and people in general, made their claim at the sharia court in person, or they were represented by a proxy (*vekil*). Judith Tucker thinks that ordinary women in court were conscious of their rights.[18] Most likely, the men who acted as legal representatives had a certain degree of knowledge of the law but did not have to be a professional lawyer.

This chapter focusses on the right to usufruct of land by women insofar as this can be traced in the records of the sharia court. My objective is to analyse the legal limitations within which women could exercise usufruct and property rights to land in the first half of the eighteenth century, which was a time of reorganisation, especially in Vidin. The court record books of Vidin from the Balkans and Antakya at the Anatolian-Syrian border, two cities where the *mîrî* system was mainly in

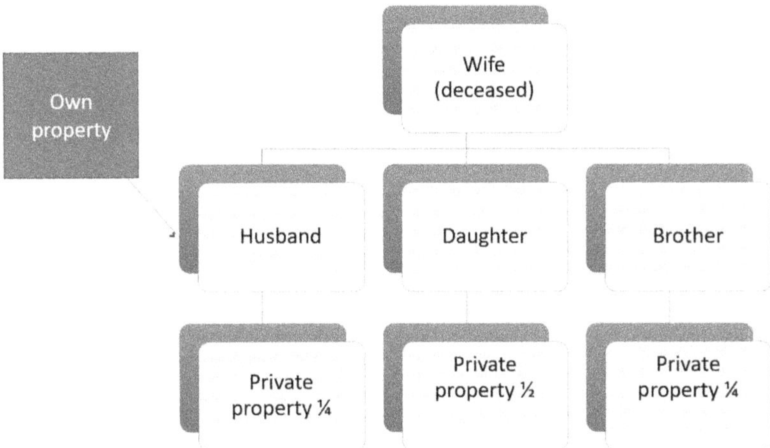

FIGURE 7.5 Inheritance pattern of private property of married women: The husband (*Ashabü'l-feraiz*) and brother (*Asabe*) receive one-fourth; the daughter (also *Ashabü'l-feraiz*) receives one-half.

Source: © Fatma Gül Karagöz.

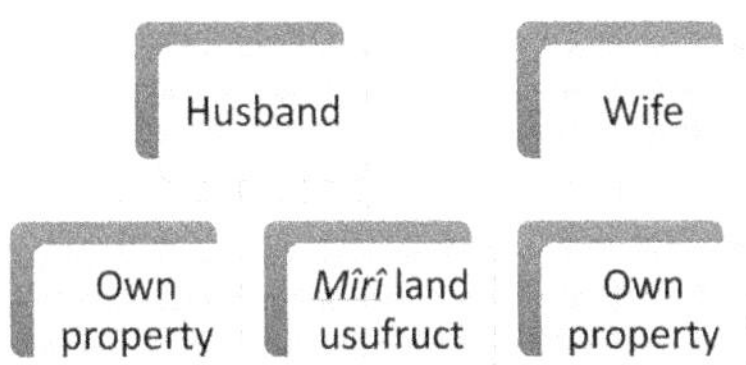

FIGURE 7.6 Property regime in marriage in Ottoman law.

Source: © Fatma Gül Karagöz.

force, will be used to analyse how gender could affect possession and usufruct of land and the distribution of agricultural labour and economic chances as a consequence. A comparative survey of these court records will illustrate the socioeconomic background of women capable of negotiating their cases in the sharia court.

II. Land politics in the eighteenth-century towns of Vidin and Antakya

Vidin, a Danubian city in today's northwestern Bulgaria, was passing through a period of reconstruction, resettlement, and refortification at the beginning of the eighteenth century. After its annexation to the Ottoman Empire in 1396, Vidin was a military border post (*serhad*) for two centuries. While the time of Suleyman I (Lawgiver, 1494–1566; r. 1520–1566) was relatively peaceful, the area was weakened towards the end of the seventeenth century. After the attempted invasion of Vienna in 1683, the Ottomans had to pull back from the Balkans for a short period. In 1689, the Habsburgs invaded Vidin for ten months.[19] Even though the control of the Balkans was re-established by the Ottomans, the city had already been deserted before the Habsburg occupation. As a consequence, legal disputes over abandoned land at the court of Vidin can be traced for at least a period of twenty years after the Habsburg invasion.[20] Vidin began to rise again as a flourishing border region and important military post of the area in the eighteenth century.[21]

The region of Antakya has a different historical background. The Ottomans secured their presence in the region around Antakya in the early sixteenth century. The city was part of the Haleb province, which had an important nomad population. The relation between the state and the nomads could be defined as unpredictable: While nomadic people were used as a military force or as a colonisation tool, they were generally seen as an uncontrollable part of the population, subject to settlement politics, especially after the late sixteenth century. At the same time, the district was highly affected by a series of rebellions, which were followed by the "Great Flight", by the end of which several villages were emptied. Some of them were used for the settlement of nomads or redistributed to other peasants. Despite the troubles of the seventeenth century, both Vidin and Antakya drew the attention of merchants in the eighteenth century. With the Treaty of Passarowitz signed between the Ottomans and the Habsburgs in 1718, commercial relations with Austria once more flourished.[22] As for Antakya, the city was an important centre for silk production. After the fall of Haleb-Iran silk commerce in 1720, the Antakya market seems to have flourished until at least 1735.[23]

In the eighteenth century, both Vidin and Antakya were administrative and judicial districts (*kaza*). The *kadi*, who had the judicial authority of each district, fulfilled multiple tasks. He was both judge and notary. Thus, people came to the sharia court to solve legal problems, to sell and buy property, and to establish a partnership or pious foundation within Islamic law (*waqf*). The *kadi* had to make decisions based on the principles of Islamic law, which was embodied in the *fetva* (legal opinion) and in the sultan's codification (*kanunnâme*).

General codes, e.g. the code of Suleyman I, which included regulations about agricultural, criminal, administrative, and tax law, were more or less in force throughout the empire.[24] Provincial codifications like the Vidin Code or the Haleb Code, both published before the eighteenth century, included regulations concerning tax law, land law, and customary fines. In the provincial codes, the influence of local custom was much more visible, especially in the legal terminology used in taxation and sometimes in the amount of tax taken. The *kadi* court had the sole authority over Muslim subjects as well as over cases between people from different religious beliefs. The Jewish population could seek the decision of their local rabbi through the institution of *responsa* in cases regarding family law or inheritance law. A similar choice was also possible for Christian subjects: Family affairs could be dealt with by the local priest. Nevertheless, members of the Christian community often came to the *kadi* court to solve problems concerning family disputes, as the Ottoman court could offer them some advantages, e.g. the divorce right for Christian women or lower trial costs. However, when the non-Muslim population had a claim or request upon *mîrî* land, the *kadi* court had the sole authority. Though the *kadi* had the decisive authority, he could not execute the decision. He recorded the verdict in the court book and gave a copy (*hüccet*) of the decision (*ilam*) to each of the parties. In criminal cases, implementation was carried out by the *subaşı* (a person responsible for the security of the city, fulfilling the function of the chief of police and the public prosecutor by summoning people to court), although the process in detail is still unknown to us.

The general principles of land law defining the rights of peasants could be found in various codes. These regulations had the primary aim of securing the continuity of land production. If the peasant left the *mîrî* land unfarmed for three successive years, or if he deserted his hometown without a legitimate reason, *sâhib-i arz* had to transfer the usufruct land to another peasant in exchange for payment of *resm-i tapu*, a title deed duty. The peasant who left the land could also be forced to return to his village. In fact, the "landlord" could pursue him and, if he found him, bring him back within a period of fifteen years. If the runaway peasant did not comply, a farm-breaking tax (*çiftbozan*) had to be paid as a penalty. Thus, the aim of the fine was the restitution of the deficit in the income of the latter.

The regulation concerning the confiscation of usufruct of the land can be found in the general code of Bayezid II (1447–1512; r. 1481–1512).[25] This regulation is repeated in the code that the chancellor (*nishandji*),[26] Celalzade (d. 1567), prepared for Süleyman I.[27] In the land code compilations of the eighteenth century, which brought together decrees, regulations, and legal opinions from the sixteenth and seventeenth centuries, there was a reference made to Celalzade in respect to this subject.[28] The approach of the state was the same in both centuries: Deserted land should be claimed first by the original usufruct or property owner in the case of a departure caused by a legitimate motive, such as occupation or bandits.[29] If the land was not claimed in the proper time, it could then be redistributed.

III. The case of the mill and the meadowland in Vidin: What could happen when the land was left?

On 23 April 1714, Mümine Hatun, a resident of Nicopolis who originated from Vidin, made a claim at Vidin court about ten acres of meadowland and a mill near the Topolovetz River.[30] Unfortunately, it is not possible to estimate Mümine's age or status.[31] She claimed that the land and the mill were part of the property of her ancestors, of which she had inherited a share, but a man named Ömer Ağa was occupying the land illegally. In his response, the defendant, Ömer Ağa, explained that he had purchased[32] the land from a man called İsmail Ağa, who himself had bought the shares from Mümine and another shareholder called Ayşe.

According to the court record, İsmail as new owner had rebuilt the mill and then sold the meadowland and mill to Ömer for 180 *kuruş*.[33] When Mümine was asked about the purchase and denied it, Ömer had to bring further proof. Two witnesses confirmed Ömer's statement that Mümine had indeed sold her share through her proxy to İsmail Ağa and had received the money for the transaction. In Islamic (and Ottoman) procedural law, a witness counted as solid proof.[34] As a result, the *kadi* decided in Ömer Ağa's favour. Nevertheless, Mümine continued to pursue her case. Only three weeks later, on 12 May 1714, Mümine appeared in Vidin court again. This time, she used a different legal argument. In her second attempt, she stated that her great-grandfather El-Hac Ömer had established a foundation (*waqf*) upon the meadowland and mill for the benefit of his children and grandchildren.[35] She stated that after the death of her great-grandfather, the rights to the *waqf* had been transferred to his three sons, El-Hac Ali, Mehmed Beşe, and Ebubekir, but during the invasion, the *waqf* and mill were destroyed. While El-Hac Ali died without an heir, Ebubekir's share went to his daughter Ayşe and Mehmed Beşe's share was handed to his granddaughter Mümine. Her opponent, Ömer Ağa, referred to the first verdict in his favour and argued that the institution of *waqfs* in the region had been annulled by many decrees since the land had been destroyed after the invasion. One of these decrees, Ömer stated, regulated that if abandoned property was not claimed within four years it would be redistributed.[36] In fact, between 1692 and 1714 there were at least three decrees regulating the distribution of empty lands after the invasion.[37] Ömer's second argument was based on the impossibility of the establishment of a *waqf* since the land in question was *mîrî*. A *waqf* could only be instituted on private property and needed the permission of the sultan (*temlik*). Nonetheless, the court tried to verify Mümine's claim but could not find any information on the issue in the royal registers where all foundations had to be entered. Ömer used the lack of documentation in his favour. As Mümine could bring neither witnesses nor any documents proving her claim, the court rejected her claim to the usufruct of the land. In spite of this second verdict against her, she took another chance. Nearly four months later, on 26 August 1714, Mümine came to the court yet again. This time she returned to her first claim. She explained that she indeed had sold her share to İsmail Ağa, as Ayşe had done. However, she had not received the money on which the parties had settled (40 *kuruş*). In the end, a reconciliation agreement (*sulh*) was offered between the two parties, and Ömer Ağa agreed to pay 25 *kuruş* to Mümine. As we can see, the plaintiff used different legal arguments to state her claim. This might mirror her gradually increasing knowledge of the ownership situation of the land in question, as she no longer lived in Vidin, or point to the fact that she operated with arguments based on pretence. The question remains, if Mümine had made a false statement in the first place, why did Ömer agree to pay 25 *kuruş*?[38] However, this case also shows a woman's determination to obtain a part of the benefit of land.

The legal background in this case in complex: Both Mümine Hatun and Ömer Ağa defined the land as *mülk-i müfevvez*, property acquired by a special contract for transferring the usufruct right of *mîrî* land (a *tefviz* or *ferağ ve tefviz*), and they used the term *mülk-i müştera*, or property bought by a sales agreement (*bey' u şirâ*), for the mill. As stated earlier, in Ottoman law, while *mîrî* land was not private property, the buildings constructed with the knowledge and permission of the *sipahi* and the trees and vineyards on *mîrî* land were. Hence, when a building like a mill on *mîrî* land was sold, the mill was transferred by a proper sale, but the usufruct of *mîrî* land was transferred by *ferağ*, a special contract that allowed the transfer of usufruct. The main difference between sale (*bey'*) and *ferağ* was that the second had to be made with the knowledge and permission of *sâhib-i arz*, who received the payment of the title deed for this transfer. The nature of rights to *mîrî* land is one of the most debated subjects of Ottoman socioeconomic and legal historiography.[39]

IV. The case of Safiye versus Saniye: A dispute over private property

On 14 March 1709, a dispute about a piece of formerly shared land by three siblings, Saniye Hatun, the late Mustafa Bey, and the late Solak Mehmed, was recorded.[40] The plaintiff was Safiye, the widow of Mustafa, who came to the court to complain about her sister-in-law, Saniye, who occupied the share of a fig garden and vineyard that had belonged to Mustafa. When one of the siblings, Mehmed, died, the other two, Mustafa and Saniye, inherited his share. Now each of them held fifty percent of the land. After the death of Mustafa, Safiye wanted to claim her husband's share as a part of his inheritance. But Saniye saw herself as the rightful user of the whole garden. First of all, after the death of her husband Hasan, she made an agreement with his sons[41] that the share of the fig garden would count as her dowry (*mehir*) and as compensation for her exclusion from heritage by mutual agreement (*teharuc*).[42] To confuse things even more, her brother Solak Mehmed had been cultivating her part of the land share, and he had also planted the fig trees that had been provided by Saniye. The trees and the necessary agricultural tools were her private property. After Solak Mehmed's death, her other brother Mustafa had continued the production. Additionally, Mustafa had sold his part of the land share to his sister Saniye before his death. Two witnesses verified all her testimonies. In the end, the *kadi* decided in Saniye's favour.

In this case, the garden in question was located next to a mulberry garden that already belonged to Saniye. In a second case, recorded on 5 September 1709, Saniye was again accused of illegal occupation of a garden. The plaintiff proved that he had bought the garden from Saniye five years prior by bringing in two witnesses.[43] Though Saniye could find two witnesses in the first case, she could not bring any proof in the second case. Saniye seems to have tried to expand her property. These cases not only show the complex connexion between land share, dowry, and private property but also that Saniye was obviously engaged in agricultural production. But she was most likely not labouring on the land herself. In the first case, she named her brother Solak Mehmed as the manager (*subaşı*) of the garden. Saniye was the private owner of the garden and employed others to manage and harvest the fruits, thus earning her living.

Although not all transfer contracts appear in court record books and not all records seem to have survived, these cases give us a good idea of female involvement in land transactions and disputes.[44] In Vidin, between 1699 and 1753, out of sixty-two records, twenty-three involved women, while in Antakya, between 1709 and 1754, women appear in thirty-one records out of eighty-seven. In Vidin, sixteen women came to court, and three women were summoned to court, and in four cases both parties were women. As for Antakya, twenty-two women came to court to sell land or to make a claim, and five women were summoned to accept a sale or to respond to an accusation, and in four of the cases both parties were women.[45] These numbers show that in both cities women appeared in almost one-third of the total records concerning land property and usufruct.[46]

In Vidin and Antakya in the eighteenth century, those who came to court on matters concerning land were from the "middle class". Men who were involved either held military titles of respect, such as *ağa* or *beşe*, or religious titles, such as *molla* or *efendi*. Most male plaintiffs in Antakya are designated *El-Hac*, *hadjı*, meaning that they had undertaken Islamic pilgrimage to Mecca. All of these men were neither members of the ruling elite nor ordinary peasants. The same is true for women who appear in our sources. Women were identified via the name of their fathers or husbands, e.g. "Fatma, daughter of Hüseyin Ağa"[47] or "Hanım, the daughter of El-Hac Ahmed, the left wife of the late Hüseyn Beşe, son of İbrahim".[48] Hence, their social and personal status could be deduced by means of their relatives.[49]

V. Ümmühan versus Mustafa Beşe: Privately owned or state-owned land?

In the case of Ümmühan versus Mustafa Beşe, Ümmühan, who was Kara Halilzade Mehmed Ağa's[50] widow, acted in the name of their daughter Fatma, who was under her tutelage and who seems to have been the rightful usufruct owner. According to the court record, Ümmühan was accused by Mustafa Beşe, son of Ömer, on 7 June 1729 of illegal usage of a meadowland and a mill in Vidin. Mustafa claimed that he had bought a piece of land by auction that was part of the late Mehmed Ağa's property. His property was sold after his death because of debts of 90 *kuru*. However, more recently Ümmühan had begun to harvest the meadow. Mehmed Beşe, the legal representative of Ümmühan, accepted that Mehmed Ağa was in debt and his inheritance was to be sold for payment of the debt. Abdullah Çelebi, who was the guardian of the inheritance, would manage the auction in which the meadow and mill in question would be left to Mustafa in exchange for 130 *kuruş*. However, Mehmed Beşe continued, noting that the meadowland in question was *mîrî*, so it could not have been transferred by sale. He also presented a title deed document (*tapu temessükü*) proving that Ümmühan had made the payment (*resm-i tapu*) three years before to the *sahib-i arz* (landlord) in the name of Fatma and was entitled to the usufruct of the meadowland. In the decision part of the record, the rule about the transfer of *mîrî* meadowland was repeated; thus, the case was concluded in Ümmühan and Fatma's favour, with reference to the regulation of the transfer of *mîrî* land from father to daughter.[51] Luckily, Ümmühan had documentation proving her statement.

In this affair, Ümmühan could claim the land in the name of her daughter because the usufruct of land was not part of property or inheritance and therefore could not be used to pay a debt. With the payment *resm-i tapu* by her mother, Fatma gained the usufruct rights to the land in question. Most likely she also had no brothers. If Fatma had died before her father, her mother, Ümmühan, could have claimed the usufruct for herself. A widow's status was secondary compared with other female relatives, as for example mothers and sisters. The status of the mother improved after the first decade of the seventeenth century, when a decree was issued stating that when a peasant died without children, the surviving parent could obtain the usufruct by payment. Parents were also secondary to siblings, whose situation was ameliorated in the seventeenth century as well. In this way, a sister who lived in her brother's village could obtain the usufruct, supposing her brother had died childless and she had no other brother. Thus, in the seventeenth century, the number of people who had the right to title deeds expanded in comparison to former codes of law.

VI. Conclusion

Court records give clues about the type of agricultural activity women could engage in. Gardening and vineyard production were significant both in Vidin and in Antakya, but according to the court records, production had much more variety in Antakya. Mulberry gardens were sold with the essentials for silk production, such as a silk mill, cauldron, and ox, and formed commercial crafting units. On 3 September 1753, Fatımahan, daughter of Hatunzade Seyyid Efendi, bought half a share of such an establishment from her husband.[52] In another example involving a purchase between a husband, Hüseyin Bey, son of Bentur Hüseyin Ağa, and his wife, Meryem, daughter of Osman, the wife bought 180 olive trees from her husband. The motive behind this purchase is not specified in the record. The reason for a sale between husband and wife could be the establishment of a sharecropping partnership or a credit relation. Shared vineyards, gardens, and trees were more frequent in Antakya than in Vidin. Some of these shares seem to have been divided by inheritance, but in some cases a partnership was probably in question. In sales between couples, separation of property seems to have been favoured by the husband either as a finance method or as a way to hide possessions from creditors.

In both Vidin and Antakya, women were more often plaintiffs than defendants, especially in disputes between family members concerning cases regarding land. This points to certain limits in the degree to which they could exercise their rights to land, property, and inheritance. The abundant claims by women at court can be read as a result of systematic practices of disinheriting women, "rendering their inheritance rights a legal fiction".[53] Additionally, some cases hint at forced consent. On 29 July 1736, Fatıma, daughter of Küçük Osman Ağa, who came to Antakya court, accused Mustafa Çavuş, son of Mehmed Ağa, of illegal occupation of a farm in Büyükburç, which, with some animals and many kinds of trees, was a unit she should have inherited from her father.[54] However, Mustafa defended himself by claiming that Fatıma had sold the property to her husband Hamamcı Mehmed Ağa. After the death of Mehmed, Mustafa bought the shares of his heirs, including Fatıma's. When the *kadi* asked her again, Fatıma denied the sale to her husband. The court demanded proof from Mustafa, who brought two witnesses. In the end, Fatıma changed her statement and accepted the existence of the sale. In this case, the sudden consent to the sale of her land and therefore the loss of her property raises questions: Had Fatıma been silenced either by a kind of compensation or deal or by threat and force? If so, why had she sold the property to her husband? Had she preferred money instead of land or had she been forced to sell by her husband? Unfortunately, we do not know her motives.

Surprisingly, the court record books for Vidin and Antakya do not contain even a single case in which a wife accused her husband of taking advantage of her own property. However, accusations between siblings were common. According to her statement, Meryas of Antakya, on 3 October 1743, accused her brothers of occupying a mulberry garden in which she had a share. Her brothers, Halil and Mehmed, stated that their father had sold the garden to Hadjı Bayezid, and that they had purchased it from the latter.[55] Interestingly, the same court record book included a list of items in the estate left by the siblings' father, and the garden Meryas laid claim to was not part of it. Similar affairs in which sons purchased their fathers' property from a third person can be seen in various cases, making the disinheritance of a sister a fact. In another record book, in the period 17–27 April 1750, a woman named Emine asked for her share from the estate of her father, and she, too, accused her brother Abdullah of occupying some berry gardens for a period of twenty years. Abdullah claimed that he had purchased Emine's share from her guardians – her brothers – in exchange for a debt.[56] The court decided in Abdullah's favour, but it most likely would have been wiser for Emine to file the case against her guardians. Again, the brothers seem to have found a way to bypass the rights of their sister to their own benefit.

The Vidin and Antakya court records of land and usufruct transfers show that women transferred *mîrî* and *mülk* property more than they obtained it. In addition, in both Vidin and Antakya, *mîrî* land was less often transmitted to women. There is only one case in both cities in which a woman obtained the usufruct of *mîrî* land by contract, and that woman was Südre Hatun. On 12 September 1733, the properties of Südre Hatun of Vidin were exchanged with the property of El-Hac Mehmed Ağa by her husband and proxy, Hüseyin Beşe. Among the properties of Südre were a shop in Vidin, a butcher shop in a village, and a vineyard in Vidin. These were exchanged for a farm situated in Kastamonu, in the western Black Sea region.[57] The farm was transferred by the permission of the *sahib-i arz*. The court record did not include the economic value of the properties in question, so it is not possible to decide if the exchange was to the advantage to Südre. Apart from this case, in

Vidin, out of twenty-seven cases, twelve women made a transfer of *mîrî* or private property. But in two cases women gained the usufruct and proprietorship. As for Antakya, out of a total of forty-eight transfers, ten women implemented transfer by sale or *ferağ*, but just three women gained the ownership or proprietorship. Islamic and Ottoman law accepted the legal capacity of women even though their status vis-à-vis property and inheritance was not equal to that of men. Examples taken from the sharia court records of Vidin and Antakya demonstrate that these rights were not a legal fiction. Still, compared to men of the same economic status, Ottoman women owned less immovable property.[58] However, the protective nature of the Ottoman code of law and the socioeconomic realities of the period affected the role of women in landownership and land production. One particular and positive aspect of the period could be the rise in utilising the sharecropping contract in the seventeenth and eighteenth centuries. This contract might have allowed women another possible activity in land production. In any case, the women who came to court in Vidin and Antakya knew how to use legal tools in their favour. In addition, while women were not totally excluded from agricultural production, the land transfers imply that they preferred, or sometimes were forced, to sell the land. Finally, the women who appeared in these sources and who engaged in agricultural activity and claimed usufruct or property rights to land were no ordinary peasants, but rather were part of the "middle class".[59] For a complete picture of property relations in the Ottoman Empire, a comparative investigation focussing on women from different socioeconomic and cultural backgrounds will be necessary.

Notes

1 This chapter is mostly based on my PhD thesis defended in June 2018: *The Practice of Land Law in The Ottoman Empire Between 1700–1750: The Example of Vidin and Antakya/1700–1750 Yılları Arasında Osmanlı Devleti'nde Arazi Hukuku Uygulamaları: Vidin ve Antakya Örneği*. For the transliterations from Ottoman Turkish, the IJMES system is used.

2 Eighty-seven percent of Ottoman lands were probably *mîrî* in the 1580s. Halil İnalcık, *The Ottoman Empire Classical Age 1300–1600*, London 1988 [Phoenix], p. 110.

3 After Ebussuud's time, *şeyhülislams* gained more power in a juridical and political respect; however, they never became part of the sultan's council.

4 Ahmet Akgündüz, *Osmanlı Kanunnâmeleri ve Hukuki Tahlilleri*, vol. 4, İstanbul 1992 [Fey Vakfı Yayınları], p. 79.

5 Ebussuud tried to eliminate potential confusion regarding the highly local legal terminology in provincial codes. Halil İnalcık, *Islamization of Ottoman Laws on land and land tax, in:* Halil Inalcık, *Essays in Ottoman History*, Istanbul 1998 [Eren Yayınları], pp. 155–169.

6 While the position of *sâhib-i arz* was originally temporary, after the sixteenth century, it became de facto hereditary, with the sons of the *sipahi*s obtaining the renewal of their fathers' post. In the eighteenth century, the economic obligations of the state resulted in extreme measures, such as the accordance of *mâlikâne*, or life lease, especially to the members of the ruling elite. *Mâlikâne*-owner landlords generally found a deputy and engaged in other agricultural or commercial activities in cities. See Bruce McGowan, "The Age of the Ayans, 1699–1812", in: Halil İnalcık and Donald Quataert (eds.), *An Economic and Social History of the Ottoman Empire, 1300–1914*, Cambridge 1994 [Cambridge University Press], pp. 637–758, pp. 713–714.

7 Baber Johansen, *The Islamic Law on Land Tax and Rent*, New York 1988 [Croom Helm], pp. 2–3.

8 Taner Timur, *Osmanlı Toplumsal Düzeni*, Ankara 2010 [İmge Kitabevi], p. 200.

9 Halil İnalcık, "Village, Peasant and Empire", in: *The Middle East and the Balkans Under the Ottoman Empire: Essays on Economy and Society*, Bloomington 1993 [Indiana University], pp. 137–160, pp. 141–142.
10 See upcoming discussion.
11 Ibid.
12 Hedda Reindl-Kiel, "A Woman Timar Holder in Ankara Province During the Second Half of the 16th Century", in: *Journal of the Economic and Social History of the Orient* 40, 2 (1997), pp. 207–238. The key was being able to cultivate the land, which Reindl-Kiel interprets as having a husband, son, or son-in-law to accomplish the task. She explains that being an unmarried woman would not be considered an ideal situation for farm production.
13 Halil Cin and Ahmet Akgündüz, *Türk Hukuk Tarihi*, İstanbul 2011 [Osmanlı Araştırmaları Vakfi], pp. 555–563. They were father, grandfather through father, siblings through mother, husband, wife, daughter, granddaughter through son, sister, sister through father, mother, and grandmother.
14 In the Quran, there are forty different options determining the share of *Ashabü'l-feraiz* members in accordance with the number and group of relatives (Mehmet Akif Aydın, *Türk Hukuk Tarihi*, İstanbul 2012 [Beta Yayınları], p. 311). See ibid. pp. 311–314 for the calculation of feraiz in Fig. 7.2, 7.3, 7.5.
15 Madeline C. Zilfi, "Introduction", in: Madeline C. Zilfi (ed.), *Women in the Ottoman Empire: Middle Eastern Women in the Early Modern Era*, Leiden 1997 [Brill], pp. 1–5, p. 1; Dror Zeevi, "The Use of Ottoman Sharīʿa Court Records as a Source for Middle Eastern Social History: A Reappraisal", in: *Islamic Law and Society* 5, 1 (1998), pp. 35–56, p. 36.
16 Ronald C. Jennings, "Women in Early 17th Century Ottoman Empire: The Sharia Court of Anatolian Kayseri", in: *Journal of the Economic and Social History of the Orient* 18, 1 (1975), pp. 53–114; Fariba Zarinebaf, "The Role of Women in the Urban Economy of İstanbul", in: *International Labor and Working-Class History* 60 (2001), pp. 141–152; Madeline C. Zilfi, *Women and Slavery in the Late Ottoman Empire*, Cambridge 2010 [Cambridge University Press], p. 55.
17 Judith Tucker, *Women, Family and Gender in Islamic Law*, New York 2008 [Cambridge University Press], p. 137.
18 Ibid., p. 64. See also: Fatma Müge Göcek and Marc David Baer, "Social Boundaries of Ottoman Women's Experience in 18th-Century Galata Court Records", in: Madeline C. Zilfi (ed.), *Women in the Ottoman Empire: Middle Eastern Women in the Early Modern Era*, Leiden 1997 [Brill], pp. 48–65, p. 51.
19 Sources regarding the Habsburg invasion seem to be scarce. Rossitsa Gradeva, "War and Peace Along the Danube: Vidin at the End of the Seventeenth Century", in: *Oriente Moderno, the Ottomans and the Sea* 81, 1 (2001), pp. 149–175, p. 153.
20 Rossitsa Gradeva, "Between Hinterland and Frontier: Ottoman Vidin, Fifteenth to Eighteenth Centuries", in: Andrew Peacock (ed.), *The Frontiers of the Ottoman World. Proceedings of the British Academy*, Oxford 2009 [Oxford University Press], pp. 331–351, p. 346.
21 Mahir Aydın, *Vidin Kalesi, Tuna Boyundaki İnci*, İstanbul 2015 [Ötüken Yayınevi], p. 131.
22 Bruce McGowan, *Economic Life in Ottoman Europe: Taxation, Trade and the Struggle for Land 1600–1800*, Cambridge 1981 [Cambridge University Press], pp. 188–189.
23 M. Sait Türkhan, *18. Doğu Akdeniz'de Ticaret ve Haleb*, 2014 (Institute of Social Sciences, Unpublished PhD thesis, İstanbul University), pp. 66, 68. For the situation at the end of the eighteenth century, see McGowan, *Economic Life in Ottoman Europe*, p. 41–42.
24 Some of the general codes could be compilations of the local codes and decrees, rather than promulgated texts.
25 Ahmet Akgündüz, *Osmanlı Kanunnâmeleri ve Hukuki Tahlilleri*, vol. 2, İstanbul 1990 [Fey Vakfi Yayınları], p. 66.
26 *Nishandjı*, a member of the sultan's council, was the mind behind the codifications and the sultan's decrees.

27 Ahmet Akgündüz, *Osmanlı Kanunnâmeleri ve Hukuki Tahlilleri*, vol. 4, İstanbul 1992 [Fey Vakfı Yayınları], p. 391.
28 *Maruzat*, Süleymaniye Library, Çelebi Abdullah 159, vr. 37–2. The reference means that Celalzade's regulations were still in force in the eighteenth century. The record date given in the Hijri (Islamic) calendar corresponds to 1756–1757 in the Gregorian calendar.
29 *Kanunnâme-i Sultan Süleyman Han*, Süleymaniye Library Y 358, vr. 15.
30 National Library of Cyril and Methodius (NLCM) S161a, vr. 72.
31 The term "Hatun" could refer to gender, old age, or status. Leslie P. Peirce, "Seniority, Sexuality, and Social Order: The Vocabulary of Gender in Early Modern Ottoman Society", in: Madeline C. Zilfi (ed.), *Women in the Ottoman Empire, Middle Eastern Women in the Early Modern Era*, Leiden 1997 [Brill], pp. 169–196, pp. 183–184.
32 Ömer used *bey' ve teslim ve kabz-ı semen ve tefviz*, which translates as "sale and deliver and exchange of money and the transfer of usufruct".
33 In the second half of the seventeenth century, Ottoman traditional currency *akçe* became less used in trade, giving way to foreign money. In the eighteenth century, following the example of Italian *grosso* and German *Groschen*, Ottomans issued a new type of coin, the *kuruş*, which corresponded to 120 *akçe* and 40 *para*, *akçe* and *para* becoming the smaller coins. Şevket Pamuk, *Osmanlı Ekonomisi ve Kurumları*, 3rd ed., İstanbul 2010, p. 35. See also Şevket Pamuk, "Kuruş", in: *DİA* 26 (2002), p. 458.
34 If both parties could bring witnesses in a *waqf* case, the court should decide according to the "credibility" of the witnesses (see Süleyman Kaya, Betül Algın, Asuman Erkan and Zeynep Trabzonlu (eds.), *Şeyhülislam Yenişehirli Abdullah Efendi. Behçetü'l-Fetava*, İstanbul 2011 [Klasik Yayınevi], p. 422).
35 NLCM, S161a, vr. 78–79.
36 Ibid.: "[B]ecause of the infidel invasion, all the charitable foundations became useless. Hence, there were multiple decrees explaining that these old cases should not be heard in court, and there were decrees explaining that after the conquest by the permission of Allah, those who laid claim within four years could use their property but the property of those who did not come should be distributed by treasury." NLCM S161a, vr. 72.
37 NLCM 38, vr. 101. A decree copied in 1707, in a court book references three orders, issued in 1692–1693 (Hijri year 1104), 1695–1696 (Hijri year 1107), and 1706, respectively, regarding the rejection of such cases, which points out that the problem of settlement in Vidin was not easily solved.
38 The amount of money seems to be moderate considering the wages of construction workers in the capital city, İstanbul. Between 1710 and 1720, their daily wages were fixed in *akçe*, and they possibly earned 1 *kuruş* after a work period of three days to one week. For this calculation, I used Şevket Pamuk, *İstanbul ve Diğer Kentlerde 500 Yıllık Fiyatlar ve Ücretler 1469–1998*, Ankara 2000 [Devlet İstatistik Enstitüsü Matbaası], pp. 193–194. In another article with Süleyman Özcumur, Pamuk notes that these numbers were taken from *waqf* registers, which means the payments were made by large institutions that could offer more than a normal wage. See Süleyman Özcumur and Şevket Pamuk, "Real Wages and Standards of Living in the Ottoman Empire, 1489–1914", in: *The Journal of Economic History* 62, 2 (2002), pp. 293–321, p. 314.
39 E. Attila Aytekin, "Agrarian Relations, Property and Law: An Analysis of the Land Code of 1858 in the Ottoman Empire", in: *Middle Eastern Studies* 45, 6 (2009), pp. 935–951. "The most evident example of legal formalism in this sense is the exaggerated importance attributed to the distinctions between categories of land as stipulated in the texts of law on the one hand, and the legal concepts of 'possession' and 'ownership', on the other." See Ibid., p. 936; Haim Gerber, *The Social Origins of the Modern Middle East*, Boulder, CO 1987 [Lynne Rienner Publishers], pp. 14–15, 24.
40 Başbakanlık Osmanlı Arşivi Meşihat Şer'iye Sicil Defterleri BOA, MŞH.ŞSC.d..1094, v. 6a-6b.
41 Saniye mentioned her family as "My husband (*zevcim*) Kuloğluca Hasan and his sons (*oğulları*) Ahmed Ağa and Mustafa Ağa". BOA, MŞH.ŞSC.d..1094, v. 6a-6b.

42 Once marriage was consummated *mehir/mehr* could be immediately paid to the wife -*mehr-i muaccel*-, or it was promised and postponed -*mehr-i müeccel*- after divorce or death of the husband. In this document, the payment was *mehr-i muahhar*, a postponed payment like *mehr-i müeccel*.
43 MŞH.ŞSC.d..1094, v. 20a, text: 2.
44 Antakya court records, including affairs from the eighteenth to the end of the nineteenth century, were brought together in the State Archives of the Turkish Republic. The records between 1711 and 1734 are missing, probably lost during the transfer from local libraries.
45 See the bibliography for the exact references of four court book records from Antakya in the State Archives of the Turkish Republic and fifteen court book records from the National Library of Cyril Methodius in Sofia. I used the translation of BOA, MŞH. ŞSC.d..1096 by Adem Kara, *Antakya'nın Üç Numaralı Şeriyye Sicili*, 2000 (Unpublished MA Thesis, Institute of Social Sciences, Department of History, Sakarya University).
46 For a similar remark about Amid (Diyarbakır), see Veysel Gürhan, "18. Yüzyıl Osmanlı Toplumunda Kadın ve Hukuk: Amid Mahkemesi'nde Kadınların Hak Arama Süreçlerine Dair Bazı Değerlendirmeler", in: *İnsan ve Toplum Bilimleri Araştırmaları Dergisi, Journal of Human and Social Sciences Researches* 6, 3 (2017), pp. 1644–1664, p. 1650.
47 NLCM S43, vr24.
48 MŞH.ŞSC.d..1094, v. 13a, text: 1.
49 On the socioeconomic situation of women seeking justice, see Fariba Zarinebaf, "Ottoman Women and the Tradition of Seeking Justice in the 18th Century", in: Madeline C. Zilfi (ed.), *Women in the Ottoman Empire: Middle Eastern Women in the Early Modern Era*, Leiden 1997 [Brill], pp. 253–263, p. 253; Suraiya Faroqhi, "Crime, Women and Wealth in the 18th-Century Anatolian Countryside", in: Madeline C. Zilfi (ed.), *Women in the Ottoman Empire: Middle Eastern Women in the Early Modern Era*, Leiden 1997 [Brill], pp. 6–27, p. 12; Margaret L. Merriwether, "Women and Waqf Revisited: The Case of Aleppo, 1770–1840", in: Madeline C. Zilfi (ed.), *Women in the Ottoman Empire: Middle Eastern Women in the Early Modern Era*, Leiden 1997 [Brill], pp. 128–152, p. 130.
50 *Zade* is used for a member or descendent of a family, probably elite. The term could be translated as "Mehmed Ağa of Black Halil's House".
51 "[M]eadow was not the type of inheritance, it is transferred to the son without payment and to the daughter by the payment of a title deed." NLCM S19, vr. 110–111, text 3.
52 BOA, MŞH.ŞSC.d..1098, vr. 37.
53 Tucker, *Women, Family and Gender*, p. 151.
54 BOA, MŞH.ŞSC.d..1095, vr. 29b.
55 Kara, *Antakya'nın Üç Numaralı Şeriyye Sicili*, pp. 56–57.
56 BOA, MŞH.ŞSC.d..1097, vr. 25b, text 1.
57 NLCM VŞS42, vr. 68, text 3.
58 Gül Akyılmaz, "Osmanlı Devleti'nde Mülkiyet Hakları ve Mülkiyet İlişkileri Çerçevesinde Kadının Hukuki Statüsü", in: Fethi Gedikli (ed.), *II. Türk Hukuk Tarihi Kongresi Bildirileri*, vol. I, İstanbul 2016 [On iki Levha Yayıncılık], pp. 195–289, pp. 230–231.
59 The statistical analysis includes Christian and Jewish subjects of the Ottoman Empire as long as they chose to come to a *kadi* court or if there was a case about *mîrî* land.

Bibliography

Archive sources

Turkey, State Archives of Turkey, Istanbul.
BOA, MŞH.ŞSC.d..1094.
BOA, MŞH.ŞSC.d..1095.
BOA, MŞH.ŞSC.d..1097.
BOA, MŞH.ŞSC.d..1098.
Bulgaria, National Library of Cyril and Methodius, Sofia.

NLCM S8.
NLCM S9.
NLCM S10.
NLCM S14.
NLCM S19.
NLCM S25a.
NLCM S38.
NLCM S41.
NLCM S42.
NLCM S43.
NLCM S60.
NLCM S67.
NLCM S81.
NLCM S161a.
NLCM S305.
Turkey, Süleymaniye Library, Istanbul.
Kanunnâme-i Cedid, Esad Efendi 854–1.
Maruzat, Çelebi Abdullah 159.
Turkey, Turkish Historical Institution Library, Ankara.
Kanunnâme-i Sultan Süleyman Han, Y 358.

Printed sources

Akgündüz, Ahmet, *Osmanlı Kanunnâmeleri ve Hukuki Tahlilleri*, vol. 2, İstanbul 1990 [Fey Vakfı Yayınları].

———*Osmanlı Kanunnâmeleri ve Hukuki Tahlilleri*, vol. 4, İstanbul 1992 [Fey Vakfı Yayınları].

Akyılmaz, Gül, Osmanlı Devleti'nde Mülkiyet Hakları ve Mülkiyet İlişkileri Çerçevesinde Kadının Hukuki Statüsü, *in: Fethi Gedikli (ed.), II. Türk Hukuk Tarihi Kongresi Bildirileri*, vol. I, İstanbul 2016 [On iki Levha Yayıncılık], pp. 195–289.

Aydın, Mahir, *Vidin Kalesi, Tuna Boyundaki İnci*, İstanbul 2015 [Ötüken Yayınevi].

Aydın, Mehmet Akif, *Türk Hukuk Tarihi*, İstanbul 2012 [Beta Yayınları].

Aytekin, E. Atilla, "Agrarian Relations, Property and Law: An Analysis of the Land Code of 1858 in the Ottoman Empire", in: *Middle Eastern Studies* 45, 6 (2009), pp. 935–951.

Cin, Halil and Ahmet Akgündüz, *Türk Hukuk Tarihi*, İstanbul 2011 [Osmanlı Araştırmaları Vakfı].

Faroqhi, Suraiya, "Crime, Women and Wealth in the 18th-Century Anatolian Countryside", in: Madeline C. Zilfi (ed.), *Women in the Ottoman Empire: Middle Eastern Women in the Early Modern Era*, Leiden 1997 [Brill], pp. 6–27.

Gerber, Haim, *The Social Origins of the Modern Middle East*, Boulder and Colorado 1987 [Lynne Rienner Publishers].

Göcek, Fatma Müge and Marc David Baer, "Social Boundaries of Ottoman Women's Experience in 18th-Century Galata Court Records", in: Madeline C. Zilfi (ed.), *Women in the Ottoman Empire: Middle Eastern Women in the Early Modern Era*, Leiden 1997 [Brill], pp. 48–65.

Gradeva, Rossitsa, "War and Peace Along the Danube: Vidin at the End of the Seventeenth Century", in: *Oriente Moderno, the Ottomans and the Sea* 81, 1 (2001), pp. 149–175.

———"Between Hinterland and Frontier: Ottoman Vidin, Fifteenth to Eighteenth Centuries", in: A. Peacock (ed.), *The Frontiers of the Ottoman World. Proceedings of the British Academy*, Oxford 2009 [Oxford University Press], pp. 331–351.

Gürhan, Veysel, "18. Yüzyıl Osmanlı Toplumunda Kadın ve Hukuk: Amid Mahkemesi'nde Kadınların Hak Arama Süreçlerine Dair Bazı Değerlendirmeler", in: *İnsan ve Toplum Bilimleri Araştırmaları Dergisi, Journal of Human and Social Sciences Researches* 6, 3 (2017), pp. 1644–1664.

İnalcık, Halil, *The Ottoman Empire Classical Age 1300–1600*, London 1988 [Phoenix].

———"Village, Peasant and Empire", in: *The Middle East and the Balkans under the Ottoman Empire: Essays on Economy and Society*, Bloomington 1993 [Indiana University], pp. 137–160.

———"Islamization of Ottoman Laws on Land and Land Tax", in: *Essays in Ottoman History*, İstanbul 1998 [Eren Yayınları], pp. 155–169.

Jennings, Ronald C., "Women in Early 17th Century Ottoman Empire: The Sharia Court of Anatolian Kayseri", in: *Journal of the Economic and Social History of the Orient* 18, 1 (1975), pp. 53–114.

Johansen, Baber, *The Islamic Law on Land Tax and Rent*, New York 1988 [Croom Helm].

Kara, Adem, *Antakya'nın Üç Numaralı Şeriyye Sicili*, 2000 [Unpublished MA thesis, Institute of Social Sciences, Department of History, Sakarya University].

Kaya, Süleyman, Betül Algın, Asuman Erkan and Zeynep Trabzonlu (eds.), *Şeyhülislam Yenişehirli Abdullah Efendi. Behçetü'l-Fetava*, İstanbul 2011 [Klasik Yayınevi].

Kiel, Hedda Reindl, "A Woman Timar Holder in Ankara Province During the Second Half of the 16th Century", in: *Journal of the Economic and Social History of the Orient* 40, 2 (1997), pp. 207–238.

McGowan, Bruce, *Economic Life in Ottoman Europe: Taxation, Trade and the Struggle for Land 1600–1800*, Cambridge 1981 [Cambridge University Press].

———"The Age of the Ayans, 1699–1812", in: Halil İnalcık and Donald Quataert (eds.), *An Economic and Social History of the Ottoman Empire, 1300–1914*, Cambridge 1994 [Cambridge University Press], pp. 637–758.

Merriwether, Margaret L., "Women and Waqf Revisited: The Case of Aleppo, 1770–1840", in: Madeline C. Zilfi (ed.), *Women in the Ottoman Empire: Middle Eastern Women in the Early Modern Era*, Leiden 1997 [Brill], pp. 128–152.

Özcumur, Süleyman and Şevket Pamuk, "Real Wages and Standards of Living in the Ottoman Empire, 1489–1914", in: *The Journal of Economic History* 62, 2 (2002), pp. 293–321.

Pamuk, Şevket, *İstanbul ve Diğer Kentlerde 500 Yıllık Fiyatlar ve Ücretler 1469–1998*, Ankara 2000 [Devlet İstatistik Enstitüsü Matbaası].

———"Kuruş", in: *DİA* 26 (2002), pp. 458–459.

———*Osmanlı Ekonomisi ve Kurumları*, 3rd ed., İstanbul 2010 [İş Bankası Kültür Yayınları].

Peirce, Leslie P., "Seniority, Sexuality, and Social Order: The Vocabulary of Gender in Early Modern Ottoman Society", in: Madeline C. Zilfi (ed.), *Women in the Ottoman Empire, Middle Eastern Women in the Early Modern Era*, Leiden 1997 [Brill], pp. 169–196.

———*Morality Tales: Law and Gender in the Ottoman Court of Aintab*, Los Angeles 2003 [University of California Press].

Timur, Taner, *Osmanlı Toplumsal Düzeni*, Ankara 2010 [İmge Kitabevi].

Tucker, Judith, *Women, Family and Gender in Islamic Law*, New York 2008 [Cambridge University Press].

Türkhan, M. *Sait, 18. Doğu Akdeniz'de Ticaret ve Haleb*, 2014 [Institute of Social Sciences, Unpublished PhD thesis, İstanbul University].

Zarinebaf, Fariba, "Ottoman Women and the Tradition of Seeking Justice in the 18th Century", in: Madeline C. Zilfi (ed.), *Women in the Ottoman Empire: Middle Eastern Women in the Early Modern Era*, Leiden 1997 [Brill], pp. 253–263.

———"The Role of Women in the Urban Economy of İstanbul", in: *International Labor and Working-Class History* 60 (2001), pp. 141–152.

Zeevi, Dror, "The Use of Ottoman Sharīʿa Court Records as a Source for Middle Eastern Social History: A Reappraisal", in: *Islamic Law and Society* 5, 1 (1998), pp. 35–56.

Zilfi, Madeline C., "Introduction", in: Madeline C. Zilfi (ed.), *Women in the Ottoman Empire: Middle Eastern Women in the Early Modern Era*, Leiden 1997 [Brill], pp. 1–5.

———*Women and Slavery in the Late Ottoman Empire*, Cambridge 2010 [Cambridge University Press].

PART IV

Women, law, and property in colonial contexts

FIGURE 8.1 Map of Jamaica, John Cary, *The West Indies, including part of Virginia, North Carolina, East Florida, South Carolina, West Florida, Georgia, Louisiana, and the Gulf of Mexico, with part of the coast of South America: From the Bay of Honduras, to the mouth of the River Oronoko. From the latest and best authorities and actual observations*, 1783.

Source: Library of Congress Geography and Map Division, Washington, D.C., U.S.A., public domain, G4390 1783. C3, www.loc.gov/resource/g4390.ar171300/?r=-0.616,0.076,2.233,0.902,0 (15.02.2020, 14:00 CET).

8

IN HER OWN RIGHT

Gender, slaveholding, and movable goods in colonial Jamaica

Christine Walker

ABSTRACT

In the eighteenth-century, Jamaica became the wealthiest and the largest slaveholding colony in the British Empire. Local adaptations to British property laws were crucial to this development. Colonists treated enslaved people as movable goods in their inheritance bequests. Buttressed by Jamaican law, this island practice was especially significant for female heirs. Women, who were the customary recipients of personal property, regularly received captive Africans. Handled as fungible, flexible and expensive assets, enslaved people commanded far more value than the movable goods such as livestock, furniture and clothing that women typically inherited. Consequently, free and freed women of European, Euro-African and African descent became critical investors in Jamaica's slavery regime. Female slaveholders capitalised on their newfound wealth to purchase more captives, thereby bolstering the Atlantic slave trade. Pervasive slaveholding among the island's female inhabitants altered the relationship between gender and property that underwrote masculine power. Determined to protect their newfound wealth, islanders used a host of legal strategies to preserve married women's property claims, especially to enslaved people. Women slaveholders preferred to bequeath their captives to other women. These colonial customs enabled families to preserve slavery from one generation to the next along female lines.

I. Ill-gotten gains: Free women and the entrenchment of slaveholding Jamaica

When Mary Penlerick made her will in 1716, the Jamaican colonist set aside £17 for a "negro young woman [. . .] to be bought" for her granddaughter "after marriage."[1] In doing so, Penlerick was following a local precedent that her family had helped to establish on the island. Penlerick's ancestor James Pennelerick, among the first English settlers in Jamaica in the seventeenth century, gave enslaved people to his wife, together with money for her to purchase more captives, who were transported to the fledgling English colony from Africa via the Atlantic slave trade.[2] A few brief lines in Mary Penlerick's will confirmed the connexion between women and slaveholding that had been established a generation earlier.

Mary Penlerick parlayed the property, including enslaved people, that she had inherited to buy more unfree African labourers. Through this bequest, Penlerick participated in several critical alterations that originated in the colonial family, yet had imperial consequences. As the directive in her will suggests, Penlerick considered participation in the slave trade to be ordinary. Moreover, she identified enslaved people, like the unnamed "negro young woman" whom she ordered her executors to purchase, as a type of movable good – one that was no different from livestock.[3] Additionally, Penlerick configured this form of personal property as an especially appropriate gift for a female heir; in this case, her granddaughter.

Penlerick's seemingly simple bequest of cash to her granddaughter hints at a larger and more radical alteration that was underway in the relationship between gender and property. Slavery was the medium through which this change occurred. The treatment of enslaved people as personal or movable property, rather than real estate or landed property, by Jamaica's lawmakers and thousands of colonists in their inheritance bequests had unintended yet significant consequences for female heirs. Defining captives as movable goods made it easier to transfer them to women. By the early eighteenth century slaves had become one of the chief assets women inherited. This local practice placed a valuable new kind of wealth into female hands. Women, in turn, capitalised on their enhanced economic stature to purchase more slaves, thus intensifying the colony's commitment to the slave labour system and its dependency upon the Atlantic slave trade.

Jamaica's property laws and the inheritance practices of ordinary colonists were designed to maximise profits through the intensive exploitation of enslaved labourers in a demographically unstable environment. These colonial circumstances were especially beneficial to free and freed women. Female legatees received larger and more valuable bequests, of which enslaved people comprised considerable portions. Slaveholding created an alternative means of wealth accumulation that was more accessible to female inhabitants than landholding. When women enslavers wrote their own wills, they used captives to offer monetary and physical support to other female kin, reinforcing the local understanding of the slave as a feminised category of personal property. These alterations marked a departure from, and in some ways posed a challenge to, older modes of patriarchal authority that emanated from men's monopolisation of landownership. Jamaican real estate, especially land in the countryside, only gained value when it was cultivated by an enslaved labor force.

The property transfers made by thousands of colonial families were shaped by and also influenced broader Atlantic and global trends. By the 1720s, Jamaica was the primary depot for the British slave trade, and the island was inhabited by the largest enslaved population in the Anglo-Atlantic world. A decade later, Jamaica became the most valuable colony in the British Empire. These developments occurred quickly. When England seized Jamaica from the Spanish in 1655, after failing to capture Hispaniola, it was a sparsely settled outpost populated by a thousand or so free and enslaved inhabitants who worked as cattle ranchers.[4] One hundred years later, 10,000 colonists and more than 100,000 enslaved people lived on the island. Jamaica's economic and strategic importance, and the financial and political power wielded by its constituents in London, was unrivalled.[5]

Britain's grip on the island was not secure, however. The colony's riches were produced by a brutal labour system. The enslaved people who produced Jamaica's wealth, suffered from malnutrition, disease, overwork, and abuse. They experienced abysmal mortality rates and never became a self-reproducing population. The terrible conditions experienced by captives provoked unrest, and frequent slave insurrections occurred on the island. Colonists, and eventually the British Army, were also engaged in a guerilla war with the Jamaican Maroons until 1739, when the British admitted defeat and signed a peace treaty with them. The Maroons were independent and self-governing communities made up of people of African and Amerindian descent. In 1760, Tacky's War, one of the largest slave-led insurgencies in the Americas, posed another serious challenge to slaveholder hegemony and control. At the same time, Jamaica's value and its location in the heart of the Caribbean meant that the island was chronically vulnerable to attacks by Britain's imperial rivals as well as privateers and pirates.[6]

Colonists lived in a violent and unstable society that they helped to construct. Chronically high mortality rates contributed to this insecurity. A host of viral and bacterial infections made Jamaica a lethal place for free and enslaved inhabitants alike. In Kingston, for instance, only one in three white infants survived past the age of five. New arrivals from Europe might survive for a few years there, and locally born inhabitants could expect to live into their forties. Despite these dangers, the lure of wealth drew a diverse population of free migrants to the island from Europe, primarily from England, Scotland, Ireland, and other colonies in British America. These migrants joined the Creoles, or island-born people of European and, increasingly, Euro-African and African descent, who were either born to free parents or manumitted from slavery. Some members of Jamaica's free population of colour achieved considerable wealth and status on the island, whereas others who had spent part of their lives in bondage occupied the lower rungs of the social ladder. An enslaved majority population, most of whom were born in Africa, significantly outnumbered the free minority. They, too, comprised an ethnically and linguistically diverse assemblage.[7]

Brought together by choice and by force, the island's free and enslaved populations comprised a remarkably heterogeneous lot, which was further diversified as a result of Jamaica's lax handling of religion. Intensively focussed on trade, the colony's chief governing bodies – the Jamaica Assembly and the Jamaica Council – and the governor never passed acts to restrict inhabitants based on their religious persuasion. The Church of England's presence on the island remained weak, allowing Protestants of all sorts, included Quakers and Baptists, who faced persecution, together with Catholics, who were viewed with contempt and occasionally barred from other colonies in the empire, to seek refuge there. The island was also home to a small but significant Jewish community. Jamaica's enslaved population brought their own diverse spiritual beliefs and practices to the colony.[8]

Local officials paid little attention to the place of birth or the spiritual persuasion of the free community members. Instead, they focussed on creating and enforcing the boundaries between legally free and enslaved people while also making enslavement a more permanent and heritable status. By the end of the seventeenth century, as the Jamaica Assembly coped with a large influx of captive Africans, they invoked racial categories, rather than religious differences, to distinguish between free and enslaved persons. The legal codes, as well as the few census records that have survived, labelled people as "white", "mulatto", "negro", and, much more rarely, "Indian". Jamaica's lawmakers participated in the creation of a racialist logic whereby only people with African or Indian ancestry could be enslaved. White people, by contrast, were assumed to be free at birth and could not be legally held in bondage.[9]

During the first half of the eighteenth century, race gained salience as a marker of legal status on the island. Gender also shaped a free person's position there, though not in the ways we might expect. Scholars have typically pointed to Jamaica as the most extreme version of the type of hypermasculine society that characterised the British West Indies. Consequently, accounts of the development of this crucial region of the empire assume that female colonists were either absent or marginal. My findings suggest otherwise, While it is true that male colonists outnumbered female colonists and controlled the majority of the wealth on the island, free and freed women of European, Euro-African, and African descent made significant contributions to Jamaica's phenomenal economic growth and, specifically, to the expansion of chattel slavery. Moreover, as the heirs and managers of family businesses, female islanders sustained colonial ventures that often appeared to be under male control on paper.[10]

A number of local conditions aided in enhancing women's positions in Jamaica. High mortality rates resulted in frequent property transfers. At the same time, colonial wills indicate that sisters tended to outlive brothers. Consequently, female heirs were often the only surviving family members who stood to inherit. Free families adapted to these demographic conditions and thereby preserved their estates by modifying gendered inheritance practices. Wives, mothers, and daughters received larger portions, especially in the form of captive Africans, than they typically did in England or British North America via inheritance. As a result, women were overrepresented as slaveholders. A few sparse census records indicate that women made up only one-third of the free adult population. Yet between the 1670s and the 1760s, one out of every ten slaveowners on the island was a woman, and an estimated eighty percent of all female property holders owned slaves.[11]

Women's investment in chattel slavery augmented their status on the island. They already lived in one of the most profitable regions of the world. Anglophone Caribbean colonists were much wealthier than Britons who resided elsewhere in the empire, and women benefited from this trend. Whereas the ordinary Briton possessed £42, a female colonist's Jamaican estate had a median value of £285 and a mean value of £803.[12] Slaveholding offered women more than material wealth. It also empowered them with new kinds of legal authority. Women were considered to be constitutive actors in the creation and maintenance of Jamaica's slave system.

The slave codes that were initially passed in the late seventeenth century, and largely upheld until emancipation in 1834, required every member of free society, irrespective of gender, to participate in the island's draconian disciplinary regime and invested them with strikingly wide-ranging legal authority. Colonists commanded the right to maim or kill enslaved people who were accused of stealing or running away or who "refuseth to submit" to their authority. By contrast, the law treated the murder of a servant as a felony that was punishable by death. The slave codes sharpened the difference between freedom, servitude, and slavery while muting the gendered, religious, ethnic, and class distinctions between members of the free minority population.[13]

II. "Not subject to his control during her life": Protecting women's property claims

The financial and legal advances free and freed women derived via their acquisition of enslaved people as a category of movable property, and whom they then commanded with nearly absolute authority, were in many respects at odds with English legal precedents that strongly favoured men. Married women living in the British Empire were subjected to the harsh English common law of coverture, or femme covert. According to the laws of coverture, husbands assumed the sole legal authority to act for married couples and legally subsumed any possessions their wives held before and during wedlock. Wives were considered to be legal dependents; they could not testify in court, author wills, sign contracts, or engage in credit and debt transactions under their own names.[14]

Widows and women who never married were not subjected to these laws. However, other common law customs, including dower, primogeniture, and entail, sought to keep property in men's hands. Under common law, widows were only entitled to their dower, or one-third of a family estate, for life; they could not then bequeath this portion as they chose. Likewise, primogeniture and entail favoured the eldest sons in families, designating them the sole beneficiaries of family estates. Alternative legal codes did mitigate the harshness of the common law. Married women, for instance, could adopt the status of "femme sole" (with the permission of their husbands), which entitled them to transact business as legally independent persons. Moreover, starting in the mediaeval period, a legal system called equity was established to offer legal remedies to common law. Equity afforded the tools to protect married women's property in the form of the trust and the separate estate. Once a woman's holdings were placed in one of these categories, they could not be touched by her husband. Additionally, the creation of equity or chancery courts meant that common law was not the sole means of settling property disputes.[15]

Equity may have softened the strictures of common law, but it did not alter the premise of the English legal system that was designed to uphold a patriarchal social order rooted in men's monopolisation of land. However, replicating this gendered model in Jamaica proved to be challenging. As the actions of the Jamaica Assembly and colonial property holders suggest, common law customs, especially the legal disabilities that marriage imposed upon women, were ill-suited to cope with the realities of a Caribbean slave society. Local husbands offered their wives far more than the common law of dower allotted, often transferring their entire estates to spouses, whom they also nominated to be sole executors, in perpetuity. Parents likewise displayed little interest in using the common laws of primogeniture or entail to favour elder sons. For families that lacked male heirs, such traditions were impractical, if not impossible, to uphold. Instead, colonists favoured island-born female heirs who possessed the local knowledge and connexions that managing a colonial business required over distant male heirs who resided in Britain.[16]

Jamaica was one of the British colonies that adopted equity law and established a court of chancery. Locals readily took advantage of equity measures, establishing trusts, separate estates, and annuities as a means of ensuring that women's property would remain at their disposal irrespective of their marital status. For instance, Lady Mary Molesworth placed £308 in a trust to pay off the debts of her niece in 1721, gave her an annuity of £46, and insisted that her niece's husband "shall have no power thereof . . . notwithstanding her coverture".[17] Molesworth used equity to countermand coverture, assuring that her legatee would maintain the right to her inheritance. Widows who had experienced the strictures of coverture in the past were especially anxious to protect their assets, and their right to bequeath them, if they remarried. The widow Elizabeth Hargrave, for example, obliquely referred to the separate estate she had established before remarrying in her 1744 will, asserting that she was "empowered" to bequeath the substantial sum of £7,142 in a trust for her daughters "notwithstanding . . . coverture".[18] She stated that the legacy she transferred to her married daughter would be kept "separate" from the daughter's husband and "not subject to his control during her life".[19] Like Molesworth, Hargrave was also careful to use equity measures to safeguard belongings she intended for her female heirs.

The influx of enslaved people into women's estates made colonists especially concerned with securing female-held property. While Molesworth and Hargrave offered money – one sort of movable goods – to their kinswomen and children, other testators turned to equity to maintain control of the captives whom they designated for their female heirs. By mitigating the absolute power husbands asserted over estates vis-à-vis coverture, the trust amplified women's authority as slaveholders, making it possible for them to possess slaves in their own right irrespective of marital status. In 1741, Margaret Tenticow left ten enslaved people, together with the rest of her estate, to her daughter. The mother established a separate estate to prevent her son-in-law "from having any right title or claim" to this legacy.[20] By insisting that her son-in-law "shall have no authority to sell or alienate her inheritance", Tenticow was also proclaiming her daughter's command of enslaved people.[21] In Jamaica, the protection of female property became intimately connected with slavery, wherein women like Tenticow sought to ensure their legal rights as slaveholders irrespective of marital status.

That same year the widow Charity Butler made her married daughter's privilege as a slaveholder even more explicit. Butler placed ten slaves in a trust for her daughter "for her sole and separate use", stating that it was her "express will" that her son-in-law would have "no power to intermeddle with the said negro slaves and that he [would] not receive any benefit from them".[22] These types of bequests accomplished several interrelated legal feats. Following British trends, they used equity to override the gendered legal disabilities experienced by married women, thereby increasing women's legal authority. Doing so undermined older laws that were designed to protect a patriarchal social order. Yet families were often motivated to make these alterations, not because they intended to enhance female rights but because they needed to safeguard their investment in enslaved people from one generation to the next.

III. "One negroe girl Savannah by name": The conflict between personal property and personhood

Jamaica's property laws were designed to maintain a labour system that commodified and profited from the bodies and the work of captive Africans. To accomplish this, the Jamaica Assembly passed laws that stripped enslaved people of all legal rights and turned them into objects. The Jamaica Slave Act – a section of laws borrowed from the 1661 Barbados slave codes – marked captives as a type of movable goods rather than persons. The colonial acts passed in 1683 labelled enslaved people as "negroes" and grouped them together with cattle, horses, and "utensils", and the amended 1684 *Laws of Jamaica* listed slaves with "all other goods and chattels".[23] By designating enslaved people as movable goods or personal estates, colonial lawmakers made it easier for slaveholders to buy, sell, and especially bequeath captives. If a person died intestate, their real estate could be subjected to the aforementioned strictures of common law, whereas personal estate, or movable goods, was not.[24]

Colonial laws complemented local inheritance practices. The majority of Jamaica's will makers designated enslaved people as movable goods and equated them with other sorts of personal estate, including livestock, furniture, cash, jewellery, and clothing. In addition to giving his wife "lands in St. Andrews", for instance, James Pennelerick offered her "one negro woman called Susanna", together with "all my moveable goods", in 1688.[25] The same year, Harstrian Hendrickson associated "negro slaves, servants, chattels" with the half of his "personal estate" that he bequeathed to his wife.[26] Interestingly, Hendrickson distinguished between "negro slaves" and "servants", who were presumably of European descent, but he still treated the servants as movable property.[27] Most colonists, however, did not identify servants as movable goods. Instead, they used phrases like the one written by Thomas Beend, who devised "all lands, negroes, chattels, houses" to his wife, carefully isolating "lands" from "negroes".[28] Similarly, in 1710 "gentleman" John Gourlaw gave a "negro woman Dafne", together with cattle, horses, household goods, money, and outstanding debts, to his wife.[29] The same year the wife of William Hunt would receive a comparable gift of a "negro woman Jane" and a "bald face horse".[30]

As these wills show, husbands categorised enslaved people as especially suitable assets for wives. Parents also treated slaves as an appropriate legacy for children, daughters in particular.[31] Equating the people whom he held in bondage with livestock, Joel White listed "twenty and seven old and young negroes" with the "thirteen horses and mares and five colts" that he then conveyed to his two daughters along with his real estate in 1678.[32] Like White, the widow Katherine Broone combined all of her personal property, including "horned cattle negro indian slaves horses, mares, goods, plate, money" and gave it to her children in her 1681 will.[33] The bequests made by parents like White and Broone turned enslaved people into a crucial form of material support for their children, ensuring the continuity of slaveholding from one generation to the next.

On the surface, these types of bequests seem to mimic European customs of providing personal property to female kin, whereas male heirs received land. On a deeper level, however, the colonial practice of treating slaves like movable goods, and offering them to women, altered European traditions in fundamental ways. Enslaved people were worth far more money than other forms of movable goods. Trevor Burnard has determined that, between 1720 and 1739, the average price of an enslaved man was £25 and the average price of an enslaved woman was £22.[34] Individual inventories, however, show a wide range in the values of individual captives. When the estate of planter Mary Elbridge was probated in 1745, an enslaved man, Eugene, was valued at £64 and a woman, Maria, at £49. The livestock on Elbridge's estate commanded lower prices. A "mare and colt" were worth £10 and sixteen mules were priced at £17 each. The movable goods in Elbridge's house were the least valuable items on her estate. Textiles such as "22 napkins, 25 towels, 12 table clothes" and a chest of drawers were each priced at roughly £3. Enslaved people were by far the most expensive assets on her plantation.[35]

Slaves offered women a potential lifetime of labour, and any children born to enslaved women in the future would also belong to them. In bequeathing captives to female relatives, testators therefore offered them an alternative and lucrative new source of wealth that enhanced women's financial and legal independence on the island. Once in command of enslaved people, women carefully guarded and directed the transmission of their newfound capital, and the accompanying benefits they derived as slaveholders, to future generations of female heirs. Mothers displayed a general preference for daughters over sons in their bequests, especially when it came to distributing captives.[36] In 1720, Mercy Bars transferred several families of enslaved people to her daughter, while she offered only five captives to her son.[37] Eight years later, Catherine Byndloss conveyed slaves that she held in a separate estate in her "own right", giving one enslaved man to her son, while one of her daughters would assume control over a woman named Betty, Betty's three daughters, and another woman named Quasheba. Her other daughter received an enslaved mother and child.[38]

Women like Bars and Byndloss aided in the process of turning slaves into a feminised type of movable good. Yet their treatment of this new kind of property was not strictly monetary in nature. Mothers frequently transferred entire captive families to their daughters. Byndloss, for instance, exploited the kinship connexion between Betty and her daughters to strengthen her emotional tie to her own daughter. As movable property, Betty's family was objectified, commodified, and used to both signify and reinforce the complex emotional bonds between slave-holding parents and their offspring. James Leller used a standard legal phrase to transfer the majority of his estate to his sons in 1700. By contrast, he penned a detailed description of the personal property he left for his daughter, offering her £560, together with sentimental family keepsakes, such as a silver tankard, a sugar box, and her mother's wedding ring. Leller's attention to his daughter may intimate a closer relationship with her. The father also included "one negroe girl Savannah by name" in the litany of objects for his daughter.[39] In doing so, he equated Savannah with his wife's wedding ring, emphasising both the child and the ring as objects that were charged with intimate meanings he and his daughter would understand. Maybe Leller's daughter perceived a close connexion with Savannah, who may have been a similar age as herself. It is even possible that Savannah was also Leller's daughter. The sexual exploitation of enslaved women was an endemic feature of colonial society. Consequently, kinship networks that traversed the boundaries of enslave-ment and liberty were commonplace in Jamaica.

Similarly, in 1718 Mary Walker offered family items, including a silver tankard, "porringers" – small bowls that were used to feed infants – and silverware, to her daughter, who would also receive several enslaved women and children, including "Hannah and her daughters, Flora, Bella, and Gibba".[40] By defining the object status of captives, Leller and Walker participated in the routinised and legally emphasised yet equally destructive process of turning people into property. Such actions underscored the lack of power women like Hannah, Flora, Bella, and Gibba exercised over their own lives. Equated with tankards, bowls, and spoons, they could not give; they were only given to others. If the women were from Africa, then the bequests also were also acts of cultural violence that forced them to assume English names. When the mariner James Neal, for example, bequeathed his estate to his wife and daughter in 1722, he carefully listed the people whom it included – "Dover, Tower Hill Kent Tour Deal Celia Mimbo Venus" – instead of merely referring to his "real and personal estate".[41] It was important for Neal to name his captives. In doing so, he recognised them as individual subjects while simultaneously enforcing their status as objects.

In addition to naming enslaved people, slaveholders acknowledged their kinship ties. The same year that Neal made his will, James Haughton assembled "all plate, chariot and horses" in a bequest to his wife. He also gave her eleven slaves, including "Imoundao and son, Nanny and children Elsy and Flora, Hercules, mulatto Quaco, Marlborough, Dorinda, and her child Betty and Mary a washerwoman".[42] When testators like Haughton referred to the familial connections between Imoundao and her son, Nanny and her children Elsy and Flora, and Dorinda and her child Betty, they asserted the principle of *partus sequitur ventrem* (offspring follows the womb), which English colonies adopted in an effort to make slavery heritable. According to this custom, which was never officially codified in law in Jamaica, the children born to enslaved women followed the status of the mother irrespective of the father's legal status. Thus, Haughton used his will not only to claim the mothers but also to assert his ownership and therefore his right to transfer their children to his family members. It was a means for him to enslavement as a heritable status.[43]

Testators leveraged slaves as personal property, thereby confirming the boundaries between legal freedom and bondage. Cumulatively, their actions contributed to the expansion and enforcement of Jamaica's slave labour system. Yet colonial wills also disclose a certain ambivalence surrounding these processes. The practice of naming individual captives, as well as the seepage of their kinship connexions into legal documents that were ostensibly intended to describe belongings, exposes the fraught nature of the enslaver-enslaved relationship. In naming specific captives and recognising their family ties, colonists implicitly acknowledged the fundamental difference between enslaved people and other kinds of movable goods. While it might be argued that enslavers referred to individual slaves as a means of reinforcing their property claims, doing so was not legally necessary. Testators knew that their estates would be probated after their death and that enslaved people would be listed by name in the probated inventories. Instead, such bequests hint at the impossibility of fully translating the de jure status of an enslaved person as a commodity, or a movable good, into de facto lived reality.

Highlighting the tensions within sources like colonial wills does not imply that slaveholders were humane. It is doubtful that colonists like James Haughton agonised over the ethical implications of their actions. Even after the antislavery movement put slaveholders on the defensive at the end of the eighteenth century, Jamaican colonists rarely expressed moral qualms about slavery. Rather, these fraught documents advance our understanding of how individuals drove the growth of Atlantic slavery, family by family, bequest by bequest. They also disclose the fragility that was embedded in the legal practices that justified slaveholding. This instability created possibilities for enslaved people to better their own conditions. As much as references like the one to "Imoundao and son, Nanny and children Elsy and Flora, Hercules, mulatto Quaco, Marlborough, Dorinda, and her child Betty" (Haughton; see previous discussion) confirm the status of these women and children as material goods, they might also offer rare glimpses of the covert, and perhaps overt, actions of enslaved people, flickering beneath the surface of the prosaic and brief sentences in wills. Such terse statements are often the only evidence of their lives that has survived – yet another facet of the violence of Atlantic slavery.[44]

On paper, all slaveholders, male and female alike, wielded absolute sovereignty over enslaved people, but daily life was messier, and bondage remained a highly unequal yet negotiated relationship. If the women like Imoundao, Nanny, and Dorinda wielded influence with their owners, then it is possible that they shaped the terms of their bondage. Some may have promised compliance in return for preferred treatment or for keeping their families intact upon the death of an owner. Slavery sought to negate the kinship ties between captives, and in the British Empire *partus sequitur ventrem* erased the genealogical link between father and child. This does not mean, however, that the enslaved were unable to manoeuvre and manipulate dire circumstances to their advantage. Opportunities may have been slim, but they existed. And slaveholder wills may unwittingly reveal the field wherein these otherwise obscured actions took place.

Notes

1 Jamaica, Island Record Office (IRO), Will of Mary Penlerick, 1716, vol. 14.
2 IRO, Will of James Pennelerick, 1668, vol. 1.
3 IRO, Will of Mary Penlerick, 1716, vol. 14.
4 Carla Pestana, *The English Conquest of Jamaica: Oliver Cromwell's Bid for Empire*, Cambridge 2017 [Harvard University Press].
5 See Edward Long, *The History of Jamaica*, vol. 1, London 1774, p. 376; Richard S. Dunn, *Sugar and Slaves: The Rise of the Planter Class in the English West Indies, 1624–1713*, Williamsburg, VA and Chapel Hill, NC 1972 [University of North Carolina Press], p. 155; Trevor Burnard, *Planters, Merchants, and Slaves: Plantation Societies in British America, 1650–1820*, Chicago 2015 [University of Chicago Press], pp. 68–70; David Eltis, "The Volume and Structure of the Transatlantic Slave Trade: A Reassessment", in: *WMQ* 58, 1 (2001), pp. 17–46; Vincent Brown, *The Reaper's Garden: Death and Power in the World of Atlantic Slavery*, Cambridge, MA 2008; Christer Petley, *Slaveholders in Jamaica: Colonial Society and Culture During the Era of Abolition*, New York 2009 [Harvard University Press].
6 Burnard, *Planters, Merchants, and Slaves*, 97–100; Trevor Burnard and John Garrigus, *The Plantation Machine: Atlantic Capitalism in French Saint-Domingue and British Jamaica*, Philadelphia 2016 [University of Pennsylvania Press]; David Barry Gaspar, "A Dangerous Spirit of Liberty: Slave Rebellion in the West Indies in the 1730s", in: Laurent Dubois and Julius Scott (eds.), *Origins of the Black Atlantic*, New York 2009 [Routledge], pp. 11–25.
7 J. R. McNeill, *Mosquito Empires, Ecology and War in the Greater Caribbean, 1620–1914*, Cambridge 2010 [Cambridge University Press], pp. 48–49; pp. 51–52; Dunn, *Sugar and Slaves*, pp. 301–303; Brown, Reaper's Garden, p. 17; Trevor Burnard, "A Failed Settler Society: Marriage and Demographic Failure in Early Jamaica", in: *Journal of Social History* XXVIII (1994), p. 67, pp. 69–70; The majority of Jamaica's African population came from Bight of Biafra, the Gold Coast, West Central Africa, Sierra Leone, the Bight of Benin, and Senegambia. See: Simon P. Newman, Michael L. Deason, Yannis P. Pitsiladis, Antonio Salas and Vincent A. Macaulay, "The West African Ethnicity of the Enslaved in Jamaica", in: *Slavery & Abolition* 34, 3 (2013), pp. 376–400, here pp. 378–379.
8 See Anonymus, *The Importance of Jamaica to Great Britain Considered*, London 1740; Charles Leslie, A New History of Jamaica: From the Earliest Accounts, to the Taking of Porto Bello by Vice-Admiral Vernon, London 1740; Nicholas Beasley, *Christian Ritual and the Creation of British Slave Societies, 1650–1780*, Athens 2009 [University of Georgia Press].
9 The Laws of Jamaica, *Passed by the Assembly and Confirmed by His Majesty in Council*, London 17 April 1684. See also: David Barry Gaspar, " 'Rigid and Inclement:' Origins of the Jamaica Slave Laws of the Seventeenth Century", in: Christopher L. Tomlins and Bruce Mann (eds.), *The Many Legalities of Early America*, Chapel Hill 2001 [University of North Carolina Press]; Hilary McD Beckles, "A 'Riotous and Unruly Lot': Irish Indentured Servants and Freemen in the English West Indies, 1644–1713", in: *WMQ* 47, 4 (1990), pp. 502–533; Edward Rugemer, "The Development of Mastery and Race in the Comprehensive Slave Codes of the Greater Caribbean during the Seventeenth Century", in: *WMQ* 70, 3 (2013), pp. 429–458.
10 Throughout this chapter, I refer to women who held legally free status, meaning they were not indentured servants or slaves, as "women," "free and freed women", or female colonists. Women were normally categorised by their marital status in legal records. Hence, I indicate if a woman was married, widowed, or never married. However, colonial record keepers were less scrupulous about categorising women by race, ethnicity, and religion. During the first half of the eighteenth century, recognisably modern racial categories were still in formation. Additionally, some women of African ancestry intentionally obscured their heritage in legal documents as a means of avoiding restrictions the colony imposed on free people of colour. Achieving "white" status could yield social and economic benefits for free women of colour and their children. For these reasons, I do not make assumptions about a woman's race unless it is identified in a record. For more on the subject of race in the early modern Anglo-Atlantic world, see Jennifer Morgan,

"'Some Could Suckle Over Their Shoulder': Male Travelers, Female Bodies, and the Gendering of Racial Ideology, 1500-1770", in: *WMQ* 54, 1 (1997), pp. 167–192; Roxann Wheeler, *The Complexion of Race: Categories of Difference in Eighteenth-Century British Culture*, Philadelphia 2000 [University of Pennsylvania Press]; Daniel Livesay, *Children of Uncertain Fortune: Mixed-Race Jamaicans in Britain and the Atlantic Family, 1733–1833*, Williamsburg, VA and Chapel Hill, NC 2018 [University of North Carolina Press], pp. 38–41; Rana Hogarth, *Medicalizing Blackness: Making Racial Difference in the Atlantic World, 1780–1840*, Chapel Hill 2017 [University of North Carolina Press].

11 Nearly eighty percent (648 of the 825) of the estates owned by women that were probated between 1674 and 1765 included slaves. See Christine Walker, *Jamaica Ladies: Female Slaveholders and the Creation of Britain's Atlantic Empire*, Chapel Hill forthcoming, June 2020, p. 201. For a survey of the scholarship that has been done on female slaveholding in the Atlantic world, see Christine Walker, "Female Slave Owners", in: Trevor Burnard (ed.), *Oxford Bibliographies in Atlantic History* [Oxford University Press], www.oxfordbibliographies.com, 2015 (accessed 06 September 2019).

12 For a comparison of the total estate values of men's and women's probated inventories, see Walker, *Jamaica Ladies*, p. 21.

13 For a more detailed analysis of women's wealth on the island, see Walker, *Jamaica Ladies*, p. 21 and p. 201. The 1684 legal codes distinguished between servants and slaves by invoking the new racial category of "white" when referring to servants. Colonial lawmakers added a deficiency clause requiring slaveholders to employ "white" male servants in proportion to the number of African captives they owned. The Laws of Jamaica, *Passed by the Assembly and Confirmed by His Majesty in Council*; see also Diana Paton, "Punishment, Crime, and the Bodies of Slaves in Eighteenth-Century Jamaica", in: *Journal of Social History* 34, 4 (2001), pp. 923–954, here pp. 923, 927, 931.

14 Marylynn Salmon, *Women and the Law of Property in Early America*, Chapel Hill, NC 1986 [The University of North Carolina Press]; Marylynn Salmon, "Women and Property in South Carolina: The Evidence from Marriage Settlements, 1730 to 1830", in: *WMQ* 39, 4 (1982), pp. 655–685; Amy Louise Erickson, *Women and Property in Early Modern England*, 1993, London and New York 1995 [Routledge]; Linda Sturtz, *Within Her Power: Propertied Women in Colonial Virginia*, New York 2002 [Routledge]; Carole Shammas, *Inheritance in America from Colonial Times to the Present*, New York 1997 [Frontier Press]; Joanne Bailey, "Favoured or Oppressed? Married Women, Property, and 'Coverture' in England, 1660–1800", in: *Continuity and Change* XVII (2002), 351.

15 Common law covered a broad range of legal subjects, from individual rights to criminal law, and tended to follow precedent instead of statute, whereas chancellors, rather than juries, decided cases in equity courts that had gained jurisdiction over trusts, land law, fraud, security for money lending, charities, the administration of estates imperilled by mental illness, and the guardianship of infants. These two systems of law were perceived as being in opposition to each other. See William Blackstone, *Commentaries on the Laws of England*, Book 3, Chapter 27, London 1765–1769, www.lonang.com/exlibris/blackstone/bla-327.htm (accessed 30 October 2019); Alison Tait, "The Beginning of the End of Coverture: A Reappraisal of the Married Woman's Separate Estate", in: *Yale Journal of Law and Feminism* XXVI (2014), p. 216.

16 For more on husbands' bequests to wives in Jamaica, see Walker, *Jamaica Ladies* [page number to be added].

17 IRO, Will of Mary Molesworth, 1721, vol. 15.

18 IRO, Will of Elizabeth Etough, Kingston, 1744, vol. 24 (Etough had remarried; prior to her remarriage she was "the widow Elizabeth Hargrave").

19 Ibid.

20 IRO, Will of Margaret Tenticow, 1752, vol. 28.

21 Ibid.

22 IRO, Will of Charity Butler, 1744, vol. 24.

23 The Laws of Jamaica, *Passed by the Assembly and Confirmed by His Majesty in Council*, London 23 February 1683, pp. 171–192; "An Act for the Better Ordering of Slaves", in: *The Laws of Jamaica, Passed by the Assembly and Confirmed by His Majesty in Council*, London 17 April 1684, pp. 140–141.

24 The Laws of Jamaica, *Passed by the Assembly and Confirmed by His Majesty in Council*; The Laws of Jamaica, *Passed by the Assembly and Confirmed by His Majesty in Council*, 1684. See also: Rugemer, "The Development of Mastery and Race"; McD Beckles, "A 'Riotous and Unruly Lot'", pp. 502–533; Gaspar, "Rigid and Inclement".
25 IRO, Will of James Pennelerick, 1668, vol. 1.
26 IRO, Will of Harstrian Hendrickson, 1668, vol. 1.
27 Ibid.
28 IRO, Will of Thomas Beend, 1678, vol. 1.
29 IRO, Will of John Gourlaw, 1710, vol. 13.
30 IRO, Will of William Hunt, 1710, 13.
31 For a comparison of parental bequests to sons and daughters, see Walker, *Jamaica Ladies*, p. 191.
32 IRO, Will of Joel White, 1678, vol. 1.
33 IRO, Will of Katherine Broone, 1681, vols. 3, 4, 5.
34 For more on the prices of slaves in Jamaica, see Trevor Burnard, "Evaluating Gender in Early Jamaica, 1674–1784", in: *The History of the Family* 12, 2 (2007), pp. 81–91.
35 Jamaica Archives, Inventory of Mary Elbridge, 1745, vol. 25, fol. 132.
36 The distribution of enslaved people by mothers to sons and daughters is explored in: Walker, *Jamaica Ladies*, p. 198.
37 IRO, Will of Mercy Bars, 1720, vol. 15.
38 IRO, Will of Catherine Byndloss, 1728, vol. 17.
39 IRO, Will of James Leller, 1700, vol. 1.
40 IRO, Will of Mary Walker, 1718, vol. 15.
41 IRO, Will of James Neal, 1722, vol. 16.
42 IRO, Will of James Haughton, 1722, vol. 22.
43 For more on the cultural violence experienced by enslaved women, and on *partus sequitur ventrem* in particular, see Jennifer L. Morgan, *Laboring Women: Reproduction and Gender in New World Slavery*, Philadelphia 2004 [University of Pennsylvania Press]; Marisa Fuentes, *Dispossessed Lives: Enslaved Women, Violence, and the Archive*, Philadelphia 2016 [University of Pennsylvania Press]; Jennifer L. Morgan, "Partus sequitur ventrem: Law, Race, and Reproduction in Colonial Slavery", in: *Small Axe* 22, 1 (2018), pp. 1–17; Kathleen M. Brown, *Good Wives, Nasty Wenches, and Anxious Patriarchs: Gender, Race, and Power in Colonial Virginia*, Williamsburg, VA and Chapel Hill, NC 1995 [University of North Carolina Press].
44 For more on archival erasure, see Morgan, *Laboring Women*; Fuentes, *Dispossessed Lives*.

Sources

Anonymous, *The Importance of Jamaica to Great Britain Considered*, London 1740.

Blackstone, William, *Commentaries on the Laws of England, Book 3*, Chapter 27, London 1765–1769, www.lonang.com/exlibris/blackstone/bla-327.htm (accessed 30 October 2019).

Leslie, Charles, *A New History of Jamaica: From the Earliest Accounts, to the Taking of Porto Bello by Vice-Admiral Vernon*, London, 1740.

The Laws of Jamaica, *Passed by the Assembly and Confirmed by his Majesty in Council*, February 23, 1683, London 1683.

The Laws of Jamaica, *Passed by the Assembly and Confirmed by his Majesty in Council*, April 17, 1684, London 1684.

Jamaica, Island Record Office (IRO):

Will of Catherine Byndloss, 1728, vol. 17, fol. 235, IRO.

Will of Charity Butler, 1744, vol. 24, fol. 196, IRO.

Will of Elizabeth Etough, Kingston, 1744, vol. 24, fol. 100, IRO.

Will of Harstrian Hendrickson, 1668, vol. 1, IRO.

Will of James Haughton, 1722, vol. 22, IRO.

Will of James Leller, 1700, vol. 1, IRO.

Will of James Neal, 1722, vol. 16, IRO.

Will of James Pennelerick, 1668, vol. 1, IRO.
Will of Joel White, 1678, vol. 1, IRO.
Will of John Gourlaw, 1710, vol. 13, IRO.
Will of Katherine Broone, 1681, vols. 3, 4, 5, fol. 20, IRO.
Will of Margaret Tenticow, 1752, vol. 28, fol. 149, IRO.
Will of Mary Molesworth, 1721, vol. 15, fol. 230, IRO.
Will of Mary Penlerick, 1716, vol. 14, fol. 228, IRO.
Will of Mary Walker, 1718, vol. 15, fol. 69, IRO.
Will of Mercy Bars, 1720, vol. 15, IRO.
Will of Thomas Beend, 1678, vol. 1, IRO.
Will of William Hunt, 1710, 13, IRO.
(if no page numbers are indicated, the sources are unpaginated.).
Jamaica Archives (JA).
Inventory of Mary Elbridge, 1745, vol. 25, fol. 132, JA.

Bibliography

Bailey, Joanne, "Favoured or Oppressed? Married Women, Property, and 'Coverture' in England, 1660–1800", in: *Continuity and Change* XVII (2002), 351–372.

Beasley, Nicholas, *Christian Ritual and the Creation of British Slave Societies, 1650–1780*, Athens 2009 [University of Georgia Press].

Beckles, Hilary McD, "A 'riotous and unruly lot': Irish Indentured Servants and Freemen in the English West Indies, 1644–1713", in: *WMQ* 47, 4 (1990), pp. 502–533.

Brown, Kathleen M., *Good Wives, Nasty Wenches, and Anxious Patriarchs: Gender, Race, and Power in Colonial Virginia*, Williamsburg VA and Chapel Hill, NC 1995 [University of North Carolina Press].

Brown, Vincent, *The Reaper's Garden: Death and Power in the World of Atlantic Slavery*, Cambridge, MA 2008 [Harvard University Press].

Burnard, Trevor, "A Failed Settler Society: Marriage and Demographic Failure in Early Jamaica", in: *Journal of Social History* XXVIII (1994), pp. 63–82.

———*Planters, Merchants, and Slaves: Plantation Societies in British America, 1650–1820*, Chicago 2015 [University of Chicago Press].

Burnard, Trevor and John Garrigus, *The Plantation Machine: Atlantic Capitalism in French Saint-Domingue and British Jamaica*, Philadelphia 2016 [University of Pennsylvania Press].

Dunn, Richard S., *Sugar and Slaves: The Rise of the Planter Class in the English West Indies, 1624–1713*, Williamsburg, VA and Chapel Hill, NC 1972 [University of North Carolina Press].

Eltis, David, "The Volume and Structure of the Transatlantic Slave Trade: A Reassessment", in: *William and Mary Quarterly* 58, 1 (2001), pp. 17–46.

Erickson, Amy Louise, *Women and Property in Early Modern England*, London 1993 and New York 1995 [Routledge].

Fuentes, Marisa, *Dispossessed Lives: Enslaved Women, Violence, and the Archive*, Philadelphia 2016 [University of Pennsylvania Press].

Gaspar, David Barry, "'Rigid and Inclement:' Origins of the Jamaica Slave Laws of the Seventeenth Century", in: Christopher L. Tomlins and Bruce Mann (eds.), *The Many Legalities of Early America*, Chapel Hill 2001 [University of North Carolina Press].

———"A Dangerous Spirit of Liberty: Slave Rebellion in the West Indies in the 1730s", in: Laurent Dubois and Julius Scott (eds.), *Origins of the Black Atlantic*, New York 2009 [Routledge], pp. 11–25.

Hogarth, Rana, *Medicalizing Blackness: Making Racial Difference in the Atlantic World, 1780–1840*, Chapel Hill 2017 [University of North Carolina Press].

Livesay, Daniel, *Children of Uncertain Fortune: Mixed-Race Jamaicans in Britain and the Atlantic Family, 1733–1833*, Williamsburg, VA and Chapel Hill, NC 2018 [University of North Carolina Press].

McNeill, J. R., *Mosquito Empires, Ecology and War in the Greater Caribbean, 1620–1914*, Cambridge 2010 [Cambridge University Press].

Morgan, Jennifer L., "'Some Could Suckle over Their Shoulder': Male Travelers, Female Bodies, and the Gendering of Racial Ideology, 1500-I770", in: *WMQ* 54, 1 (1997), pp. 167–192.

———*Laboring Women: Reproduction and Gender in New World Slavery*, Philadelphia 2004 [University of Pennsylvania Press].

———"Partus Sequitur Ventrem: Law, Race, and Reproduction in Colonial Slavery", in: *Small Axe* 22, 1 (2018), pp. 1–17.

Newman, Simon P., Michael L. Deason, Yannis P. Pitsiladis, Antonio Salas and Vincent A. Macaulay, "The West African Ethnicity of the Enslaved in Jamaica", in: *Slavery & Abolition* 34, 3 (2013), pp. 376–400.

Paton, Diana, "Punishment, Crime, and the Bodies of Slaves in Eighteenth-Century Jamaica", in: *Journal of Social History* 34, 4 (2001), pp. 923–954.

Pestana, Carla, *The English Conquest of Jamaica: Oliver Cromwell's Bid for Empire*, Cambridge 2017 [Harvard University Press].

Petley, Christer, *Slaveholders in Jamaica: Colonial Society and Culture during the Era of Abolition*, New York 2009 [Routledge].

Rugemer, Edward, "The Development of Mastery and Race in the Comprehensive Slave Codes of the Greater Caribbean during the Seventeenth Century", in: *WMQ* 70, 3 (2013), pp. 429–458.

Salmon, Marylynn, "Women and Property in South Carolina: The Evidence from Marriage Settlements, 1730 to 1830", in: *WMQ* 39, 4 (1982), pp. 655–685.

———*Women and the Law of Property in Early America*, Chapel Hill, NC 1986 [The University of North Carolina Press].

Shammas, Carole, *Inheritance in America from Colonial Times to the Present*, New York 1997 [Frontier Press].

Sturtz, Linda, *Within Her Power; Propertied Women in Colonial Virginia*, New York 2002 [Routledge].

Tait, Alison, "The Beginning of the End of Coverture: A Reappraisal of the Married Woman's Separate Estate", in: *Yale Journal of Law and Feminism* XXVI (2014), pp. 165–216.

Walker, Christine, "Female Slave Owners", in: Trevor Burnard (ed.), *Oxford Bibliographies in Atlantic History*, September 2019 [Oxford University Press], www.oxfordbibliographies.com, 2015.

———*Jamaica Ladies: Female Slaveholders and the Creation of Britain's Atlantic Empire*, Chapel Hill June 2020 [University of North Carolina Press].

Wheeler, Roxann, *The Complexion of Race: Categories of Difference in Eighteenth-Century British Culture*, Philadelphia 2000 [University of Pennsylvania Press].

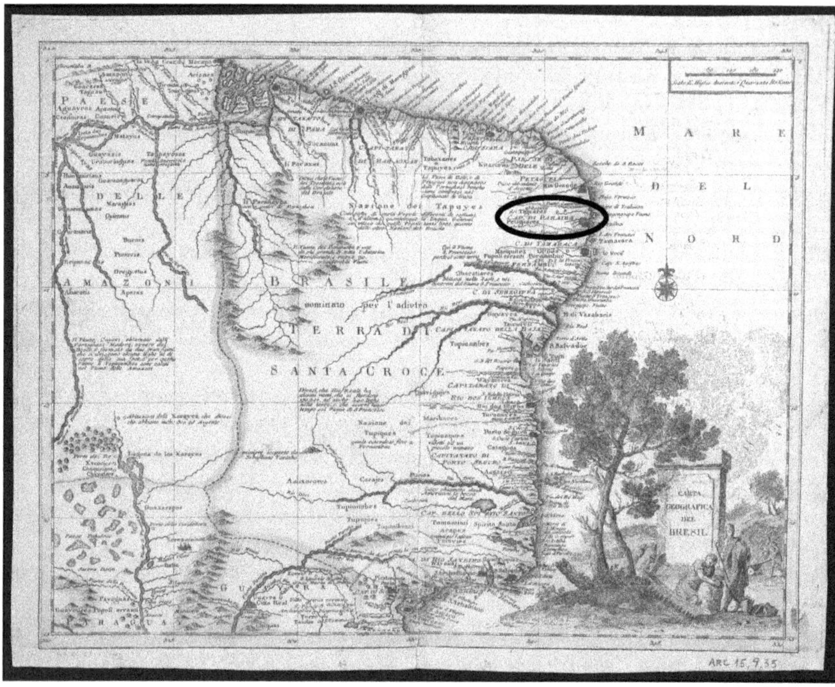

FIGURE 9.1 Map of Brazil, showing the location of Paraíba, *Carta geografica del Bresil*, *c.* 1740.

Source: Biblioteca Nacional (Brasil), Biblioteca digital Luso-Brasileira, Acervo da Fundação Rio de Janeiro, Brazil, public domain, ARC.030,02,012 - Cartografia, http://acervo.bndigital.bn.br/sophia/index.asp?codigo_sophia=2282, http://objdigital.bn.br/objdigital2/acervo_digital/div_cartografia/cart551648/cart551648.html (accessed 25.08.2020, 10:15 CET).

9

LAND, SLAVES, AND HONOUR

Women's ownership and possession in colonial Brazil (Paraíba)

Luisa Stella de Oliveira Coutinho Silva

ABSTRACT

Portuguese overseas expansion extended to many places around the globe. Different cultures from America, Africa, and Europe encountered each other during the colonisation of Brazil, one part of the Portuguese Empire. Recent developments in feminist legal history, women's history, and postcolonial theory focus on women's agency and seek to transcend the description of women within fixed racialised stereotypes of the nineteenth and early twentieth centuries. Based on primary sources from Portuguese and Brazilian archives, an interdisciplinary approach to legal history in respect to women during the colonisation of Brazil is adopted here, comparing these documents with the norms in force during colonisation. The archival sources, such as donation charters and requests of royal confirmations, reveal that women were owners and administrators of land. This mere fact compels us to expand the traditional image of the colonial northeast of Brazil, seemingly occupied only by large mills and their purported solely male owners. In some captaincies (administrative units), the number of requests for royal confirmations of women's land possessions was as common as those made by men. In addition, wills demonstrate that women were owners not only of land but also of various movable goods and especially of slaves. The latter counted neither as a mobile nor an immobile good but formed a third category of property – *semoventes*, "half-movables".

I. Introduction

During the Portuguese overseas expansion, different cultures from America, Africa, and Europe clashed during the colonisation of Brazil. As a consequence, different normative orders coexisted beside each other. Existing side by side with the *ius commune*, Portuguese norms expanded on a global scale in the sixteenth century, also reaching Paraíba, in the northeast of Brazil.[1] After the independence of Brazil in

1822, scholars from the nineteenth and early twentieth centuries described women in terms of racialised stereotypes, which idealised women according to fixed gender roles.[2] During the last thirty years, feminist jurisprudence,[3] women's history,[4] and postcolonial theory[5] have fostered a different interpretation of agency of women in the colonies and unveiled the limitations of this previous understanding.[6] Based on this combined methodological approach, and by looking at primary sources, the chapter will analyse the different kinds of ownership and possession available to women principally of a certain "status" and "condition", frequently from a social elite, during the colonisation of Brazil in the captaincy of Paraíba.[7]

Based on documents from Portuguese and Brazilian archives, I will consider women's access to land and their options to accumulate wealth and how they could protect it. A key research question is, How do women appear as agents in wills, donations, royal charters, and general requests to the king (*requerimentos*) between the 1580s (the years of the Portuguese military conquest of Paraíba) and 1822 (the year of Brazilian independence)? Furthermore, the study of women's complaints in cases of "rape" (which had a different meaning than today) sheds light on contemporary ideas of virtue and honour. Moreover, in situations in which women were not formally married, or lived in concubinage (*concubinato*), a term summarising different types of cohabitation, how could they and how did they try to protect their property? How could a woman protect the inheritance of an illegitimate child? Based on these sources and questions, the chapter will show that women actively and of their own accord used a variety of tools of the normative system in support of their own causes in the captaincy of Paraíba.

II. Possessing land: The *cartas de data e sesmaria*

During the colonisation of Brazil, the Portuguese administration divided the land into captaincies, a system that was first applied in different places of the Portuguese Empire, such as Madeira and the Azores Islands. But in contrast to these sites, Brazil was much bigger and populated by natives. This presented difficulties previously unknown.

In colonial Brazil, the captaincies were handed over to hereditary *donatários* by the Portuguese king. The *donatários* did not own these lands but exercised administrative and jurisdictional rights over them. They had the obligation and responsibility to populate and develop them in an economic sense, mostly by means of their own resources. To enable this, the land was divided into land grants called *sesmarias* based on an institution of agricultural law from 1375 (*lei das sesmarias*), reproduced in the *Ordenações Afonsinas*,[8] the compilation of Portuguese laws from the fifteenth century. According to further developments of the institution in the *Ordenações Manuelinas*[9] and *Filipinas*,[10] in the sixteenth and seventeenth centuries, as soon as a *sesmaria* was granted, the person who received the donation was obliged to cultivate it. This law reflected the shortage of certain goods, such as wheat, as a result of natural catastrophes and the plague. Feeding the subjects was key and crucial, so the Portuguese authorities desperately needed landowners to produce agricultural goods.[11] The colonisers implemented the *sesmarias* system in the colony along with the Portuguese normative system.

So how could one precisely obtain possession of a plot of land in Brazil? The process to obtain a grant over a parcel of land in the colony required an official inquiry of the interested party to the captain and governor of the captaincy. This was followed by a thorough investigation of the request by the crown judge (*ouvidor*), according to issued edicts, and, depending on the case, testimonials of witnesses and the applicant's certificates. Based on the outcome of this process, the *sesmaria* would or would not be granted. If awarded, it was registered in the governmental secretariat. After this procedure, the beneficiary had a year to request royal confirmation through the Lisbon Overseas Council (*Conselho Ultramarino*), the Portuguese council that dealt with overseas issues. The beneficiary of the land would then have five years to make the land productive.[12] If the person in possession of the land did not succeed in rendering it productive during this time, they could lose the land grant, as the plot would be considered vacant (*devolutas*). The captains were in charge of controlling the productivity and administering and exercising jurisdiction in the colonial land on behalf of the king, if necessary. King Filipe II of Portugal (r. 1598–1621), for instance, issued a statute in 1609 and gave orders to the new administrator of Paraíba (Francisco Coelho de Carvalho, who governed the captaincy of Paraíba as *provedor* between 1608 and 1612) to report the number of inhabitants and the productivity of the lands.[13]

The first *sesmaria* in the captaincy of Paraíba was granted by Martim Leitão, the crown judge (*ouvidor*) of the captaincy of Bahia and responsible for the conquest of Paraíba in 1585, and by João Tavares, the first provisory governor of the recently conquered Paraíba, even before the captaincy's recognition by the king, to João Affonso Pamplona on 10 January 1586.[14] Leitão and Tavares conceded the land for the construction of a sugar plantation at the request of the beneficiary himself on the grounds that he had supported the conquest of Paraíba against the natives at the risk of his own life and expenses. As a major export, sugar cane plantations were the gold mines of the Portuguese colonial economy, and the captaincy of Paraíba had the perfect soil for growing sugar plants.

*II.a Women and possession of land (*sesmarias*)*

However, not only men claimed the possession of land, or *sesmarias*. In Brazil, a small number of women (unmarried, married, and widowed) also possessed land. In some captaincies, claims by women were as common as requests for royal confirmations of *sesmarias* by men. However, this was not so in Paraíba. Between 1586 and 1624 – before the Dutch occupation – the captains granted twenty-four *sesmarias* in the captaincy of Paraíba.[15] Of these grants, only one was appointed to a woman, Izabel Caldeira, who claimed the *sesmaria* of Restinga Island (also known as Conceição Island and Camboa) as her daughter's dowry. Izabel had been the wife of Manoel de Azevedo, who must have been the first ombudsman of the royal estate of the captaincy of Paraíba. Archival documents show that Manoel first built a camp to supply himself and the city and then a fort to protect the land, preventing raids by the natives. The land had not been previously granted to him – he had simply taken control of it on his own account and populated the island (*povoou a ilha*), making it impossible to inherit it automatically.[16] The island of Restinga was located on the Paraíba River, in front of the river bar ("*boca do Rio Parahiba de fronte da Barra do Cabedelo*").[17] After Frutuoso Barbosa (gov. 1582–1594) assumed the position of captain of the captaincy, the most important fortification was dismantled, which weakened the protection of the fort. Without protection, the island was left to "the mercy of the enemy", as the same document states. The natives destroyed what had been built by Izabel's husband and killed him and also one of his sons. Izabel became a widow with five daughters and two sons to support. She claimed the donation of the island of Camboa for herself as an inheritance, as she had been the wife of Manoel de Azevedo and his successor, and in respect and recognition of the services rendered by Azevedo in the conquest of the captaincy of Paraíba. Izabel claimed possession of the land in her name, referencing the protection of a widow's inheritance as it was laid down in the law.[18] As was a quite common argument, which we will see later, Izabel argued in addition that the land would serve a "greater good", as it would function as the dowry of one or two of her daughters.[19] The granting of the land to Izabel in 1586 should be understood as recognition of her difficult situation as a widow with several children and the strategically important position of the territory and as a reward for the brave actions of her husband.

The captain agreed to the donation of the island "until the end of time" (*para todo o sempre*)[20] to Izabel Caldeira in acknowledgement of the heroic deeds of Manoel in the early years of the colonisation of Paraíba. The registration and demarcation of geographical borders of the donation were made in the *Livro dos Registos da Fazenda de Sua Majestade* on 11 April 1596.[21] Later, the land was passed on to Izabel's son-in-law, Manoel Homem da Sylva, as the dowry of her daughter by a legal act of transfer of domain (*carta de trespaçassão*). In this case, the domain, the right of administration, and usufructus of the *sesmaria* were transferred.

After the Dutch occupation in northeastern Brazil ended in 1654, several other women asked the king for confirmation of *sesmarias*. In 1717, Clara Spindola claimed a *sesmaria* where her cattle and horses grazed. She argued that she was the legitimate mistress (*senhora*) of the land, which meant that she had occupied it according to the law, and needed the king's confirmation. This information is very important because according to the *ius commune*'s principle of *possidentis*, in claims the position of the possessor is fundamental: Whoever retained the land in good faith would have more chance to stay in possession of the property.[22] Because she was a *moça donzela* (which meant a virgin, honourable, and suitable to marry well), she claimed the land to use as her dowry on the occasion of her marriage (*tomar estado*). But she also challenged the geographical extension of the *sesmaria*. According to her, the land measured three leagues (a linear measure that amounted to 6.172 metres per league) in length and one in width, but Bento Araújo, her neighbour, alleged to the king that the limits were extrapolated. After two years, in 1719, the king confirmed her concession, but she had the obligation to take possession, measure, demarcate, and pay the obligatory tithe. The confirmation was written down in the royal chancellery. This document proves that Clara acted as a young and unmarried woman who owned movable property (cattle and horses) and who – in her own name – requested the concession of the land she used to graze her cattle from the monarch.[23]

On 23 January 1806, Jozefa Francisca de Medeiros demanded from the king the confirmation of a *carta de data e sesmaria*, a letter of concession of the land with its precise location. The land had been given to her by the governor of Paraíba, Luiz Motta Feo, "by his pure and irrevocable will" (*de pura e irrevogável vontade*). According to the *carta de data e sesmaria*, Jozefa lived in the village of Pombal and had an abundance of cattle but no land to breed them upon. She petitioned some land in provincial Cariri from the king.[24] The land mentioned was part of the backwoods (*sertão*), a region between the littoral areas of the coast and the northwest of Brazil. This region was inhabited by the Tapuias, who were considered to be "wild Indians" of Brazil, in contrast with the Tupi, who used to cooperate more with the Portuguese colonisers. It was important for the Portuguese administration to dominate this territory. For this reason, the king donated land in this area to better control the Indians and to facilitate access to the interior of Brazil.

In total, from 1580 to 1822, around 1,178 *sesmarias* were granted to persons in the captaincy of Paraíba. Fifty-four of these land grants were requested only by women, while forty-three were requested by women and men together.[25] Unfortunately, the documents give no evidence with regard to the status and condition of the applicants, but presumably they originated in the local elite. Furthermore, seen sociologically from a micro perspective, the approach to the topic reveals female agency of women of all ages and status, but statistically their total numbers as possessors of land were low. Less than five percent of *sesmarias* were accorded to women alone. Women who claimed land appear to have been either not married (yet) or widowed. For women, the possession of real estate donated by the Portuguese king was legally possible but remained comparably rare.

III. Transferring and inheriting: Succession, wills, "charters of halves", and dowry contracts

The general succession rights in the Portuguese Empire were regulated in the *Ordenações Filipinas*, although much commented on in the *doutrina comum*, and offered two ways to inherit property, mobile or immobile. The first was the succession without a testament (*abinstestado*), which meant that the inheritance had to follow a succession line established by the law. First, the sons and daughters inherited equally. Then came the descendants of the offspring, followed by the parents of the deceased. Finally, the wife, in the case of the death of the husband, or the husband, in the case of the death of the wife, would inherit only if the deceased had no relative to the tenth degree, counted according to civil law.[26] The second option was to draw a testament in which the deceased could distribute only one-third of their property according to their own wishes.

Marriages and the division of patrimony chosen in the marriage were essential in the characterisation of the patrimony left by a deceased person. There were two main possibilities: Charters of halves (*cartas de ametade*) and dowry. These were the two options a couple had to divide or share property and possessions within marriage and would influence the division of the couple's possessions in case of one spouse's death.

The most common division was the charters of halves (*cartas de ametade*), according to which both spouses were heirs of one another if one of them died. This meant that because of their communion, the surviving spouse retained as co-owner (not as heir) for half of the couple's property as well as possession of the total property until it was divided with the heirs. This option was the general rule in the kingdom.[27] By contrast, the dowry contract (written as well as oral), as part of a premarital agreement, characterised certain goods and objects that were given to the bride by her family as material and economic support and defined explicitly as her dowry. This dowry was kept separate from the property the couple owned in common and generally was to be returned intact to the widow after the husband's death – which meant it did not count as the inheritance of the husband. If she died first, her heirs inherited the dowry. In case she had no heirs, the destiny of the dowry would depend on what was established in the contract; it could be given back to the one who had provided the dowry, or it could be left to the husband or another person designated in a clause. In both legal forms – the *cartas de ametade* and the dowry contract – the husband had the right to administer the goods. Despite this, in the dowry system, the wife remained the owner of the dowry. The husband could neither trade nor sell her goods, nor could he conclude any kind of legal business with her property, even with her permission. The *cartas de ametade* system was much more favourable to the husband, as he had absolute power to dispose of the couple's movable and immovable property, although, with respect to the latter, there was a legal condition for the act to be perfect – the authorisation of the wife.[28]

This means that, with regard to immovable property, husbands needed the authorisation of the spouse in the case of *cartas de ametade*, but not the dowry, which could not be sold by the husband.[29] However, husbands could administer and sell movable property as they wanted in the *cartas de ametade* regime. Notwithstanding, for these goods, the subject was controversial among jurists and legislators in the dowry system.

III.a Immovable property in the captaincy of Paraíba

In the captaincy of Paraíba, Gaspar Cardozo and his wife sold land to the monastery of São Bento on 7 January 1602. The sale was executed in front of a notary (*taballiam*) in the presence of the vendor and his wife, Maria da Sylva. The document mentions explicitly that husband and wife sold the land together (*elles marido e molher vendiáo*).[30] The presence and consent of the wife were thus a crucial prerequisite to render the business legally binding.[31] A similar case was recorded the year before, when Manoel Lopes de Praya sold a parcel of land on Varadouro Street in Paraíba in the presence of his wife, Maria dos Reys. The public notary here, too, emphasised that husband and wife were jointly selling their land.[32]

The presence and consent of the wife were necessary at the time of the transmission and purchase of an estate that was seen as belonging to the couple. However, it seems possible that the consent was a mere formality since the Catholic Church expected women's subordination to the authority of her husband. The necessity of female consent to property transactions can be seen not only as protection of the economic well-being of the married women but also as a mode of protection of the very institution of marriage.

III.b Mobile goods and half-movables: Household items and slaves

In her will from 1671, Anna da Silveira de Moraes left 150,000 *réis* (the currency of the day), which was equivalent to the cost of a small house or a strong slave, as dowry to enable each of her two granddaughters to marry – on the prerequisite of proper behaviour. In early modernity, a gendered code of conduct was central to the life of young women of the social elites so as to be considered "marriageable".[33] This applied to Portugal as well as to its colonies. Anna also owned slaves and freed two *mulatas* called Perpétua and Bárbara, who were both daughters of one of her slaves, by the act of manumission. The latter was freed on the condition that she light a candle for the deceased every Saturday for the rest of her life.[34]

When the widowed Catharina da Silva Lopes died in 1751, she left a will in which she specified numerous goods and detailed recommendations on the use of her goods according to her third of assets, in view of the fact that she married by *cartas de ametade*. Catharina owned animals, household goods, and garden tools (oxen, hoes, scythes, an axe, and a copper basin) as well as slaves. In her will, Catharina listed each slave she possessed and their appointed destiny. Like Anna above, she also granted some of them their freedom. The act of making a slave free on the death of the owner was not uncommon and was sometimes even accompanied by a pension. Since she had no children, she privileged other women and left instructions on the payment of dowries.[35] Thirty *arrobas* of sugar (one *arroba* was equivalent to 14.7 kilograms) were to be given to the dowry of her goddaughter, who also bore the same name (Catharina da Silva). By law, her possessions would have been handed over to her next of kin. Instead, she deliberately decided to act in favour of her own sex, using the third she could dispose of so as to improve their chances in life and to free some of her slaves. As these two documents show, black and "mixed-race" enslaved women were subject to ownership rights and comprised an important part of a woman's possessions and wealth besides sundry household items.[36] Unfortunately, the records that have survived do not allow us to quantify the total number of wills drawn up in Paraíba, but a thorough investigation (still necessary) of what is left could highlight more information regarding the personal status of women (unmarried, married, widowed).

III.c Privileges and dowries

A marriage was the standard biographical option. The aim was to be as attractive as possible in an economic sense. The higher the value of the dowry – the wealth women brought into marriage – the better the chances of a good match and a prosperous life.

A woman's dowry in colonial Brazil consisted of different categories of goods. Often, titles and privileges were hereditary. Under certain circumstances, women could claim the privileges of their fathers as their dowries. In 1807, Luiza Maria Rodrigues de Bandeira petitioned the king for the property (*propriedade*) and income of the office of the scribe (*escrivão*) of the royal treasury, customs, and warehouse of Paraíba as her legitimate inheritance. Her father, Bento Bandeira de Melo, had occupied this administrative post, and since she was his firstborn daughter and entitled to succeed him, she needed royal confirmation of the inheritance of the privilege.[37] But Luiza did not seek to claim the office for herself. Rather, she intended the privilege to become an attractive component of her dowry for any future husband.[38] However, since she and her sister were orphans, she requested the income of the office to be granted to her immediately so that she could support herself and her sister. The practice of including an office or privilege as part of a dowry was common in colonial Brazil. Luiza demanded the inheritance, but as a woman she could never have exercised it herself. However, it could provide her and her sister with a living.

As was the case with Luiza Rodrigues, other daughters in the captaincy of Paraíba obtained their fathers' office, a position of authority or post in the administration, as dowries. After the "reconquest" of northeastern Brazil, which was occupied by the Dutch in the seventeenth century, the Portuguese kings began to grant several titles as rewards for the services of colonial officials and colonisers in the fight against the Dutch. Baltazar Pereira de Mattos was one of the men who fought to regain the territories of the colony in the wars of Pernambuco and Paraíba.[39] He married the daughter of Fernão de Moraes Daltro, who had the post of public notary as well as the responsibility for the demarcation of the land (*Tabalião do publico, judicial e nottas e escrivão das demarcações*) of the captaincy of Paraíba. His rightful heir was his eldest son, Francisco Vieira Daltro, who renounced his father's office in favour of his sister's husband. Baltazar, Francisco's brother-in-law, wrote to the king in his capacity as husband of Officer Daltro's daughter and requested confirmation of the transmission of the office by marriage. After a thorough investigation of the matter by the Lisbon Overseas Council, the prince regent Pedro (1648–1706) eventually agreed and effectively granted the title to Baltazar in 1681.[40]

Turning privileges into dowries meant that the administration of Paraíba and the crown in Portugal, by means of their permission or rejection of claims (*graça*), brought influence to bear on the marriage market and on the formation of colonial elite society.

IV. Abstract goods: "Virginity" and honour

Equally important to the dowry with regard to the prospect of marriage was the reputation and honour (*fama e honra*) and assumed virginity of a woman. Its loss (meaning sexual intercourse with or without her consent before marriage) diminished the chances of women who did not possess a reasonable dowry to negotiate a good marriage. Virginity had almost the status of being good. Rape, on the contrary, had a slightly different meaning than today and can be translated as taking away the virginity or morally devaluing the reputation of a woman by the use of promises. Virginity as a legal good or "possession" could be disputed in a lawsuit. It represented an abstract value, not a physical condition.

In the *Ordenações Filipinas*, there are two sections (*títulos*) on the subject of the rape of a virgin and an honest widow.[41] The first deals with those who had sexual intercourse (*dormir*) with a virgin or honest widow (who most likely was no longer a virgin) up to twenty-five years of age and who were still under the authority of their father or paternal grandfather.[42] In this case, a woman could, if she so desired, and the man was deemed appropriate according to her social position, marry him. If a woman did not want to enter matrimony, however, the man could be forced to pay the amount that corresponded to the woman's virgin dowry – a monetary compensation for the now lost female honour – as a punishment for the transgression. In such cases, a judge would settle the exact amount according to the status and wealth of the respective woman. The punishment for the seducer or rapist also depended on the social status of his family. If a man was unable to pay the fine but was a so-called *fidalgo*, a Portuguese nobleman, he could be exiled to Africa. If the offender was not of noble origin, he would first be flogged with a noose around the neck while publicly announcing the crime (*com baraço e pregão*) before also being sent into exile. The procedure was a form of public humiliation and was staged in front of the whole village.

Thus, Portuguese norms, ideals of virtue, and social convention dictated that without virginity, marriage plans could be compromised. And the solution, as we saw, was twofold: Either the man had to enter marriage or he had to offer a financial compensation for depriving the woman of her honour.[43] The accusation of rape could also come in handy if a couple wanted to force the consent of parents, who would probably rather accept an unwanted son-in-law than the damaged reputation of a daughter.

The verdicts varied, however, when the woman had not consented to the sexual act.[44] A man who had sexually abused a woman (raped, in the modern sense of the term) was to receive the penalty of *morra por ello* – literally "to die for this". This could mean "a civil death" (*morte civil*), loss of property, exile, or being forced to do galley service.[45] In this case, even if the rapist married the victim, the very fact of the rape, which was different from the staining of a woman's honour, meant that he was not relieved of the penalty. Only if the victim was a prostitute or his slave was execution not to be carried out unless the crown authorised it. So the letter of the law did not treat all victims equally.

In the Lisbon Overseas Historical Archive, two cases show the application of the law in the captaincy of Paraíba. Josefa Rois Pires wrote to the king explaining that she had been a decent and modest woman in her parents' house when Manoel Malheiro de Mello seduced her under the promise of marriage in 1765. Josefa had consented to sexual intercourse with him, lost her virginity, and believed that he was going to marry her.[46] But Mello did not comply and, to complicate matters, he publicly announced in church that he wanted to marry another woman named Anna Escolástica Portela. Josefa sued him under the accusation of rape. The verdict she demanded from the judge was either financial compensation for the loss of her virginity, corresponding to the value of her dowry, or a sentence that forced Mello to marry her. The last information recorded about this case is that he not only paid the value of her dowry but also married Anna Escolástica *clandestinamente* – not following the procedure established by the Council of Trent. In the end, Mello and Anna were condemned in the ecclesiastical jurisdiction to excommunication not because of Josefa but because they were cousins.

Another record from 1769 details the seduction and rape of Thereza Maria do Espírito Santo. She was sleeping in her parents' house when José Pinto Coelho forced himself into the house and kidnapped her. Her father asked the king to punish José according to the *Ordenações* and to condemn him to the penalty of *morra por ello*. After the event, Thereza was sent to a house of retreat (*recolhimento*), where she remained for more than ten years. These *recolhimentos* were alternatives to convents and functioned to keep women apart from the world without having to take a religious vow or to provide a place for the family to "keep them safe" – for example while a husband was travelling – and prevent adultery or hide them. They were also an option for women who wanted to live a secluded life, especially considering that since 1603 the king had forbidden the construction of monasteries to stimulate the growth of the population.[47] Again, we cannot be sure if Thereza's situation described a rape scenario in the modern sense. It could well be possible that the couple tried to steal away without the father's consent, and the daughter might have been punished by banning her to the house of retreat. As far as we know, based on the archival material, the case was not solved. However, in the first case, it was the woman who sought justice for a false promise, and in the second it was the father who obviously considered his daughter ruined. These two cases in colonial Paraíba prove that the Portuguese norm was applied to the Brazilian colony to a certain extent.

V. Protecting property outside of marriage: Concubinage and illegitimate children

So far, we have encountered cases that focussed on couples within the institution of marriage or on women who fought for the prerequisites to marriage. As stated, marriage as an institution was the most common and recommended biographical model for men and women. However, in the colony, couples often cohabitated and constituted families in a much wider sense. In the case of women who had relations with married men and even children outside of marriage, such as concubines (called *barregãs* in the *Ordenações*), none of their possessions, common or not, were protected, and the woman's position against the legitimate wife was weak.[48] Legally, relations outside of marriage were sanctioned. In the context of these informal familial arrangements, women developed strategies to protect the inheritance of their sons and daughters.

The inheritance laws of succession mentioned earlier applied only to legitimate children. If a couple had children from a relation that had not been blessed by ecclesiastical authorities – if the parents were adulterers, if they lived together despite religious impediments, or if the father was a member of a religious order – there was only one option to save their children's inheritance: A process of affiliation (*legitimação* or *perfilhação*). Under the king's right of grace (*direito de graça*), they could become entitled to the rights of succession even though they had not been born of a legitimate marriage. In the captaincy of Paraíba, in spite of celibacy, priests lived in concubinage (*concubinato*) with women and had families with many children. As their children could not be considered legally entitled to inherit, priests petitioned the king for the right to elevate their children to the status of legitimate heirs. Men issued the majority of requests of affiliation. But there is one document from the captaincy of Paraíba that was written by a woman.

In 1792, the priest João Batista Barreto demanded from Queen Maria I (1734–1816) legitimisation of the daughter he had with Catherine de Melo Monteiro – Francisca Xavier de Sales. The main purpose of the request, he argued, was for the daughter to succeed him according to the law.[49] Francisca's mother backed the request and also sent a formal petition to the queen. In 1794, the crown judge (*ouvidor*) of Paraíba, António Filipe Soares de Andrade e Brederode (*c.* 1755–1818), wrote a letter to Portugal in which he replied to the queen's request for his position on the case. By the time Brederode wrote to Europe, the priest had already died, but Brederode argued that the request was still fair, and he supported the legitimisation because of the mother's lack of relatives and descendants.[50] In 1802, Catherine reiterated the request. She stated that her daughter might have been born of a "sacrilegious coitus", but since Catherine had no other ascendants or descendants, she underlined the need to heal "any defect of Francisca's birth" by royal order. The crown, in turn, sought to clarify the situation and ordered a hearing with the supplicant and Francisca's brothers, as her only possible heirs.[51] In 1803, Catherine reiterated the request to the prince regent, João VI (1767–1826), arguing that the crown judge of Paraíba had already issued a report, but that it had been lost on a ship seized by the French. The date of the request also reveals how long these requests for legitimisation could take. Begun in 1794, almost ten years passed without a final decision.[52] This document provides information about a woman who, like many, had lived in concubinage with a man of the church and who, in spite of her behaviour against the moral order of the day, claimed the legitimisation of her child to protect the father's inheritance and the future of her offspring. Unfortunately, there is no extant record of the outcome of this plea.

There were also other legal instruments mothers could use to hand down their property to illegitimate children. In 1804, Francisca Maria do Carmo, with the consent of her husband, Francisco José dos Santos, in the city of Paraíba do Norte, demanded from the prince regent a *carta de insinuação* for the recognition of a donation made by her natural mother. This tells us that Francisca was an illegitimate child.[53] This kind of letter was needed to confirm donations over the amount of 300 *cruzados* in case the beneficiary was male and over 150 *cruzados* in case the beneficiary was female, arguably in view of their "fragile mood" and "lack of intellect" in managing their own properties.[54] Donations could be made only during a person's lifetime. As the value of the donation exceeded the legally allowed amount, Francisca needed the consent of the crown. Since Francisca was a natural but not a legitimate daughter, the mother guaranteed the financial security and future of her daughter by means of the donation, which was nothing but a disguised inheritance before death. This example demonstrates how women used different mechanisms in the legal system to protect their inheritance and to transfer it to whomever they wanted.

VI. Conclusion

In this chapter, on the basis of archival sources, I have analysed the ways women used to claim, protect, and distribute their property and possessions in a colonial territory within and without marriage. In Brazil, women owned different kinds of property, movable and immovable assets, albeit not to the extent men did; they also owned slaves, considered neither movable nor immovable, but *semoventes*. Movable goods were those that could be moved from one place to another without being damaged; these types of goods included jewellery, agricultural tools, and money. Immovable goods could not be physically relocated without undoing and changing their nature and shape; these types of goods included houses, farms, and trees. The second category also included rights, such as annual rents or pensions.[55] *Semoventes*, which literally means "half-moveables", were considered those goods that could move by themselves, like animals and slaves. Slaves belonged to the land but could be easily moved from one place to the next. This division between mobile, immobile, and half-mobile was essential, for instance, if, according to the law in a certain business, a husband needed the authorisation of his wife to sell.

Women, in the form of mistress and administrator, were among the beneficiaries of the land and were in possession of large estates in their own right. Women – before, within, and after marriage – were landholders and requested royal confirmations of the *sesmarias*. They seem to have benefited in phases of administrative reorganisation – for example after the recovery following the Dutch occupation of the northeast of Brazil that ended in 1654. The dowry system in force protected goods that belonged only to women in marriage, although the widely popular model of property distribution within marriage served to benefit the surviving spouse by the law of the charter of halves. Women in the colonies also held privileges as part of their dowries that guaranteed their ability to marry well. Women played an active role in the economy of the colony, buying and selling estates, inheriting property, and petitioning for their own dowries so as to keep up and improve their livelihood and social status.

All examples in this chapter appear to portray women who were part of the "white" social elite. They had access to a certain kind of education and to the legal instruments of the Portuguese administration. Nonetheless, women never formed a homogeneous group – not even those in this elite society. In a colonial society, the intersectionality of condition and status, gender and religion mattered greatly and shaped and determined options of agency.[56] Norms privileged the institution of marriage; they privileged men over women, husbands over wives, and white women of Portuguese noble descent over native and black women. But to establish a more complete picture of female agency in colonial Brazil, the property and possessions of native and African women as well as their customs of property transfer would need thorough investigation.

Notes

1 Although "northeast" is not a concept used in this time period, we will use it to refer to the geographical region of Brazil. Instead, in the colonial period it was common to use the expression "captaincies of the North". "Northeast" is a modern conceptual term.

2 See among many Francisco Adolpho Varnhagen, *Historia Geral do Brazil*, Rio de Janeiro 1857 [E. e H. Laemmert]; Capistrano de Abreu, *Capítulos da História Colonial*, Rio de Janeiro 2009 [Biblioteca Virtual de Ciências Humanas do Centro Edelstein de Pesquisas Sociais]; Oliveira Viana, *Populações meridionais*, Brasília 2005 [Senado Federal]; Gilberto Freyre, *Casa Grande e Senzala: formação da família brasileira sob o regime da economia patriarcal*, São Paulo 2006 [Global].

3 Such as Carol Smart, *Feminism and the Power of Law*, London and New York 1989 [Routledge]; Ann Scales, *Legal Feminism: Activism, Lawyering, and Legal Theory*, New York and London 2006 [New York University Press].

4 See among others Maria Odila Leite da Silva Dias, "Novas subjetividades na pesquisa histórica feminista: uma hermenêutica das diferenças", in: *Estudos Feministas* 2 (1994), pp. 373–382; Mary del Priore, *Ao sul do corpo: condição feminina, maternidade e mentalidades no Brasil colonial*, Rio de Janeiro 1995 [José Olympio]; Rachel Soihet and Joana Maria Pedro, "A Emergência da Pesquisa da História das Mulheres e das Relações de Gênero", in: *Revista Brasileira de História* 27, 54 (2007), pp. 281–300; Leila Mezan Algranti, *Honradas e devotas: Mulheres da colônia. Estudo sobre a condição feminina através dos conventos e recolhimentos do sudeste 1750–1822*, São Paulo 1992 [Tese, Universidade de São Paulo], p. 41; Eni de Mesquita Samara, *A família brasileira*, São Paulo 2004 [Brasiliense]; Maria Beatriz Nizza da Silva, *Sistema de casamento no Brasil colonial*, São Paulo 1984 [T.A. Queiroz/EDUSP]. Regarding women and properties rights, see Mariana Candido and Eugénia Rodrigues, "African Women's Access and Rights to Property in the Portuguese Empire", in: *African Economic History* 43 (2015), pp. 1–18; Mariana Candido, "Women, Family, and Landed Property in Nineteenth-Century Benguela", in: *African Economic History* 43 (2015), pp. 136–161; Alida Metcalf, "Women and Means: Women and Family Property in Colonial Brazil", in: *Journal of Social History* 24, 2 (1990), pp. 277–298.

5 Edgardo Lander, *La colonialidad del saber: eurocentrismo y ciencias sociales. Perspectivas Latinoamericanas*, Buenos Aires 1993 [CLASCO]; Mabel Moraña, Enrique Dussel and Carlos A. Jáuregui, *Coloniality at Large: Latin America and the Postcolonial Debate*, Durham and London 2008 [Duke University Press].

6 Ratna Kapur, *Erotic Justice: Law and the New Politics of Postcolonialism*, Great Britain 2005 [The Glass House Press]; Piyel Haldar, *Law, Orientalism and Postcolonialism. The Jurisdiction of the Lotus Eaters*, London and New York 2007 [Routledge]; Ann Laura Stoler, *Carnal Knowledge and Imperial Power. Race and the Intimate in Colonial Rule*, Berkeley and Los Angeles 2010 [University of California Press].

7 Paraíba was one of the oldest captaincies of Portuguese Empire, "Status and condition" is the phrase used in the empire to refer to what we designate nowadays as race, ethnicity, or class. Instead of these words, the expression meant the place of the person in the order of the world (*ordem do mundo*), in terms of liberty, "civil" status, and family. From these, all rights and duties would accrue. Nonetheless, all conditions and status cannot be analysed as static concepts; instead, they must be seen as connected and dependent on each other. See António Manuel Hespanha, Como os juristas viam o mundo.

1550–1750: Direitos, estados, pessoas, coisas, contratos, ações e crimes, 2015 [Create Space Independent Publishing Platform]

8 *Ordenações Afonsinas*, Livro IV, Reprodução «fac-simile» da edição de 1792. Lisboa 1998 [Fundação Calouste Gulbenkian], título LXXXI.

9 *Ordenações Manuelinas*, Livro IV, Reprodução «fac-simile» da edição de 1797. Coimbra 2006 [Fundação Calouste Gulbenkian], título LXVII.

10 *Código Filipino ou Ordenações e Leis do Reino de Portugal*, Livro IV. Reprodução «fac-simile» da 14ª edição de 1870, com introdução e comentários de Cândido Mendes de Almeida. Brasília 2004 [Senado], título XLIII.

11 Tabir Dal Poggetto Oliveira Sueyoshi, "As Sesmarias nas Ordenações do Reino", in: *Revista da Faculdade de Direito da Universidade de São Paulo* 102 (jan./dez. 2007), pp. 695–711.

12 *Ordenações Manuelinas*, Livro IV, título LXVII, §3 e título XLIII, §3.

13 "Sabereis quantos moradores ha na dita Capitania, e se tem todos terras para cultivar, que lhe fossem dadas de sesmaria, e se as tem aproveitadas, e os engenhos são feitos; e procurareis por os ajudares e favorecerdes, para effeito de se ir abrindo e cultivando a terra. E porque fui informado que muitas pessoas, a quem se deram as ditas terras de sesmaria com condição de as beneficiarem em tempo limitado, o não tinham feito, e estão devoluto, sendo-lhes passado o tempo em que tinham obrigação de as beneficiarem, vos mando que saibaes isto muito em particular, e quantas e quaes sejam as pessoas que tenham terras, e as não tenham aproveitado, e se lhe é passado o tempo que lhe foi limitado para as beneficiar; e a qualidade e quantidade das ditas terras", in: Portugal, Lisbon, Biblioteca da Ajuda, Regimento que S. Magestade mandou dar a Francisco Coelho de Carvalho, que vai por provedor da Capitania da Paraíba nas partes do Brasil. Lisboa, 09 de maio de 1609, Doc 339, 51-VII-11, fl. 172.

14 These land grants charters are published in: Regina Célia Gonçalves, *Guerras e Açúcares Política e economia na Capitania da Paraíba – 1585–1630*, Bauru 2007 [EDUSC]; Guilherme Gomes da Silveira d'Avila Lins, *Um Erro Elementar de Interpretação Histórica, Referente às Primeiras Sesmarias da Capitania da Paraíba.* (Século XVI), João Pessoa 2005 [Edição do autor].

15 Gonçalves, *Guerras e Açúcares*, p. 234, anexo II.

16 Transcript of the donation charter in: Brazil, João Pessoa, Arquivo do Instituto Histórico Geográfico Paraibano, *Livro do Tombo do Mosteiro de São Bento da Paraíba*, Recife 1948 [Imprensa Oficial]. pp. 66–69.

17 Ibid., p. 66.

18 *Código Filipino*, Livro IV, título XCIV. Widows demanded the land grants through attorneys. Maria Beatriz Nizza da Silva, *Donas e plebeias na sociedade colonial*, Lisboa 2002 [Editorial Estampa], p. 66.

19 Ibid.

20 All translation from Portuguese sources into English by the author.

21 Lins, *Um Erro Elementar de Interpretação Histórica*.

22 Rudolf Schüßler, "Moral Self-Ownership and IUS Possessionin Scholastics", in: V. Mäkinen and P. Korkman (eds.), *Transformations in Medieval and Early-Modern Rights Discourse. The New Synthese Historical Library* (Texts and Studies in the History of Philosophy), vol 59, Dordrecht 2006 [Springer], pp. 149–172.

23 Portugal, Lisbon, Torre do Tombo, Carta de Sesmaria. Chancelaria de D. João V, tomo 55, fólios 24V – 26.

24 Among them were parts of the counties (*sítios*) Loango, Buraco, Salinas, São Bento, Juá, Acaracuzinho, Catolé and Bodocongó. Portugal, Lisbon, Arquivo histórico Ultramarino Paraíba (=AHU-Paraíba), AHU_CU_014, Cx. 46, D. 3248.

25 These numbers were organised by the project and online platform SILB – Sesmarias do Império Luso-Brasileiro, www.silb.cchla.ufrn.br (accessed 09.01.2020). The project lists the requests, but not the confirmations and does not inform and qualify the social background of the applicants.

26 *Código Filipino*, Livro IV, títulos XCVI and XCIV.

27 According to the Ordenações Manuelinas: "Todos os casamentos que forem feitos em Nossos Reynoos, e Senhorios, se entendem seer feitos por carta de metade, saluo quando

antre as partes outra cousa for acordado e contractado, porque entonce se guardará o que antre elles for concertado." Ordenações Manuelinas, Livro, título VII, p. 23.

28 *Código Filipino*, título XLVIII.

29 Ibid., título LXIV.

30 Brazil, João Pessoa, *Livro do Tombo*, 3ª parte, p. 105.

31 *Código Filipino*, Livro IV, título XLVIII.

32 "E logo por elles ambos e dous marido, e molher foi dito, e cada um por si em presença de mi . . . publico Tabaliam ao deante nomeado, e das testemunhas abaixo escriptas, e assignadas que elles, marido e molher, vendiam, como de feito logo venderam". Brazil, João Pessoa, *Livro do Tombo*, p. 521.

33 Maria Beatriz Nizza da Silva, *Donas e plebeias na sociedade colonial*, Lisboa 2002 [Editorial Estampa].

34 Adauto Ramos and Zilma Ferreira Pinto, *Processo do Pio Legado de Anna da Silveira 1671–1847*. João Pessoa 2012 [Sal da Terra].

35 AHU-Paraíba, AHU_CU_014, Cx. 40, D. 2810, fls. 14 and 15.

36 On the agency of slaves, see Silva, História do Direito e Colonização do Brasil; Ana Maria Bandeira de Mello Magaldi and Figueiredo, Luciano Raposo de Almeida,"Quitandas e Quitutes: estudo sobre rebeldia e transgressão femininas numa sociedade colonial", in: *Cad. Pesq.*, 54 (1985), pp. 50–61.

37 The primogeniture, *morgados*, and inheritance were topics widely discussed in the period, especially in doctrine. There were competing ideas and a rivalry between "equal share" and "primogeniture". See Hespanha, *Como os Juristas viam o Mundo* and Anthony Gilissen, *Introdução Histórica ao Direito*, Lisboa 1995 [Gulbenkian].

38 AHU-Paraiìba, AHU_CU_014, Cx. 48, D. 3378.

39 AHU-Paraíba, AHU_CU_014, Cx. 2, D. 115.

40 Ibid., f. 2.

41 *Código Filipino*, Livro V., título XXIII. "Do que dorme com mulher virgem, ou viuva honesta per sua vontade."

42 Sons and daughters would be under the *pátrio poder* until their father's death or their marriage and, for men, if they entered a religious order, were ordained, or became magistrates.

43 Virginity as the honour of a woman was so important that the *Ordenações* evaluated even its assumption. If a man (in this example a tutor of an orphan) raped a woman who was not a virgin but had the reputation to be one, he was ordered to pay double the value of her dowry. *Código Filipino*, Livro V, título XXI, §1.

44 Ibid., título XVIII. "Do que dorme per força com qualquer mulher, ou trava della, ou a leva per sua vontade."

45 Antonio Vanguerve Cabral, *Epilogo juridico de varios casos civeis, e crimes concernentes ao especulativo, & pratico controvertidos, disputados e decididos a mayor parte delles no Supremo Tribunal da Corte, & Casa da Supplicação com humas insignes annotaçoens à ley novissima da prohibição das facas, & mais armas promulgada em 4 de Abril de 1719*, Lisboa Occidental 1729 [Na Officina de Antonio Pedroso Galram] and *Código Filipino*, livro V, p. 1170.

46 AHU-Paraíba, Pernambuco AHU_CU_014, Cx. 23, D. 1765.

47 Carta Régia 02 de setembro de 1603. Não se fundem Mosteiros de Freiras na Baía e Pernambuco, mas sim Recolhimentos para donzelas e órfãs; and Carta Régia 16 de outubro de 1609. Não se fundem Mosteiros no Brasil. Both in: José Justino de Andrade Silva, *Collecção Chronologica da Legislação Portugueza 1603–1612*, Lisboa 1854 [Imprensa de F. X. de Souza].

48 If the concubine stole something from the husband, his legitimate wife could sue her and demand its return. Furthermore, the wife could sue the husband for anything he gave to his concubine as a gift. *Código Filipino*, Livro V., título XXIX, "Das barregaãs, que fogem áquelles, com que vivem, e lhes levão o seu", p. 1180.

49 AHU-Paraíba, AHU_CU_014, Cx. 31, D. 2271.

50 AHU-Paraíba, AHU_CU_014, Cx. 32, D. 2312.

51 AHU-Paraíba, AHU_CU_014, Cx. 40, D. 2779.

52 AHU-Paraíba, AHU_CU_014, Cx. 40, D. 2847.
53 AHU-Paraíba, AHU_CU_014, Cx. 42, D. 2932, f. 1.
54 "E as doações feitas por mulheres, que vivam per si, quer solteiras, quer viuvas, que passarem de cento e cincoenta cruzados, ou sua valia, que cada huma valer ao tempo, que for feita, serão insinuadas; e a que o não for, valha somente em quanto chegar á quantia de cento e cincoenta cruzados, e no que passar, não valha, nem tenha effeito, como se feita não fosse". *Codigo Filipino*, p. 862.
55 Ibid., título XLVIII, §8 and Livro III., título XLVII.
56 Chandra Talpade Mohanty, "Under Western Eyes: Feminist Scholarship and Colonial Discourses", in: *Feminist Review* 30 (1988), pp. 61–88. My assumption is that women, in contrast to the traditional historiographical constructed image, actively interfered in their own future. They married against their parents' wishes; they decided against marriage and led a secluded, religious life; they wrote to the king claiming the offices and positions of their parents; and they had property and land of their own. Moreover, they built social networks and rebuilt family relations that contravened the recommendations of the church – for instance by living with or having different sexual partners or by engaging in same-sex relations or performing other sexual acts beyond what was considered "natural" intercourse, behaviors that could at the time be considered acts of sodomy and were also criminalised by the Inquisition. See Luisa Stella de Oliveira Coutinho Silva, *História do Direito e Colonização do Brasil: as Mulheres da Capitania da Paraíba, 1661–1822*, Lisboa 2018 [Tese, Universidade de Lisboa].

Sources

Portugal, Lisbon, Biblioteca da Ajuda, Regimento que S. Magestade mandou dar a Francisco Coelho de Carvalho, que vai por provedor da Capitania da Paraíba nas partes do Brasil. Lisboa, 09 de maio de 1609, Doc 339, 51-VII-11, f. 172.

Portugal, Lisbon, Arquivo histórico Ultramarino Paraíba, AHU_CU_014, Cx. 2, D. 115.

Portugal, Lisbon, Arquivo histórico Ultramarino Paraíba, Pernambuco AHU_CU_014, Cx. 23, D. 1765.

Portugal, Lisbon, Arquivo histórico Ultramarino Paraíba, AHU_CU_014, Cx. 31, D. 2271.

Portugal, Lisbon, Arquivo histórico Ultramarino Paraíba, AHU_CU_014, Cx. 32, D. 2312.

Portugal, Lisbon, Arquivo histórico Ultramarino Paraíba, AHU_CU_014, Cx. 40, D. 2810.

Portugal, Lisbon, Arquivo histórico Ultramarino Paraíba, AHU_CU_014, Cx. 40, D. 2779.

Portugal, Lisbon, Arquivo histórico Ultramarino Paraíba, AHU_CU_014, Cx. 40, D. 2847.

Portugal, Lisbon, Arquivo histórico Ultramarino Paraíba, AHU_CU_014, Cx. 42, D. 2932.

Portugal, Lisbon, Arquivo histórico Ultramarino Paraiiba, AHU_CU_014, Cx. 46, D. 3248.

Portugal, Lisbon, Arquivo histórico Ultramarino Paraiiba, AHU_CU_014, Cx. 48, D. 3378.

Portugal, Lisbon, Torre do Tombo, Carta de Sesmaria. Chancelaria de D. João V, tomo 55, fls. 24V – 26, https://digitarq.ahu.arquivos.pt/details?id=1119379 (accessed 23 August 2020).

Published sources

Brazil, João Pessoa, *Arquivo do Instituto Histórico Geográfico Paraibano, Livro do Tombo do Mosteyro de São Bento de Olinda*, Recife 1948 [Imprensa Oficial].

———*Arquivo do Instituto Histórico Geográfico Paraibano, Livro do Tombo do Mosteiro de São Bento da Paraíba*, Recife 1948 [Imprensa Oficial].

Cabral, Antonio Vanguerve, *Epilogo juridico de varios casos civeis, e crimes concernentes ao especulativo, & pratico controvertidos, disputados e decididos a mayor parte delles no Supremo Tribunal da Corte, & Casa da Supplicação com humas infignes annotaçoens à ley novissima da prohibição das facas, & mais armas promulgada em 4 de Abril de 1719*, Lisboa Occidental 1729 [Na Officina de Antonio Pedroso Galram].

Legal sources

Código Filipino ou Ordenações e Leis do Reino de Portugal, Livro III. Reprodução "fac-simile" da 14ª edição de 1870, com introdução e comentários de Cândido Mendes de Almeida, Brasília 2004 [Senado].

Código Filipino ou Ordenações e Leis do Reino de Portugal, Livro IV. Reprodução "fac-simile" da 14ª edição de 1870, com introdução e comentários de Cândido Mendes de Almeida, Brasília 2004 [Senado].

Código Filipino ou Ordenações e Leis do Reino de Portugal, Livro V. Reprodução "fac-simile" da 14ª edição de 1870, com introdução e comentários de Cândido Mendes de Almeida, Brasília 2004 [Senado].

Ordenações Afonsinas, Livro IV. Reprodução "fac-simile" da edição de 1792, Lisboa 1998 [Fundação Calouste Gulbenkian].

Ordenações Manuelinas, Livro IV. Reprodução "fac-simile" da edição de 1797, Coimbra 2006 [Fundação Calouste Gulbenkian].

Silva, José Justino de Andrade, *Collecção Chronologica da Legislação Portugueza. 1603–1612*, Lisboa 1854 [Imprensa de F. X. de Souza].

Bibliography

Abreu, Capistrano de, *Capítulos da História Colonial*, Rio de Janeiro 2009 [Biblioteca Virtual de Ciências Humanas do Centro Edelstein de Pesquisas Sociais].

Algranti, Leila Mezan, *Honradas e devotas: Mulheres da colônia. Estudo sobre a condição feminina através dos conventos e recolhimentos do sudeste 1750–1822*, São Paulo 1992 [Tese, Universidade de São Paulo].

Candido, Mariana, "Women, Family, and Landed Property in Nineteenth-Century Benguela", in: *African Economic History* 43(2015), pp. 136–161.

Candido, Mariana and Eugénia Rodrigeus, "African Women's Access and Rights to Property in the Portuguese Empire", in: *African Economic History* 43 (2015), pp. 1–18.

Dias, Maria Odila Leite da Silva, "Novas subjetividades na pesquisa histórica feminista: uma hermenêutica das diferenças", in: *Estudos Feministas* 2 (1994), pp. 373–382.

Freyre, Gilberto, *Casa Grande e Senzala: formação da família brasileira sob o regime da economia patriarcal*, São Paulo 2006 [Global].

Gilissen, Anthony, *Introdução Histórica ao Direito*, Lisboa 1995 [Gulbenkian].

Gonçalves, Regina Célia, *Guerras e Açucares. Política e economia na Capitania da Paraíba – 1585–1630*, Bauru 2007 [EDUSC].

Haldar, Piyel, *Law, Orientalism and Postcolonialism. The Jurisdiction of the Lotus Eaters*, London and New York 2007 [Routledge].

Hespanha, António Manuel, *Como os juristas viam o mundo. 1550–1750: Direitos, estados, pessoas, coisas, contratos, ações e crimes*, 2015[Create Space Independent Publishing Platform].

Kapur, Ratna, *Erotic Justice: Law and the New Politics of Postcolonialism*, Great Britain 2005 [The Glass House Press].

Lander, Edgardo, *La colonialidad del saber: eurocentrismo y ciencias sociales. Perspectivas Latinoamericana*, Buenos Aires 1993 [CLASCO].

Lins, Guilherme Gomes da Silveira d'Avila, *Um Erro Elementar de Interpretação Histórica, Referente às Primeiras Sesmarias da Capitania da Paraíba* (Século XVI), João Pessoa 2005 [Edição do autor].

Magaldi, Ana Maria Bandeira de Mello Magaldi and Luciano Raposo de Almeida Figueiredo, "Quitandas e Quitutes: estudo sobre rebeldia e transgressão femininas numa sociedade colonial", in: *Cad. Pesq.*, 54 (1985), pp. 50–61.

Metcalf, Alida, "Women and Means: Women and Family Property in Colonial Brazil", in: *Journal of Social History* 24 (1990), pp. 277–298.

Mohanty, Chandra Talpade, "Under Western Eyes: Feminist Scholarship and Colonial Discourses", in: *Feminist Review* 30 (1988), pp. 61–88.

Moraña, Mabel, Enrique Dussel and Carlos A. Jáuregui, *Coloniality at Large: Latin America and the Postcolonial Debate*, Durham and London 2008 [Duke University Press].

Priore, Mary del, *Ao sul do corpo: condição feminina, maternidade e mentalidades no Brasil colonial*, Rio de Janeiro 1995 [José Olympio].

Ramos, Adauto and Zilma Ferreira Pinto, *Processo do Pio Legado de Anna da Silveira 1671–1847*, João Pessoa 2012 [Sal da Terra].

Samara, Eni de Mesquita, *A família brasileira*, São Paulo 2004 [Brasiliense].

Scales, Ann, *Legal Feminism: Activism, Lawyering, and Legal Theory*, New York and London 2006 [New York University Press].

Schüßler, Rudolf, "Moral Self-Ownership and IUS Possession in Scholastics", in: V. Mäkinen and P. Korkman (eds.), *Transformations in Medieval and Early-Modern Rights Discourse. The New Synthese Historical Library*, vol. 59 (2006), Dordrecht [Springer], pp. 149–172.

Silva, Luisa Stella de Oliveira Coutinho, *História do Direito e Colonização do Brasil: as Mulheres da Capitania da Paraíba, 1661–1822*, Lisboa 2018 [Tese, Universidade de Lisboa].

Silva, Maria Beatriz Nizza da, *Sistema de casamento no Brasil colonial*, São Paulo 1984 [T.A. Queiroz/EDUSP].

———*Donas e plebeias na sociedade colonial*, Lisboa 2002 [Editorial Estampa].

Smart, Carol, *Feminism and the Power of Law*, London and New York 1989 [Routledge].

Soihet, Rachel and Joana Maria Pedro, "A Emergência da Pesquisa da História das Mulheres e das Relações de Gênero", in: *Revista Brasileira de História* 27, 54 (2007) pp. 281–300.

Stoler, Ann Laura, *Carnal Knowledge and Imperial Power. Race and the Intimate in Colonial Rule*, Berkeley and Los Angeles 2010 [University of California Press].

Sueyoshi, Tabir Dal Poggetto Oliveira, "As Sesmarias nas Ordenações do Reino", in: *Revista da Faculdade de Direito da Universidade de São Paulo* 102 (jan./dez. 2007), pp. 695–711.

Varnhagen, Francisco Adolpho, *Historia Geral do Brazil*, Rio de Janeiro 1857 [E. e H. Laemmert].

Viana, Oliveira, *Populações meridionais. Edições do Senado Federal*, Brasília 2005 [Senado Federal].

PART V

Women and property in transitory zones

FIGURE 10.1 Map of Sicily/Stromboli, Guillaume de L'Isle, Philippe Buache, *Carte d' Europe*, 1769 (detail).

Source: Library of Congress Geography and Map Division, Washington, D.C., U.S.A., public domain, G5700 1724. L5 TIL, http://hdl.loc.gov/loc.gmd/g5700.ct000045 (15.02.2020, 15:15 CET).

10

WOMEN AND MOVABLE GOODS IN A MARITIME BORDER ECONOMY IN NINETEENTH-CENTURY SICILY (AEOLIAN ISLANDS)

Ida Fazio

ABSTRACT

This chapter focusses on women possessing material goods, and on their informal administration, use, production, maintenance, and transformation in a small Sicilian island, Stromboli in the Aeolian Archipelago, in the first half of the 19th century. To explore this diverse social practices such as work, assistance, personal and familial relationships, and the informal management of money in transactions should all be taken into account. In areas such as Southern Italy, where Roman Law heritage predominated in Mediaeval and Early Modern age, women's property rights were quite strong: although they were subject to special restrictions, they enjoyed, at the same time, special protections, as in the case of the dowry system. The new Bourbon Civil Code enacted under the Restoration was quite flexible and allowed to balance the transmission of property to women and men. Archival sources such as judicial proceedings, marriage contracts, wills and post-mortem inventories give the possibility to shed some light on the everyday life of women of the lower classes and on their relationship with movable goods, personal objects, household goods, and working tools. Women in Stromboli owned and used objects for agricultural and fishing activities and fully participated to the economic life of the island with its licit and illicit trades.

I. Introduction: Women's wealth and material goods

International and Italian historiography on property, its conveyance and management within families, specifically focussing on women's roles and accomplishments in the early modern period and in the first half of the nineteenth century, has yielded considerable results. Sources have included, above all, notarial acts, such as testaments, dowry certificates, marriage contracts, transfers of goods, donations, and inventories. For many reasons, however, both the theory and the sources examined have been particularly affected and complicated by the question of women's property rights.

First, everywhere in Europe women's property rights during the ancien régime were shaped by peculiar conditions. In Italy two peculiar legal systems, the German and the Roman one, broadly shaped the civil laws of the many states in which its territory was divided before the political unification of the 1860s. The two systems entitled women to different property rights, in general more favourable under the Roman law, which was hegemonic in southern Italy, although the systems were entwined and blurred in a variety of local specific features brought about by the shared history and geographical proximity of the ancien régime Italian states.[1]

As regards in particular Sicily, until the adoption of the new Civil Code of 1819 after the institutional reform following the unification of the Bourbon kingdoms of Sicily and Naples in the Kingdom of the Two Sicilies, a number of local urban customary laws (the *Consuetudini*) were applied.[2] Almost all of them, from the early Middle Ages, in the case of intestate succession, allowed both sons and daughters to inherit the same share of inheritance. Married children, both males and females, also inherited from their parents in equal parts, taking into account the wealth they had already received at the time of the wedding.[3] If the family lived under the Longobard and French Law (the Normans conquered Sicily in 1061), the mother, father, and children were part of the *comunione tripartita* (tripartite community property state) that assigned one-third of the family wealth, which merged when the first child was born, to each of them. If one of the spouses died without a will, his or her third part of the wealth (possessions, belongings) was inherited by all the children; but if the father died leaving a will, he was free to devolve his share, while the mother could freely dispose of only movable goods.[4] The marriage law based on the community property state was called *alla Latina* because the "people from northern Europe" married according to the rites of the Latin Church. On the contrary, if the family lived under Roman law, according to the rituals of the Greek

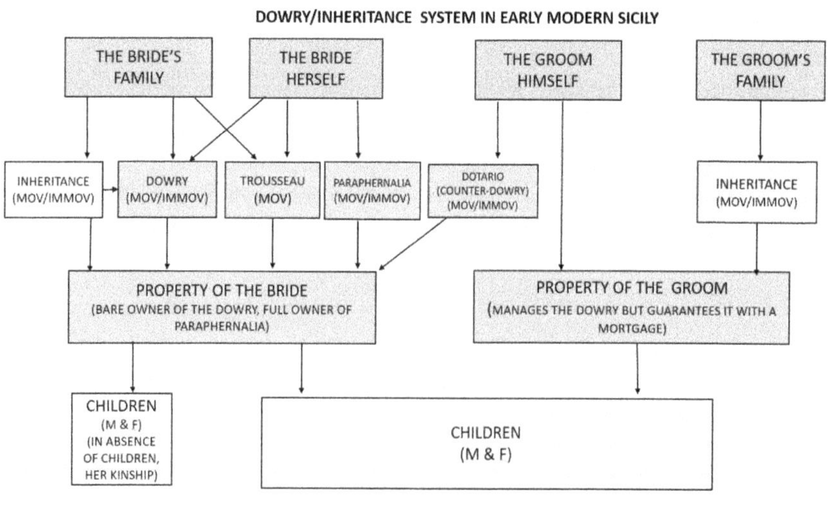

FIGURE 10.2 Dowry and inheritance system in early modern Sicily.

Source: © Ida Fazio.

Catholic Church, which persisted in some parts of southern Italy, the marriage entailed the separation of assets (marriage *alla Greca*). If this was the case, married women received the dowry from their parents and a wedding gift (*dotario*) from the husband. In the dowry system, the wife was the bare owner of the dowry, while the husband was the administrator, and he secured refund to the widow by a mortgage on his wealth. The dowry was inalienable, but over time in the early modern age it became possible to sell some immovable assets if the couple was able to demonstrate to the civil court that they were compelled to sell them for extreme need.[5]

Sicilian dowries were made up of both movable and immovable assets, such as tools, furniture, jewels, and money as well as houses and plots of land. Bed linen, clothes, and lingerie were part of the trousseau, a real treasure that could be either jealously guarded or sold to make some money instead.[6] Igor Mineo has shown that through the introduction of the Roman dowry as specific female inheritance, the ruling class families tried to avoid the effects of the *comunione tripartita* (equal inheritance rights for male and female members of a household) that prevented the possibility of agnatic development of kinship reproduction.[7] Beginning in the first half of the fifteenth century the dowry system began to replace the *comunione tripartita* over time and became the typical matrimonial property regime in the Kingdom of Sicily. During the nineteenth century, the wealthier the family, the more immovable goods began to be handed over by means of inheritance to sons, whereas brides enjoyed a dowry made of money, credits, clothes, or jewels, for example. By contrast, peasants transmitted their small, poor houses via the dowry of the brides to attract young workers, the grooms, towards the fields of the brides' villages.[8]

From the time of Emperor Frederick II (in the beginning of the thirteenth century), Sicilian noblewomen were also allowed to inherit fiefs or to receive them as a dowry. However, since the feudal laws were settled *more Francorum*, sons were preferred to daughters; nevertheless, daughters were preferred to collateral relatives. Male heirs had to give their sisters the *dote di paraggio*, i.e. a dowry proportionate to the family standard of living; but if she became a nun, she had to renounce it and receive a smaller sum of wealth.[9] Not every type of wealth owned by women was secured by the dotal bounds. Women could also be free owners of paraphernalia, movable and immovable goods held as unbound property before being awarded with the dowry (inheritances, gifts).

Everywhere in Italy in the early modern age women were subject to the rule of the *Senatusconsultum Velleianum* (the impossibility to act as guarantee on behalf of others due to *fragilitas sexus*) until the abolition of this rule in the Italian states where the Napoleonic civil code came into force at the beginning of the nineteenth century. Before that time, notarial practice usually allowed women to renounce the limit of the *Senatusconsultum Velleianum* to validate their deeds, and then the authorisation by their husbands, fathers, and other relatives or by a *mundualdus* to conclude a contract replaced this custom.[10] In general, widows who did not choose to marry again were free of the protection of fathers and husbands and enjoyed a legal autonomy that wives and mothers lacked.[11] In Sicily, however, the high rate of widows' remarriages in early modern times suggests that Roman laws allowed them a better capacity for legal agency as property owners.[12]

To sum up, we can state that in Italy (and also in Sicily, despite their relatively better position), until the reforms of the civil laws that took place under Napoleonic rule and the restoration, women, though not excluded, were in a particular position, subject to special restrictions, but enjoyed, at the same time, special protections. They were the rightful owners of their property, but management was restricted and subject to complex procedures, including authorisation by the husband or a male relative. By law, they were deemed incapable of being autonomous and thus in need of protection (see the case of dowry as a woman's inalienable property) from fraud, deception by strangers, and squandering on the part of their own husbands. In her study on women's juridical capability during the ancien régime, Simona Feci described them as "fish out of water".[13]

Second, an analysis of women's economic position cannot be fully understood if the analysis of property is not integrated with other elements, such as work, assistance, personal and familial relationships, and the informal management of money in commercial and credit transactions. This explains why, to understand women's economic role, Angela Groppi has proposed the term "resources", as opposed to "work", as more appropriate.[14] Notarial archives have allowed only a partial study of the economic resources available to women, as these archives mainly contain certificates regarding goods of a certain value and duration aimed at specifically identifying property deeds and conveyance procedures for future transfers or claims. For these reasons, such sources allow us to analyse, for example, a property itself, rather than its use or ownership; immovable goods, as opposed to movable goods; houses and lands, not objects; and precious objects, such as jewels, paintings, and new clothes, instead of tools, working utensils, and second-hand and everyday linen and clothes. Although notarial archives are a vast and valuable resource for the study of women's economic role in history, the exclusive use of such sources has given rise to the difficulty of providing a complete, dynamic report on women's agency and its connexion with property, conveyance, consumption, and labour. These sources need a transversal interpretation, aimed at acquiring new information, beyond the original purpose of documents examined, that, if analysed innovatively and in combination with other sources, will prove their real value.

Research has, in fact, recently had to widen its range of interpretative models thanks to an increased interest in women's studies and examine certain aspects of law and juridical procedures involving less customary subjects, sources, and methods. This has created new perspectives in the analysis of relationships of subjects with the world of objects, with a deeper insight into the experience of possessing material goods – so obviously characterised by gender – as well as an array of related social practices, such as informal administration of goods, their use, possession, production (including home production), maintenance, and transformation.

These new perspectives, which include studies focussing on men's and women's relationships with the world of objects, allow us to reconsider the three earlier mentioned elements, i.e. the specificity of women's juridical condition, new research topics, and use of sources. In Italy, these studies, prompted by the initial results obtained from international historiography and the fruit of the work of researchers working on the history of women and gender differences, have examined topics like men's and women's distinct, intertwined roles in social and economic practices related to the world of objects and their evolution as well as gender-related logics, determining their meaning and circulation.[15] The possibility of focussing on the everyday life of the lower classes – of ordinary people – and their relationship with personal household goods or working tools and also on the intermediary classes, which Renata Ago, in her history of goods in seventeenth-century Rome, calls "the mediocre class", made up of traders, lawyers, well-to-do craftsmen, and officers, has been of particular relevance.[16] As explained by Sandra Cavallo and Isabelle Chabot in the introduction to *Oggetti* (objects) in *Genesis: Rivista della Società italiana delle storiche*, it is everyday objects that, above all, play an important role in the configuration and evolution of the relationship between genders.[17]

The route followed by studies on objects has been distinct from that followed by research on consumption. The latter has indeed contributed to a significant shift in historiography, including women and gender-related aspects of economic practices. However, research carried out on the relationship between women and objects has expressed criticism towards the binary identification of men and women as "Mr Breadwinner" and "Mrs Consumer"[18] and the interpretation of the evolution of the historical relationship of individuals with objects primarily as "a revolution in consumption" and modernisation.[19]

Seen from this perspective, women's relationship with movable goods and objects may also be traced back by means of subjective, qualitative sources, such as letters, diaries, and publications; various kinds of legal acts, from sumptuary laws to regulations regarding jobs and professions; administrative documents, such as tax forms and governmental surveys; and judiciary sources of various kinds conceived to punish infringements. There are also, of course, notarial acts, which may conceal information incidentally contained in procedures designed for other purposes, such as those describing and listing objects as securities[20] or acts on widows with usufruct of their deceased husbands' goods or acts regarding women administering goods inherited by their underage children. Managing objects is often intertwined with the autonomous use of money on the part of women. Among the range of documents available, wills and post-mortem inventories are the most suitable for analysing the relationship between women and objects, and in fact they have been used in the most significant studies on late mediaeval and early modern times.[21] These documents, however, contain mainly information concerning well-to-do people, who had to ensure that their movable and immovable goods of a certain value would be passed down to their heirs. The bulk of objects and goods involved in exchanges, use, gifts, production, and work on the part of country or city women from the lower classes is more difficult to trace back, considering the scanty genealogical and patrimonial contribution of these women. Their lives left fleeting traces, and, even more so, the objects they used and owned – things of little value or of limited duration – were destined to be dissolved in oblivion, together with their owners, within the space of one or at most two generations. These objects would wear out quickly and be altered by the work carried out with them; they were of low value and circulated widely in small, everyday transactions. Yet these goods – as in the case of single items, originally part of trousseaus, pawned in Jewish market stalls in eighteenth-century Turin or objects pawned by women in Naples between the nineteenth and twentieth centuries[22] – represent a crucial resource for the family economy, both in pre-industrial economies and in strongly commercial, capitalist contexts. Being able to identify their traces is very important for observing economies and societies in a less conventional but equally indispensable way for relevant analyses.

The starting point of this chapter stems from these unanswered questions. How is it possible to give meaning to the diverse, ephemeral traces of ordinary women's relationship with movable goods and other objects?

II. Owning and devolving goods in Stromboli

The context that has prompted these reflections is the volcanic isle of Stromboli, one of the seven islands in the Aeolian archipelago, in the southern Tyrrhenian Sea, between Sicily and Calabria, in the first decades of the nineteenth century. The archipelago was part of the Kingdom of Sicily, while Calabria was part of the Kingdom of Naples. Both kingdoms were under the rule of the Bourbon dynasty beginning in 1734, and under the restoration they merged in the Kingdom of the Two Sicilies until the unification of Italy in 1860.

Like many other coastal and island communities of the Mediterranean, this seemingly unimportant place, in the nineteenth century, occupied a strategic geopolitical and commercial position. Stromboli was in the centre of an ideal triangle of maritime space formed by the important Sicilian ports of Palermo and Messina and, on the Italian coast, the peninsula of Sorrento, between the gulfs of Salerno and Naples. The economy of Stromboli in the nineteenth century was rather complex, in that farmers were also fishermen and sailors, transporting their produce by boats.[23] Agriculture relied on special grape varieties to produce raisins and *Malvasia* (Malmsey) wine for export. Figs and capers were also grown and were sold dried and packed. Wheat for local consumption was grown on terraced plots of land on the slopes of the volcano. Fishing was carried out regularly for the local market, delivering top-quality fish to Messina and Palermo.[24] There were some small shipyards, where boats used for fishing, cabotage, and trade were built. Trading activity, both legal and illegal, was intense, mainly due to the island's position between the two kingdoms of Naples and Sicily. Illicit activities included smuggling salt produced in Trapani or on the island of Salina, which was also part of the Aeolian archipelago. Moreover, during the Napoleonic wars, when Sicily was an English protectorate, the islanders fraudulently traded prizes that had been captured by privateers raiding ships on behalf of the Bourbon king.[25]

According to the testimony of nineteenth-century travellers, the women of Stromboli appeared to have played a leading role in the management of the island's economic activities, fishing and farming as much as men did. From 1869 onwards, the Aeolian archipelago was visited and observed by Archduke Ludwig Salvator of Habsburg-Lorraine (1847–1915), son of Leopold II of Tuscany, traveller, naturalist, and amateur anthropologist, who sailed the Mediterranean in his yacht, staying along the coasts and on the islands. Observations and illustrations from his travels were recorded in many books, eight of which are about the Aeolian Islands.[26] The archduke wrote that on Stromboli "quite often, the entire family, father, mother, sons and daughters, would go out on a fishing boat which, as they say here, is like a home".[27] Alexis de Tocqueville (1805–1859), half a century earlier, in 1826, blocked by a storm on Stromboli during a trip to Sicily, saw a boat coming in to moor with three generations of men and women rowing, all belonging to the same family.[28] Women, as pointed out by the archduke, would normally be seen rowing, hauling fishing nets, and working in fields, sometimes on their own or in a group, without the men of their families. On Stromboli

> after five o'clock in the afternoon . . . a merry crowd of girls and women, swimming and laughing, would bring their boats ashore for the night, or come back from fishing, or from tilling the soil on the distant slopes of the volcano.[29]

The archduke observed that "it is the women themselves who sail their boats stern forward, so that it is not difficult to identify a boat sailed by women, even if from a distance."[30] The same thing would happen all over the islands of the archipelago. Botanist Michele Lojacono Pojero (1853–1919), who was on the Aeolian Islands in 1877 to study the flora on behalf of the Botanical Gardens of Palermo, observed that

> it is not only the men who carry out the work on the Aeolian Islands, but also women work. They till the soil most meticulously and perform the manliest tasks. They hoe the ground, and look after their vines with the highest expertise, and harvest capers, grapes and muscadine with the utmost care. On Panarea, one can see women rowing their tiny boats, and going fishing; on Lipari . . . little girls can be seen carrying heavy loads of pumice stones on their shoulders. . . . They work merrily and fast, all on their own.[31]

The earliest statistical surveys carried out during the mid-nineteenth century show that women outnumbered men on Stromboli. Figures from the 1861 census show that, in a population of 1,828 inhabitants, women outnumbered men ten to seven; in the suburb of San Vincenzo, inhabited by fishermen, sailors, and "boat owners", this dropped to ten to 5.8.[32]

Transmission of property during the Bourbon monarchy, made possible by laws that allowed bilateralism in transmitting goods by descent, saw women in Stromboli holding, even in their legal status of daughters or mothers, a position regarded as almost equal to that of men.[33] Bourbon legislative norms, which were also included in the new Civil Code of 1819, were quite flexible, allowing passage and exchange of goods to either men or women on basically equal terms just as previous norms did.[34] Sometimes, however, children would be treated differently according to sex, order of birth, or individual projects – for instance to reward help offered by a son or daughter to old parents or to make it easier for children to migrate or settle elsewhere. In the case of the inhabitants of Stromboli, if there were any preferences they did not seem related to sex or birth order, but rather to personal events preceding a transfer of property or to family strategies devised by one or more members. Passing possessions on to children took place through wills, which should be considered, when possible, alongside dowries. On the parents' death, the shares of the family's patrimony already given as dowries to the daughters on their marriage were counted as part of each daughter's legitimate share or even balanced with other items of the available bulk of goods. In the case of a division in equal shares, previous donations could even be included as part of the entire legacy; the same also applied to previous sales or donations in favour of sons. A wife/mother, who quite often outlived her husband, received a share of the legacy equal in value to her dowry and became administrator of most or the entire patrimony on behalf of the children. If named as special heir, a widow could also inherit certain goods, which she would then own freely. Often, goods passing from one generation to the next were equally shared, as was the case in more than fifty percent of the examined wills issued in Stromboli (1809–1814, 1829–1868).[35]

In a previous article, I have shown how, for this reason, in Stromboli a high number of notarial acts certified trades of estates among relatives who were reorganising ownership of houses and land, which had been fragmented by wills into equal or comparable portions. Shares of immovable property were often of small dimensions and reduced value due to the accentuated divisibility of ownership of the plots, which often bordered on one another as a result of divisions between brothers and sisters or cousins of the same piece of land or group of houses or stores or warehouses. So many women and men from Stromboli used to trade items of limited economic value, such as pieces of land that had become too small after excessive fragmentation, with their relatives or neighbours.

Other times, it was simply a case of selling some property to buy property somewhere else, or a different piece of land, more suitable to their business; or, ultimately, to invest in movable goods and objects suitable for different activities, such as sea trade.[36]

To understand the local economy and women's roles, it is also necessary to reconstruct the flow of cash and objects, only in part documented by notarial acts. On observing, together with notaries' registers, other sources concerning the island, it is possible to identify traces and interesting information regarding items – objects, materials, tools – managed informally by women. It is particularly important to obtain information regarding those goods that would not usually be listed in inventories or marriage settlements (clothes, linen, or jewels) as part of a bride's trousseau and dowry. Women did, in fact, manage, own, pass on, buy, or sell other types of movable goods that passed through informal or even, on specific occasions, clandestine networks. A good methodological approach to preventing this information regarding possession, use, and trade of movable goods carried out by women from disappearing is historical microanalysis.

III. Trading with privateers

A document issued in the early nineteenth century reporting illegal trading on the island of Stromboli seemed to me of particular importance in understanding the management by women of movable goods as objects, tools, and foodstuff. The source is exceptional – namely, an investigation carried out by the prize court of the Kingdom of Sicily in 1811 to verify and punish the continual frauds carried out by corsairs sailing the Tyrrhenian Sea on behalf of King Ferdinand of Bourbon during the Napoleonic Wars. This court, as in other European countries, worked to legitimate the capture of prizes by privateers armed by the warring parties in the Mediterranean during the Napoleonic Wars and to regulate the resale of the captured goods. These corsairs, together with the inhabitants of Stromboli, unloaded raided goods onto the island to sell them without paying any duty to the Crown on goods ransacked from enemy ships. At the time, in the Tyrrhenian Sea, pro- or anti-France (the former the Kingdom of Naples, fallen under Napoleonic rule; the latter, the Kingdom of Sicily, under the British protectorate) privateer ships fought one another, looting the cargoes of their enemies. Wars fought by privateers represented a further, yet still quite anomalous, form of trade in the years when the continental blockade had enacted an embargo between French-controlled ports and British ports and canals.[37]

The *Camerale processo ammannito per la vendita delle robbe fatte dai corsari nell'Isole di Lipari* (investigation set up for the sales of stolen goods carried out by privateers in the Aeolian Islands)[38] allows us to reconstruct various forms of circulation as well as the identity of those who traded goods with privateers on Stromboli. It also helps us to understand the nature of the transactions of the people involved (including authorities in charge of maritime surveillance, trade, and health and also ordinary people) as well as their networks. There is information regarding personal relationships (godparentship of children, care and hospitality given during an illness)[39] and business associations, such as partnerships in cattle-breeding[40]; small maintenance and repair jobs given to people from Stromboli[41]; depository trusts of personal objects or navigation tools[42]; credits, in cash or in kind,[43] such as in the form of supplies for privateer ships[44]; and proxies.[45] From the traffic of privateer ships, Stromboli obtained supplies of food and other items, which were also traded with the other islands, including Lipari, the most important and most populated of the archipelago, whose administrators could obtain cattle, olive oil, and wheat.

This document contains statements gathered during investigations by the court, revealing new information regarding the personal life of people from the island. Conceived as a tool to gather information and take measures against the aforementioned illegal trading, including also an intricate case of corruption involving privateers and local superintendents and health and maritime officers, the *camerale processo* provides new insight into the circulation of objects and goods loaded onto ships sailing around the Mediterranean and subject to attacks by privateers all over the area.[46] Furthermore, this file shows the involvement of some women from Stromboli, alongside the men, in managing purchases and sales and working the materials brought onto the island. They made their statements as witnesses, or were variously involved and named, in a total of seventy-two witness statements gathered in the file. Twenty-one women were identified (among 148 subjects recorded) as engaged in certain activities that were mentioned much more rarely in notarial acts, such as certain informal jobs, businesses, trading, and other pursuits used by women to acquire and use goods, objects, and resources. Among these, the manufacturing of materials and the exchange of objects, tools, and food supplies held an important position.

IV. Typology of objects owned, used, and traded by women

Integrating the information obtained from this precious source with details gathered from notarial acts of the first half of the nineteenth century, I have attempted a grouping according to the typology of objects to obtain some diverse, though significant, details relevant to the knowledge of women's relationship with movable goods of varying value in the island's economy before the unification of Italy. The first type of movable goods and materials owned, used, and traded by women is linked with the world of work. Sea trade activities were predominant: The wives of well-to-do "boat owners" could become their heirs when they died and be free owners (and not just life tenants or administrators on behalf of their sons named as heirs) of fishing or passenger boats. In 1830, on the death of her husband, Simone Pajno, Provvidenza Renna, received, before (in *antiparte*) the dividing of the inheritance (together with a parcel of land and the family house, with its furniture and supplies), "the new *palamatara*[47] with its attached boat" and a fifty percent share of another *palamatara* co-owned with Baron Rodriquez.[48] After the death of Giuseppe Alajmo, a "boat owner", his widow, Marianna Restuccia, who then remarried a well-to-do man, Gaetano Renna, sold two-thirds of a 40-ton *paranzello*, of which she was the exclusive owner, to a great-grandchild of hers – Giuseppe Pajno, sailor.[49] Boats that were part of the small local fleet could therefore be owned and passed on by women, who would be seen actively rowing and fishing, as witnessed by travellers who visited the island.[50]

Women also owned tools for processing agricultural produce. The final products were then sold, and this activity was of crucial importance to the economy of the island. Among the main products were raisins, produced with a variety of grapes called *minutilla*, considered top quality among the Aeolian Islands at that time.[51] It was, again, Marianna Ristuccia, named in her husband's will in 1848,[52] who received, together with the estates she received in *antiparte*, "*caldara, cannizzi e cofina*"[53] – tools used to blanch, spread out, sun-dry, and transport the raisins. Eleonora Pirera married Francesco Di Matina in 1812. Her dowry, which consisted of various pieces of cultivated land with pergolas and the usual trousseau of linen and jewels, also included ten *cannizzi*, ten *cofina*, and a promised inheritance, on her father's death, of a few empty wine barrels.[54] In the same year, Mr and Mrs Moleta signed a "mutual codicil" in the notary's office, according to which each would be heir of the other. In the same act, they bequeathed a *pinnata* (a large porch used for storage) to one of their two daughters, Giuseppa. This act included the *littera* (a yard used for processing agricultural produce) in front, in the neighbourhood of Ficogrande. It specified also that the other daughter, Maria, could use these areas to process raisins, availing herself of the necessary tools – five *cannizzi* for each sister – to dry the raisins under the sun, and to be kept, after use, below the aforementioned *pinnata*.[55]

Women's jobs implied the possession of materials, along with specific tools. On Stromboli, women wound and wove silk for themselves or on behalf of others in their clients' houses or their own. They bought and sold it, worked as mediators in business transactions, and estimated and valued the material coming, more or less legally, from neighbouring Calabria through coastal trade or privateers. The *Camerale processo* allows the identification of at least twelve women, whose names appear constantly in the aforementioned period, who identified the origin and verified the quality of the silk and then worked it, twisting and winding it onto spools.[56]

A further analysis of the same document allows us to acquire more information regarding the role played by women in the informal trading of objects and other movable goods on Stromboli. More specifically, some of the illicit trading of goods brought onto the island by privateers, in the same way as silk, was managed by women who bought and traded objects and commodities. Sister Maria Galletti bought an empty vat from privateer Gaetano Gambardella, who, together with his brother Domenico and another privateer, Michele Pulpo, sold three more vats to another nun, Maria Tesoriero, who in turn bought olive oil from other privateers, which was traded for some wine on the island. These nuns were *bizzoche*, or "monache di casa" (literally house nuns); that is, women who took their vows without joining any order, born into well-to-do families, but destined neither to marry nor to join a convent. After being consecrated, they continued to live in their own houses. They made active use of their monastic dowry money, which they personally administered. When another woman, also named Maria Tesoriero, was questioned in 1811, she was thirty-three years old, widow of Giuseppe Pajno, and remarried to Antonino Panittieri. She admitted trading quite often with privateers, in collusion with the health authority deputy, and mediating frequently in big purchases of raisins and barrels of olive oil.[57] Giuseppa Moleti, together with her husband, Master Pietro D'Albora, also traded goods with privateers using an elaborate network of exchanges of credits in cash and kind as well as food supplies with the captains of the ships. She was one of the most active in the clandestine silk trade, and her name appears in the papers of the *Camerale processo* regarding a bale of silk that was at the centre of an intricate case of corruption and six vats of wine supplied to privateers.[58]

V. Conclusion: "Women of the sea" and their material world

Such evidence is not enough for a systemic study, but it does lead to some considerations. In coastal and maritime societies,[59] agriculture (or other trades, when examining towns)[60] is integrated with sea trade (transport, fishing, trade, smuggling) and with the manufactured processing of the produce of these activities in frontier areas at intersections between town, country, and sea. The character of such open spaces, which are continually changing, can be better understood by considering alternative systems of allocation and acquisition of resources to those applied to standard typologies of trade, labour, and use. These contexts could be understood by applying the concept of *shadow economy*, or *economie sombre*. In these systems, formal and informal spheres – the licit and illicit spheres – are mutually related and include an infinite range of intermediate grey areas.[61]

These are, moreover, border economies. Borders between land and sea and between states, jurisdictions, and economic spheres are all involved, where the term "border" no longer means a separation, but rather crossroads and communication. Contact with other economies, both near and far, was made through navigation, war, piracy, or privateering. In these border economies, the areas of formal and informal, but also licit and illicit, would fade into one another. They generated tasks, knowledge, practices, and specific opportunities, which can now be closely studied using the tools generated by border studies in social and economic sciences and in geography.

It is from such contexts that examination, even if fragmentary or coincidental, of possession and circulation of movable goods, objects, and materials is particularly significant since it allows us to observe more informal and particularly less evident aspects – even more so when women are involved in the possession, use, and trade. The observations made in this study on the island of Stromboli in the nineteenth century allow us to confirm that women were strongly involved in every kind of relationship regarding objects and movable goods in use on the island. They inherited working tools and supplies that they would then use to perform many tasks on land or at sea, ranging from processing agricultural produce to managing maritime enterprises and being boat owners. On their own, or together with their husbands, they would buy, lend, and trade goods and supplies. In addition, a more specifically female activity revolved around trading and working raw silk that arrived by ship and that was assessed, wound, and woven by expert women – the silk-winding "mistresses".

This is important evidence of the roots of what anthropologists still observed many years later, in the twentieth century.[62] Anthropologist Macrina Marilena Maffei, writing on the *donne di mare* (women of the sea) from the Aeolian Islands, suggests the historical value and chronological depth of practices and behaviours that are currently studied by ethnographers. Introducing a brief ethnographic study of fisherwomen from the Aeolian Islands in the twentieth century, she wrote,

> [T]he memory of women who set their boats afloat, rowed day and night, hauled the fishing nets in, set their creels, brought their boats ashore is being lost. Women who would go fishing at night, and who, during the day, would sow the land, pick olives and capers, and salt fish. Women who would sail great distances to sell their fish, and who would look after their families, washing their clothes, keeping their houses in order and cooking.[63]

Fragmentary but real evidence of the objects used in all these activities two centuries ago has emerged today, from documents of various origins, showing the actual work that contributed to building a frontier world of trade – quite demanding but at the same time dynamic and open to opportunities.

Notes

1 Paolo Ungari, *Storia del diritto di famiglia in Italia 1796–1945*, Bologna 1974 [Il Mulino]; Thomas Kuehn, *Family and Gender in Renaissance Italy, 1300–1600*, Cambridge 2017 [Cambridge University Press]. Kuehn points out that the comparison between northern and central Italy and southern Italy and Sicily is "problematic for lack of printed versions, but the work of scholars such as Andrea Romano and Igor Mineo makes possible some points of comparison" (p. 18).

2 *Codice per lo Regno delle Due Sicilie* (2 vol.), Naples 1819.

3 Vito La Mantia, *Leggi civili del Regno di Sicilia (1130–1816)*, Palermo 1895 [Reber], pp. 66–78. However, in Siracusa the daughter who already had her dowry was excluded from the inheritance, and in Caltagirone the surviving spouse got the usufruct and the children just the bare ownership, pp. 72–75.

4 Ibid., pp. 178–193.

5 Ibid., pp. 157–176.

6 Jane Schneider, "Trousseau as Treasure. Some Contradictions of Late Nineteenth Century Change in Sicily", in: E. B. Ross (ed.), *Beyond the Myths of Culture. Essays in Cultural Materialism*, New York 1980 [Academic Pr], pp. 323–355; Ida Fazio, "Valori economici e valori simbolici. Il declino della dote nell'Italia dell'Ottocento", in: *Quaderni storici* 79 (1992), pp. 291–316.

7 E. Igor Mineo, "Formazione delle élites urbane nella Sicilia del tardo medioevo. Matrimonio e sistemi di successione", in: *Quaderni storici* 88 (1995), pp. 9–41.

8 Ida Fazio, "Famiglia, matrimonio, trasmissione della proprietà. Ipotesi di lavoro a partire dal caso siciliano", in: Benedetto Meloni (ed.), *Famiglia meridionale senza familismo. Reti di relazione e parentela*, Roma 1997 [Donzelli], pp. 3–24.

9 La Mantia, *Leggi civili*, pp. 104–119.

10 Cristina Fenu, "La clausola giuridica di rinuncia ai benefici del senatoconsulto velleiano e la tutela pupillorum materna in un documento inedito dell'Archivio notarile antico di Udine", in: *Metodi e Ricerche* XXXIII, 1–2 (2014), pp. 3–14, esp. pp. 5–8. On the contradictions of the shift to the Napoleonic legal systems for married women, see Ida Fazio, "Complicità coniugali. Proprietà e identità nella Torino napoleonica", in: *Quaderni storici 33, Gestione dei patrimoni e diritti delle donne* (1998), pp. 333–360; Simona Feci, *Pesci fuor d'acqua. Donne a Roma in età moderna. Diritti e patrimoni*, Rome 2004 [Viella], pp. 36–37.

11 Sandra Cavallo and Lyndan Warner (eds.), *Widowhood in Medieval and Early Modern Europe*, Harlow 1999 [Routledge], gives a comparative perspective on widowhood and on the links between dowry, succession, agency in Early Modern Europe. The most complete update on Renaissance Tuscany in Isabelle Chabot, *La dette des familles. Femmes, lignage et patrimoine à Florence aux XIVe et XVe siècles*, Rome 2011 [École française de Rome].

12 Francesco Benigno, "The Southern Italian Family in the Early Modern Period. A Discussion of Coresidential Patterns", in: *Continuity and Change* 4 (1989), pp. 165–194, p. 173. He stresses also that widows were more likely to remarry in southern than in northern Italy, and that the average period of widowhood was shorter, as Livi Bacci pointed out, for the nineteenth century (Massimo Livi Bacci, "On the Frequence of Remarriage in Nineteenth-century Italy. Methods and Results", in: Jacques Dupaquier et al. (eds.), *Marriage and Remarriage in the Populations of the Past*, London 1981 [Academic Press Inc.], pp. 347–360). For a comparison between early modern Mediterranean legal systems in the sixteenth century, see Jutta Sperling, "Dowry or Inheritance? Kinship, Property, and Women's Agency in Lisbon, Venice, and Florence (1572)", in: *Journal of Early Modern History* 11 (2007), pp. 197–238.

13 Feci, *Pesci fuor d'acqua*.

14 Angela Groppi, "Il lavoro delle donne. Un questionario da arricchire", in: Simonetta Cavaciocchi (ed.), *La donna nell'economia. Secc. XIII – XVIII*, Firenze 1990 [Le Monnier], pp. 143–154; Angela Groppi (ed.), *Il lavoro delle donne*, Roma and Bari 1996 [Laterza],

see also Anna Bellavitis, *Women's Work and Rights in Early Modern Urban Europe*, London 2018 [Palgrave Macmillan].

15 It is important to stress the shift from the study of the cultures of consumption to the analysis of the meaning of objects, i.e. the "world of goods". See John Brewer and Roy Porter (eds.), *Consumption and the World of Goods*, London and New York 1993 [Routledge]. Gender as a category of analysis is used by Amanda Vickery, "Women and the world of goods: A Lancashire consumer and her possessions, 1751–81", pp. 274–303; The Società Italiana delle Storiche and the Dottorato internazionale in Storia delle donne e delle identità di genere of the University of Naples "L'Orientale" fostered plenty of new research. See, in particular: Giulia Calvi and Isabelle Chabot (eds.), *Le ricchezze delle donne. Diritti patrimoniali e poteri familiari in Italia* (XIII – XIX secolo), Torino 1998 [Rosenberg & Sellier]; Angiolina Arru, Laura Di Michele and Maria Stella (eds.), *Proprietarie. Avere, non avere, ereditare, industriarsi*, Napoli 2002 [Liguori]; Angiolina Arru and Maria Stella (eds.), *I consumi. Una questione di genere*, Rome 2003 [Carocci]. For an overview, see in Giulia Calvi (ed.), *Innesti. Donne e genere nella storia sociale*, Roma 2004 [Viella], Daniela Lombardi- (Famiglie di antico regime, pp. 199–221) and Alessandra Pescarolo (Genere e famiglia in età contemporanea, pp. 223–255).

16 Renata Ago, *Gusto for Things: A History of Objects in Seventeenth-Century Rome*, Chicago 2013 [University of Chicago Press] (Italian edition Roma 2006).

17 Sandra Cavallo and Isabelle Chabot (eds.), "Oggetti", special issue of: Genesis. *Rivista della società italiana delle storiche* V/1 (2006).

18 Arru and Stella, *I consumi, Introduzione*, p. 12.

19 A critique on the "trickle-down approach" to the history of consumption, i.e. the diffusion from upper to middle and lower classes of the consuming habits of the élite (Neil McKendrick, John Brewer and J. H. Plumb, *The Birth of a Consumer Society: The Commercialization of Eighteenth-Century England*, Bloomington 1982 [Europa Publications Limited]) has been discussed by many historians who stressed the importance of many other ways of interacting with the "world of goods" (John Brewer and Roy Porter (eds.), *Consumption and the World of Goods*, London and New York 1993 [Routledge]) by the means of multiple strategies (Giovanni Levi, "Comportements, ressources, procés. Avant de la «révolution» de la consommation", in: Jacques Revel (ed.), *Jeux d'échelles. La mycroanalyse à l'experiénce*, Paris 1996 [Gallimard], pp. 187–207). For a discussion see Renata Ago, *Gusto for things*, Introduction.

20 Renata Ago, *Economia barocca. Mercato e istituzioni nella Roma del Seicento*, Roma 1998, and "Oltre la dote: i beni femminili", in: Angela Groppi (ed.), *Il lavoro delle donne*, Roma and Bari 1996 [Donzelli]; Maria Rosaria De Rosa, *A tempo debito. Donne, uomini, relazioni di credito a Napoli tra Ottocento e Novecento*, Rome 2017 [Viella].

21 Cavallo and Chabot, "Oggetti", "Introduzione".

22 Luciano Allegra, "Corredi smembrati. Donne e credito in ancien régime", in: Angiolina Arru and Maria Stella (eds.), *I consumi. Una questione di genere*, Rome 2003 [Carocci]; De Rosa, *A tempo debito*.

23 Ludwig Salvator von Österreich-Toskana (1893–1896), *Die Liparischen Inseln* (8 vol.), Prag. Italian translation: *Le isole Lipari. Riproduzione litografica dall'originale con traduzione in italiano*, edit. by Pino Paino, Lipari 1979–1987, VII, Stromboli, VIII, Allgemeiner Theil.

24 Ettore Barnao, *Appunti per servire alla storia di Stromboli*, Lipari 2017 [Edizioni del Centro Studi eoliano], p. 233.

25 Ida Fazio and Rita Loredana Foti, "Scansar le frodi. Prede corsare nella Sicilia del decennio inglese", in: *Quaderni storici* 143, 2 (2013), pp. 497–539; Rita Loredana Foti, *Giudici e corsari nel Mediterraneo. Il Tribunale delle prede di Sicilia 1808–1813*, Palermo 2016 [Istituto Poligrafico Europeo].

26 Wolfgang Löhnert, *Vienna: 'Hinaus, hinaus aufs weite blaue Meer', Auf den Spuren von Erzherzog Ludwig Salvator*, Vienna [Ludwig Salvator-Gesellschaft], www.ludwigsalvator.com/ital/basis.htm (accessed 22 October 2019).

27 von Österreich-Toskana, *Le isole Lipari*, VII, p. 120.

28 Alexis de Toqueville, *Correspondance et oeuvres posthumes de Alexis de Tocqueville*, Paris 1866 [Michel Lévy Frères], pp. 149–153.
29 von Österreich-Toskana, *Le isole Lipari*, VII, p. 6.
30 Ibid., VIII, p. 120. Also, on the very nearby island of Panarea the women "having finished work in the fields did not disdain giving themselves over to fishing, to earn something". (VIII, p. 20).
31 Michele Lojacono Pojero, *Le isole Eolie e la loro vegetazione*, Palermo 1878 [Losnaider], pp. 15–16.
32 von Österreich-Toskana, *Le isole Lipari*, VII, *Apparato*; VIII, pp. 12–13. Data refers to people on the cencus (present + absent) as at 31.12.1861.
33 Ida Fazio, "Parentela e mercato nell'isola di Stromboli", in: Renata Ago and Benedetta Borello (eds.), *Famiglie. Circolazione di beni, circuiti di affetti in età moderna*, Rome 2008 [Viella], pp. 141–184, pp. 158–161.
34 According to the new Bourbon Code of 1819, women's hereditary rights were equivalent to men's, both in intestate inheritance and inheritance through testament. If there was no will, all children had the same right to equal shares of the parents' property. If children inherited by will, they had the right to equal shares of the "legitimate portion", equal to fifty percent of the inheritance. The remaining half, the so-called available portion, could be transferred to anyone and could therefore be used by the testator to make distinctions among children. Dowries provided to daughters, or donations made to sons on the occasion of their marriages, were to be counted ("collated") among the inheritance assets, in the absence of a will. By contrast, if sons and daughters inherited by will, the goods advanced before the death of the testator could be considered anticipation of their final share. Or, if one wanted to favour one child, the "advanced share" (*anteparte*) could be counted in the "available portion". However, if its value exceeded the total available portion of the inheritance, the excess had to be shared equally among all heirs, making it impossible to disinherit children. Heirs could agree not to divide the inheritance and to administer it together. *Codice per lo Regno delle Due Sicilie, Parte prima, Leggi civili*, Libro III.
35 Archivio di Stato di Messina (herein ASM), Notarile Messina (herein NM), Notary Angelo Florio, voll. 2458–2461 (1809–1814) and voll. 2472–2492 (1829–1868); Notary Angelo Florio Pajno, voll. 3318–3319 (1860–1861). See, for example, in 1812, the reciprocal codicil of the spouses Francesco Moleta and Francesca Lo Curcio of 16.11.1812.
36 Regarding 1829–1868, see cases examined in Fazio, *Parentela e mercato*, pp. 147–161; "Brothers, Sisters and the Rearrangements of Property on the Sicilian Island of Stromboli in the Nineteenth Century", in: *European Review of History. Revue europeenne d'histoire* 17, 5 (2010), pp. 805–815.
37 Silvia Marzagalli, *Les Boulevards de la fraude. Le négoce maritime et le Blocus continental 1806–1813*, Villeneuve D'Ascq 1999 [Presses universitaires du Septentrion].
38 Archivio di Stato di Palermo, (herein ASPa), Consultore del Governo, Tribunale delle Prede del Regno di Sicilia (herein TP), vol. 270.
39 ASPa, TP, vol. 267, *Memoriale del Deputato Capitano Gianbattista Manti*; ASPa, TP, Camerale processo, cc. 61, 67v.
40 Camerale processo, cc. 16–16v, 26, 48.
41 Ibid., p. 41.
42 Camerale processo, cc. 23, 26, 37v–38.
43 ASM, NM, Notary Angelo Florio, vol. 2458, 17.5.1810, proxy for Fr. Don Gaetano Tesoriero given to Don Francesco Saracino of Palermo to claim a sum due to him from the privateer Ambrosio Piatti; 31.5.1810, proxy for Pietro Costa to his brother Giovanni to claim a debt from the privateer Spiro Magri.
44 ASM, NM, Notary Angelo Florio, vol. 2458, 28.5.1810, a debt of the Dalmatian privateer Giovanni Radonic in favour of Giuseppe Pajno for "bread, wine, pasta and money" to sustain the crew and to sail for a value of 39 onze; 31.5.1810, Radonic admits to being in debt for 36 onze lent him "to continue his trip in the gulf of Venice".
45 ASM, NM, Notary Angelo Florio, vol. 2458, 11.5.1810, proxy of privateer Filippo Carpanzano to Aniello Di Gregorio; 31.5.1810, proxy of Giuseppe Pajno to Giovanni Costa, and guarantee for Pietro Costa.

46 Foti, *Giudici e corsari*.
47 A *palamatara* is a large boat used both to catch fish and for transport.
48 ASM, NM, Notary Angelo Florio, vol. 2475, 53, Will of Simone Pajno, 53, 24.4.1830.
49 ASM, NM, Notary Angelo Florio Pajno, vol. 3320, n. 44, 20.5.1862. Two-thirds of the boats are sold for the sum of 226 onze and 20 tarì, equivalent to Lire 2850.
50 Ida Fazio, "Rematrice o filatrice? Donne in un'economia di frontiera (Isole Eolie, inizio dell' Ottocento)", *Storica* 72 (2020), pp. 55–84, pp. 70–73.
51 According to De Welz (1822), p. 67, raisins produced on Stromboli were the highest quality.
52 ASM, NM, Notary Angelo Florio, vol. 2486, 21.3.1848.
53 Cauldron, cane grids used to sun-dry grapes and figs, large baskets to transport produce.
54 ASM, NM, Notary Angelo Florio, vol. 2460, 10.11.1812.
55 Ibid.
56 Among them Maria Russo, daughter of a sergeant, thirty-four, and Francesca Giannone, sixty, wife of a soldier of the garrison of Lipari, are silk-winding "mistresses".
57 *Camerale processo* (1811), cc. 33, 45v, 68.
58 *Camerale processo* (1811), cc. 14, 16 v., 38, 40, 54 v., 70 v.
59 Gérard Le Bouëdec, Francis Ploux, Christophe Cérino and Aliette Geistdoerfer, (eds.), *Entre terre et mer. Sociétés littorales et pluriactivités* (XVe – XXe siècle), Rennes 2004 [PU]; Emmanuelle Charpentier, *Le littoral et les hommes. Espaces et sociétés des côtes nord de la Bretagne au XVIIIe siècle*, Rennes 2009 [Université Rennes 2, Université Européenne de Bretagne]; Mathias Tranchant (ed.), "Face aux risques maritimes. La pluriactivité et la mutualisation comme stratégies individuelles et collectives (XIIIe – XVIIIe siècle)", in: *Annales de Bretagne et des Pays de l'Ouest* 120, 2 (2013); Alida Clemente, "Il mare e la città. Comunità pescherecce e trasformazione urbana nella Napoli contemporanea", in: *Società e storia* 97 (2012), pp. 542–579; Gilbert Buti, *Les chemins de la mer. Un petit port méditérranéen: Saint Tropez, XVII – XVIII siècles*, Rennes 2010 [PUR]; Alessandro Carassale and Luca Lo Basso, Piero Vernassa, *Sanremo, giardino di limoni. Produzione e commercio degli agrumi dell'estremo Ponente ligure* (secoli XII – XIX), Milano 2008 [Carocci]; Luca Lo Basso, *Capitani, corsari e armatori. I mestieri e le culture del mare dalla tratta degli schiavi a Garibaldi*, Novi Ligure 2011 [Città del silenzio].
60 Clemente, "Il mare e la città".
61 Thomas Buchner and Philip R. Hoffmann-Rehnitz (eds.), *Shadow Economies and Irregular Work in Urban Europe: 16th to Early 20th Centuries*, Vienna and Münster 2011 [LIT]; Anne Montenach, "Une économie de l'ombre? La fraude dans le commerce alimentaire à Lyon au XVIIe siècle", in: Gérard Béaur, Hubert Bonin and Claire Lemercier (eds.), *Fraude, contrefaçon et contrebande de l'Antiquité à nos jours*, Genève 2016 [DROZ], pp. 515–538.
62 Macrina Marilena Maffei, *Donne di mare. Una storia sommersa dell'arcipelago eoliano*, Patti 2013 [Pungitopo].
63 Ibid., pp. 12–13.

Sources

Archives

Italy, Messina, Archivio di Stato di Messina (ASM), Notarile Messina (NM):
———Notary Angelo Florio: voll. 2458–2461 (1809–1814); voll. 2472–2492 (1829–1868).
———Notary Angelo Florio Pajno: voll. 3318–3319 (1860–1861).
Italy, Palermo, Archivio di Stato di Palermo (ASPa), Consultore del Governo, Tribunale delle Prede del Regno di Sicilia (TP):
———vol 270.
———vol 267, Memoriale del Deputato Capitano Gianbattista Manti.
———Camerale processo, cc. 14, 16, 23, 26, 33, 37–38, 40, 41, 45, 48, 54, 61, 67, 68, 70.

Printed

Codice per lo Regno delle Due Sicilie, 2 vol, Napoli 1819 [Angelo Trani].
de Toqueville, Alexis, *Correspondance et oeuvres posthumes de Alexis de Tocqueville*, Paris 1866 [Michel Lévy Frères].
Michele Lojacono Pojero, *Le isole Eolie e la loro vegetazione*, Palermo 1878 [Losnaider].
von Österreich-Toskana, Ludwig Salvator, *Die Liparischen Inseln (8 vol.)*, Prag [H. Mercy]. Italian translation: *Le isole Lipari. Riproduzione litografica dall'originale con traduzione in italiano*, ed. Pino Paino, Lipari 1979–1987 [Edinixe].

Bibliography

Ago, Renata, "Oltre la dote: i beni femminili", in: Angela Groppi (ed.), *Il lavoro delle donne*, Rome and Bari 1996 [Laterza].
———*Economia barocca. Mercato e istituzioni nella Roma del Seicento*, Rome 1998 [Donzelli].
———*Gusto for Things: A History of Objects in Seventeenth-Century Rome*, Chicago 2013 [University of Chicago Press] (Italian edition Roma 2006).
Allegra, Luciano, "Corredi smembrati. Donne e credito in ancien régime", in: Angiolina Arru and Maria Stella (ed.), *I consumi. Una questione di genere*, Rome 2003 [Carocci].
Arru, Angiolina and Maria Stella (eds.), *Proprietarie. Avere, non avere, ereditare, industriarsi*, Naples 2002 [Liguori].
———(eds.), *I consumi. Una questione di genere*, Rome 2003 [Carocci].
Barnao, Ettore, *Appunti per servire alla storia di Stromboli*, Lipari 2017 [Edizioni del Centro Studi eoliano].
Bellavitis, Anna, *Women's Work and Rights in Early Modern Urban Europe*, London 2018 [Palgrave Macmillan].
Brewer, John and Roy Porter (eds.), *Consumption and the World of Goods*, London and New York 1993 [Routledge].
Buchner, Thomas and Philip R. Hoffmann-Rehnitz (eds.), *Shadow Economies and Irregular Work in Urban Europe: 16th to Early 20th Centuries*, Vienna and Münster 2011 [LIT].
Buti, Gilbert, *Les chemins de la mer. Un petit port méditérranéen: Saint Tropez, XVII – XVIII siècles*, Rennes 2010 [PUR].
Calvi, Giulia and Isabelle Chabot (eds.), *Le ricchezze delle donne. Diritti patrimoniali e poteri familiari in Italia* (XIII–XIX secolo), Torino 1998 [Rosenberg & Sellier].
Carassale, Alessandro, Luca Lo Basso and Piero Vernassa, *Sanremo, giardino di limoni. Produzione e commercio degli agrumi dell'estremo Ponente ligure* (secoli XII–XIX), Milan 2008 [Carocci].
Cavallo, Sandra and Isabelle Chabot (eds.), "Oggetti, special issue of Genesis", *Rivista della società italiana delle storiche* V, 1 (2006).
Cavallo, Sandra and Lyndan Warner (eds.), *Widowhood in Medieval and Early Modern Europe*, Harlow 1999 [Routledge].
Chabot, Isabelle, *La dette des familles. Femmes, lignage et patrimoine à Florence aux XIVe et XVe siècles*, Rome 2011 [École française de Rome].
Charpentier, Emmanuelle, *Le littoral et les hommes. Espaces et sociétés des côtes nord de la Bretagne au XVIIIe siècle*, Rennes 2009 [Université Rennes 2, Université Européenne de Bretagne].
Clemente, Alida, "Il mare e la città. Comunità pescherecce e trasformazione urbana nella Napoli contemporanea", in: *Società e storia* 97 (2012), pp. 542–579.
De Rosa, Maria Rosaria, *A tempo debito. Donne, uomini, relazioni di credito a Napoli tra Ottocento e Novecento*, Rome 2017 [Viella].

De Welz, Giuseppe, *Saggio su i mezzi da moltiplicare prontamente le ricchezze della Sicilia*, Paris 1822 [Firmin Didot], www.ludwigsalvator.com/ital/basis.htm (accessed 22 October 2019).

E. Igor Mineo, "'Formazione delle élites urbane nella Sicilia del tardo medioevo. Matrimonio e sistemi di successione", in: *Quaderni storici* 88 (1995), pp. 9–41.

Fazio, Ida, "Valori economici e valori simbolici. Il declino della dote nell'Italia dell'Ottocento", in: *Quaderni storici* 79 (1992), pp. 291–316.

———Famiglia, matrimonio, trasmissione della proprietà. Ipotesi di lavoro a partire dal caso siciliano", in: Benedetto Meloni (ed.), *Famiglia meridionale senza familismo. Reti di relazione e parentela*, Rome 1997 [Donzelli], pp. 3–24.

———"Complicità coniugali. Proprietà e identità nella Torino napoleonica", in: *Quaderni storici 33, Gestione dei patrimoni e diritti delle donne* (1998), pp. 333–360.

———"Parentela e mercato nell'isola di Stromboli", in: Renata Ago and Benedetta Borello (eds.), *Famiglie. Circolazione di beni, circuiti di affetti in età moderna*, Rome 2008 [Viella], pp. 141–184.

———"Brothers, Sisters and the Rearrangements of Property on the Sicilian Island of Stromboli in the Nineteenth Century", in: *European Review of History. Revue europeenne d'histoire* 17, 5 (2010), pp. 805–815.

———"Rematrice o filatrice? Donne in un'economia di frontiera (Isole Eolie, inizio dell'Ottocento)", in: *Storica* 72 (2020), pp. 55–84.

Fazio, Ida and Rita Loredana Foti, "Scansar le frodi. Prede corsare nella Sicilia del decennio inglese", in: *Quaderni storici* 143 (2013), pp. 497–539.

Feci, Simona, *Pesci fuor d'acqua. Donne a Roma in età moderna. Diritti e patrimoni*, Rome 2004 [Viella].

Fenu, Cristina, "La clausola giuridica di rinuncia ai benefici del senatoconsulto velleiano e la tutela pupillorum materna in un documento inedito dell'Archivio notarile antico di Udine", in: *Metodi e Ricerche* XXXIII, 1–2 (2014), pp. 3–14.

Foti, Rita Loredana, *Giudici e corsari nel Mediterraneo. Il Tribunale delle prede di Sicilia 1808–1813*, Palermo 2016 [Istituto Poligrafico Europeo].

Francesco Benigno, "The Southern Italian Family in the Early Modern Period. A Discussion of Coresidential Patterns", in: *Continuity and Change* 4 (1989), pp. 165–194.

Groppi, Angela, "Il lavoro delle donne. Un questionario da arricchire", in: Simonetta Cavaciocchi (ed.), *La donna nell'economia* (Secc. XIII–XVIII), Firenze 1990 [Le Monnier], pp. 143–154.

———(ed.), *Il lavoro delle donne*, Rome and Bari 1996 [Laterza].

Kuehn, Thomas, *Family and gender in Renaissance Italy, 1300–1600*, Cambridge 2017 [Cambridge University Press].

La Mantia, Vito, *Leggi civili del Regno di Sicilia (1130–1816)*, Palermo 1895 [Reber].

Le Bouëdec, Gérard, Francis Ploux, Christophe Cérino and Aliette Geistdoerfer (eds.), "Entre terre et mer. Sociétés littorales et pluriactivités Gérard", in: Francis Ploux, Christophe Cérino, Aliette Geistdoerfer (eds.), *Entre terre et mer. Sociétés littorales et pluriactivités* (XVe–XXe siècle), Rennes 2004 [PU].

Livi Bacci, Massimo, "On the Frequence of Remarriage in Nineteenth-Century Italy. Methods and Results", in: Jacques Dupaquier et al. (eds.), *Marriage and Remarriage in the Populations of the Past*, London 1981 [Academic Press Inc.], pp. 347–360.

Lo Basso, Luca, *Capitani, corsari e armatori. I mestieri e le culture del mare dalla tratta degli schiavi a Garibaldi*, Novi Ligure 2011 [Città del silenzio].

Lombardi, Daniela, "Famiglie di antico regime", in: Giulia Calvi (ed.), *Innesti. Donne e genere nella storia sociale*, Rome 2004 [Viella], pp. 199–221.

Maffei, Macrina Marilena, *Donne di mare. Una storia sommersa dell'arcipelago eoliano*, Patti 2013 [Pungitopo].

Marzagalli, Silvia, *Les Boulevards de la fraude. Le négoce maritime et le Blocus continental 1806–1813*, Villeneuve D'Ascq 1999 [Presses universitaires du Septentrion].

Montenach, Anne, "Une économie de l'ombre? La fraude dans le commerce alimentaire à Lyon au XVIIe siècle", in: Gérard Béaur, Hubert Bonin and Claire Lemercier (eds.), *Fraude, contrefaçon et contrebande de l'Antiquité à nos jours*, Genève 2016 [DROZ], pp. 515–538.

Pescarolo, Alessandra, "Genere e famiglia in età contemporanea", in: Giulia Calvi (ed.), *Innesti. Donne e genere nella storia sociale*, Rome 2004 [Viella], pp. 223–255.

Schneider, Jane, "Trousseau as Treasure: Some Contradictions of Late Nineteenth Century Change in Sicily", in: E.B. Ross (ed.), *Beyond the Myths of Culture. Essays in Cultural Materialism*, New York 1980 [Academic Pr], pp. 323–355.

Sperling, Jutta, "Dowry or Inheritance? Kinship, Property, and Women's Agency in Lisbon, Venice, and Florence (1572)", in: *Journal of Early Modern History* 11 (2007), pp. 197–238.

Tranchant, Mathias (ed.), "Face aux risques maritimes. La pluriactivité et la mutualisation comme stratégies individuelles et collectives (XIIIe – XVIIIe siècle)", in: *Annales de Bretagne et des Pays de l'Ouest* 120, 2 (2013).

Ungari, Paolo, *Storia del diritto di famiglia in Italia 1796–1945*, Bologna 1974 [Il Mulino].

Vickery, Amanda, "Women and the World of Goods. A Lancashire Consumer and Her Possessions (1781–1881)", in: John Brewer and Roy Porter (eds.), *Consumption and the World of Goods*, London and New York 1993 [Routledge], pp. 274–303.

FIGURE 11.1 Map of Greece, Guillaume de L'Isle, Philippe Buache, *Carte d' Europe*, 1769 (detail).

Source: Library of Congress Geography and Map Division, Washington, D.C., U.S.A., public domain, G5700 1724. L5 TIL, http://hdl.loc.gov/loc.gmd/g5700.ct000045 (15.02.2020, 15:15 CET).

11

STAMP DUTY AND THE TRANSFORMATION OF THE DOWRY IN NINETEENTH-CENTURY GREECE

Evdoxios Doxiadis

ABSTRACT

In 1843 the newly established Greek kingdom imposed a stamp duty on dowry contracts calculated on the value of the dowry described. Although this change has been little discussed in Greek historiography and is often seen simply as an attempt by the bankrupt Greek state to raise revenue, its effect was near revolutionary. In the first place, it added a significant cost to marriage arrangements, possibly forcing many poorer Greeks to avoid notarised dowry contracts. Since the law mandated that only notarised dowry contracts were enforceable in the new Greek courts, such an outcome would have been particularly detrimental to women who owned their dowry but did not control it. Second, while dowry contracts throughout the Ottoman period usually described the goods and land assigned rather than their value, the stamp duty forced the reconceptualisation of the dowry in monetary terms. Alongside other social transformations in the early nineteenth century, this development led to the eventual monetarisation of the dowry and the increasing alienation of the dowry from its principal owner, the wife, to the benefit of her husband. Although this was a long process, the establishment of the stamp duty helped transform how Greeks perceived the dowry, from a set of productive properties to a monetary value. This chapter will discuss the dowry and other marriage payments prior to the establishment of the modern Greek state and the impact of the new laws, and especially of the stamp duty, following Greece's independence in 1829, with a particular focus on the effects of such laws on the composition of the dowry.

I. Introduction

On 18 February 1983 the first socialist government of Greece issued a comprehensive revision of family law abolishing the dowry and transferring the ownership of existing dowries from husbands to their wives unless they were monetary.[1] This was the formal end of an institution that had seen radical changes since the establishment of the modern Greek state in 1829. This chapter examines part of these transformations, focussing on the first formative decades of modern Greece, when the laws and institutions of the state were being formulated, with a particular focus on an 1843 law and its impact on dowry practices. My main argument is that transformation of the dowry, in particular a trend that saw an increased monetisation compared to the Ottoman period, was a complex affair. Certainly, social and economic transformations had an enormous impact on dowry practices, as other scholars have suggested, but so did certain policies of the new state whose initial purposes were quite different. In this case I am examining the imposition of a stamp duty on notarised documents, itself one of several measures taken by the Greek government of the time to raise income to forestall a looming bankruptcy. My sources are primarily dowry contracts from the town of Leonidio in the immediate post-independence period, but I also use notarial documents from other regions (Mykonos, Naxos, Athens) to establish the conditions prior to independence as well as documents from the Athens courts of appeals in an effort to detect possible changes in legal practice following the establishment of the Greek state.

II. The dowry in Ottoman times

When discussing the dowry in Ottoman Greece, the most fundamental aspect that has to be kept in mind is the extreme variety of practices, even within the limited space of the regions that participated in the Greek war of independence and composed the subsequent Greek state. It often appears as if every region, island, and village had its own customs that varied dramatically from all others. Customs ranged from the extreme of the island of Karpathos, where firstborn daughters received nearly the entire immovable wealth of their mothers, with the rest of the female offspring being thus rendered essentially propertyless, to inner Mani, where daughters were excluded from all immovable property. Moreover, in many regions there was more or less equitable division of the property of the parents among all offspring regardless of gender. Some scholars have even argued that in certain areas brideprice rather than dowry was the norm. Some regions clearly favoured matrilocal/uxorilocal marriage, while others practiced patrilocality, and occasionally both types existed side by side.[2]

Marriage for Greek women was an imperative, even when compared to other Mediterranean societies. As late as 1880, ninety-seven percent of Greek women of marriageable age were indeed married compared to eighty-eight percent in Italy and eighty percent in Portugal. Most Greek women married young, between the ages of fifteen and twenty-one, and at that moment received the bulk of their wealth in the form of a dowry.[3] Traditions originating in Roman/Byzantine law considered the dowry inviolate and inalienable, and husbands' properties stood as surety for it. Any change to the dowry, as, for example, to augment the dowries of offspring, required the consent of the wife and, depending on the situation, frequently some form of compensation. Women did not manage their wealth, nor did they profit from any income generated from the dowry. The dowry remained under the control of their husbands, who also enjoyed its fruits. Even the proceeds of the labour of a married woman belonged to her husband, who "sustains the burdens of matrimony", as the *Corpus Juris Civilis* put it, although this was disputed in some parts of Greece.[4] In general, women were able to gain full control of their wealth only after the end of their marriage through death or divorce, the latter being legal in Orthodox Christianity under certain conditions.

Women also received wealth through other vehicles, such as inheritances, donations, and gifts, mostly from relatives without offspring in return for support in their old age.[5] Husbands sometimes bequeathed properties to their wives (thirty-five percent of male wills in Mykonos, thirty-three percent in Naxos), often with the stipulation that their widows would "stand by his honor" and not remarry.[6]

In Athens women were also promised a *donatio propter nuptias* (*progamiaia dorea*) by their husbands that he or his heirs were to give to the wife if the marriage was subsequently dissolved. The legal status of the *donatio* was not very clear, but its inclusion in the dowry contracts ensured that it could be legally pursued. Similarly, although inheritances, donations, and other such forms of wealth were not under the same legal restrictions as the dowry, husbands, who managed those as well, were supposed to compensate their wives for any alienation, as is evident from the documents of Ottoman Greece in which husbands regularly compensated their wives for the sale of their properties, either in the bills of sale themselves or in separate documents called *antikatastatika* (replacements).[7] The properties of men and women were thus kept separate even after decades of marriage.[8] Prohibitions regarding donations between spouses, prohibitions that can be traced to the introduction of the *donatio propter nuptias*, further strengthened the principle of separation of properties.[9]

Women in Ottoman Greece owned a great variety of properties, including substantial real estate, but it is difficult to compare the wealth of women to that of men because dowries were descriptive and did not assign values.[10] Since the actual value of an individual property could vary substantially, a comparison is not possible except from areas where women were excluded from real property, such as Mani, in which case their disadvantage is obvious. Nevertheless, it is evident that women in some regions received wealth that appears comparable to that of men. My earlier research indicated that most women in the four regions I investigated received in their dowries some real property in the form of structures (sixty-seven percent of women in Naxos, ninety-eight percent in Mykonos, and thirty-six percent in Athens) or agricultural land (ninety-five percent in Naxos, ninety-six percent in Mykonos, and ninety-one percent in Athens).[11] Of course, movable goods were ubiquitous in dowry contracts and usually composed of household items and clothing. Actual money was scarce, especially in areas like agricultural Naxos, and even when relatively common, as in Athens, money was never the dominant component, but rather of symbolic value.[12]

III. The modern Greek state

The state that emerged following the ten-year Greek war of independence (1821–1829) was of course very different from the previous Ottoman administration. The short-lived Bavarian regency (1832–1835) that ruled Greece until King Otto's maturity established the foundations of a modern, bureaucratic, hierarchical state mechanism, especially as far as the legal structures of the state were concerned. With remarkable speed Greece acquired a European judicial system, with justices of the peace, courts of first instance, two appeals courts, a supreme court, a commercial court, and so on. The regency also produced a new criminal code based in part upon the Bavarian one, a code of criminal jurisprudence, and a commercial code based upon the French one.[13] It failed, however, to produce a civil code in part due to the conviction by the famed legalist and regent Georg Ludwig von Maurer and his associates that foreign codes like the Napoleonic one were inapplicable to Greek circumstances and that Greece should develop its own code based upon the customary practices that had evolved over the centuries.[14] Thus, custom assumed the power of law with regard to civil law and was enforced by the Greek courts, as numerous cases over the next thirty years indicate.[15]

In addition to their attempts to "modernise" the Greek system of justice, the regency was also quite aware of the difficulty in convincing the Greek public to accept and trust such a different system, especially when many of the new judges would be strangers to the insular Greek communities of the time. Even during the Greek war of independence local notables were outraged by the decisions of governors appointed by the revolutionary authorities, who often wielded judicial as well as executive powers because they showed a complete disregard or ignorance of local customs and practices.[16] To gain the trust of a suspicious population for the new regime and the institutions of the new state, the foreign regents introduced a series of measures aimed at appealing to the Greek public, including essentially mandatory primary education for boys and girls, free access to midwives for those who could not afford them, and exemption from legal fees and costs for the indigent.[17] The latter was a clearly successful measure, as the numbers of Greeks who sought to use the courts to settle various disputes indicate.

Unfortunately, the Greek kingdom also emerged from its war of independence bankrupt. The revolutionary governments had, by 1827, ceased servicing two foreign loans they had contracted in London a couple of years earlier, and the Bavarian king had accepted the Greek crown on behalf of his young second son, Otto, only after Britain, France, and Russia had agreed to guarantee a 60 million franc loan to the new state.[18] Bavaria also provided some loans, but even so the fiscal situation was desperate. Not only was the Greek economy utterly devastated by a brutal ten-year war, but Greece also had to rebuild all state institutions from scratch, settle thousands of refugees from areas that had revolted to the Greek state, rebuild the destroyed towns and villages, and impose some order to a territory that by 1829 had deteriorated into chaos. To make matters worse, the Greek state was saddled with some additional costs, including a Bavarian army meant to restore order and a rather large bureaucracy originally staffed to a great degree by foreigners in part because educated locals were in short supply.[19] As a result of all these difficulties, as well as many unfortunate economic decisions and practices, the Greek state throughout the nineteenth century was in perpetual fiscal difficulties and repeatedly defaulted on its foreign loans and as a result was frozen out of the European money markets for most of the century.

Among the many economic difficulties of the Greek state, the inability to develop an effective taxation system was particularly problematic for the Greek governments, who were in desperate need of funds to cover the near-perpetual budget deficits.[20] Greece relied overwhelmingly on agricultural taxes, originally continuing the Ottoman system in the form of a tithe,[21] with only various tariff duties and indirect taxation to sustain the budget since the state was more or less unable to assess the wealth of its inhabitants.[22] Even with regard to the simplistic agricultural tithe, however, the Greek governments faced difficulties because much of the land was technically state-owned, being the property of former Muslims who had been massacred or expelled during the course of the war. Ambitious plans to redistribute the land to the peasantry did not come to fruition until the 1870s, leaving landownership and land use in limbo.[23]

After the ascension of Otto to the throne and his assumption of full powers upon his maturity in 1835, Greece tried to avoid its foreign financial obligations by unilaterally refusing to honour the two revolutionary loans that had not been negotiated by the subsequent monarchical regime.[24] The holders of those bonds quite naturally protested, and Greece, utterly reliant upon the continued financial guarantees of the great powers, had no choice but to capitulate and implement "austerity" measures by slashing government spending and increasing revenues.[25] In addition to firing bureaucrats and cutting expenditures, the state also introduced a new stamp tax in 1843 that was required for all notarised documents in order for them to be recognised in court.[26] Thus, dowry contracts from 1843 onwards had to be notarised and had to be expressed in monetary values so that the stamp duty could be assessed.

IV. Women, dowry, and the modern state

The dowry remained the most significant component of women's wealth in early modern Greece and continued to be managed by their husbands. As in earlier times, women continued to actively defend their rights in the new courts. Even as late as 1860 over forty percent of the civil cases heard by the courts of appeals of Athens between January and October 1860 involved women, most related to dowry disputes. Many of the defendants were widows – a pattern also seen in Ottoman Greece – like Anthi, who successfully sued her brothers-in-law for her dowry as well as a bequest of 1,000 drachmas set by her late husband in his last will.[27] Women also proved quite adaptable to new economic conditions, as exemplified by the widow Kouzi, who confronted the Hellenic Bank over a mortgage her late husband had taken on a house that he had also relinquished to her as compensation for some dowered properties he had sold.[28] As this case indicates, new economic tools such as a mortgage could potentially compromise the property of wives, who were apparently not consulted by the bank prior to the loan, although the courts, as the case of Kouzi indicates, generally defended the rights of widows.

As in the Ottoman period, these women often found support from their natal families, especially their fathers, who intervened when they perceived their daughters' dowries were being threatened or compromised. However, although fathers clearly considered it their duty to defend their daughters' wealth, the courts were less certain about their role. In two cases in 1860, the courts allowed fathers to act as guardians of their married daughters because the latter were still under the legal age of maturity. In a third case, however, when the daughter was legally an adult, the court was uncertain about the rights of the father.[29] The importance assigned to the legal age of maturity indicates that new stricter lines were being drawn, slowly eroding the flexibility in Ottoman times that frequently worked in a woman's favour.

If women continued to receive and defend their dowries, it does not mean that dramatic changes were not taking place in Greece. I have argued elsewhere that although women continued to defend their rights, the new structure of the judicial system meant that they did so by proxy and not in person, as was often the case in the Ottoman period.[30] Furthermore, if their husband was alive, because of his role as manager of the dowry only he could pursue a case in court since, as the appeals court in Athens determined in the case of Maria Semerikou from Mykonos, only he, and not his wife, had a private interest.[31] That change had not been an outcome of ideological imperatives, but rather a result of the hierarchical and formalised nature of the new judicial process. Similarly, the transformation of the dowry I will discuss later was in part an outcome of the new emerging economic and social realities but was given an immediate and important boost by the 1843 stamp duty imposition, itself a measure taken to shore up Greek finances in view of an impending default.

The dowry contracts from the agricultural region around the new town of Leonidio and from the capital Athens show that the dowry had begun to change from the very beginning of the kingdom of Greece. In Athens, references to destroyed houses and fields indicate the destruction of the Greek war of independence, but they also point to the inevitable changes such destruction would have had on the valuation of properties.[32] More significantly, the rapid growth of Athens from a town of some 10,000 inhabitants in 1820 to one of some 65,000 by 1860 was accompanied by a rapid rise in the value of houses, which now became a crucial component in fifty-five percent of dowry contacts compared to thirty-six percent in pre-independence Athens.[33] The significance of a dowered house was even more crucial because Athenian women in the new state frequently married non-local men. Of the marriages in the immediate post-independence period, fifteen percent involved non-Athenian men, a percentage that probably increased, as Athens grew rapidly.[34] Over the same period researchers have noted the increasing monetisation of the dowry in Athens and other parts of the Greek world as well as a dowry inflation that spurred the ecclesiastical and municipal authorities to attempt to impose limits.[35]

Various explanations for this transformation have been suggested in the past.[36] Among the most convincing has been the tying of this monetisation to the urbanisation of Greece and the growth of cities like Athens, Ermoupolis, Patras, and Piraeus. Although, by allowing the household to begin its existence on a firm economic foundation, a dowry of predominantly immovable properties was of great value to agricultural communities, the post-independence rapid urbanisation and the transformation of the economy may have spurred many newly married couples to relocate to urban centres, especially if the war had damaged the productive capacity of the land, making it unproductive for the immediate future. This relocation, even if it was only to a neighbouring community, would require the disinvestment from land that was impractical to cultivate. It is noteworthy that the record reveals several marriages whose celebration was followed by a flurry of sales of dowered properties and the required compensation for the properties thus alienated. From October 1835 to November 1850, the notarial records in Leonidio, a small, newly founded provincial town at the time, contain ninety-six such exchanges of properties. A typical example is that of Konstantinos K Pougias and his wife, Thomais D. Karamanou, who sold a vineyard from Thomais's dowry to Dimitrios Ilias Kordogouras for twenty-two goats and sheep; in the same document Konstantinos secured the dowry with 7 drachmas per sheep and 5 drachmas per goat.[37] It has also been noted in earlier studies that new migrant women to cities like Athens had trousseaux composed of higher than normal concentrations of such valuable portable items as jewellery, possibly for reasons similar to those just described.[38]

This monetisation, however, was both an urban and a rural phenomenon, as other researchers have determined. Eleftherios Alexakis, for example, has calculated that the monetary component of dowries among the Albanian-speaking Arvanites of southeastern Attica rose from seventeen percent in the second half of the nineteenth century to thirty-five percent in the first half of the twentieth.[39] This expansion of the monetary component of dowries in the latter half of the nineteenth century was confirmed by Dimitris Psychogios and others and points to a continuous trend from the establishment of the modern Greek state.[40] This contradicts earlier assertions that had linked the monetary dowry to non-agricultural regions[41] but fits quite well with the monetisation of the Greek economy following independence.[42]

Leonidio, however, provides us with stronger evidence regarding the transformation of the dowry because of the completeness of the notarial archive after the imposition of the stamp duty on dowries in 1843. Although the state had required the detailed valuation of each component and the whole of the dowry of all notarised dowry contracts as early as 1836,[43] the imposition of the stamp duty made certain the enforcement of the earlier law if only to calculate the appropriate surcharge. Furthermore, the 1843 law included a provision that made only such notarised dowries defensible in court. In agricultural Leonidio the dowry continued to be composed of a mixture of different movable and real properties,[44] but the 1843 law still had a significant impact on the composition of the dowry and perceptions surrounding the dowry itself.

First of all, by insisting on the formal draughting of the dowry contract by a notary and by levying a duty on it, the law significantly increased the cost of formally dowering a daughter, especially if one considers the impoverished nature of much of the Greek population at the time. Whereas in Ottoman Greece dowry contracts were drafted by all sorts of people of varying economic standing, and it should be noted that Greece lacked at the time the social and class distinctions of Western Europe,[45] the dowry contracts from post-independence Leonidio seem to be drafted predominantly by wealthier individuals, who could most easily afford the added expense.[46] Poorer families seem grossly underrepresented in the documents, which can only mean that those of lesser means dowered their daughters informally outside the legal framework of the new state. If that was indeed the case it would mean that these women would have been particularly vulnerable to the potential that their husbands would abuse their position as managers of the dowry and erode their wives' dowries without the latter having recourse to the courts. Essentially, the law may have reduced the ability of most women to defend their property rights and may have led to the amalgamation of their wealth with that of their husbands.

A second long-term effect of the law was the start of the transformation of the way Greeks perceived the dowry and its role. It is certainly the case that the dowry assumed increasingly negative connotations in the nineteenth century, being transformed in the mindset of people, and women in particular, from a vehicle for the protection of the wife to one for the enrichment of the husband. Thus, by the second half of the century the institution of the dowry came under attack by early feminists and even by foreign travellers, both of whom excoriated the greed and avarice of men, and in particular men in urban settings like Athens, who demanded ever-larger dowries from hapless fathers-in-law. In their writings, dowry-hunting (*proikotheria*) was portrayed as a scourge of nineteenth- and twentieth-century Athens, destroying marriages and impoverishing families.[47]

The role of the 1843 law has not been considered in this process but should not be underestimated. By insisting upon the monetary valuation of the dowry, the law helped transform perceptions about the dowry in Greece away from clearly defined, predominantly immovable property to an abstract monetary value. Increasingly, the exact composition of the dowry was less significant than its total value expressed in the new currency, the drachma. The change was not merely semantic. As mentioned, in Ottoman Greece husbands who for some reason had expropriated a piece of property from their wives' dowries usually replaced it with another piece of immovable property, presumably of equal value. In post-independence Greece women continued to insist on being compensated for such expropriations using essentially the same legal vehicle, the documents called *antikatastatika*, or through notarised documents that placed real properties of the husband as surety.[48] In Leonidio, from June 1839 to August 1850, couples drafted fifty-five *antikatastatika*, some indicating significant prior alienation of a wife's dowry, as was the case with

Stamatou, whose husband, Konstas, had gone through a dowry worth 9,000 drachmas![49] Over time, however, husbands would substitute real properties of their wives' dowry with the equivalent monetary value rather than with other real property. This substitution had a number of benefits for the husband. First of all, it kept the immovable wealth of the husband intact, avoiding the alienation of his patrimony to compensate his wife. The undiminished property could also serve as collateral for the assumption of larger loans from the new, impersonal, commercial banks, which would be unaware of such circumstances, as the case of the widow Kouzi discussed earlier indicates.

Furthermore, a monetary substitution acted more as a promissory note than anything else since all property remained under the control of the husband for the duration of the marriage. Essentially the husband would not have to actually pay anything until the dissolution of the marriage through death or divorce. An added benefit to this was that over time the real value of the initial sum would have been reduced due to inflation, which, under the circumstances of the Greek economy, with its persistent loose monetary policies, was significant.[50] Finally, monetary dowries were easier for husbands to alienate, hide, or spend, further eroding their wives' wealth over a period of decades, leaving widows with the unenviable task of attempting to extract the value of their dowry from the estate of the deceased husband, often through legal action against his former creditors, as the court records indicate.[51]

Such outcomes would not have been noticeable immediately in the archival record, but the numerous complaints and protests of women in the latter half of the nineteenth century and in the twentieth century demonstrate that these dangers inherent in the monetisation of dowry had indeed taken place. This is a process that modern anthropologists also observed in twentieth-century rural Greece, where the alienation of the movable dower was common and merely required the informal consent of the wife, unlike the case of immovable property, which required a notarised contract, rendering the latter more secure.[52] The transformation of the dowry from immovable to movable has often been seen as a sign of the disinheritance of women through the belief that real estate was too valuable to be lost to daughters, as seen in Greece, even in Ottoman Greece in areas like Mani.[53] Although that was not generally the case in Greece, and certainly not as far as the law was concerned, the transformation of the dowry to a monetary one raised the real threat of the merging of the wife's dowry with the husband's estate, as has been seen elsewhere.[54] An early decision by the court of appeals in Athens that is indicative of the first steps towards this process is the case in which the court refused to consider an estate (*tsifliki*) bought by the husband of Despoinous Karagiannopoulas with money from her dowry as a dowered property, considering that it was irrelevant with whose money the estate was purchased. As far as the court was concerned, the only relevant point was who had received the estate according to the contract. Thus, a creditor could indeed confiscate the estate for the debts of her husband.[55]

The law mandating the draughting of dowries in a notary may have had an even more sinister, though hidden, consequence. As the notarised dowries concluded in the town of Leonidio seem to indicate, and as noted earlier, it was predominantly the wealthier segments of the population that were willing to undertake the added expense of a notarised dowry.[56] Poorer families may have eschewed the cost, leaving these women without the benefit of legal recourse in case of a husband's despoliation of the dowry. Thus, the law may have also inadvertently reduced the capacity of most women to defend their property rights. In addition, some researchers have tied the monetisation of the dowry to female hypergamy, though that is a complex argument in the rather socially fluid Greek society of the nineteenth century.[57]

The transformations experienced in Greece during the reign of King Otto were too varied and dramatic to allow for simple explanations of complex processes such as the material transformation of dowry practices. State structures, economic processes, social transformations, and political developments all impacted the composition of the dowry. What I have tried to present here, however, is the impact of state actions that on face value had little to do with the dowry per se. The Greek state certainly had no intention of weakening women's rights over their dowries, but its decision to attempt to increase its revenues to forestall a default added pressure to an institution that was already being buffeted by social and economic transformations. More research is needed to determine the transformation of the dowry over the course of the nineteenth century as well as whether the Greek courts conformed to the stipulations of the 1843 law or proved more flexible, as was the case in other instances. Although the process may have taken some time, by the turn of the century not only had the dowry been compromised, but the state also felt obliged to intervene to defend the women whose husbands had abused their roles, wasted their dowries, and then abandoned them. Of course, the way the Greek state reacted to this problem was by constraining the right to divorce, which would become another focal point of Greek feminists in the ensuing decades and up to the twenty-first century.[58]

Notes

1 Efemeris tes Kyverneseos tes Ellenikes Demokratias, Athens, 18 February 1983, issue 1, No 25. See esp articles 56 to 59 page 444.

2 Giorgos Michailidis-Nouaros, "Paratereseis Sti Kleronomiko Ethimo Tes Karpathou", in: *Etaireia Karpathiakon Meleton* 3 (1984), pp. 7–27, p. 11; Eleftherios P. Alexakis, *Ta Gene Kai E Oikogeneia Sten Paradosiake Koinonia Tes Manis* (Athens 1980), p. 205; Eleftherios P. Alexakis, *Ta Paidia Tes Siopes: Oikogeneia, Syggeneia Kai Gamos Stous Arvanites Tes Na Attikes – Lavreotikes 1850–1940,* Athens 1996 [Parousia], p. 36; Aglaia E. Kasdagli, "Family and Inheritance in the Cyclades, 1500–1800: Present Knowledge and Unanswered Questions", in: *The History of the Family* 9 (2004), pp. 257–274, p. 268.

3 Eleni Varikas, *E Exegerse Ton Kyrion*, Athens 2004 [Katarti], p. 123; Matoula Tomara-Sideri and Nikos Sideris, *Syghrotese Kai Diadoche Ton Geneon Sten Ellada Tou 19ou Aiona,* Athens 1986 [AthensIstoriko Archeio Ellinikis Neolaias, Geniki Grammateia Neas Genias], p. 155.

4 Alan Watson, ed. *The Digest of Justinian*, Philadelphia 1998 [University of Pennsylvania Press], vol. 2, book 24, Ulpianus, On Sabinus Book 32 and Book 31, p. 238. In 1810 two brothers, Nikolas and Geronimos Kornaros, sued their father, demanding in addition to their mother's dowry the value of her labour since she had been commercially weaving for over forty years. Historical and Ethnological Society of Greece Mykonos Archive (hereafter IEEE Mykonos), No. 22565, 23 March 1810.

5 General State Archives of Greece, Mykonos Notarial Archive, (hereafter GAK Mykonos), F96, No. 95, 28 September 1807.
6 IEEE Mykonos, No. 22597, 12 November 1761; Historical and Ethnological Society of Greece Naxos Archive (hereafter IEEE Naxos), No. 3954, 3 July 1783; among many. Women also inserted similar clauses (IEEE Mykonos, No. 22612, 21 February 1780; GAK Mykonos, F4, No. 031, 25 December 1781; GAK Mykonos, F4, No. 042, 26 July 1785; IEEE Naxos, No. 5274, 31 December 1812); IEEE Naxos, No. 3954, 3 July 1783.
7 GAK Mykonos, F18, No. 069, 7 February 1764; GAK Mykonos, F96, No.72, 17 May 1806 among many.
8 Eva Kalpourtzi, *Syggenikes Scheseis Kai Strategikes Antallagon. To Paradeigma Tes Naxou Ton 17o Aiona*, Athens 2001 [Ellinika Grammata], p. 83.
9 Nikolaos K. Pharmakopoulos, *Peri Progamiaias Doreas*, Athens 1886 [Spyridon Kousoulinos], p. 83. See also Dianne Owen Hughes, "From Brideprice to Dowry in Mediterranean Europe", in: *Journal of Family History* 3, 3 (1978), pp. 262–296, p. 277; Aysu Dincer, "Wills, Marriage and Business Contracts: Urban Women in Late-Medieval Cyprus", in: *Gender & History* 24, 2 (2012), pp. 310–332, p. 316.
10 Aglaia E. Kasdagli, *Land and Marriage Settlements in the Aegean*, Venice 1999 [Hellenic Institute of Byzantine and Post-Byzantine Studies], p. 225.
11 Evdoxios Doxiadis, *The Shackles of Modernity: Women, Property, and the Transition from the Ottoman Empire to the Greek State (1750–1850)*, Cultural Politics, Socioaesthetics, Beginnings, Cambridge 2011 [Cambridge Department of Classics, Harvard University], p. 263.
12 Ibid., p. 45.
13 Georg Ludwig von Maurer, *O Ellenikos Laos*, Athens 1976 [Afoi Tolidi], p. 70; Nikolaos I Pantazopoulos, *Apo Tes "Logias" Paradoseos Eis Ton Astikon Kodika*, Thessaloniki 1965 [Aristoteleion Panepistemion Thessalonikis], p. 157; Alexandros Svolos, *Ta Ellinika Syntagmata 1822–1975/1986. I Syntagmatiki Istoria Tis Ellados*, Athens 1998 [Stochastis], pp. 119, 131, 149; Nikolaos I Pantazopoulos, "Georg Ludwig Von Maurer, E Pros Evropaika Protypa Oloklerotike Strofe Tes Neoellenikes Nomothesias", in: *Epistemonike Epeteres Scholes Nomikon kai Oikonomikon Epistemon* 13 (1968), pp. 1346–1506, p. 1366.
14 Gustav Karl Geib, *Parousiase Tes Katastases Tou Dikaiou Sten Ellada*, Athens 1990 [Govostis], p. 67; Maurer, *O Ellenikos Laos*, p. 627.
15 Pantazopoulos, *Apo Tes "Logias" Paradoseos Eis Ton Astikon Kodika*, p. 160; Nikolaos I. Pantazopoulos, "To Neoelleniko Dikaio 2. E Dikaiodotike Politike Kata Ten Epanastase Kai Ten Kapodistriake Periodo (1821–1832)", in: *Epistemonike Epeteris Scholes Nomikon kai Oikonomikon Epistemon, Aristoteleio Panepistemion Thessalonikis* 10 (1978), p. 1231f.; Nikolaos I. Pantazopoulos, "E Entaxe Tes Elladas Sten Evropaike Koinoteta. E Symvole Tes Antibasileias Kai Tou Othona (1833–1843)", in: *E Krise Ton Thesmon Tou Kratous, Symmeikta Pros Timen Faidonos Th. Vegleri*, Athens 1988 [Ant. N. Sakkoulas], p. 572; General State Archives of Greece, Politikes Apofaseis Efeteiou Athinon (hereafter GAK Efeteio), vol. 120, no. 18145, pg. 897, 14 May 1860; GAK Efeteio, vol. 119A, no. 17935, pg. 281, 16 March 1860; GAK Efeteio, vol 119A, no. 17974, pg. 725, 26 March 1860.
16 IEEE, Naxos, No. 6481, 31 August 1826.
17 G A. Rallis and M. Potlis, *Oi Ellenikoi Kodikes Meta Ton Tropopoiounton Autous Neoteron Nomon Kai Vasilikon Diatagmaton Eis Prosetethesan to Politiko Syntagma Tes Ellados*, vol. A, Athens 1844 [G Chartofylakas], p. 3.
18 See Convention, "Convention between Great Britain, France, and Russia, on the One Part, and Bavaria on the Other, Relative to the Sovereignty of Greece", in: *The American Journal of International Law* 12, 2 (1918 [1832]).
19 G B Dertilis, *Epta Polemoi, Tesseris Emfylioi, Epta Ptochevseis 1821–2016,* Athens 2016 [Polis], p. 37.
20 Jon V. Kofas, *Financial Relations of Greece and the Great Powers, 1832–1862*, Boulder, CO 1981 [East European Monographs], p. 26.
21 Socratis Petmezas, *E Ellenike Agrotike Oikonomia Kata Ton 19o Aiona. E Perifereiake Diastase*, Herakleio 2003 [Panepistimiakes Ekdoseis Kritis], p. 58.
22 Michalis Psalidopoulos, "The Greek 'Society for the Freedoms of Trade' (1865–67): Rise, Activities, Decline", in: *Journal of the History of Economic Thought* 27, 4 (2005).

pp. 383–398, p. 386, p. 393; Sophia Lazaretou, "The Drachma, Foreign Creditors, and the International Monetary System: Tales of a Currency During the 19th and the Early 20th Centuries", in: *Explorations in Economic History* 42, 2 (2005), pp. 202–236, p. 209.

23 See William W. McGrew, *Land and Revolution in Modern Greece, 1800–1881: The Transition in the Tenure and Exploitation of Land from Ottoman Rule to Independence,* Kent, OH 1985 [Kent State University Press].

24 Demetrius Bikelas, "Statistics of the Kingdom of Greece", in: *Journal of Statistical Society of London* 31, 3 (1868), pp. 265–298, p. 285.

25 Kostas Kostis, *Ta Kakomathemena Paidia Tes Istorias: E Diamorfose Tou Neoellenikou Kratous 18os-21os Aionas*, Athens 2013 [Polis], pp. 195–196; G. B. Dertilis, *Istoria Tou Ellenikou Kratous 1830–1920*, Heraklaio 2017 [Panepistimiakes Ekdoseis Kritis], p. 214.

26 Pavlos Kalligas, *Systema Romaikou Dikaiou*, vol. B, Athens 1930 [Georgios Fexis kai Yios], p. 76.

27 GAK Efeteio, vol. 121, no. 18299, pg. 1131, 30 June 1860.

28 GAK Efeteio, vol. 120, no. 18132, pg. 777, 25 May 1860.

29 GAK Efeteio, vol. 121, no. 18257, pg. 645, 21 June 1860; GAK Efeteio, vol 120, no. 18166, pg. 1121, 4 June 1860, GAK Efeteio, vol. 121, no. 18276, pg. 847, 25 June 1860.

30 Evdoxios Doxiadis, "Standing in Their Place: The Exclusion of Women from the Judicial System in the First Decades of the Modern Greek State, 1821–1850", in: *Journal of Modern Greek Studies* 25 (2007), pp. 75–97.

31 GAK Efeteio, vol. 4, no. 747, pg. 9457, 24 May 1838.

32 Doxiadis, *The Shackles of Modernity*, p. 61.

33 Kostis Moskoff, *E Ethnike Kai Koinonike Syneidese Sten Ellada, 1830–1909. Ideologia Tou Metapratikou Chorou*, Thessaloniki 1972 [Nea Poreia], p. 152; Doxiadis, *The Shackles of Modernity*, p. 62.

34 Doxiadis, *The Shackles of Modernity*, p. 62f.

35 Paul Sant Cassia and Constantine Bada, *The Making of the Modern Greek Family*, Cambridge 1992 [Cambridge University Press], p. 70f.; Marina Maropoulou, "E Politike Ton Ekklesiastikon Kai Koinotikon Archon Sto Zetema Tes Avjeses Tou Posou Tes Proikas", in: Colette Piault (ed.), *Oikogeneia Kai Periousia Sten Ellada Kai Ten Kypro*, Athens 1994 [Vivliopoleio tis Estias], p. 113, 117, 120; Eleni Kyrtsi-Nakou, "Ai Peri Proikodosion 'Nomothetikai' Rythmeseis Vasei Ton Kanonikon Diataxeon Tou Oikoumenikou Patriarcheiou 1701–1844", in: *Epistemonike Epeterida tou Dekegorikou Syllogou Thessalonikis* 1 (1980), pp. 11–27; Haris Symeonidou-Alatopoulou, "E Exelixe Tou Thesmou Tes Proikas Sthn Ellada 1956–1974", in: *Epitheorisi Koinonikon Erevnon* 36–37 (1979), pp. 322–340, p. 323.

36 See Cassia and Bada, *The Making of the Modern Greek Family*, p. 177f.

37 General State Archives Leonidio Notarial Archive (hereafter GAK Leonidio), No. 2552, 21 September 1843.

38 Cassia and Bada, *The Making of the Modern Greek Family*, p. 109.

39 Alexakis, *Ta Paidia Tes Siopes*, p. 35.

40 Dimitris Psychogios, *Proika, Foroi, Stafida, Kai Psomi. Oikonomia Kai Oikogeneia Sten Agrotike Ellada Tou 19ou Aiona*, Athens 1995 [Ethniko Kentro Koinonikon Erevnon], p. 178; Maropoulou, "E Politike Ton Ekklesiastikon Kai Koinotikon Archon Sto Zetema Tes Avjeses Tou Posou Tes Proikas", pp. 113, 123; Maria Couroucli, ed., "Dot Et Societe En Grece Moderne", in: *Femmes Et Patrimoine Dans Les Societes Rurales De L'europe Mediterraneenne*, Paris 1987 [Editions du CNRS]; Maria Couroucli, "Dot Et Société En Grèce Moderne", in: G Ravis-Giordani (ed.), *Femmes Et Patrimoine Dans Les Sociétés Rurales De L'europe Méditerranéenne*, Paris 1983 [L'Harmattan], pp. 327–348, p. 327.

41 See for instance Nora Skouteri-Didaskalou, *Anthropologika Gia to Gynaikeio Zetema*, Athens 1984 [Politis]; Eva Kalpourtzi, "Ina Pragmatopoiethe E Dia Ton Gamou Syzeuxis", in: *Greek Society* 1 (1987), pp. 81–86.

42 Dertilis, *Istoria Tou Ellenikou Kratous 1830–1920*, p. 321; see also Sophia Lazaretou, "Greek Monetary Economics in Retrospect: The Adventures of the Drachma", in: *Economic Notes* 34, 3 (2005).

43 Pavlos Kalligas, *Systema Romaikou Dikaiou*, vol. D, Athens 1930 [Georgios Fexis kai Yios], p. 76.
44 Doxiadis, *The Shackles of Modernity*, pp. 61, 266.
45 Polly Thanailaki, *Gender Inequalities in Rural European Communities During 19th and Early 20th Century, a Historical Perspective*, Cham 2018 [Springer International Publishing], p. 51.
46 Doxiadis, *The Shackles of Modernity*, p. 70.
47 Dimitra Samiou, "To Feministiko Kinema Sten Ellada (1860–1960)", in: Eutychia Leontidou and Sigrid R Ammer (eds.), *E Ellada Ton Gynaikon*, Athens 1992 [Enallaktikes Ekdoseis/Gaia], pp. 57–63, p. 59; Edmond About, *E Ellada Tou Othonos*, Athens 1992 (1855) [Athens Ekdoseis Afon Tolidi], pp. 57, 141; Varikas, *E Exegerse Ton Kyrion*, p. 60.
48 GAK Leonidio, no. 201, 10 June 1848; GAK Leonidio, no. 515, 12 November 1849.
49 GAK Leonidio, no. 2041, 15 July 1842.
50 see Lazaretou, "The Drachma, Foreign Creditors", pp. 202–236, p. 211, p. 213.
51 GAK Efeteio, vol. 2, no. 485, pg. 5655, 27 July 1837; GAK Efeteio, vol. 2, no. 529, pg. 6157, 30 August 1837, GAK Efeteio, vol. 3, no. 601, pg. 7085, 7 December 1837; GAK Efeteio, vol. 4, no. 747, pg. 9457, 24 May 1838; GAK Efeteio, vol. 119A, no. 17928, pg. 221, 10 March 1860; GAK Efeteio, vol. 119A, no. 17950, pg. 445, 23 March 1860 among many.
52 Ernestine Friedl, *Vasilika, a Village in Modern Greece*, New York 1962 [Holt, Rinehart and Winston], p. 55.
53 Hughes, "From Brideprice to Dowry in Mediterranean Europe", p. 281; Marie A. Kelleher, "Hers by Right: Gendered Legal Assumptions and Women's Property in the Medieval Crown of Aragon", in: *Journal of Women's History* 22, 2 (2010), pp. 34–55, p. 37; Maria Agren, *Domestic Secrets: Women & Property in Sweden 1600–1857*, Chapel Hill 2009 [The University of North Carolina Press], p. 102.
54 Hughes, "From Brideprice to Dowry in Mediterranean Europe", p. 282.
55 GAK Efeteio, vol. 4, no. 653, pg. 7677, 11 February 1838.
56 Doxiadis, *The Shackles of Modernity*, p. 70.
57 Cassia and Bada, *The Making of the Modern Greek Family*, p. 78.
58 Konstantinos L Triantafyllopoulos, *Ekthesis Kai Proschedion Nomou Peri Ton Logon Tou Diazygiou Kai Synepeion Tinon Avtou*, Athens 1918 [Ypourgeio Dikaiosynes, Epitroph tou Astikou Kodikos], p. 11f., p. 14.

Sources

Archival sources

Historical and Ethnological Society of Greece Mykonos Archive.
Historical and Ethnological Society of Greece Naxos Archive.
General State Archives of Greece, Mykonos Notarial Archive.
General State Archives of Greece, Politikes Apofaseis Efeteiou Athinon (Civil Decisions of the Court of Appeals of Athens).
General State Archives Leonidio Notarial Archive.

Bibliography

About, Edmond, *E Ellada Tou Othonos*, Athens 1992 (1855) [Ekdoseis Afon Tolidi].
Agren, Maria, *Domestic Secrets: Women & Property in Sweden 1600–1857*, Chapel Hill 2009 [The University of North Carolina Press].
Alexakis, Eleftherios P., *Ta Gene Kai E Oikogeneia Sten Paradosiake Koinonia Tes Manis*, Athens 1980 [privately published Dissertation, University of Ioannina].
———*Ta Paidia Tes Siopes: Oikogeneia, Syggeneia Kai Gamos Stous Arvanites Tes Na Attikes – Lavreotikes 1850–1940*, Athens 1996 [Parousia].
Bikelas, Demetrius, "Statistics of the Kingdom of Greece", in: *Journal of Statistical Society of London* 31, 3 (September 1868), pp. 265–298.

Cassia, Paul Sant and Constantine Bada, *The Making of the Modern Greek Family,* Cambridge 1992 [Cambridge University Press].
Convention, "Convention Between Great Britain, France, and Russia, on the One Part, and Bavaria on the Other, Relative to the Sovereignty of Greece", in: *The American Journal of International Law* 12, 2 (1918 [1832]), pp. 68–74.
Couroucli, Maria, "Dot Et Société En Grèce Moderne", in: G. Ravis-Giordani (ed.), *Femmes Et Patrimoine Dans Les Sociétés Rurales De L'europe Méditerranéenne,* Paris 1983 [L'Harmattan].
———(ed.), "Dot Et Societe En Grece Moderne", in: G. Ravis-Giordani (ed.), *Femmes Et Patrimoine Dans Les Societes Rurales De L'europe Mediterraneenne,* Paris 1987 [Editions du CNRS].
Dertilis, G. B., *Epta Polemoi, Tesseris Emfylioi, Epta Ptochevseis 1821–2016,* Athens 2016 [Polis].
———*Istoria Tou Ellenikou Kratous 1830–1920,* Heraklaio 2017 [Panepistimiakes Ekdoseis Kritis].
Dincer, Aysu, "Wills, Marriage and Business Contracts: Urban Women in Late-Medieval Cyprus", in: *Gender & History* 24, 2 (August 2012), pp. 310–332.
Doxiadis, Evdoxios, "Standing in Their Place: The Exclusion of Women from the Judicial System in the First Decades of the Modern Greek State, 1821–1850", in: *Journal of Modern Greek Studies* 25 (2007), pp. 75–97.
———*The Shackles of Modernity: Women, Property, and the Transition from the Ottoman Empire to the Greek State (1750–1850),* Cultural Politics, Socioaesthetics, Beginnings, Cambridge 2011 [Cambridge Department of Classics, Harvard University].
Friedl, Ernestine, *Vasilika, a Village in Modern Greece,* New York 1962 [Holt, Rinehart and Winston].
Geib, Gustav Karl, *Parousiase Tes Katastases Tou Dikaiou Sten Ellada,* Athens 1990 [Govostis].
Hughes, Dianne Owen, "From Brideprice to Dowry in Mediterranean Europe", in: *Journal of Family History* 3, 3 (1978), pp. 262–296.
Kalligas, Pavlos, *Systema Romaikou Dikaiou,* vol. B, Athens 1930 [Georgios Fexis kai Yios].
———*Systema Romaikou Dikaiou,* vol. D, Athens 1930 [Georgios Fexis kai Yios].
Kalpourtzi, Eva, "Ina Pragmatopoiethe E Dia Ton Gamou Syzeuxis", in: *Greek Society* 1 (1987), pp. 81–86.
———*Syggenikes Scheseis Kai Strategikes Antallagon. To Paradeigma Tes Naxou Ton 17o Aiona,* Athens 2001 [Ellinika Grammata].
Kasdagli, Aglaia E., *Land and Marriage Settlements in the Aegean,* Venice 1999 [Hellenic Institute of Byzantine and Post-Byzantine Studies].
———"Family and Inheritance in the Cyclades, 1500–1800: Present Knowledge and Unanswered Questions", in: *The History of the Family* 9 (2004), pp. 257–274.
Kelleher, Marie A., "Hers by Right: Gendered Legal Assumptions and Women's Property in the Medieval Crown of Aragon", in: *Journal of Women's History* 22, 2 (2010).
Kofas, Jon V., *Financial Relations of Greece and the Great Powers, 1832–1862,* Boulder, CO 1981 [East European Monographs].
Kostis, Kostas, *Ta Kakomathemena Paidia Tes Istorias: E Diamorfose Tou Neoellenikou Kratous 18os-21os Aionas,* Athens 2013 [Polis].
Kyrtsi-Nakou, Eleni, "Ai Peri Proikodosion 'Nomothetikai' Rythmeseis Vasei Ton Kanonikon Diataxeon Tou Oikoumenikou Patriarcheiou 1701–1844", in: *Epistemonike Epeterida tou Dekegorikou Syllogou Thessalonikis* 1 (1980), pp. 11–27.
Lazaretou, Sophia, "The Drachma, Foreign Creditors, and the International Monetary System: Tales of a Currency During the 19th and Early 20th Centuries", in: *Explorations in Economic History* 42, 2 (2005), pp. 202–236.
———"Greek Monetary Economics in Retrospect: The Adventures of the Drachma", in: *Economic Notes* 34, 3 (2005), pp. 331–370.
Maropoulou, Marina, "E Politike Ton Ekklesiastikon Kai Koinotikon Archon Sto Zetema Tes Avjeses Tou Posou Tes Proikas", in: Colette Piault (ed.), *Oikogeneia Kai Periousia Sten Ellada Kai Ten Kypro,* Athens 1994 [Vivliopoleio tis Estias], pp. 111–123.

Maurer, Georg Ludwig von, *O Ellenikos Laos,* Athens 1976 [Afoi Tolidi].

McGrew, William W., *Land and Revolution in Modern Greece, 1800–1881: The Transition in the Tenure and Exploitation of Land from Ottoman Rule to Independence,* Kent, OH 1985 [Kent State University Press].

Michailidis-Nouaros, Giorgos, "Paratereseis Sti Kleronomiko Ethimo Tes Karpathou", in: *Etaireia Karpathiakon Meleton* 3 (1984), pp. 7–27.

Moskoff, Kostis, *E Ethnike Kai Koinonike Syneidese Sten Ellada, 1830–1909. Ideologia Tou Metapratikou Chorou,* Thessaloniki 1972 [Nea Poreia].

Pantazopoulos, Nikolaos I., *Apo Tes "Logias" Paradoseos Eis Ton Astikon Kodika,* Thessaloniki 1965 [Aristoteleion Panepistemion Thessalonikis].

———"Georg Ludwig Von Maurer, E Pros Evropaika Protypa Oloklerotike Strofe Tes Neoellenikes Nomothesias", in: *Epistemonike Epeteres Scholes Nomikon kai Oikonomikon Epistemon* 13 (1968), pp. 1346–1506.

———"To Neoelleniko Dikaio 2. E Dikaiodotike Politike Kata Ten Epanastase Kai Ten Kapodistriake Periodo (1821–1832)", in: *Epistemonike Epeteris Scholes Nomikon kai Oikonomikon Epistemon, Aristoteleio Panepistemion Thessalonikis* 10 (1978), pp. 1230–1330.

———"E Entaxe Tes Elladas Sten Evropaike Koinoteta. E Symvole Tes Antibasileias Kai Tou Othona (1833–1843)", in: *E Krise Ton Thesmon Tou Kratous, Symmeikta Pros Timen Faidonos Th. Vegleri,* Athens 1988 [Ant. N. Sakkoulas], pp. 545–583.

Petmezas, Socratis, *E Ellenike Agrotike Oikonomia Kata Ton 19o Aiona. E Perifereiake Diastase,* Herakleio 2003 [Panepistimiakes Ekdoseis Kritis].

Pharmakopoulos, Nikolaos K., *Peri Progamiaias Doreas,* Athens 1886 [Spyridon Kousoulinos].

Psalidopoulos, Michalis, "The Greek 'Society for the Freedoms of Trade' (1865–67): Rise, Activities, Decline", in: *Journal of the History of Economic Thought* 27, 4 (December 2005), pp. 383–398.

Psychogios, Dimitris, *Proika, Foroi, Stafida, Kai Psomi. Oikonomia Kai Oikogeneia Sten Agrotike Ellada Tou 19ou Aiona,* Athens 1995 [Ethniko Kentro Koinonikon Erevnon].

Rallis, G. A. and M. Potlis, *Oi Ellenikoi Kodikes Meta Ton Tropopoiounton Autous Neoteron Nomon Kai Vasilikon Diatagmaton Eis Prosetethesan to Politiko Syntagma Tes Ellados,* vol. A, Athens 1844 [G Chartofylakas].

Samiou, Dimitra, "To Feministiko Kinema Sten Ellada (1860–1960)", in: Eutychia Leontidou and Sigrid R. Ammer (eds.), *E Ellada Ton Gynaikon,* Athens 1992 [Enallaktikes Ekdoseis/Gaia].

Skouteri-Didaskalou, Nora, *Anthropologika Gia to Gynaikeio Zetema,* Athens 1984 [Politis].

Svolos, Alexandros, *Ta Ellinika Syntagmata 1822–1975/1986. I Syntagmatiki Istoria Tis Ellados,* Athens 1998 [Stochastis].

Symeonidou-Alatopoulou, Haris, "E Exelixe Tou Thesmou Tes Proikas Sthn Ellada 1956–1974", in: *Epitheorisi Koinonikon Erevnon* 36–37 (1979).

Thanailaki, Polly, *Gender Inequalities in Rural European Communities During 19th and Early 20th Century, a Historical Perspective,* Cham 2018 [Springer International Publishing].

Tomara-Sideri, Matoula and Nikos Sideris, *Syghrotese Kai Diadoche Ton Geneon Sten Ellada Tou 19ou Aiona,* Athens 1986 [Athens Istoriko Archeio Ellinikis Neolaias, Geniki Grammateia Neas Genias].

Triantafyllopoulos, Konstantinos L., *Ekthesis Kai Proschedion Nomou Peri Ton Logon Tou Diazygiou Kai Synepeion Tinon Avtou,* Athens 1918 [Ypourgeio Dikaiosynes, Epitroph tou Astikou Kodikos].

Varikas, Eleni, *E Exegerse Ton Kyrion,* Athens 2004 [Katarti].

Watson, Alan (ed.), *The Digest of Justinian,* Philadelphia 1998 [University of Pennsylvania Press].

FIGURE 12.1 Romania/Wallachia, Johann Baptist Homann, *Imperium Turcicum in Europa, Asia et Africa Regiones Proprias Tributarias, Clientelares sicut et omnes eusdem Beglirbegatus seu Praefecturas Generales exhibens*, 1737.

Source: Bibliothèque nationale de France, département Cartes et plans, CPL GE DD-2987 (5839 BIS), public domain, https://gallica.bnf.fr/ark:/12148/btv1b59622189?rk=407727;2 (15.02.2020, 17:15 CET).

12

STARTING A MARRIED LIFE

Women and goods in the mid-nineteenth-century Romanian towns of Piteşti and Câmpulung

Nicoleta Roman

ABSTRACT

Today's Romania used to be a territory of the Ottoman Empire, lying at the south-east margin of Europe as a last zone of known civilisation before the veil of the Orient settled.[1] Until the early nineteenth century, the region was theatre to many armed conflicts and a buffer zone between the Ottoman, Russian, and Habsburg empires.[2] The principality of Wallachia was a peripheral province, bordering on the Austrian Empire, enjoying a status of autonomy that had long enabled it to keep its Orthodox faith and Byzantine legal heritage while at the same time honouring its fiscal and political obligations to the Porte.[3] Wallachia thus experienced a degree of controlled freedom. Despite the slow modernisation of the peripheral Ottoman provinces and a visible Europeanisation of the elites, the provincial towns especially remained attached to tradition and custom more than to law.[4] This delay becomes evident when looking at the transfer of familial property from one generation to the next. The chapter looks at property and goods women in nineteenth-century Wallachia received upon marriage as dowry and its meaning for the individual and the family as well as its position within the distribution of wealth.[5] The chapter is based on a quantitative and qualitative analysis of archival sources (inventories and dowry registers) of Argeş and Muscel counties in the north of Wallachia.

I. The legal institution of the dowry in the Romanian principality of Wallachia

Generally, in matters of inheritance (and thereby the transmission of wealth), the letters of the law, state administration, and the particularities of the geographical region, such as economic development and customary practices, seem to collide with the interests of families and individuals.[6] This results in "transitional zones" in southeast Europe that impose variations of the "official" and favoured system of succession.[7] Sources also show different ways of relating to Napoleon's civil code as a legal model; nonetheless, this did not displace customary practices or the continuity of the interfamilial pattern.[8] There was a process of adaptation, distortion, and transformation of this model that continued in the nineteenth century, leading to a broad variety of legal frames across Europe.[9] The authority of the father in directing land and a considerable part of his wealth towards his son is associated with the rural environment and the economic dependence of peasants on this resource for income and hence the exclusion of women from receiving land and immovable property.[10] If we turn our attention to the towns and other social classes, things are much more nuanced. The urban family was starting to undergo structural transformation in the nineteenth century, even in traditionally agrarian societies like the Romanian principalities. There was still an economic partnership and understanding between families, but this also exposed affective bonds that had previously been less visible; in other words, the family was restructuring itself.[11]

Matters concerning the family, such as marriage, dowry, divorce, and control of inheritance, were managed almost exclusively by the Orthodox Church in Wallachia until the mid-nineteenth century. The Byzantine-influenced *Îndreptarea Legii* (The guide to the law, 1652) known as *Pravila* (codex) continued to be taken into account until 1818, when it was partially replaced by *Legiuirea Caragea* (Caradja's legislation).[12] At the beginning of the eighteenth century, Metropolitan Antim of Iviria (1650–1716), who was considered the head of the Orthodox Church in the principality of Wallachia, made a first draught of a dowry contract, accompanied by recommendations. In his version, the dowry contract divided goods by categories.[13] Parents and guardians of girls had to value each object given in monetary terms and even calculate a general total to avoid quarrels afterwards. This had to be reinforced by the signatures of parents, witnesses, and the recipient of the dowry.[14] The conversion of objects into abstract monetary values already hints at the dowry perceived as a form of provisional inheritance. Alexander Ypsilantis (1725–1805) issued *Pravilniceasca condică* (The legal register) in 1780, which added two important factors. First, it specified that this monetary evaluation concerned only movable goods; second, it stated that any dowry contract had to be entered in the register of the parish in which the marriage took place either before its celebration or, at the most, two months after. In case of the death of her husband, a woman was obliged to draw an inventory of her husband's property and all things missing from her original dowry within six (or twelve) months. Her claims to the restitution stayed valid for twenty years and had to be fulfilled by her husband's heirs.[15] This inventory was the prerequisite to any claim.[16]

In the Romanian realm, and thus also in Wallachia, the dowry contract included both the dowry proper and the trousseau, i.e. both immovable and movable goods. By law, property transmitted as dowry remained protected from creditors.[17] The husband usually became its administrator, but he could not engage in transactions with it or modify it without the consent of his wife. Should he alienate any item, he had to replace it with something of the same value and utility – likewise with his wife's agreement – in a process known as *andipricon*.

In 1831, through the introduction of *Regulamentul Organic* (Organic Regulation), the first law with the character of a constitution in the principalities, the discourse on dowries was renewed. With this regulation, the state took over the traditional role of the church and charged the courts with keeping stricter records than those that had hitherto been kept by parish priests. From now on, each county court had to maintain a special register for dowry contracts (including *andipricon* papers), and the office of the *Marele Logofăt* (chief minister) was to receive a certified copy within three days.[18]

The institutional correspondence that followed the issue of the Organic Regulation highlights the manner in which the couple, and particularly the wife, could judicially influence the procedure to protect the wife's property against possible (future) creditors by "hiding" her husband's property beneath the legal umbrella of the dowry and declaring his property hers simply by raising the total monetary value of the dowry. Consequently, in 1839, the office of the chief minister instructed the courts to verify the truthfulness of the information entered.[19] In the following decades, all trials in which a dowry was lacking or creditors were involved were announced in the state gazette, *Buletin: Gazeta officială*. In 1839, the state issued a circular that regulated that dowry contracts drawn up thereafter would be valid only if they were authenticated by the local law court. Thenceforth, the official gazette would regularly record the number of trials for loss of dowry brought before county law courts.

In general, endowment must be seen in relation to inheritance, in which there was a clear gender difference, privileging the son over the daughter and the son's children over the daughter's children.[20] The holding and transmission of the family name were thus subject to a transmission of the residence of the family – of the lineage. The nobility, including the Romanian boyar class, laid claim to their origin and built their wealth around a primary property (estate). Because of the connexion between name and estate, women appear to have been excluded from the inheritance of land, although in some areas of the Balkans this was accepted in the absence of sons or if the girl was the firstborn.[21] The process of transmission of goods was flexible and adaptable to local and regional realities and especially prone to manipulation on the part of the individual, depending on the social class to which they belonged.[22] In Wallachia we cannot speak of an exclusion of daughters from inheritance so much as of a "privilege of masculinity".[23] For the sixteenth and seventeenth centuries, it has been demonstrated that equal division and substitution were permitted by custom, and though initially women could inherit on an equal basis, in time endowment became a specific process, a kind of gift made separately from inheritance by way of testament.[24] They remained connected, however, because the testament would refer to the share given to the daughter on her marriage,[25] recalling what had been given and when, and if no dowry had been given (yet), the new head of the family (brother, uncle, grandfather, widow of the deceased) was obliged by law to provide it. The legal protection of the dowry became a preoccupation of lawmakers, and the legislation of the nineteenth century reaffirmed it while at the same time it did no more than confirm what was happening in practice.[26] In general, the dowry was perceived as the share of the parental wealth that went to daughters.[27]

II. Two town settings in Wallachia: Câmpulung and Piteşti

The two towns, Câmpulung and Piteşti, administrative centres of the neighbouring counties of Argeş and Muscel, respectively, had different pasts. Câmpulung was one of the oldest urban settlements in the principalities, dating to before the founding of Wallachia in the thirteenth century and home to a significant community of Roman Catholics.[28] Lying on the road towards Braşov in Hungarian Transylvania, it was the location of intense trade, supported by the establishment of an annual fair in July.[29] Gradually, the two communities, Orthodox and Catholic, blended together, and while in 1682 there were 200 Catholics in the town, within a century (1773) their numbers had fallen to thirty.[30] This process has been explained as the result of confessional-cultural pressure on the part of the majority population of Orthodox Romanians, continuous wars, and excessive taxation.[31] Piteşti, by contrast, was a new town, first documented in the sixteenth century, when it was known to foreigners as Nuwestad or Nieuwere.[32] Like Câmpulung, it also owed much to the trade the principality engaged in with Transylvania and Hungary and, later, areas south of the Danube.[33] Consequently, the market towns in the neighbouring counties sold their produce at Piteşti and also at Câmpulung.[34]

Visitors to Wallachia in the early nineteenth century had a vague appreciation of the size of its towns and the number of their inhabitants and also of their degree of Europeanisation, for although the Romanian towns did not bear visible signs of Islamisation, as was the case in other areas in the Balkans subject to the Ottoman Empire, they nevertheless seemed to have an Oriental look.[35] At the beginning of the century, Wallachia had thirty-seven towns, including small market centres, and by means of the first complete census (1838), it is possible to form a detailed impression of the urban population in terms of marital status, occupation, nationality, ethnicity, and wealth.[36]

The growth of the urban population was belated compared with the West; it was closely connected to political and economic factors and became constant after 1830.[38] The populations of the two towns show slight growth even if the rural population remained in the majority at the county level.[39]

III. Sources and methodology

The present investigation is based on one hundred dowry contracts from the period 1831 to 1856 registered by the courts of two counties, Argeş and Muscel, whose

TABLE 12.1 Number of households according to the census-like surveys made in 1838.

Census-like survey	*Argeş County (number of households)*		*Muscel County (number of households)*	
	Piteşti	*The rest of the county (Piteşti excluded)*	*Câmpulung*	*The rest of the county (Câmpulung excluded)*
1,838	779	21,739	1,494	12,301

Source: © Nicoleta Roman.[37]

administrative seats were Piteşti and Câmpulung, respectively; today these registers are preserved in the Argeş county branch of the national archives.[40] In the context of dowry contracts a range of other related documents, such as marriage certificates, purchase contracts for the properties that are mentioned, and parents' testaments, appear in the archives. The dowry contracts do not cover women of every social strata, as villagers were exempt from this obligation due to a lack of property.[41] Furthermore, every contract exceeding the sum of 1,000 lei had to state movable and immovable property in detail, including their respective monetary value.[42] This official threshold was not at all high given that 1,000 lei, equivalent to approximately 25 Austrian ducats, the most common currency of exchange, represented just ten months' pay for a county midwife.[43] Thus, the possibility opened up of knowing the situation of a relatively wide segment of the urban population in the two counties mentioned but not of the large peasantry. Wallachia was a preponderantly agricultural area in which there were both free peasants (*moşneni*) and dependent peasants tied to the land (*clăcaşi*). The 1831 law, although it was innovative from an administrative point of view, strengthened even more the authority of the boyars, named as landowners, and the dependence of the peasants on them. The *clăcaşi* continued to be numerous, and they were now obliged to work "according to old custom" twelve days per year in the service of the landowner, four days in each season, with their cattle and their tools or else with their hands.[44] Their freedom of movement was restricted. The land they received depended on how many animals they held, and historians have concluded that they often received poor land.[45] On top of all this, they had to pay the *dijmă*, a tenth part of their harvest, to work for one day at the plough and to fulfil other obligations, which invariably affected the wealth they could accumulate and the means by which it was transmitted. The peasantry lacked either the financial means or the knowledge, literacy, and interest to make out a dowry contract. In the two county towns where the courts were situated, the number of both free and dependent peasants was reduced in relation to the rest of the population: 879 *moşneni* and 176 *clăcaşi* in Câmpulung (out of 6,278 inhabitants)[46] and 405 *moşneni* and three *clăcaşi* in Piteşti (out of 4,015 inhabitants).[47]

The dowry-givers did not always specify to which social category they belonged, but starting from those who did and identifying others by matching their names with those in other sources, the majority belonged to the bourgeoisie and represent tradesmen, clerks, great merchants (designated by the term *hagi*), shopkeepers (bakers, butchers) officers, and petty boyars. Also, not all marriages concluded in this period in Piteşti and Câmpulung were followed by the presentation in court and registration of the dowry contract. The reasons are unclear – negligence or distrust of a system still in its early days, litigation in the family regarding the goods, or the simple fact that the family did not want the value of their property to be known. What is important to highlight is that although this system of registering the dowry contract in a town court rather than in a parish was in its beginnings, a number of dowry-givers came from outside the towns. This shows an inner mobility within the county and that the new legal developments started to reach a part of the rural areas as well. The documents mention especially Piteşti and Câmpulung as places of residence for the dowry-givers, but some also refer to those coming from the capital, the town of Târgovişte, or nearby villages, while others neglect to give this information.[48]

IV. What women get: A quantitative analysis of Piteşti and Câmpulung's dowry registers

Immovable goods entered in the dowry contracts include land (the estate or part thereof measured in *stânjeni* house, shop, and orchards/vineyards), while movable goods include clothes, tableware, silverware, and jewellery. Money may or may not be included in the dowry contract.[49] The inclusion of money in dowry contracts was no rarity in the corpus from Argeş and Muscel counties. The better off opted for imperial ducats, while others used the local leu currency. In a regional economy, stability was provided by the Austrian currency rather than the currency of the Ottoman Empire, which entered a decline in the 1830s. Even in a territory under the domination of the Porte, in provincial Wallachian towns like Piteşti and Câmpulung, things could not be different. The leu, based on the Dutch leeuwendaalder, was merely an "abstract" currency of calculation established by the same Organic Regulation of 1831 mentioned earlier. Also, the Ottoman reform of 1843 did not displace Austrian domination in this field.[50] In 1834, 8½ Austrian Zwanziger was equivalent to 19 lei at the rate of exchange a widow with two sons and a marriageable daughter used when she put on sale "a small shop front in the market of Piteşti, with its plot".[51] The trading space was bought by another woman for 3,370 lei, and the money became the daughter's dowry.[52] In spite of this general tendency, for Argeş and Muscel counties, the preferred currency for the valuation of goods in dowry contracts was the leu and not the ducat, although the leu (also known as the thaler) was only a unit of account.

TABLE 12.2 Relation between dowry-giver and endowed in Piteşti and Câmpulung. "Family combinations" include grandmother/grandfather, grandmother and son, mother and brother, mother and uncle, father and aunt.

Dowry-giver	*No.*
Father	33
Mother	32
Both parents	14
Family combinations	7
Wife to husband	7
Brother	4
Epitrop (guardian)	2
Nephew to aunt	1
Total	100

Source: © Nicoleta Roman.[53]

The majority of dowry-givers were parents, either the mother or the father (in almost equal numbers) or both; in some cases in which the father drew up the document, his wife was present and entered as a witness. Mothers often appeared as widows or as substitutions for the fathers as legal persons; sometimes there were also brothers among the witnesses. In 1831, Ioana from Piteşti, for example, received 300 thalers "to be able to buy a plot of land for a house in the district". Her three brothers were present when their mother appeared in court to have the document, which had been draughted much earlier, together with her deceased husband, confirmed. The various combinations of family members who granted a dowry, either singly or together, testify to family solidarity and prior agreement regarding the division of goods between the children.

Occasionally, the prenuptial gift, even in an old, Hellenised form (*progamia dora*), is mentioned in the dowry contracts. It is a gift offered by the woman to her future husband without specifying whether it is part of inherited property.[54] Moreover, as stated earlier, in addition to money, the dowry consisted of immovable property and movable goods.

IV.a Immovable property

In the analysis of our corpus of one hundred dowry contracts, 152 properties are mentioned. Frequently, land, such as estates or parts of estates measured in *stânjeni* (fathoms), was granted (fifty-eight times); and vineyards and orchards (thirty-nine times), houses (thirty-seven mentions), and properties of a commercial character, such as inns, taverns, shops, or mills, appeared eighteen times.[55] It seems daring to deduce agency from the fact that women were owners of a property such as a tavern or shop. Nonetheless, their position within the family of the husband was strengthened.

Women made use of their power over their own property. In 1831, Anica endowed her husband Iuliu Enghel with a considerable quantity of movable and immovable goods in the town of Piteşti – "a house plot on the boyar street" and an inn with six shops and a kitchen, to which was added a tavern and a vineyard in the vicinity. She also gave him two estates (Ciomăjeşti and Vlăşcuţa), "as I have had [full] ownership of them until now" and her share of a third estate owned in common with a female cousin.[56] But that is not all. Additionally, four estates, together with the right of use over part of a mill, were conveyed. For these, no value is stated, but their future is specified:

> All these, according to the agreement we have made, he is permitted to sell by public auction, [he] not having knowledge of their market value and skill of administration, and the money realized from their sale to be entered in this same document.[57]

The document also mentions fifteen animals and a very special category of property – twenty gypsy slaves. These are not priced, but the movable goods, such as a carriage, jewellery, dresses, and "the bedding and other small items of the house", add up to a total of about 8,800 lei. The court did not record a later price on the dowry contract or any decision in this regard. Properties are very rarely priced – in only three cases in fact, where the items in question are a vineyard, a house still under construction, and a shop, for the purchase of which money is given. No price is ever given for an estate or a portion of an estate. One possible explanation could be the continually fluctuating price of land and the insecurity of the area, which lay in a zone of regional conflict between the Porte, Russian, and Austrian empires. However, we may get an idea of the relatively higher value of such properties in comparison with other types of immovable goods. In the same year, 1831, the wife of a deacon brought a dowry contract before the court to replace an earlier one. The illiterate woman declared (through the handwriting of another person) that the original contract "not having been made according to the proper order, has been torn up by myself". Via the new document, she handed over part of an estate to her daughter that a few years later, in 1840, would be sold for 5,500 lei. At the end of the file, the transaction is mentioned together with the fact that the money is treated as *andipricon* in place of the land.[58] The variety of goods and their combinations may be read as an indicator distinguishing between the elite, the lesser boyar class, and the townsfolk. Money functioned as a substitute for property.[59] The lower down the social scale, the greater the tendency to invest in animals rather than any other goods, as animals had a high economic value and helped with the maintenance and development of the household, the working of the land, and the obtaining of additional income.

In some cases, girls received land, house, shop, and money in addition to the objects in their trousseau – in other words, something from each category of goods. For one cloth merchant's daughter, the most important items were "a small shop front with a back room and with its yard on the main street of Piteşti", five strips of vineyard, and 1,600 lei.[60] Basically, the small merchant granted her a selling space (the shop front) and a sum of money that might have been sufficient for the start of a household. Sometimes parents specified the destiny of a particular item (e.g. the land might be for the construction of a house and the money for buying clothes and jewellery), but most of the time they did not. It is worth mentioning that they might also reserve for themselves the right to live in the house they granted to their daughter, which would become her full property upon their death, as is illustrated by the case of a furrier in 1839:

> The large house and the shop on the street with their plot measured as six *stânjeni* and two palms . . . and as many buildings as are on this plot are given to our daughter, we being to stay in this house and shop until the end of our lives and then it will remain in the full possession of our abovementioned daughter. And let it be known that the gate and yard of these houses are common to the small house, which is given to our grandson.

"Reserving one's right of rest"[61] is a provision by which parents sought security for their old age and that, although it frequently appears in testaments, may be encountered in this type of document too. Even though the power relations between parents and children changed, the parental home continued to be shared between the generations, and the full cession of property rights over it took place by stages. In such circumstances, the transmission of the immovable property was negotiated between the two parties, and the endowment, as a process assimilated to inheritance, was completed on the parent's death.[62]

In our sample, a total of 152 properties are mentioned in sixty-six dowry contracts, but most commonly the reference is in general terms. When no documentary proof can be produced it is simply affirmed, in the presence of witnesses, that the properties are owned by the dowry-giver, who is entitled to dispose of them according to the law. Thus, in twenty-six cases the provenance of the properties is not specified, but analysis of those that remain reveals a variety of appropriations, such as purchase, inheritance from parents, mother's dowry, or gift.[63]

IV.b A special category of immobile property: Gypsy slaves

In the Romanian principalities, gypsy slaves were owned privately, princely by the state or by the church or monasteries. In Wallachia, gypsies were considered slaves (*robi*) who lived in family or kinship groups (*sălașe*). Legally unfree, they could be bought and sold, although they enjoyed limited customary rights to own and inherit property themselves. Although they were legally objectified as immobile property, this was not understood in an absolute sense. There were calls for a concept of animate property (*res animata*) to justify the limited rights they enjoyed.[64] Beginning in the eighteenth century, the status of *robi* gradually became a matter of political and intellectual debate, and in the first half of the nineteenth century, an effort to redeem the Wallachian slave population was undertaken by the state despite the vehement opposition of the Orthodox Church, the largest slaveholder in the principality.[65] Nomadism, characteristic of those gypsies who practised various trades, and vagrancy as a result of flight from a master became concerns of the ruling class in the mid-nineteenth century. For this reason, the imposition of a sedentary lifestyle was associated with the emancipation laws, and in the case of Wallachia, the emancipation law of 1856 required nomads and emancipated gypsies to settle in a locality of their choice, from which they were not to move for ten years; at the same time they were encouraged to turn to occupations connected with agriculture.[66]

Gypsy slaves were included in dowry contracts as immovable goods, although in their case transmission as a *sălaș*, or family, rather than as individuals, was preferred. They were considered a property with economic value and were not appointed to agricultural work, but rather comprised a specific domestic apparatus similar to servants such as cooks and coachmen. Their value was assessed according to their age, gender, and the trades they knew. In our corpus of dowry contracts, gypsies are mentioned fourteen times, representing 151 individuals. On thirteen occasions they are clearly specified to be extended families of over four members, but they are also transmitted separately, as individuals. A recurrent practice in the period, which can also be observed in our documents, is the exchange of gypsies, a type of barter that replaced the notion of price.[67]

IV.c Movable goods: Between homemade and luxury

The mobile items within the dowry constituted a more flexible resource in the domestic economy in comparison to immobile property.[68] Often referred to as "feminine goods", these were assimilated to the trousseau and served to furnish, equip, and decorate the house.[69] The top five categories of movable goods entered in dowry contracts are clothing, bedding, tableware, costume accessories, and kitchen accessories (Table 12.3). Such objects related to the woman's body and to the well-being of the household and the couple. Tableware included silver items; drams of silver could be reused to make ornaments or cutlery. We also find mirrors, vases, and irons alongside dowry chests from Braşov, carpets from Ţarigrad (Constantinople), and Lipsca (Leipzig) trays. In addition, the contracts testify to the coexistence of the old and the new in clothing and of items made in the home

TABLE 12.3 Movable and immovable items included in dowry contracts in Piteşti and Câmpulung.

Category of items (movable and immovable) included in dowry contracts	*Number of items*
Clothes	651
Bed linen	349
Tableware	330
Accessories	231
Properties	152
Gypsy slaves	151
Kitchen accessories	147
Jewels	137
Money	123
Hygiene supplies	116
Objects for godparents and parents-in-law	110
Carpets, rugs	86
Tools	62
Dowry chests	49
Candlesticks	48
Animals	44
Pots	35
Footwear	27
Patch of materials	13
Drams of silver	8
Religious items	7
(Indecipherable words)	7
Furniture	6
Transportation (carriage/wagon)	6

Source: © Nicoleta Roman.[75]

(blouses), some previously worn and others made from new material. They point to the bond between generations, between mothers and daughters,[70] but also to cultural symbiosis.

Usually, the value of movable goods was considerably lower than that of immovable properties, and these goods often came from local workshops or commercial centres like Leipzig or the Russian realm. At the same time, we may observe another important process, the "devaluing" of certain articles – formerly luxury items worn, for example, by the princely family but now ordered by townsfolk and petty boyars. These were still seen as expensive prestige items but were now accessible both in terms of price and as a result of the gradual disappearance of the sumptuary laws. The *malotea*, for instance, is frequently mentioned as being included as part of these movable goods, or money is given to have one made. The *malotea* was a long Oriental coat made of *ghermesit*,[71] with fur lining, collar, and cuffs. If there were no pretensions regarding the fur, the monetary "help" to have a *malotea* made was around 100 lei, while for a coat with Russian sable the reference price rose to 300. The provenance, degree of wear, and material from which the item was made were important in establishing the price. Women dowry-givers were more attentive to its detailed description, referring not only to the aforementioned criteria but also to the design (flowery or checked, with or without lace, etc.). Among the classic accessories that completed the image of a bourgeois woman up-to-date with the latest novelties – gloves, fan, umbrella, and vanity set[72] – only the first are to be found, but they are complemented by the existence of hats, sometimes described as being "of English muslin and with lace".[73] Only four mentions of garments clearly refer to a bride's dress of silk (two), a blouse (one), and a veil (one), while a wedding ring "with diamonds"[74] is listed only once. The infrequency of such mentions is significant and points to a late diffusion of the Western model of specialisation in certain types of clothing and at the same time a specifically bourgeois type of consumption. However, as the bourgeoisie itself was in the process of forming in the Romanian space, the interpenetration of the various goods of the former elite of the late eighteenth century and what was produced at home, or typical of the peasantry, or copied from the various cultural spaces that served as models (Vienna, Paris) became a natural phenomenon. Townsfolk were still searching for the look on which to model themselves, and they remained bound to the rural space and to old customs.

V. Conclusion

This investigation of dowry contracts in two provincial towns of Wallachia has highlighted important aspects of the connexion between women, family, and property. In an environment marked by inner mobility and continuous cultural transfer, an ensemble of strategies was developed through which families found a middle way between law and custom, manipulating the transmission of goods according to their own interests and the needs of the family group. The dowry-giver might be the father, but a dowry could also be given by the mother or by other members of the family acting in solidarity to create a new family alliance. The dowry remained a result of prior negotiations and was the woman's share of the inheritance granted to her in advance. She could receive properties or parts of the family estate, or money to buy these, and at the same time could impose conditions on their management by her husband. Immovable goods, however, remained preponderantly bound to an intergenerational accord between parents and children – the "right of rest" – with being cared for in old age solicited as a final guarantee before the children's property rights turned from usufruct to ownership. In towns and in the case of the well-off, the absence of real estate was compensated for with money or goods of high value that enabled a possible equivalence between the shares granted to sons and daughters.[76] The relations between siblings and between parents and children should be seen as part of a much wider network of kinship in which other members, too (grandparents, aunts, and uncles), had something to say from an economic point of view. These were not occasional decision makers but "agents of a daily solidarity".[77] As the family was not a fixed structure,[78] and the woman remained a channel through whom goods were transmitted and recovered,[79] a discussion of the dowry should be seen in this context as negotiation in a family enlarged by alliance and, at the same time, as the manifestation of affective bonds.[80] Seen as a homogeneous corpus belonging to a region, the dowry contracts from Piteşti and Câmpulung also reflect aspects of consumption and material culture, and in particular an interpenetration of clothing styles, seen in the selective adoption of the garments of the earlier elite, the homemade clothes of the peasantry, and items brought through merchants acting as intermediaries. They testify to a belated and relative diffusion of the fashions launched in a West seen as civilising. The state sought to control the population administratively through the norms introduced by the Organic Regulation (1831) and later revisions regarding the valuation of goods, the obligatory registration of dowry contracts in court, and the informing of creditors of the content of the documents. All the same, there were departures from the norm, and the practice of distributing goods did not result in an absolute exclusion of women from inheritance.

Notes

1 This study is part of research conducted within the ERC project Luxury, Fashion and Social Status in Early Modern South-Eastern Europe (LuxFaSS), project no. 646489, hosted by New Europe College – Institute for Advanced Study (Bucharest). I am grateful to James Christian Brown for translating the text from Romanian.
2 After being until the eighteenth century, to a large extent, a continual theatre of armed conflict in the Russian–Austrian–Turkish wars, following the peace of Kuchuk Kainarji (1774), and especially the Treaty of Adrianople (1829), this territory began to gain in terms of both economic development and juridical status. On the Black Sea and the Danube, ports such as Odessa, Brăila, and Galați acquired the status of free ports, and the straits of the Bosphorus and the Dardanelles were opened to all commercial shipping. On this matter, see the results of the international project dedicated to the Black Sea region, https://blacksea.gr (accessed 2 February 2020).
3 Viorel Panaite, "Wallachia and Moldavia from the Ottoman juridical and political viewpoint, 1774–1829", in: Antonis Anastasopoulos and Elias Kolovos (eds.), *Ottoman Rule*

and the Balkans, 1750–1860: Conflict, Transformation, Adaptation, Rethymno 2007 [University of Crete], pp. 21–44; Viorel Panaite, *Război, pace şi comerţ în Islam: Ţările Române în dreptul otoman al popoarelor*, Iaşi 2013 [Polirom].

4 About the influence of Phanariot Greeks see Pompiliu Eliade, *De l'influence française sur l'esprit public en Roumanie. Les origines, étude sur l'état de la société roumaine à l'époque des règnes phanariotes*, Paris 1898 [Ernest Leurex]; Ioan Constantin Filitti, *Rôle diplomatique des Phanariotes de 1700 à 1821*, Paris 1901 [L. Larose]; Fatma Müge Göcek, *East Encounters West: France and the Ottoman Empire in the Eighteenth Century*, New York 1987 [Oxford University Press]; Daniel Chirot, "Causes and Consequences of Backwardness", in: Daniel Chirot (ed.), *The Origins of Backwardness in Eastern Europe: Economics and Politics from the Middle Ages Until the Early Twentieth Century*, Berkeley, Los Angeles and London 1989 [University of California Press], pp. 1–14, pp. 4–9; Suraiya Faroqhi and Fikret Adanır, "Introduction", in: Fikret Adanır and Suraiya Faroqhi (eds.), *The Ottomans and the Balkans: A Discussion of Historiography*, Leiden and Boston 2002 [Brill], pp. 1–56, pp. 21–28 for an overview of the current state of research.

5 Ida Fazio, "Percorsi coniugali nell'Italia moderna in Storia del matrimonio", in: Christiane Klapisch-Zuber and Michela De Giorgio (eds.), *Storia dell Matrimonio*, Rome 1996 [Laterza], pp. 166–170.

6 Karl Kaser and Olga Katsiardi-Hering, "Introduction", in: *The History of the Family* 9, 3 (2004), pp. 253–255, p. 254.

7 Karl Kaser, "Power and Inheritance: Male Domination, Property, and Family in Eastern Europe, 1500–1900", in: *History of the Family* 7, 3 (2002), pp. 375–395, p. 377; Violetta Hionidou, "Independence and Inter-dependence: Household Formation Patterns in Eighteenth Century Kythera, Greece", in: *The History of the Family* 16, 3 (2011), pp. 217–234, p. 232.

8 Gérard Beaur, "Le contrat de mariage dans les sociétés européennes. Enjeux familiaux et pratiques des acteurs", in: *Annales de Démographie Historique* 121, 1 (2011), pp. 5–21, p. 7; Didier Lett, *Freres et sœurs. Histoire d'un lien*, Paris 2009 [Payot & Rivages], pp. 119–120.

9 Evdoxios Doxiadis, "From Legal Diversity to Centralization. Marriage and Wealth in Nineteenth-century Greece", in: Anna Bellavitis and Beatrice Zucca Micheletto (eds.), *Gender, Law and Economic Well-Being in Europe from the Fifteenth to the Nineteenth Century. North Versus South?* London and New York 2018 [Routledge], pp. 91–105, p. 97; Nicole Arnaud-Duc, "Les contradictions du droit", in: Genevieve Fraisse and Michelle Perrot (eds.), *Histoire des femmes en Occident*, vol. IV. Le XIXe siècle, Paris 2002 [Perrin], pp. 101–139, here pp. 132–133; Heide Wunder and Grethe Jacobsen, "Introduction", in: Grethe Jacobsen and Heide Wunder (eds.), *East Meets West: A Gendered View of Legal Tradition*, Kiel 2015 [Solivagus], pp. 9–22; Margarida Durães and Antoinette Fauve-Chamoux (eds.), *The Transmission of Well-Being. Gendered Marriage Strategies and Inheritance Systems in Europe (17th – 20th Centuries)*, Bern 2009 [Peter Lang]; Anna Bellavitis and Beatrice Zucca Micheletto, "Introduction", in: Anna Bellavitis and Beatrice Zucca Micheletto (eds.), *Gender, Law and Economic Well-Being in Europe from the Fifteenth to the Nineteenth Century, North Versus South?* London and New York 2018 [Routledge], pp. 1–27.

10 James Marten, "Family Relations", in: Colin Heywood (ed.), *A Cultural History of Childhood and Family, vol. V. In the Age of Empire*, London 2014 [Bloomsbury], pp. 19–38, p. 23; Ulf Brunnbauer, "Families and Mountains in the Balkans. Christians and Muslim Household Structures in the Rhodopes, 19th–20th Century", in: *History of the Family* 7, 3 (2002), pp. 327–350, p. 341.

11 Marten, "Family Relations", p. 21; David Warrean Sabean and Simon Teuscher, "Kinship in Europe. A New Approach to Long Term Development", in: David Warren Sabean, Simon Teuscher and Jon Mathieu (eds.), *Kinship in Europe. Approaches to Long-Term Development (1300–1900)*, New York 2007 [Berghahn Books], pp. 1–32, p. 3; Susan Kellogg and Steve Mintz, *Domestic Revolutions: A Social History of American Family Life*, New York 1988 [Free Press].

12 Chronologically, Constanţa Vintilă-Ghiţulescu, "Zestrea între normă şi practică. Ţara Românească în secolul al XVII-lea", in: *Studii şi materiale de istorie medie* XVIII (2000), pp. 51–75 and XIX (2001), pp. 255–265 (continued in În şalvari şi cu işlic, pp. 148–184);

Violeta Barbu, "De la comunitatea patrimonială la comunitatea de destin: zestrea în Ţara Românească în secolul al XVII-lea", in: Violeta Barbu, Florina Manuela Constantin et al. (eds.), *De la comunitate la societate: studii de istoria familiei din Ţara Românească în Vechiul Regat*, Bucharest 2007 [Institutul Cultural Român], pp. 19–93 (continued in *Ordo amoris: o istorie a instituţiei căsătoriei în Ţara Românească în secolul al XVII-lea*, Bucharest 2011 [Editura Academiei Române], pp. 204–258); Angela Jianu, "Women, Dowries, and Patrimonial Law in Old-Regime Romania (c. 1750–1830)", in: *Journal of Family History* 34, 2 (2009), pp. 189–205.

13 "[S]ilver or gold jewels, copper products, clothes, animals or anything of the sort, the parents should price them and put the total amount and the total number of the items at the end of the dowry." "Mijlocirile cu care pot să rămâie foiţele zestrilor temeinice şi nestrămutate", in: G. Ştrempel (ed.), *Antim Ivireanul. Opere*, Bucureşti 1972 [Minerva], pp. 393–394. The text is addressed to priests, and this section dedicated to the dowry follows that referring to the drawing up of testaments.

14 Ibid.

15 *Pravilniceasca condică* (1780), Bucureşti 1957, cap. XIX. On dowry, 8, pp. 96–98. The same interval of time is granted to the other heirs to make any claims.

16 Barbu, "De la comunitatea patrimonială", pp. 73–78; Constanţa Ghiţulescu, "Mariage et parenté à travers les actes dotaux roumains (1700–1865)", in: *Annales de Démographie Historique* 1 (2011), pp. 141–160.

17 *Pravilniceasca condică* (1780), cap. XIX, 4, p. 94 shows that only expenses arising from the making of income were deducted from it, not those relating to the maintenance of the house or other buildings or resulting from the illness of gypsies.

18 P. Negulescu, G. Alexianu and A. Sava (eds.), *Regulamentul Organic al Valahiei şi al Moldovei*, vol. I, Bucharest 1944 [Întreprinderile Eminescu], secţia VIII. For the entry in the registry of dowry contracts and guarantees, see p. 123, art. 337.

19 Arhivele Naţionale Istorice Centrale (National Archives of Romania. Main Headquarters, hereafter ANIC), Ministerul Justiţiei. Extrajudiciare, 35/1839, f. 29. A quite common habit, if we take into consideration the situation in Italy. Beatrice Zucca Micheletto, "A qui sert la dot? Aliénations dotales, économie familiale et stratégies des couples à Turin au XVIIIe siècle", in: *Annales de Démographie Historique* 1 (2011), pp. 165–168.

20 *Legiuirea Caragea* (1818), critical edition, Bucharest 1955, p. 118, cap. III. For inheritance or "clironomie", gl. 17 c): "When they have boys and girls, only the boys inherit equally, and if the girls are not provided with a dowry, it is their duty to provide them with a dowry and to see them married." In the earlier draught it was provided that girls would inherit together with boys.

21 Maria N. Todorova, *Balkan Family Structure and the European Pattern. Demographic Developments in Ottoman Bulgaria*, Budapest and New York 2006 [CEU Press], pp. 119–120. Todorova argues that as a general rule the daughter received only the dowry and the mother's goods. Only Russia stands out, from a legislative point of view, as a special case; by the end of the eighteenth century, women of the nobility were guaranteed seven percent of the immovable property of their parents and an eighth part of their personal goods, and in the absence of sons, daughters could inherit equal shares. Michelle LaMarche Marrese, "Gender and the Legal Order in Imperial Russia", in: Dominic Lieven (ed.), *Russia, vol. I. Imperial Russia, 1689–1917*, Cambridge 2006 [Cambridge University Press], pp. 326–343, p. 327 and her extensive research on this subject in *A Woman's Kingdom: noblewomen and the control of property in Russia, 1700–1861*, Ithaca and London 2002 [Cornell University Press], in which she argues that many women had and controlled landed property, especially given that from 1753 the law changed and they did not have to request permission from their husbands to sell.

22 Angela Groppi and Agnès Fine, "Femmes dot et patrimoine", in: *Clio. Femmes, Genre, Histoire* 7 (1998), p. 3.

23 Ion Peretz, *Privilegiul masculinităţii în Pravilniceasca Condică Ipsilanti şi în Legiuirea Caragea*, Bucharest 1905 [Tipografia Clementa]; Ovidiu Sachelarie and Nicolae Stoicescu (eds.), *Instituţii feudale din Ţările Române: dicţionar*, Bucharest 1988 [Editura Academiei Române], pp. 521–522; Andrei Rădulescu, "Pagini despre Legiuirea Caragea", in: *Pagini*

inedite din istoria dreptului vechi românesc, Bucharest 1991 [Editura Academiei Române], p. 86. Rădulescu shows that the custom of the land and some law codes had recognised the equality of the sexes, but the privilege of masculinity was preferred (note 16). Subsequent to the adoption of Caradja's legislation, the inheritance of the parental home by daughters, in the absence of sons and with the approval of the ruling prince, was accepted to avoid the disintegration of the property.

24 Violeta Barbu, "Familia şi sistemele succesorale în ţara obiceiului. Substituţia", in: Violeta Barbu (ed.), *De bono coniugali. O istorie a familiei din Ţara Românească în secolul al XVII-lea*, Bucureşti 2003 [Meridiane], pp. 100–118, using sixty-seven documents from *Documenta Romaniae Historica*. Seria B. Ţara Românească collection for the period 1400–1653. Barbu, *Ordo amoris: o istorie a instituţiei căsătoriei în Ţara Românească în secolul al XVII-lea*, Bucharest 2011 [Editura Academiei Române], p. 210.

25 Beaur, "Le contract de marriage", p. 13; Lett, *Frères et sœurs*, p. 116, who mentions the exclusion of daughters from the will because they had already received their share of inheritance as dowry.

26 Barbu, *Ordo amoris*, pp. 214–215.

27 Nicoleta Roman, "Dowry Contracts, Women's Objects and the Circulation of Goods in Mid-Nineteenth Century Oltenia", pp. 105–140; R. Romanelli, "Donne e patrimoni", in: Angela Groppi (ed.), *Il lavoro delle donne*, Rome 1996 [Laterza], p. 356; Margareth Lanzinger, "Marriage Contracts in Various Contexts: Marital Property Rights, Socio-cultural Aspects and Gender-Specific Implications. Late-Eighteenth-Century Evidence from Two Tirolean Court Districts", in: *Annales de Démographie Historique* 2 (2011), pp. 69–98, p. 81; Elisabeth Joris, "Kinship and Gender. Property, Enterprise, and Politics", in: David Warren Sabean, Simon Teuscher and Jon Mathieu (eds.), *Kinship in Europe. Approaches to Long-Term Development (1300–1900)*, New York 2007 [Berghahn Books], pp. 231–257, p. 239; Hionidou, "Independence and Inter-dependence", p. 220.

28 Laurenţiu Rădvan, *At Europe's Borders: Medieval Towns in the Romanian Principalities*, Leiden and Boston 2010 [Brill], pp. 264–267.

29 Ibid., p. 271; George Ioan Lahovari, Constantin I. Brătianu and Grigore G. Tocilescu, *Marele Dicţionar Geografic al României*, vol. II, Bucharest 1899, p. 484.

30 Rădvan, *At Europe's Borders*, pp. 266–267; Alexandru Ciocâltan, "Comunităţile catolice din Câmpulung şi Bucureşti (1688–1763)", in: Ileana Căzan and Bogdan Mateescu (eds.), *Timp, societate şi identitate culturală. "Miniaturi" istorice*, Cluj-Napoca 2015 [Academia Română-Centrul de Studii Transilvane], pp. 137–237, p. 145.

31 Alexandru Ciocâltan, *Comunităţile germane la sud de Carpaţi în Evul Mediu (secolele XIII-XVIII)*, Istros 2015 [Brăila], pp. 273–297.

32 Rădvan, *At Europe's Borders*, p. 159, pp. 164–165.

33 Ibid., p. 285.

34 George Ioan Lahovari, Constantin I. Brătianu and Grigore G. Tocilescu, *Marele Dicţionar Geografic al României*, p. 785; Ştefan Meteş, *Relaţiile comerciale ale Ţării Româneşti cu Ardealu până în veacul al XVIII-leal*, Sighişoara 1921 [Tipografia W. Krafft], pp. 180–181.

35 Alexandra Yerolympos, *Urban Transformations in the Balkans (1820–1920): Aspects of Town Planning and the Rethinking of Thessaloniki*, Thessaloniki 1996 [University Studio Press], p. 20.

36 Dan Berindei (ed.), *Istoria Românilor, vol. VII, tom. 1. Constituirea României moderne (1821–1878)*, Bucureşti 2003 [Editura Enciclopedică], p. 157: a ranking of the populations of towns, including Bucharest (60, 567 inhabitants), Ploieşti (15, 897), and Craiova (11, 885). The figures are from the survey of 1831; the town in second place varied over time. Other Balkan capitals were smaller, according to the estimates produced by similar surveys. Yerolympos, p. 17: Sofia (50,000 inhabitants in 1853), Athens (14,000 in 1836), Belgrade (12,900 in 1838).

37 Spiridon Cristocea, *Oraşul Piteşti în catagrafia din 1838*, Piteşti 2011 [Ordessos], p. 11; Bogdan Mateescu, *Census-like material preserved in the Romanian archives, for the former principalities of Moldavia, Wallachia and for Romania before 1914*, Mosaic Working Paper WP2013–001, pp. 33–34. It should be added that besides Piteşti, Argeş county had another major town, Curtea de Argeş. The estimated number of persons per household

in 1838 is 5.2 for Piteşti and 4.2 for Câmpulung. The calculation has been made taking into consideration the number of inhabitants: 4,015 for Piteşti and 6,278 for Câmpulung.

38 Keith Hitchins, *The Romanians, 1774–1866*, Oxford 1996 [Clarendon Press], pp. 172–174, who links population growth to the end of the wars between the neighbouring powers (Austria, Russia, the Ottoman Empire) that had been a constant of the eighteenth century; fiscal stability through the removal of restrictions and of certain economic privileges; population flow; and reduced mortality (through the introduction of sanitary measures).

39 There is evidence of immigration, especially in Piteşti. In Piteşti, Serbs (960 individuals) were the largest immigrant group. These were in fact Bulgarians who had taken refuge here after the Russian–Turkish war of 1828–1829 but who preferred to assume another nationality to avoid being sent back. Serbia had gained autonomy in relation to the Ottoman Empire in 1812, while Bulgaria continued to be an Ottoman province. Cristocea, *Oraşul Piteşti în catagrafia din 1838*, p. 14.

40 Muscel county was abolished in an administrative reform in 1950 and its territory divided between the present Argeş and Dâmboviţa counties. Arhivele Naţionale. Serviciul Judeţean Argeş (hereafter DJAN Argeş): Eight registers from Tribunalul Argeş (139/1831, 639/1833, 2761/1833, 1521/1834, 14618/1835, 12176/1836, 13/1838, 27/1839) and seven from Tribunalul Muşcel (8/1834, 6/1835, 8/1838, 9/1837, 7/1850, 4/1855, 8/1856). The consideration of these documents from the courts of two neighbouring counties as one single corpus is also due to the fact that in some cases the inhabitants of one town would register a dowry contract in the other. Such juridical mobility was determined by the marriage of a family member to a local and their resulting move.

41 Negulescu, Alexianu and Sava (eds.), *Regulamentul Organic al Valahiei şi al Moldovei*, vol. I, Chapter VII, Section VIII, art. 341.

42 Ibid., Chapter VII, Section X. The duties of the chief minister, p. 331, art. 384.

43 The salary per month for an assistant clerk or a county midwife in Wallachia was 100 lei, cf. Nicoleta Roman, "Deznădăjduită muiere n-au fost ca mine". *Femei, onoare şi păcat în Valahia secolului al XIX-lea*, Bucharest 2016 [Humanitas], p. 198, raised from 80 lei. The midwives from the quarantine points received 50–60 lei, cf. Negulescu, Alexianu and Sava (eds.), *Regulamentul Organic al Valahiei şi al Moldovei*, pp. 99–100.

44 Hitchins, *The Romanians*, p. 177 argues for 75% of the population.

45 Negulescu, Alexianu and Sava (eds.), *Regulamentul Organic al Valahiei şi al Moldovei*, vol. I, Chapter III, Section VII. Reciprocal rights and duties between the landowner and his villager, in particular art. 140–144, in which it is specified that "the tenant's working day is calculated according to the extent of the land". Hitchins, *The Romanians*, p. 179, with a reference to M. Constantinescu, *L'évolution de la propriété rurale et la réforme agraire en Roumanie*, Bucharest 1925 [Cultura Naţională].

46 Spiridon Cristocea, Ştefan Trâmbaciu, *Câmpulung Muscelului*, p. 14.

47 Cristocea, *Oraşul Piteşti*, p. 19.

48 Capital (two), the town of Târgovişte (one), or nearby villages: Bădiceni (one), Brăneşti (one), Dealu ot Valea Bălenilor (one), Româneşti (one), Stoiceni (two dowry contracts made by the same person, Maria Slăviteasca, in 1836 to her daughters, Lucsandra and Joiţa), Valea lui Enache (one). Without information (thirty-two).

49 *Stânjen* – unit of length used before the introduction of the metric system. It varied between 1.96 and 2.23 metres. A similar study carried out on the records of Craiova in Dolj county, a merchant town, has brought to light a distinctive characteristic: The preference of merchant families for giving money, listed with the trousseau and silverware, in combination with land and shop, cf. Roman, "Dowry Contracts, Women's Objects and the Circulation of Goods in Mid-Nineteenth Century Oltenia", pp. 105–140.

50 The new lira of 7.216 grams was equivalent to 9 Austrian florins, cf. Pamuk Sevket, *A Monetary History*, Cambridge 2000 [Cambridge University Press], pp. 188–209;

Edhem Eldem, *A History of the Ottoman Bank*, Istanbul 1999 [Osmanlı Bankası Arşiv Ve Araştırmalar Merkezi], p. 21.

51 DJAN Argeş, Tribunalul Argeş, 1366/1834, f. 2.

52 Ibid., f. 11.

53 DJANArgeş,TribunalulArgeş 139/1831,639/1833,2761/1833,1521/1834,14618/1835, 12176/1836, 13/1838, 27/1839; Tribunalul Muşcel (8/1834, 6/1835, 8/1838, 9/1837, 7/1850, 4/1855, 8/1856.

54 DJAN Argeş, Tribunalul Argeş, 239/1831, dowry contract no. 3 of 25 October 1831 given by Theodoriţa sin Ştefan Cocul to her second husband, Dumitru Slăvian: A share inherited from her first husband.

55 DJAN Argeş, Tribunalul Argeş 139/1831, 639/1833, 2761/1833, 1521/1834, 14618/1835, 12176/1836, 13/1838, 27/1839 and Tribunalul Muscel, 8/1834, 6/1835, 8/1838, 9/1837, 7/1850, 4/1855, 8/1856.

56 It is highly likely that Anica is entering a second marriage or talks about the fortune she has established herself. In this case, the bride "endows" herself.

57 DJAN Argeş, Tribunalul Argeş, ds. 139/1831, dowry contract no. 4 of 6 December 1831.

58 DJAN Argeş, Tribunalul Argeş, 139/1831, dowry contract no. 5 of 12 January 1831. Women were present when the dowry contracts were made. They either signed or put their thumb beside their name while at least three witnesses were in the room. These people also signed or put their thumbs down but only after the dowry-giver and before the recipient of the goods. This hierarchised order of signatures and testimonies showed that all of them acknowledged and understood what was written and given.

59 Marrese, *A Woman's Kingdom*, p. 140, where it is observed that for Moscow the dowry contracts from 1703 to 1714 included mainly land and serfs, while after 1731 there is a preference for a sum of money; Micheletto, "A qui sert la dot?" p. 164 who analyses the 1760–1780 period for Turin.

60 Ilinca, daughter of the cloth merchants Nicolaie and Paraschiva.

61 DJAN Argeş, Tribunalul Muşcel, 8/1856, by which the giver of the dowry also specifies that the girl must "give us for ourselves two resting rooms for our old age, for as long as I have days and as long as I live", or DJAN Argeş, Tribunal Argeş, 12176/1836, dowry contract no. 5 of 28 October 1836, in which the mother specifies that "as long as I, the undersigned, the mother of the girl, live, I shall be able to stay in a room to have my rest".

62 Hionidou, "Independence and Inter-dependence", p. 221.

63 Properties and their previous ownership as mentioned in the dowry contracts: Without property 34%, with property 66%; previous ownership undefinded 38%; property formerly owned by father 9%, owned by parents 8%, owned by mother 8%, gift 2%. Source: DJAN Argeş, Tribunalul Argeş, 139/1831, 639/1833, 2761/1833, 1521/1834, 14618/1835, 12176/1836, 13/1838, 27/1839 and Tribunalul Muşcel, 8/1834, 6/1835, 8/1838, 9/1837, 7/1850, 4/1855, 8/1856.

64 Florina Manuela Constantin, "Modalităţi de transmitere a dreptului de stăpânire asupra robilor ţigani. Vânzarea şi schimbul (Ţara Românească, secolul al XVII-lea)", in: *Miscellanea historica in honorem Professoris Marcel-Dumitru Ciucă septuagenarii*, Istros and Ordessos 2013 [Brăila – Piteşti], pp. 313–328, an idea developed in her forthcoming article in Studii şi materiale de istorie medie (2019), starting from her doctoral thesis.

65 On gypsies in Romanian society, see Viorel Achim, *The Roma in Romanian History*, Budapest 2004 [Central European University Press]; Florina Manuela Constantin, "Liens de parenté et liens sociaux chez les esclaves tsiganes de Valachie. Le sălaş au XVIIe siècle", in: Roger Botte and Alessandro Stella (eds.), *Couleurs de l'esclavage sur les deux rives de la Méditerranée (Moyen Âge – XXe siècle)*, Paris 2012 [Karthala], pp. 283–296; Bogdan Mateescu, "Mixed Marriages Involving Gypsy Slaves in Nineteenth Century Wallachia: State and Church Policies", in: Luminiţa Dumănescu, Daniela Mârza and Marius Eppel (eds.), *Intermarriage Throughout History*, Newcastle-upon-Tyne 2014 [Cambridge Scholars Publishing], pp. 212–231; Nicoleta Roman, "Caught between Two Worlds:

The Children from Gypsy and Romanian – Gypsy Families in Wallachia (1800–1860)", in: *Romanian Journal of Population Studies* 8, 1 (2014), pp. 63–86.

66 *Buletin oficial*, nr. 13/1856, p. 49. Viorel Achim, "Transformări sociale în cadrul populației țigănești în epoca dezrobirii: sedentarizarea și legarea de ocupația agricolă", in: Venera Achim and Viorel Achim (eds.), *Modernizarea socială și instituțională în Principatele Române, 1831–1859*, Bucharest 2016 [Editura Academiei Române], pp. 156–166.

67 There are references to one exchange of gypsy slaves, with the dowry-giver mentioning in the contract only the "new" gypsy slaves, from whom he bought them, and that they were acquired without any suit of clothes, but this was not the reason for the transaction. The reference is to a man (bought from Costache Lipoianu) and a pregnant woman (bought from Catinca, Baroness Sachelarie). DJAN Argeș, Tribunal Argeș, 27/1839, dowry contract no. 4.

68 Micheletto, "A qui sert la dot?" p. 172.

69 Jane Hamlett, *Material Relations. Domestic Interiors and Middle-Class Families in England, 1850–1910*, Manchester 2010 [Manchester University Press], pp. 79–80.

70 Ibid., p. 81.

71 *Ghermesit* = material of silk or atlas, the expression used being "help towards the malotea".

72 Ariel Beaujot, *Victorian Fashion Accessories*, London and New York 2012 [Berg].

73 *o boneță de tul angle cu horboți*, cf. Tribunal Argeș, ds. 2761/1833, dowry contract no. 1 given by mother Elenca Viișoreanu to her daughter Zinca; or *pălărie de tulpan angle cu horbote*, cf. Tribunal Argeș, 12176/1836 dowry contract no. 7, mother Sultana Hristodor to her daughter Anica.

74 *Una verighetă cu diiamanțele*, cf. Tribunal Muscel, ds. 8/1856, dowry contract no. 1 given by mother Ecaterina Trandafiroaia to her daughter Filotea.

75 Source: DJAN Argeș, Tribunalul Argeș, 139/1831, 639/1833, 2761/1833, 1521/1834, 14618/1835, 12176/1836, 13/1838, 27/1839 and Tribunalul Mușcel, 8/1834, 6/1835, 8/1838, 9/1837, 7/1850, 4/1855, 8/1856. With respect to gypsy slaves, see Source: DJAN Argeș, Tribunalul Argeș, as follows: Dowry contracts no. 2, 4, 11, 14 from file 139/1831 (for five, twenty, three, and one gypsy slave), dowry contract no. 20 from file 12176/1836 for seventy-four individuals (mentioned both as families and unmarried men), dowry contracts no. 2 and 3 from file 12/1838 (for six and eleven gypsy slaves), and dowry contract no. 1 from file 1521/1834 for six gypsy slaves. For Tribunalul Mușcel, dowry contract no. 1 from file 8/1834 (two gypsy slaves), dowry contract no. 2 from file 14/1838 (two gypsy slaves), dowry contracts no. 2 and 4 from file 7/1850 (ten and five gypsy slaves), dowry contract no. 7 from file 4/1855 (six gypsy slaves), and dowry contract no. 2 from file 8/1856 (ten gypsy slaves).

76 Ida Fazio, "Brothers, Sisters and the Rearrangements of Property on the Sicilian Island of Stromboli in the Nineteenth Century", in: *European Review of History: Revue européenne d'histoire* 17, 5 (2010), pp. 805–815, pp. 808–809.

77 Vincent Gourdon, *Histoire des grands-parents*, Paris 2001 [Perrin], p. 57.

78 Carolina Blutrach-Jelin and Giulia Calvi, "Sibling Relations in Family History: Conflicts, Co-operation and Gender Roles in the Sixteenth to Nineteenth Century. An Introduction", in: *European Review of History: Revue européenne d'histoire* 17, 5 (2010), pp. 695–704, p. 702.

79 Fazio, "Percorsi coniugali", pp. 193–194; Renata Ago, "Oltre le dote: i beni femminili", in: Angela Groppi (ed.), *Il lavoro delle donne*, Rome 1996 [Laterza], pp. 164–182, p. 169.

80 Blutrach-Jelin and Giulia Calvi, "Sibling Relations in Family History", p. 703; Benedetta Borello, "Prossimi e lontani: fratelli aristocratici a Roma e Siena (secoli XVII – XIX)", in: Renata Ago and Benedetta Borello (eds.), *Famiglie. Circolazione di beni, circuiti di affetti in eta moderna*, Rome 2008 [Viella], pp. 117–140, p. 118; Joanne M. Ferraro, "Courtship, Marriage and Divorce", in: Peter N. Stears (ed.), *Encyclopedia of European Social History from 1350 to 2000*, Detroit and New York 2001 [Charles Scribner's & Sons], pp. 145–160, p. 150; Sabean and Teuscher, *Kinship in Europe*, p. 18.

Sources

Arhivele Naţionale. Serviciul Judeţean Argeş (Piteşti).
Tribunalul Argeş.
139/1831.
239/1831.
639/1833.
2761/1833.
1366/1834.
1521/1834.
14618/1835.
12176/1836.
13/1838.
27/1839.
8/1856.
13/1856.
Tribunalul Muşcel.
8/1834.
6/1835.
9/1837.
8/1838.
7/1850.
4/1855.
8/1856.
Arhivele Naţionale Istorice Centrale, National Archives of Romania (Bucharest).
Ministerul Justiţiei. Extrajudiciare.
35/1839.

Published sources

Alexianu, G., P. Negulescu and A. Sava (eds.), *Regulamentul Organic al Valahiei şi al Moldovei*, vol. I, Bucharest 1944 [Întreprinderile Eminescu].
Antim Ivireanul, *Opere*, ed. G. Ştrempel, critical edition, Bucharest 1972 [Minerva].
Cristocea, Spiridon, *Oraşul Piteşti în catagrafia din 1838*, Piteşti 2011 [Ordessos].
Cristocea Spiridon and Ştefan Trâmbaciu, *Câmpulungul Muscelului reflectat în catagrafia din 1838*, Piteşti 2007 [Ordessos].
Lahovari, George Ioan, Constantin I. Brătianu, Grigore G. Tocilescu, *Marele Dicţionar Geografic al României*, vol. II, Bucharest 1899 and vol. IV, Bucharest 1901 [Socec].
Legiuirea Caragea, critical edition, Bucharest 1955 [1818] [Editura Academiei Române].
Pravilniceasca condică, Bucharest 1957 [1780] [Editura Academiei Române].

Bibliography

Achim, Viorel, *The Roma in Romanian History*, Budapest 2004 [Central European University Press].
———"Transformări sociale în cadrul populaţiei ţigăneşti în epoca dezrobirii: sedentarizarea şi legarea de ocupaţia agricolă", in: Venera Achim and Viorel Achim (eds.), *Modernizarea socială şi instituţională în Principatele Române, 1831–1859*, Bucharest 2016 [Editura Academiei Române], pp. 156–166.

Ago, Renata, "Oltre le dote: i beni femminili", in: Angela Groppi (ed.), *Il lavoro delle donne*, Rome 1996 [Laterza], pp. 164–182.

Arnaud-Duc, Nicole, "Les contradictions du droit", in: Genevieve Fraisse and Michelle Perrot (eds.), *Histoire des femmes en Occident*, vol. IV. Le XIXe siècle, Paris 2002 [Perrin], pp. 101–139.

Barbu, Violeta, "Familia şi sistemele succesorale în ţara obiceiului. Substituţia", in: Violeta Barbu (ed.), *De bono coniugali. O istorie a familiei din Ţara Românească în secolul al XVII-lea*, Bucharest 2003 [Meridiane], pp. 100–118.

———"De la comunitatea patrimonială la comunitatea de destin: zestrea în Ţara Românească în secolul al XVII-lea", in: Violeta Barbu, Florina Manuela Constantin et al. (eds.), *De la comunitate la societate: studii de istoria familiei din Ţara Românească în Vechiul Regat*, Bucharest 2007 [Institutul Cultural Român], pp. 19–93.

———*Ordo amoris: o istorie a instituţiei căsătoriei în Ţara Românească în secolul al XVII-lea*, Bucharest 2011 [Editura Academiei Române].

Beaujot, Ariel, *Victorian Fashion Accessories*, London and New York 2012 [Berg].

Beaur, Gérard, "Le contrat de mariage dans les sociétés européennes. Enjeux familiaux et pratiques des acteurs", in: *Annales de Démographie Historique* 121, 1 (2011), pp. 5–21.

Bellavistis, Anna, *Famille, Genre, Transmission à Venise au XVIe siècle*, Rome 2008 [École Française de Rome].

Bellavitis, Anna and Beatrice Zucca Micheletto, "Introduction", in: Anna Bellavitis and Beatrice Zucca Micheletto (eds.), *Gender, Law and Economic Well-Being in Europe from the Fifteenth to the Nineteenth Century. North Versus South?* London and New York 2018 [Routledge], pp. 1–27.

Berindei, Dan (ed.), *Istoria Românilor, vol. VII, tom. 1. Constituirea României moderne (1821–1878)*, Bucharest 2003 [Editura Enciclopedică].

Blutrach-Jelin, Carlina and Giulia Calvi, "Sibling Relations in Family History: Conflicts, Co-operation and Gender Roles in the Sixteenth to Nineteenth Century. An Introduction", in: *European Review of History: Revue européenne d'histoire* 17, 5 (2010), pp. 695–704.

Borello, Benedetta, "Prossimi e lontani: fratelli aristocratici a Roma e Siena (secoli XVII – XIX)", in: Renata Ago and Benedetta Borello (eds.), *Famiglie. Circolazione di beni, circuiti di affetti in eta moderna*, Rome 2008 [Viella], pp. 117–140.

Brunnbauer, Ulf, "Families and Mountains in the Balkans. Christians and Muslim Household Structures in the Rhodopes, 19th – 20th Century", in: *History of the Family* 7, 3 (2002), pp. 327–350.

Chirot, Daniel, "Causes and Consequences of Backwardness", in: Daniel Chirot (ed.), *The Origins of Backwardness in Eastern Europe: Economics and Politics from the Middle Ages Until the Early Twentieth Century*, Berkeley, Los Angeles and London 1989 [University of California Press], pp. 1–14.

Ciocâltan, Alexandru, "Comunităţile catolice din Câmpulung şi Bucureşti (1688–1763)", in: Ileana Căzan, Bogdan Mateescu (eds.), *Timp, societate şi identitate culturală. "Miniaturi" istorice*, Cluj-Napoca 2015 [Academia Română-Centrul de Studii Transilvane], pp. 137–237.

———*Comunităţile germane la sud de Carpaţi în Evul Mediu (secolele XIII–XVIII)*, Brăila 2015 [Istros].

Constantin, Florina Manuela, "Liens de parenté et liens sociaux chez les esclaves tsiganes de Valachie. Le sălaş au XVIIe siècle", in: Roger Botte and Alessandro Stella (eds.), *Couleurs de l'esclavage sur les deux rives de la Méditerranée (Moyen Âge – XXe siècle)*, Paris 2012 [Karthala], pp. 283–296.

———"Modalități de transmitere a dreptului de stăpânire asupra robilor țigani. Vânzarea și schimbul (Țara Românească, secolul al XVII-lea)", in: *Miscellanea historica in honorem Professoris Marcel-Dumitru Ciucă septuagenarii*, Brăila and Pitești 2013 [Istros and Ordessos], pp. 313–328.

Constantinescu, Mitiță, *L'évolution de la propriété rurale et la réforme agraire en Roumanie*, Bucharest 1925 [Cultura Națională].

Davidova, Evguenia, *Balkan Transitions to Modernity and Nation-States: Through the Eyes of Three Generations of Merchants (1780s–1890s)*, Leiden and Boston 2013 [Brill].

Doxiadis, Evdoxios, "From Legal Diversity to Centralization. Marriage and Wealth in Nineteenth-century Greece", in: Anna Bellavitis and Beatrice Zucca Micheletto (eds.), *Gender, Law and Economic Well-Being in Europe from the Fifteenth to the Nineteenth Century. North versus South?* London and New York 2018 [Routledge], pp. 91–105.

Durães, Margarida and Antoinette Fauve-Chamoux (ed.), *The Transmission of Well-Being. Gendered Marriage Strategies and Inheritance Systems in Europe (17th – 20th Centuries)*, Bern 2009 [Peter Lang].

Eldem, Edhem, *A History of the Ottoman Bank*, Istanbul 1999 [Osmanlı Bankası Arşiv Ve Araştırmalar Merkezi].

Eliade, Pompiliu, *De l'influence française sur l'esprit public en Roumanie. Les origines, étude sur l'état de la société roumaine à l'époque des règnes phanariotes*, Paris 1898 [Ernest Leurex].

Faroqhi, Suraiya and Fikret Adanır, "Introduction", in: Fikret Adanır and Suraiya Faroqhi (eds.), *The Ottomans and the Balkans: A Discussion of Historiography*, Leiden and Boston 2002 [Brill], pp. 1–56.

Fazio, Ida, "Percorsi coniugali nell'Italia moderna in Storia del matrimonio", in: Christiane Klapisch-Zuber and Michela De Giorgio (eds.), *Storia dell Matrimonio*, Bari 1996 [Laterza], pp. 151–214.

———"Brothers, Sisters and the Rearrangements of Property on the Sicilian Island of Stromboli in the Nineteenth Century", in: *European Review of History: Revue européenne d'histoire* 17, 5 (2010), pp. 805–815.

Ferraro, Joanne M., "Courtship, Marriage and Divorce", in: Peter N. Stearns (ed.), *Encyclopedia of European Social History from 1350 to 2000*, Detroit and New York 2001 [Charles Scribner's & Sons], pp. 145–160.

Filitti, Ioan Constantin, *Rôle diplomatique des Phanariotes de 1700 à 1821*, Paris 1901 [L. Larose].

Fontaine, Laurence, "Il posto delle donne nella piccola economia finanziaria in eta moderna", in: *Quaderni storici* 2 (2011), pp. 513–532.

Ghițulescu, Constanța, "Forme juridice și practici de transmitere a patrimoniului. Femeia și zestrea sa în Țara Românească a secolului al XVIII-lea", in: *Revista Istorică* 5–6 (2003), pp. 197–216.

———"Mariage et parenté à travers les actes dotaux roumains (1700–1865)", in: *Annales de Démographie Historique* 1 (2011), pp. 141–160.

Göcek, Fatma Müge, *East Encounters West: France and the Ottoman Empire in the Eighteenth Century*, New York 1987 [Oxford University Press].

Gourdon, Vincent, *Histoire des grands-parents*, Paris 2001 [Perrin].

Groppi, Angela and Agnès Fine, "Femmes dot et patrimoine", in: *Clio. Femmes, Genre, Histoire* 7 (1998).

Gruber, Siegfried, "Children and their Parental Households in Central Serbia in the 19th Century", in: Slobodan Naumovič and Miroslav Jovanovič (eds.), *Childhood in South Eastern Europe. Historical Perspectives on Growing Up in the 19th and 20th Century*, Münster 2004 [Lit], pp. 111–124.

Hamlett, Jane, *Material Relations. Domestic Interiors and Middle-Class Families in England, 1850–1910*, Manchester 2010 [Manchester University Press].
Hionidou, Violetta, "Independence and Inter-Dependence: Household Formation Patterns in Eighteenth Century Kythera, Greece", in: *The History of the Family* 16, 3 (2011), pp. 217–234.
Hitchins, Keith, *The Romanians, 1774–1866*, Oxford 1996 [Clarendon Press].
Jacobsen, Grethe and Heide Wunder, "Introduction", in: Grethe Jacobsen and Heide Wunder (eds.), *East Meets West: A Gendered View of Legal Tradition*, Kiel 2015 [Solivagus], pp. 9–22.
Jianu, Angela, "Women, Dowries, and Patrimonial Law in Old-Regime Romania (c. 1750–1830)", in: *Journal of Family History* 34, 2 (2009), pp. 189–205.
Joris, Elisabeth, "Kinship and Gender. Property, Enterprise, and Politics", in: David Warren Sabean, Simon Teuscher and Jon Mathieu (eds.), *Kinship in Europe. Approaches to Long-Term Development (1300–1900)*, New York 2007 [Berghahn Books], pp. 231–257.
Kaser, Karl, "Power and Inheritance: Male Domination, Property, and Family in Eastern Europe, 1500–1900", in: *History of the Family* 7, 3 (2002), pp. 375–395.
Kaser, Karl and Olga Katsiardi-Hering, "Introduction", in: *The History of the Family* 9, 3 (2004), pp. 253–255.
Kellogg, Susan and Steve Mintz, *Domestic Revolutions: A Social History of American Family Life*, New York 1988 [Free Press].
Lanzinger, Margareth, "Marriage Contracts in Various Contexts: Marital Property Rights, Sociocultural Aspects and Gender-Specific Implications. Late Eighteenth-Century Evidence from Two Tirolean Court Districts", in: *Annales de démographie historique* 1, 121 (2011), pp. 69–98.
Lett, Didier, *Freres et sœurs. Histoire d'un lien*, Paris 2009 [Payot & Rivages].
Marrese, Michelle LaMarche, "Gender and the Legal Order in Imperial Russia", in: Dominic Lieven (ed.), *Russia, vol. I. Imperial Russia, 1689–1917*, Cambridge 2006 [Cambridge University Press], pp. 326–343.
———*A Woman's Kingdom: Noblewomen and the control of property in Russia, 1700–1861*, Ithaca and London 2002 [Cornell University Press].
Marten, James, "Family Relations", in: Colin Heywood (ed.), *A Cultural History of Childhood and Family, vol. V. In the Age of Empire*, London 2014 [Bloomsbury], pp. 19–38.
Mateescu, Bogdan, "Mixed Marriages Involving Gypsy Slaves in Nineteenth Century Wallachia: State and Church Policies", in: Luminița Dumănescu, Daniela Mârza and Marius Eppel (eds.), *Intermarriage Throughout History*, Newcastle-upon-Tyne 2014 [Cambridge Scholars Publishing], pp. 212–231.
———*Census-like material preserved in the Romanian archives, for the former principalities of Moldavia, Wallachia and for Romania before 1914*, Mosaic Working Paper WP2013–001.
Meteş, Ştefan, *Relaţiile comerciale ale Ţării Româneşti cu Ardealu până în veacul al XVIII-leal*, Sighişoara 1921 [Tipografia W. Krafft].
Pamuk, Sevket, *A Monetary History of the Ottoman Empire*, Cambridge 2000 [Cambridge University Press].
Panaite, Viorel, "Wallachia and Moldavia from the Ottoman juridical and political viewpoint, 1774–1829", in: Antonis Anastasopoulos and Elias Kolovos (eds.), *Ottoman Rule and the Balkans, 1750–1860: Conflict, Transformation, Adaptation*, Rethymno 2007 [University of Crete], pp. 21–44.
———*Război, pace şi comerţ în Islam: Ţările Române în dreptul otoman al popoarelor*, Iaşi 2013 [Polirom].
Peretz, Ion, *Privilegiul masculinităţii în Pravilniceasca Condică Ipsilanti şi în Legiuirea Caragea*, Bucureşti 1905 [Tipografia Clementa].

Rădulescu, Andrei, "Pagini despre Legiuirea Caragea", in: *Pagini inedite din istoria dreptului vechi românesc*, Bucharest 1991 [Editura Academiei Române].

Rădvan, Laurențiu, *At Europe's Borders: Medieval Towns in the Romanian Principalities*, Leiden and Boston 2010 [Brill].

Roman, Nicoleta, "Caught Between Two Worlds: The Children from Gypsy and Romanian – Gypsy Families in Wallachia (1800–1860)", in: *Romanian Journal of Population Studies* 8, 1 (2014), pp. 63–86.

———"Deznădăjduită muiere n-au fost ca mine". *Femei, onoare și păcat în Valahia secolului al XIX-lea*, Bucharest 2016 [Humanitas].

———, "Women in Merchant Families, Women in Trade in Mid-19th Century Romanian Countries", in: Constanța Vintilă-Ghițulescu (ed.), *Women, Consumption, and the Circulation of Ideas in South-Eastern Europe 17th – 19th Centuries*, Leiden and Boston 2017 [Brill], pp. 169–199.

———, "Dowry Contracts, Women's Objects and the Circulation of Goods in Mid-Nineteenth Century Oltenia", in: *Revista Istorică* 1–2 (2018), pp. 105–140.

Romanelli, R., "Donne e patrimoni", in: Angela Groppi (ed.), *Storia delle donne in Italia. Il lavoro delle donne*, Bari 1996 [Laterza], pp. 345–367.

Sabean, David Warrean and Simon Teuscher, "Kinship in Europe. A New Approach to Long Term Development", in: David Warren Sabean, Simon Teuscher and Jon Mathieu (eds.), *Kinship in Europe. Approaches to Long-Term Development (1300–1900)*, New York 2007 [Berghahn Books], pp. 1–32.

Sachelarie, Ovidiu and Nicolae Stoicescu (eds.), *Instituții feudale din Țările Române: dicționar*, Bucharest 1988 [Editura Academiei Române].

Todorova, Maria N., *Balkan Family Structure and the European Pattern. Demographic Developments in Ottoman Bulgaria*, Budapest and New York 2006 [CEU Press].

Vintilă-Ghițulescu, Constanța, "Zestrea între normă și practică. Țara Românească în secolul al XVII-lea", in: *Studii și materiale de istorie medie* XVIII (2000), pp. 51–75 and XIX (2001), pp. 255–265.

———*În șalvari și cu ișlic. Biserică, sexualitate, căsătorie și divorț în Țara Românească a secolului al XVIII-lea*, 2nd ed., Bucharest 2011 [Humanitas].

Yerolympos, Alexandra, *Urban Transformations in the Balkans (1820–1920). Aspects of Town Planning and the Rethinking of Thessaloniki*, Thessaloniki 1996 [University Studio Press].

Zucca Micheletto, Beatrice, "A qui sert la dot? Aliénations dotales, économie familiale et stratégies des couples à Turin au XVIIIe siècle", in: *Annales de Démographie Historique* 1 (2011), pp. 165–168.

PART VI

Synthesis

FIGURE 13.1 Map of Central Europe, Guillaume de L'Isle, Philippe Buache, *Carte d' Europe*, 1769.

Source: Library of Congress Geography and Map Division, Washington, D.C., U.S.A., public domain, G5700 1724. L5 TIL, http://hdl.loc.gov/loc.gmd/g5700.ct000045 (15.02.2020, 17:30 CET).

13

MOVABLE GOODS AND IMMOVABLE PROPERTY

Interrelated perspectives

Margareth Lanzinger

ABSTRACT

Movable and immovable goods are in and of themselves complex entities that are historically related to a multitude of social, economic, cultural, legal, and gender-specific repertoires of actions, transactions, processes, and implications. With this in mind, the following chapter is organised into three central parts. First, with regard to historical reconstruction and analysis, movable and immovable goods not only *can* but in fact *must* be viewed in relation to the contexts and situations mentioned. Second, it is by no means always evident exactly what was considered movable or immovable in past centuries. Third, the matter becomes even more complex when we bring movable and immovable into a dialogue with each other, seeing the interrelation between them. One objective here is to develop a systematic approach for addressing such issues. Another will be to establish exactly what kinds of knowledge we gain from first contextualising movable and immovable goods and then conceiving of them as interrelated and intertwined, in particular with regard to specific legal and gendered contexts and practices. The emphasis here is on developing a broad panorama and framework of parameters for thinking about movable and immovable goods. The focus will be on Western Europe from the late Middle Ages to the end of early modernity.[1]

I. Movable goods and immovable property: Seen separately and in comparison

A common feature of both movable and immovable goods is that they can create a basis for subsistence and generate income. They achieve this in the form of workshops and tools, looms and spinning wheels, offices and retail shops, and also as spaces of knowledge, such as the home or academies of sciences.[2] This also encompasses their associated instruments, equipment, preparations, and collections. They facilitate subsistence and income, thereby securing a person's existence.[3] Movable and immovable goods were part of a diverse range used in everyday life and economic activity. Both functioned not only as means of production but also as status symbols. They could also represent containers of value, as they had the ability to procure or collateralise credit.[4] They came with a variety of legal properties, connected with specific rights of use or disposal, and were objects of a broad spectrum of transfer.[5] These were also objects that were coveted and sometimes fought over. Despite all these commonalities, there were also differences between movable and immovable goods. The first part of this chapter investigates each separately using a comparative perspective that allows for the development of a series of questions for further examination. In the second part, movable and immovable goods will be interrelated with each other. As Renata Ago has emphasised, "jurists' discourses" accord movables far less importance than real estate; however, "the social practice" of individuals, and especially of testators, demonstrates that the former are "fundamentally complementary" to the latter.[6] Both movable property and immovable property had the potential to represent belonging in a family and the continuation of family or lineage.

I.a Immovable goods

What exactly are immovable goods? We may think of buildings, encompassing a broad variety of structures, from simple huts to palaces. Or, we may think of parts of buildings, individual levels, apartments, and the associated spaces – workshops and offices, warehouses, and structural additions as well as stables, barns, and sheds. Parcels of land, gardens, meadows, fields, vineyards, and forests also come to mind. The list goes on and on. In many respects, immovable goods represented a basic economic resource. At the same time, immobile property – especially in the form of buildings and parts thereof – was a visible expression of the social status that reflected the social milieu. It was also a resource that expressed and reproduced social prestige. The presence or absence of this resource as well as the question of available alternatives – in the form of short-term and long-term tenancy, for example – shaped personal biographies and family reputations on an intergenerational level and had the potential to represent social establishment and consolidation as well as upward or downward social mobility.[7]

Fundamentally related issues include the question of the legal circumstances surrounding immovable goods, which was a decisive factor in determining various courses of action, especially with regard to the transfer of property. What kinds of immovable goods could be transferred from whom to whom, and in what form? Repertoires of action and actual practice were politically and legally structured, as were gradual changes in these repertoires and the respective time periods in which they were expected to be executed. We also need to consider the fact that it was not until the late Middle Ages, and above all at the beginning of the early modern period, that the inheritability of immovable goods became established as a legal practice. However, this was by no means the case everywhere. The case of the early modern countries in northern Europe – Finland and the northern part of Sweden – shows that only movable property could be inherited, whereas immobile property remained in the ownership of the king and could not be handed down.[8] In the German-speaking world, the right to bequeath agrarian estates to the next generation was an achievement that must be considered with respect to the gradual strengthening of farmers' property rights in relation to their landlords more generally.[9] In earlier legal forms of ownership, the manorial lords or overlords granted tenure for one year perhaps, or at best for an individual's lifetime, as in the system known as *Freistiftrecht*. This indicates that we must carefully consider legal spaces and distinguish, moreover, between primary ownership held by landlords and ownership in the sense of the power of disposal. These were all factors that remained relevant in some regions up to as late as the mid-nineteenth century.[10]

If there was a fundamental right to inherit immovable goods, this was generally associated with specific rules of transfer. Noble fiefdoms, for example, were usually handed down in male succession – unless they were so-called women's fiefdoms, or *Kunkellehen*.[11] In the early modern German-speaking areas, by contrast, allodial goods could be bequeathed freely and thus likewise passed on to daughters.[12] This was in contrast to custom among the late mediaeval Franconian nobility, where allodial goods were to be divided among all children.[13] In legal spaces that had a feudal character, the landlord's consent was necessary for each individual succession process and intergenerational transfer and included the obligatory payment of a transfer fee above and beyond regular taxes. In some regions where male succession predominated, the amount of this fee varied in accordance with whether it was a son or daughter who took over the properties. Additional fees could be levied if a son-in-law married into the property.[14] What can these criteria tell us? First, they shaped power relations within marriage, family, and community. Second, they indicate situated practices based on particular concepts of gender that came into play, especially in instances in which the criteria were of a gender-specific nature.

Thus, the essential questions in regard to gender differences are as follows: Who had access to immovable property, and to what kind of immovable property? Were there certain patterns of succession associated with specific time periods, places, and social milieus? Was it the oldest son who took over a farm or the practice of a trade, merchant business, or manor; or was it the youngest child, the firstborn child, or the best-suited successor? What did younger brothers receive – immovable goods, movable goods, money? And what did daughters receive? Did brothers jointly assume possession of their father's or parents' property? In other words, what significance was tied to gender and birth order? To what extent did law preconfigure and establish such patterns? And what were the preferences on behalf of fathers, parents, or kin groups in terms of specific interests or logics that favoured particular succession patterns? This could include arrangements that ensured provision in old age or rewards for providing care and support.

In general, there are three issues that are especially important with regard to property. The first concerns a fundamental prerequisite that has been a basic framework in the agendas of those studying gender and legal cultures: the need to approach and define norms and practices, both situationally and contextually, in relationship to one another. In what ways did norms, statutes, etc., structure practice? How much latitude for negotiation did normative requirements allow? And in what ways were they used – including perhaps counter to the original intention? The description of this relationship offered by Levi in "On Microhistory" still seems very suitable here. He recommends an

> action and conflict model which recognizes [the] – relative – freedom beyond, though not outside, the constraints of prescriptive and oppressive normative systems. Thus all social action is seen to be the result of an individual's constant negotiation, manipulation, choices and decisions in the face of a normative reality which, though pervasive, nevertheless offers many possibilities of personal interpretations and freedoms.[15]

The emphasis here is on "beyond, though not outside": Women and men took advantage of leeway and gaps in legislation, by so doing instrumentalising legal norms for their own ends.

The second issue relates to modalities of transfer and the relationships between various modalities, such as inheritance or purchase. How much immobile property was transferred between generations, on the one hand, and through purchase or sale outside the family, on the other, in the respective time periods, legal spheres, and social milieus? Since the beginning of family history research in the 1960s, a comparatively large amount of work has been carried out focussing on these questions.[16] What is often still missing from this research is a systematic approach to inheritance patterns and practices that incorporates considerations of the marital property regimes upon which these transfers were based and the gender-specific implications thereof. This broadened perspective is indispensable for providing an understanding of exactly what resources were at the disposal of married and widowed women, along with the social and legal positions they occupied and the agency they thus possessed in the context of family and kin as well as the "real estate market". The significance and implications of legal regimes concerning property in marriage are crucial to our understanding of negotiations and claims, arrangements and disputes. After all, they in large part determined whether wealth – particularly inherited wealth – was considered to belong to one's own line of descent, thus going preferentially to one's offspring and blood relatives (as in systems featuring dowries or separation of goods); or, by contrast, whether it was defined as mutual marital goods (as in joint property systems). In the latter case, spouses – widowers as well as widows – had first priority among claims to the deceased partner's wealth. There were also a range of variants and combinations of these two property models, such as the community of accrued gains, in which wealth acquired prior to the marriage was held separately, while wealth generated or acquired during the marriage belonged to both partners equally.[17] A different grouping logic governed wealth mutually acquired during marriage in Ingelheim, in the Electoral

Palatinate, during the late Middle Ages: Assets acquired after the wedding were considered joint property (*Zuerwerb*). If the couple died without children, the joint property was returned to their respective parent families, although not in equal shares. Two-thirds went to the husband's family, the so-called share of the sword (*Schwertteil*), while just one-third went to the wife's family, the so-called share of the skirt (*Rockteil*).[18]

Important also are the conditions under which immobile property was leased, exchanged, or passed on as a gift. And what did it mean when immobile property was lost at an auction or confiscated as a result of debt or bankruptcy,[19] or even political or confessional oppression?[20]

The third issue highlights the significance of immovables and movables, a point that simultaneously leads us to movable goods and their relationship to immovables. The questions here are as follows: Did certain aspects of the status of movable goods shift in relation to immovable goods? What were the consequences if the immovable goods present were considered particularly significant? What followed if the movable goods accounted for the majority of the estimated value of an estate, or if access to the movable goods tended to be unequally distributed in a structural sense – for example according to gender or birth rank? Was the existential and symbolic value of movable goods higher in cases of little immobile wealth? Did the prevailing laws define specific rules that came into play in such situations?

I.b Movable goods

What were movable goods? The typical movable goods, as noted in inventories, include furniture and household items, clothing, undergarments, household textiles, all manner of accessories, silver and jewellery, books and paintings, and weapons and tools as well as livestock and foodstuffs, money and securities.[21] And last but not least, the extant documents themselves – contracts, wills, inventories, promissory notes, etc. – also possessed a certain material character that can be considered a subject of interest in its own right. Some items had special significance in the context of marriage and the family. Most important was one object in particular: the bed. It included not only the usually wooden piece of furniture but all its accompanying accessories – the mattress, pillows, blankets, etc. Beds were classic trousseau components that women brought into their marriages. Since the Middle Ages, women, men, and couples had also bequeathed beds to "poor girls" to enable them to marry.[22] The bed simultaneously symbolised union and proper order in a marriage and in the family. In less wealthy households, the bed that was brought into the marriage by the woman was often the most valuable of all the inventoried movables. Movable goods thus had the potential to be charged with symbolic significance, representing perhaps personal links or adherence to societal convention. Immovable goods were no doubt symbolically charged as well. However, the symbolic attributes associated with movable objects were potentially more diverse than those associated with immovable goods. Immobile property – above all the "ancestral home" – could, for example, represent constructions of continuity and "anciennity" (deep ancestry along a line of descent) with regard to lineage and kinship.[23]

Movable goods, like immovable goods, raise the question of whether they were really owned or more tenurial in nature, meaning that the rights to their usage were limited in some way, such as duration or how these goods could be used or disposed of. The difference between those modes of ownership could be decisive when the time came for the object to be bequeathed or sold. Was the pearl necklace given by a husband to his wife actually owned by the wife? Was it a gift that had been given to her during his lifetime? Could she keep the necklace after his death and bequeath or sell it, or did it belong to the husband's estate? Questions such as these formed a subject in court more often than one might suspect.[24]

The question of object ownership was, accordingly, especially crucial in contexts characterised by separation of property. In this model, not only immovable but also movable goods were transferred from ancestors to their descendants in a largely linear mode, with as little as possible being allowed to flow from the male to the female line or vice versa. So what exactly served to indicate object ownership in situations in which the transaction was neither documented in writing nor had taken place before witnesses as an explicit act of gifting? Public visibility might have been one criterion, at least for items of a more everyday utilitarian character. One indication that public visibility may have been an important factor for proving ownership is a specification that appears in the sixteenth-century Tyrolean law *Tiroler Landesordnung* for noble women as well as in the contracts and other comparable documents of ordinary women. It defined ownership of clothing and jewellery "as worn on one's person to church and in the streets".[25]

The variable legal quality of movable goods was also of potential significance in intergenerational transfers. In her piece entitled "Inheritance as a Concept of Transferral",[26] Karin Gottschalk emphasised an important distinction between the early modern period and the present-day "universal succession" principle, pointing out that during the former there were certain elements of parental wealth that were *not* transferred as inheritance to the next generation. Rather, they followed preordained "routes of transfer" that did *not* fall under the definition of inheritance. The distinctions she has drawn between different types of wealth in the early modern period are primarily related to movable goods attributed to women and men. These include the *Gerade*, which consisted of bed and table linens, household items, clothing, and jewellery, as mentioned in the thirteenth-century *Sachsenspiegel*.[27] The *Gerade* was passed on to female relatives, daughters in particular. In the absence of daughters, it would go to a niece born to one of the woman's sisters, but not to one born to a brother. This was because the link between the giver and recipient also had to be a woman. The tradition of handing down items in strict accordance with the female line persisted in Leipzig up until the Thirty Years' War. The masculine counterpart to this practice was the *Heergewäte*, which included swords, horses, clothing, "basic beddings", and pots and was passed from fathers to their sons.[28] So now the question is, What is there to suggest that we should indeed accept Karin Gottschalk's means of distinguishing between inheritance (according to the legal understanding of the early modern period) and other modes of transfer? And is it necessary to distinguish between inheritance and the ways in which it is transferred? There is no question that it makes sense to do so in cases in which goods that are not part of the inheritance can be identified and in cases in which goods are listed separately from the inheritance and transferred as so-called *Voraus* (advance) rather than listed with the inventory along with their estimated values. Upon first consideration, these circumstances may make the objects concerned seem less important. However, such goods may in fact have offered room for manoeuvring that made it possible to reduce or heighten inequalities or to reward or indicate preference for individual children. This is, in any case, a topic that deserves very close attention.

I.c Modes of transfer

Movable goods, like immovable goods, were also passed between owners or users via various routes: They could be inherited and bequeathed, sold and bought, given as gifts, exchanged, lent, or pawned. Movable goods could function as stores of value but also had the potential to lose value if they became worn out or broken. They could be hoarded or used up completely or be lost or stolen. The nature of the transfer of mobile goods and the changes through which they had the potential to progress represented a perhaps greater range of possibilities and situations within a shorter time span than applied to immovable goods. We should also keep in mind that the respective shares of movable objects inherited, acquired, and received as gifts seem to have been, at least in terms of numbers, higher than was the case with immovable goods. Questions of use, acquisition, and consumption arise far more frequently with regard to movable goods than with respect to immovable goods. These questions, in turn, point to specific research fields and concepts – to the history of consumption, to research on material culture, and to the much debated concept of the Industrious Revolution.[29]

According to the *Tiroler Landesordnung*, widows were required to grant access to their "locked chests" for the purpose of inventories,[30] presumably to demonstrate that it was only their own property that was contained within. Personal items were stored in a container that, as the sources repeatedly note, was secured with a "lock and strap" that allowed it to be locked away. Other trousseau objects brought by women into their marriages – such as tables and bed linens and beds themselves – were, by contrast, in daily and visible household use. Nonetheless, these objects remained the property of the women to whom they belonged and were to be returned to them should they be widowed. Contracts and similar documents from the sixteenth century contain far more frequent mention of such movable goods than those from the eighteenth century.[31] This leads us to question whether, over the course of the centuries, movable goods became more or less fixed elements – or properties – of a house or household. This is a question we will look at in Section III, which addresses entanglements between mobile and immobile wealth.

It should also be noted that both immovable and movable goods were involved in various axes of relatedness: in relationships between spouses, among siblings, between generations, among relatives, and also in relationships that went beyond the family, such as in the "real estate" and credit markets, in pawn shops, and at second-hand markets, many of which were also structured by interpersonal relationships. I hasten to emphasise that movable goods – just like immovable ones – were constructed and structured by their legal qualities. This becomes particularly apparent when wc look at the situational and contextual ambiguity of movable and immovable goods. The structure of inventories also reveals much about the weighting and sorting of objects: Whether objects were registered by room or grouped according to usage, materiality, value, or, not least of all, legal framing – such as the aforementioned widows' chests, for example – or listed under an entirely separate heading, such as cash or cattle.

II. The ambiguity of movable and immovable goods

Studies have shown that in some legal, socioeconomic, and situational contexts, objects usually considered immovable goods were declared to be and treated in various ways as movable goods and vice versa. This means that the attributes "movable" and "immovable" were not set in stone and could vary. Looking further into the reasons behind this, one can presume that "transformability"[32] was likely a strategic practice, although caution should be exercised with regard to the notion of "strategy", as this could easily lead to an overinterpratation. As Martha Howell has shown with regard to Ghent during the late Middle Ages, more and more immovable goods were classified as movable after the fourteenth century, a factor that applied above all to buildings and lots within towns and the associated incomes. This shift took place against the backdrop of a prevailing marital property regime in which all movable goods belonged to both spouses together, and thus, in the case of the death of a spouse, these goods went to the widowed party and their mutual children. Immovable goods, by contrast, remained the property of the spouse who had brought them into the marriage and upon his or her death went to the children, including those from earlier marriages. In cases of childlessness, these goods went to the relatives of the deceased spouse (Ghent). This means that movable goods were situated in relation to marriage, while immovable goods existed in relation to an individual spouse's line of descent.

As more and more goods were added to the category of mobile goods, the wealth that belonged to a couple as a unit and was used by them grew remarkably. This circumstance strengthened, at the same time, the positions of widows and widowers, in that said wealth was decoupled from its attachment to specific lines of descent. By contrast, however, rural fiefs remained immobile wealth and functioned as important social status markers for urban burghers.[33] Howell has identified an increasing "structural tension" between marriage and lineage and associates this transformation with the "change in the nature of wealth and the proliferation of its meanings, in all senses – economic, legal, social, and cultural – as movable wealth exploded in quantity and kind".[34]

Anna Bellavitis has identified the reverse situation in Venice and its *Terraferma* – namely, one in which rural buildings were declared to be movable goods.[35] The blurring of boundaries between movable and immovable goods has also been documented in the Swiss canton of Grisons (Graubünden). During the eighteenth century, movable goods belonging to each individual in a couple became part of their joint assets one year and one day after their marriage. There were limits, however, on what was considered movable. Money and loaned capital were excluded from this definition and were classified as immovable goods instead.[36] This shows that we must be careful to distinguish between negotiable and non-negotiable goods, with the latter pointing to the issue of the feasibility of bypassing pre-structured routes of transfer.

This transformability is a central aspect in the relationship between norms and practice in the consideration of repertoires of action and in the potency of different interests. Once again, the outlined process of transformation indicates very different, essentially contrary prioritisations; namely, the axis of competition between the marriage and the line of descent. In Ghent, for example, the transformation of marital goods prioritised marriage over other family members.

III. Movable and immovable property: Interrelated

There are numerous perspectives from which one can consider the issue of links and entanglements between movable and immovable goods. The following section will concentrate on two: First, on the convertibility of movable and immovable goods and, second, on the linkage between movable goods and the house.

III.a Convertibility within movable goods or between movable and immovable goods

In her article "Le ricchezze delle donne", Ida Fazio took a critical view of focussing on the dowry as means of installing or eliminating women as heirs and thus as an indicator of bilateralism in the transfer of goods.[37] Instead, she advocated expanding the relational axis beyond women and family assets and using microhistorical methods to research the character of the process of transferring goods. In other words, she demanded that the practices of adaptations, transfer mechanisms, and wealth management by men and women should be placed in the forefront instead of focussing primarily on women's dowries. We should employ a broad notion of wealth and wealth-related processes that includes agreements, arrangements, and contractual obligations for the understanding of the relationships between movable and immovable assets.[38] In this same vein, Angiolina Arru emphasised a central characteristic of dowries – namely, that they had the character of loans. Thus, if the heirs of the deceased husband could not repay the dowry to the widow in monetary form, she might be granted immovable assets or rights of residence and usufruct in compensation.[39] The Italian dowry – like the marriage portion in southern Tyrol – placed a mortgage of sorts on the entire wealth of the husband.

In the dowry system, as in other separate marital property regimes, immovables served as collateral that could "convert" dowries or marriage portions (and thus money and unpaid debts) into pieces of land and therewith into immobile wealth if the heirs of the deceased husband were not able to repay the widow's dowry or marriage portion. This being the case, we can see that there were credit relations within marriage. And insofar as a woman's assets had yet to be secured by collateral at the point at which she married – usually as part of the marriage contract – this could also be accomplished after the fact. The following procedure serves as an actual example of eighteenth-century Graubünden/Grisons: If a husband paid debts out of his wife's assets that he managed, or if the wife paid debts owed by her husband, she could, in turn, place a mortgage on his landholdings.

Angiolina Arru also demonstrated the convertibility of mobile wealth with regard to donations between living people (*inter vivos*), as was the case for the widow Consola Ambron in late eighteenth-century Rome. She gifted her dowry to three of her deceased husband's nephews, but it had yet to be paid back to her and existed as a liability on their inheritance. Ambron's only condition was that they should provide her with two *scudi* per week, which represented an interest rate of 12.5 percent, a far higher rate than she would have received had she invested the money otherwise. Arru interprets the fact that Ambron's nephews accepted this "gift" with that stipulation not as a gesture of generosity, but rather as an attempt to prevent Ambron from demanding the return of her complete dowry. which she would have had the right to do. We find in this situation a good example of how a dowry loan could be converted into an obligation to provide for the widow until the end of her life. Houses or pieces of land could be donated or transferred to future heirs in much the same way. During this process they were converted into provisions or benefits, in the form of monetary payments, as was the case for Ambron; or into room and board or care and provision in case of illness and in old age.[40] In the sample of donation contracts for the years 1745, 1794–1796, and 1836, evaluated by Arru, we find clear gender-specific differences: Seventy percent of the donations given by men were immovable goods – houses, vineyards, etc. – while nearly ninety percent of women donated their dowry assets, with the beneficiaries being predominantly male.[41]

Donations and property transfers of these kinds were not limited to the familial context. Agreements to exchange possessions for guarantees of provision were an option for single and widowed women and men alike and could also be made between individuals that shared no blood or affinal relation. In January 1574, for instance, the burgher's widow, Barbara Latticherin, willed her monetary assets, in the form of two promissory notes and "her entire bed and bedclothes as well as all her current and future possessions including inheritances and immovable and movable goods", to Christian Taler, a carpenter and burgher in Brixen/Bressanone, and his wife, Catharina. The reason Latticherin gave for this decision was that she was old and no longer confident of her ability to "acquire" her own daily bread.

In return, she would receive lodging (*Herberg*) with the couple, which also entailed that she be provided "her whole life long, whether healthy or ill, with alimentation, clothing, shoes, a place to sleep, help rising and lying down, baths, and the satisfaction of all her other physical needs". She was also to receive a sum of money for her use as an "allowance" on a quarterly basis, and the couple were obligated to cover her funeral costs.[42] Upon her death, which came about in March of that same year, Christian Taler was also designated the heir to her estate because the widow "had no heirs, neither blood-related nor otherwise".[43]

III.b What was considered integral to a house?

In contrast to the previously discussed cases of Ghent and Venice, the movable quality of objects might be revoked without causing the need to differently define these goods. The 1532 and 1573 editions of the *Tiroler Landesordnung* applied a comparable regulation in connexion with widows' endowments.[44] Tyrolean widows had no system of provision in their late husbands' places of residence; rather, the norm was that their marriage portion and everything else they had brought into the marriage – including the morning gift, provided she had received one from her husband – were returned. This procedure was the same in both cases – the *Tiroler Landesordnung* and the Italian dowry system. The widows also had claim to one-third of their households' movable goods. Another paragraph of the *Tiroler Landesordnung* was dedicated to specifying that what was to be "construed of and recognised as" movable goods, with regard to widows' endowments, as the paragraph's title put it.[45] However, this paragraph primarily addresses what was *not* to be considered movable goods – namely, borrowers' notes, cash, gold, and silver tableware and all items that could be attributed to the deceased husband personally (which essentially correspond to what Karin Gottschalk has defined as having been excepted from inheritance), that is, his clothing, including all accessories, as well as his horse, weapons, gunpowder, protective gear, books, and merchandise. Additionally, the range of items included the means of agricultural production: livestock and all equipment necessary for working the fields as well as stores of wine, grain, and any other foodstuffs. None of these could be considered or recognised as movable goods, which were limited to the bed and its accessories (*Bedtgewanndt*), kitchen utensils, and the like.

From this we can conclude that in addition to personal goods that belonged to individuals and goods that were actually considered movable in the sense that it was possible for them to leave the house, there were also things that were considered as belonging to the house, things that simply came with it.[46] The fact that merchandise and agricultural tools fell within the latter category can be attributed to the commercial and subsistence economy based in the house. By contrast, promissory notes, money, and items made of precious metals represented mediums of exchange and stores of value, and stores of foodstuffs assured the survival of the house's inhabitants. Household items are of special interest here: Kitchen utensils,[47] the bed, and bedding, all of which are movable items[48] explicitly mentioned in the paragraph.

Nineteenth-century deeds of sale for houses explicitly indicated all items that were held fast "with nails and trusses".[49] For example, in Johann Heinrich Zedler's *Universal Lexicon* from the first half of the eighteenth century, we find that the lemma *Tisch* (table) contains mention of immovable and movable tables. Some tables could be nailed down, in which case they were not considered movable goods.[50] Household items could be objects that belonged to people or to the house itself. We find mention of household items in various documents from sixteenth-century Tyrolean households; namely, in affirmations of what women had brought into their marriages and in widows' endowments. By comparison, household items are rarely mentioned in a sample of eighteenth-century marriage contracts and therefore are hardly discernible. By the late eighteenth century, contracts had become dominated by arrangements that assumed widows would be provided for in their late husbands' houses on the basis of a property transfer, a widow's or usufruct contract, which was far from the case in the sixteenth century. In this regard, there are indications of a stronger link between household items and the house during the eighteenth century: Widows received "the necessary household and kitchen items . . . for their use", which is to say that the only real right widows had to these goods was that of usufruct. They were only allowed to use these items provided they were "returned in due time".[51] In other words, these items remained appurtenances of the house. A possible explanation for this may be that these former trousseau components, the movable items that women brought with them into their marriages,[52] had become increasingly integral components of the house – fixed elements of a home's accessories and furnishings. If this is true for household items above all, it may also hold true for beds. This can be construed as an indication that both the gender-specific attributions of goods and widows' claims to portions of the movable goods were beginning to weaken. The reasons for this may have been, on the one hand, that the widow's claim to a third of a household's movables was often converted into money and, on the other, that contracts increasingly allowed widows to remain in their late husbands' households. And with this, the relationship between mobile and immobile property likewise began to change, though the question is for whom? In neo-local households, for instance, the situation seemed different. Here the contribution of furniture to a newly founded household continued to be an important component of a bride's trousseau.[53]

The question of what might have been considered movable or immovable property was also important with regard to debt and the seizure of property and goods by the court.[54] This was certainly the case, for example, among nineteenth-century Swiss lawmakers, as Michael Suter has shown in his recent book. The quandary that arose in this instance involved permanently installed objects – industrial machines such as the weaving looms, twisting machines, and beaming machines that were common in the nineteenth century. According to Zurich's 1715 *Stadt- und Landrecht* legal code, buildings comprised not just structures themselves but also "[e]verything attached by slot or nail" to them. By 1844, the Zurich high court conceded that "views [regarding this definition] differ[ed] greatly" and in 1852 noted that in cases of unpaid debt there were frequent conflicts over whether objects such as machines were subject to confiscation as movable or immovable goods. This issue was especially complicated because different officials were responsible for the respective categories of goods. The mayor was responsible for seizing movable goods, while immovable goods were the responsibility of the local clerks. The unclear status of proto-industrial raw materials was an additional source of uncertainty. The materiality of seized animals and food, which the mayor was required to store, posed particular difficulties because they both had to be maintained and kept from spoiling.[55]

IV. Conclusion

The aims of this chapter are to portray a spectrum of differing logics that governed the transfer of goods from the late Middle Ages to the nineteenth century and, in doing so, to examine and interrelate movable and immovable goods from legal, practical, and gender-specific perspectives. This approach helps to clarify complex processes and sequences of events that resist quick-and-easy categorisation, not to mention clear characterisation as advantageous, disadvantageous, or preferential. What we uncover instead is something much more nuanced: Mutuality, shared interests, and obligations that were negotiated via and bound to movable and immovable goods. We also find differences between bodies of law and how law was implemented in actual practice. In light of all of their legal, gender-specific, social, and economic features, it is clear that the status of objects must be considered multidimensional in nature;[56] objects could also maintain symbolic and affective value.[57]

We need to emphasise the idea that ambiguity, a situational nature, transformability, and convertibility are all important aspects of movable and immovable goods. To appreciate this, it is helpful, if not indeed essential, to work with a broad definition of wealth in mind as well as in consideration of the broadest possible contexts for legal and social practices.[58] It is in these very qualities of movable and immovable goods that I see the potential for a productive exchange between social, economic, and legal history and material culture studies. The latter has only just begun to integrate consideration of objects' legal significance, implications, and structures into its research agenda. The legal character and quality of objects could, for example, be meaningfully integrated into object biographies. Such biographies could, for instance, be extended to elaborate on the legal and administrative procedures to which objects were subject and which influenced their status – procedures such as appraisal for monetary value, evaluation of quality, classification, and correlation with a particular legal status. At the same time, we must keep in mind that these were also procedures in which value, quality, and legal status were questioned, in which competing claims were negotiated, and in which movable and immovable goods became objects of conflict or pledges and objects listed in inventories, bequeathed in wills, etc. Research that focusses on movable and immovable goods in the contexts of marriage, family, kin, and beyond shows us that there is great potential for cooperation and synergy between material culture studies and legal and gender history.

Notes

1 I will partly refer to our ongoing research project The Role of Wealth in Defining and Constituting Kinship Spaces from 16th to the 18th Century, which looks at southern Tyrol. This project is funded by the FWF Austrian Science Fund (2016–2020, P29394) and based at the University of Vienna; see http://kinshipspaces.univie.ac.at/en/ (accessed 17 October 2019). For early results, see the contribution by Janine Maegraith in this volume; Christian Hagen, Margareth Lanzinger and Janine Maegraith, "Competing Interests in Death-related Stipulations in South Tirol ca. 1350–1600", in: Mia Korpiola and Anu Lahtinen (eds.), *Planning for Death: Wills, Inheritance and Property Strategies in Medieval and Reformation Europe*, Leiden and Boston 2018 [Brill], pp. 88–118; Margareth Lanzinger and Janine Maegreaith, "Houses and the Range of Wealth in Early Modern Gender- and Intergenerational Relationships", in: *Jahrbuch für Europäische Geschichte / European History Yearbook* 18 (2017), pp. 14–34, open access https://doi.org/10.1515/9783110532241-002.

2 cf. Sebatian Kühn's, Contribution on "Scholarly Households", in: Joachim Eibach and Margareth Lanzinger (eds.), The Routlegde History of the Domestic Sphere in Europe: 16th to 19th Century, forthcoming; Sebastian Kühn, *Wissen, Arbeit, Freundschaft. Ökonomien und soziale Beziehungen in den Akademien von London, Paris und Berlin um 1700*, Göttingen 2011 [V & R Unipress].

3 See John Broad and Anton Schuurman (eds.), *Wealth and Poverty in European Rural Societies from the Sixteenth to Nineteenth Century*, Turnhout 2014 [Brepols Publisher].

4 See Renata Ago, *Gusto for Things. A History of Objects in Seventeenth-Century Rome*, Chicago 2013 [University of Chicago Press], p. 4.

5 See Karin Gottschalk, "Erbe und Recht. Die Übertragung von Eigentum in der frühen Neuzeit", in: Stefan Willer, Sigrid Weigel and Bernhard Jussen (eds.), *Erbe. Übertragungskonzepte zwischen Natur und Kultur*, Frankfurt a. M. 2013 [Suhrkamp], pp. 85–125, 94.

6 Renata Ago, "Les biens meubles. Une propriété qui ne crée pas d'appartenance?" in: Sami Bargaoui, Simona Cerutti and Isabelle Grangaud (eds.), *Appartenance locale et propriété au nord et au sud de la Méditerranée*, [Institut de recherches et d'études sur les mondes arabes et musulman] Aix-en-Provence 2015, p. 3, http://books.openedition.org/iremam/3419.

7 Simone Derix and Margareth Lanzinger, "Housing Capital. Interdisciplinary Perspectives on a Multifaceted Resource", in: *Jahrbuch für Europäische Geschichte / European History Yearbook* 18 (2017), pp. 1–13, open access https://doi.org/10.1515/ 9783110532241-001.

8 Beatrice Moring and Richard Wall, *Widows in European Economy and Society 1600–1920*, Woodbridge 2017 [Boydell & Brewer], pp. 116, 128. See the contribution of Susann Anett Pedersen on Norway in this volume.

9 See Markus Cerman, "Social Structure and Land Markets in Late Medieval Central and East-Central Europe", in: *Continuity and Change* 23, 1 (2008), pp. 55–100.

10 Moring and Wall, *Widows*, pp. 116, 128.

11 Hedwig Röckelein, "De feudofemineo – Über das Weiberlehen", in: Peter Aufgebauer and Christine van den Heuvel (eds.), *Herrschaftspraxis und soziale Ordnungen im Mittelalter und in der frühen Neuzeit. Ernst Schubert zum Gedenken*, Hannover 2006 [Hahnsche Buchhandlung], pp. 267–284.

12 Michaela Hohkamp, "Eine Tante für alle Fälle. Tanten-Nichten-Beziehungen und ihre Bedeutungen für die reichsfürstliche Gesellschaft der Frühen Neuzeit", in: Margareth Lanzinger and EdithSaurer (eds.), *Politiken der Verwandtschaft. Beziehungsnetze, Geschlecht und Recht*, Göttingen 2007 [V & R Unipress], pp. 147–169, pp. 153–154.

13 Joseph Morsel, "Geschlecht und Repräsentation. Beobachtungen zur Verwandtschaftskonstruktion im fränkischen Adel", in: Otto G. Oexle and Andrea von Hülsen-Esch (eds.), *Die Repräsentation der Gruppen. Texte – Bilder – Objekte*, Göttingen 1998 [Vandenhoek & Ruprecht], pp. 259–325, pp. 299–310.

14 According to the manorial statutes of Innichen/San Candido of 1555, the seigniorial fee (*Ehrung*) to be paid on the occasion of property transfers was higher in cases in which

a daughter rather than a son assumed the holding; an additional fee was payable for the enfeoffment of a son-in-law. Freistifts Ordnung aines Ehrwürdigen Capitls zur Iniching, 1555, cit. from Oswald Strobl, *Geschichte des Kollegiatkapitels Innichen von 1690 bis 1785*, Innsbruck 1973 [PhD Dissertation], pp. 384–395.

15 Giovanni Levi, "On Microhistory", in: Peter Burke (ed.), *New Perspectives on Historical Writing*, Cambridge 1991 [Penn State University Press], pp. 93–113, p. 94.

16 cf. for example Margarida Durães, Antoinette Fauve-Chamoux and Llorenç Ferrer iAlòs and Jan Kok (eds.), *The Transmission of Well-Being: Gendered Marriage Strategies and Inheritance Systems in Europe (17th–20th Centuries)*, Bern et al. 2009 [Peter Lang]; Anne-Lise Head-König (ed.), *Inheritance Practices, Marriage Strategies and Household Formation in European Rural Societies*, Turnhout 2012 [Brepols].

17 With regard to the three marital property regimes mentioned, see Margareth Lanzinger, Gunda Barth-Scalmani, Ellinor Forster and Gertrude Langer-Ostrawsky, *Aushandeln von Ehe. Heiratsverträge der Neuzeit im europäischen Vergleich*, Cologne, Weimar and Vienna 2010 [Böhlau] (2nd ed., 2015).

18 cf. Regina Schäfer, "Inheritance Disputes from Ingelheim Court Records on the Threshold of the Early Modern Period (Fourteenth to Fifteenth Centuries)", in: Margareth Lanzinger, Janine Maegraith, Siglinde Clementi, Ellinor Forster and Christian Hagen (eds.), *Stipulating – Litigating – Mediating. Negotiations of Gender and Property*, Leiden and Boston [Brill], forthcoming.

19 cf. Michael Suter, "The Boundaries of Debt: Bankruptcy between Local Practices and Liberal Rule in Nineteenth-Century Switzerland", in: Chia Yin Hsu, Thomas Luckett and Erika Vause (eds.), *The Cultural History of Money and Credit. A Global Perspective*, Lanham, MD 2016 [Lexington Books], pp. 51–65.

20 A specialised area of research from a local perspective would be that of jointly used goods, the so-called commons, like pastures, forests, and water. Who enjoyed access to these? And what consequences did their devolution entail?

21 cf. Maxine Berg and Helen Clifford (eds.), *Consumers and Luxury. Consumer Culture in Europe 1650–1850*, Manchester 1999 [Manchester University Press]; Janine Maegraith and Craig Muldrew, "Consumption and Material Life", in: Hamish Scott (ed.), *Oxford Handbook of Early Modern European History*, Oxford 2015 [Oxford University Press], vol. I, ch. 14, pp. 369–397; Craig Muldrew, *Food, Energy and the Creation of Industriousness. Work and Material Culture in Agrarian England, 1550–1780*, Cambridge 2011 [Cambridge University Press]; Sheilagh Ogilvie, Markus Küpker and Janine Maegraith, "Household Debt in Early Modern Germany. Evidence from Personal Inventories", in: *Journal of Economic History* 3, 1 (2012), pp. 134–167; Jane Whittle, "Enterprising Widows and Active Wives. Women's Unpaid Work in the Household Economy of Early Modern England", in: *The History of the Family* 19, 3 (2014), pp. 283–300.

22 cf. Gerhard Jaritz, "Arme Jungfrauen, Betten und das Seelenheil", in: *Beiträge zur Rechtsgeschichte Österreichs* 1 (2011), pp. 78–84.

23 cf. Simone Derix, "Haus und Translokalität. Orte der Macht – Orte der Sehnsucht", in: Joachim Eibach, Inken Schmidt-Voges, Simone Derix, Philip Hahn, Elizabeth Harding and Margareth Lanzinger (eds.), *Das Haus in der Geschichte Europas. Ein Handbuch*, Berlin 2015 [De Gruyter], pp. 589–604.

24 On the ownership of jewellery, cf. Ago, *Gusto for*, pp. 179–180; regarding court debate, cf. Margareth Lanzinger, "Von der Macht der Linie zur Gegenseitigkeit. Heiratskontrakte in den Südtiroler Gerichten Welsberg und Innichen 1750–1850", in: Margareth Lanzinger, Gunda Barth-Scalmani, Ellinor Forster and Gertrude Langer-Ostrawsky, *Aushandeln von Ehe. Heiratsverträge der Neuzeit im europäischen Vergleich*, Cologne, Weimar and Vienna 2010 [Böhlau] (2nd ed., 2015), pp. 205–367, pp. 365–366.

25 Tiroler Landesordnung (TLO), 1532, 1573, book III, section 40, § 1; Südtiroler Landesarchiv (SLA), Verfachbuch (VfB) Neumarkt (Montan) 1528, fol. 21v–22v. Christian Hagen, Margareth Lanzinger and Janine Maegraith, "Verträge als Instrumente der Vermögensabsicherung im südlichen Tirol vom 14. bis zum 18. Jahrhundert", in: *Historische Anthropologie* 25, 2 (2017), pp. 188–212, p. 209.

26 Gottschalk, "Erbe und Recht".
27 The *Sachsenspiegel*, literally "Saxon Mirror", was the most important law book of the German Middle Ages.
28 Karin Gottschalk, *Eigentum, Geschlecht, Gerechtigkeit. Haushalten und Erben im frühneuzeitlichen Leipzig*, Frankfurt am Main and New York 2003 [Campus], pp. 13–14; Gottschalk, "Erbe und Recht", pp. 93–96.
29 Jan de Vries, *The Industrious Revolution. Consumer Demand and the Household Economy, 1650 to Present*, Cambridge 2008 [Cambridge University Press]; Daniel Roche, *A History of Everyday Things. The Birth of Consumption in France, 1600–1800*, Cambridge 2000 [Johns Hopkins University Press]; Ago, *Gusto for Things*; Tara Hamling and Catherine Richardson, *A Day at Home in Early Modern England. Material Culture and Domestic Life, 1500–1700*, New Haven 2017 [Yale University Press]; Roberta Sassatelli, *Consumer Culture. History, Theory and Politics*, Los Angeles 2007 [Sage].
30 TLO, 1532, 1573, book III, section 40, § 2.
31 This is a result of the research project mentioned in note 1.
32 "Transformability" in this sense refers to the legal capacity to render immobile goods mobile and vice versa in accordance with social or societal interests, cf. Gottschalk, "Erbe und Recht", pp. 108–113.
33 Martha C. Howell, "Movable/Immovable, What's in a Name? – The Case of Late Medieval Ghent", in: Lawrin Armstrong, Ivana Elbl and Martin M. Elbl (eds.), *Money, Markets and Trade in Late Medieval Europe*, Leiden and Boston 2007 [Brill], pp. 538–571, pp. 559–564.
34 Howell, "Movable/Immovable", p. 264.
35 cf. Anna Bellavitis, *Famille, genre, transmission à Venise au XVIe siècle*, Rome 2008 [École Française de Rome]; also see her contribution to this volume.
36 Jon Mathieu, "Vermögensarrangements und Verwandtschaft im frühneuzeitlichen Graubünden. Grundmuster, Wandel, Einordnung", in: *Geschichte & Region / Storia e regione* 2 (2018), pp. 149–168, p. 154.
37 Ida Fazio, "Le ricchezze delle donne: verso una riproblematizzazione", in: *Quaderni Storici* 101 (1999), pp. 539–550.
38 The concept of the research project is based on the linkage of a broad definition of wealth, including rights and claims, credit relations, practices of inheritance, and marital property arrangements, with notions of kinship as well as aspects of material culture and consumption across a wide range of social milieus. See Lanzinger and Maegreaith, "Houses and the Range of Wealth", p. 25.
39 Angiolina Arru, "'Schenken heißt nicht verlieren'. Kredite, Schenkungen und die Vorteile der Gegenseitigkeit in Rom im 18. und 19. Jahrhundert", in: *L'Homme. Z.F.G.* 9, 2 (1998), pp. 232–251.
40 Ibid., p. 233.
41 Ibid., p. 240; Christine Fertig, "Stem Families in Rural Northwestern Germany? Family Systems, Intergenerational Relations and Family Contracts", in: *The History of the Family* 23, 2 (2018), pp. 196–217; Moring and Wall, *Widows in European Economy*, in particular chapter 4; Dana Štefanová, *Erbschaftspraxis, Besitztransfer und Handlungsspielräume von Untertanen in der Gutsherrschaft. Die Herrschaft Frýdlant in Nordböhmen, 1558–1750*, Vienna 2009 [Böhlau], chapter 4.
42 SLA, VfB Brixen Stadtgericht, 1574, part 1, fol. 53v–55v. Margareth Lanzinger and Janine Maegraith, "Konkurrenz um Vermögen im südlichen Tirol des 16. Jahrhunderts", in: *L'Homme. Z.F.G.* 27, 1 (2016), pp. 15–31, pp. 23–24. The Brixen data sample was compiled by Janine Maegraith.
43 SLA, VfB Brixen Stadtgericht VB 1574, Teil 2, fol. 65v–66r. On the inheritance of childless women and men in the late Middle Ages, see Gabriela Signori, *Vorsorgen – Vererben – Erinnern. Kinder- und familienlose Erblasser in der städtischen Gesellschaft des Spätmittelalters*, Göttingen 2001 [Vandenhoek & Ruprecht].
44 TLO 1532, 1573, book III, section 38.
45 Ibid., section 41.

46 See Lanzinger and Maegreaith, "Houses and the Range of Wealth", pp. 14–34.
47 On kitchen "stuff", see Sara Pennell, *The Birth of the English Kitchen, 1600–1850*, London 2016 [Bloomsbury], pp. 87–112.
48 The corresponding term is *Varende Hab*, or "movable property". In many languages the word for "furniture" is actually synonymous with the word "movable". The term "furniture" is unique to English; most other European languages derive their term for this element from the Latin word *mobile*. It was not until rather late, however, that this latter term, *Möbel*, came into wider usage in the German language. Krünitz's encyclopaedia, for instance, issued between 1773 and 1858, still followed the French spelling, *Meuble*; see www.kruenitz1.uni-trier.de/. The Grimms's dictionary states that terms such as *mubel*, *mübel*, and *möbel* were in use as early as the fifteenth and sixteenth centuries in the Mosel region near the French border. Before that time, the term in common usage had been *Fahrhabe*, or "movable property", which encompassed general household items as well as furniture. http://woerterbuchnetz.de/cgi-bin/WBNetz/wbgui_py?sigle=DWB&mode=Vernetzung&lemid=GM06404#XGM06404
49 cf. Niederösterreichisches Landesarchiv, Kreisgericht St. Pölten, 151, Stiftsherrschaft Seitenstetten, Amtsbücher 6: Kaufprotokoll 1808–1826, fol. 223–224, 223.
50 Johann Heinrich Zedler (ed.), *Grosses vollständiges Universal Lexicon aller Wissenschafften und Künste, Halle and Leipzig 1732–1754*, 2020 [Zedler], digital edition, www.zedler-lexikon.de/index.html?c=blaettern&id=395202&bandnummer=44&seitenzahl=0215&supplement=0&dateiformat=1'.
51 For example, SLA, VfB Kastelruth 1781, widow's usufruct contract, fol. 521–530, 527: "[A]uch zu ihrer weitternWürtschaft und Gebrauch das benothigte hausgerath und Kuchelgeschir . . . aber gegen kunftiger Restitution abgegeben werden".
52 cf. Raffaella Sarti, *Europe at Home. Family and Material Culture 1500–1800*, New Haven and London 1999 [Yale University Press], chapter 2.
53 Nikola Langreiter (ed.), *Tagebuch der Wett Teuschl (1870–1885)*, Cologne, Weimar and Vienna 2010 [Böhlau], pp. 96, 146.
54 Movable goods also "served as assets in times of need, to be sold at auction or taken to the pawnshop," or what Daniel Lord Smail refers to as "objects of legal plunder," and could be used toward "debt recovery". Beginning in the fourteenth and fifteenth centuries, goods "entangled households in complex relationships of credit and debt". Daniel Lord Smail, *Legal Plunder. Household and Debt Collection in Late Medieval Households in Europe*, Cambridge, MA and London 2016 [Harvard University Press], p. 4, synopsis.
55 Mischa Suter, *Rechtstrieb. Schulden und Vollstreckung im liberalen Kapitalismus 1800–1900*, Konstanz 2016 [Konstanz University Press], pp. 250–252, note 128.
56 Anu Pylkkänen emphasises that "the different items in the inventories should not only be seen as economic capital but also as vital part of social consumption", in the sense of "consumption that manifests status in various ways". Thus, "[t]o a strict economic value must be added a social value, and every item had a *use* value as well as a *status* value". Anu Pylkkänen, "Forming the Marital Economy in the Early Modern Finnish Countryside", in: Maria Ågren and Amy Louise Erickson (eds.), *The Marital Economy in Scandinavia and Britain 1400–1900*, Aldershot 2005 [Ashgate], pp. 57–73, p. 59.
57 Ago, "Les biens meubles".
58 Margareth Lanzinger and Janine Maegraith, "Vermögen als Medium der Herstellung von Verwandtschaftsräumen vom 16. bis zum 18. Jahrhundert – ein Projektbericht mit Objektperspektive", in: *Frühneuzeit-Info* 28 (2017), pp. 202–208.

Bibliography

Ago, Renata, *Gusto for Things. A History of Objects in Seventeenth-Century Rome*, Chicago 2013 [University of Chicago Press].

———"Les biens meubles. Une propriété qui ne crée pas d'appartenance?" in: Sami Bargaoui, Simona Cerutti and Isabelle Grangaud (eds.), *Appartenance locale et propriété au nord et au sud de la Méditerranée*, [Institut de recherches et d'études sur les mondes arabes et musulman] Aix-en-Provence 2015, http://books.openedition.org/iremam/3419 [Open Edition].

Arru, Angiolina, "'Schenken heißt nicht verlieren'. Kredite, Schenkungen und die Vorteile der Gegenseitigkeit in Rom im 18. und 19. Jahrhundert", in: *L'Homme. Z.F.G.* 9, 2 (1998), pp. 232–251.

Bellavitis, Anna, *Famille, genre, transmission à Venise au XVIe siècle*, Rome 2008 [École Française de Rome].

Berg, Maxine and Helen Clifford (eds.), *Consumers and Luxury. Consumer Culture in Europe 1650–1850*, Manchester 1999 [Manchester University Press].

Broad, John and Anton Schuurman (eds.), *Wealth and Poverty in European Rural Societies from the Sixteenth to Nineteenth Century*, Turnhout 2014 [Brepols Publisher].

Cerman, Markus, "Social Structure and Land Markets in Late Medieval Central and East-Central Europe", in: *Continuity and Change* 23, 1 (2008), pp. 55–100.

De Vries, Jan, *The Industrious Revolution. Consumer Demand and the Household Economy, 1650 to Present*, Cambridge 2008 [Cambridge University Press].

Derix, Simone, "Haus und Translokalität. Orte der Macht – Orte der Sehnsucht", in: Joachim Eibach, Inken Schmidt-Voges, Simone Derix, Philip Hahn, Elizabeth Harding and Margareth Lanzinger (eds.), *Das Haus in der Geschichte Europas. Ein Handbuch*, Berlin 2015 [De Gruyter], pp. 589–604.

Derix, Simone and Margareth Lanzinger, "Housing Capital. Interdisciplinary Perspectives on a Multifaceted Resource", in: *Jahrbuch für Europäische Geschichte/European History Yearbook* 18 (2017), pp. 1–13, https://doi.org/10.1515/ 9783110532241–001.

Durães, Margarida, Antoinette Fauve-Chamoux, LIorenç Ferrer I Alòs and Jan Kok (eds.), *The Transmission of Well-Being. Gendered Marriage Strategies and Inheritance Systems in Europe (17th–20th Centuries)*, Bern et al. 2009 [Peter Lang].

Fazio, Ida, "Le ricchezze delle donne. verso una riproblematizzazione", in: *Quaderni Storici* 101 (1999), pp. 539–550.

Fertig, Christine, "Stem Families in Rural Northwestern Germany? Family Systems, Intergenerational Relations and Family Contracts", in: *The History of the Family* 23, 2 (2018), pp. 196–217.

Gottschalk, Karin, *Eigentum, Geschlecht, Gerechtigkeit. Haushalten und Erben im frühneuzeitlichen Leipzig*, Frankfurt a. M. and New York 2003 [Campus].

———"Erbe und Recht. Die Übertragung von Eigentum in der frühen Neuzeit", in: Stefan Willer, Sigrid Weigel and Bernhard Jussen (eds.), *Erbe. Übertragungskonzepte zwischen Natur und Kultur*, Frankfurt a. M. 2013 [Suhrkamp], pp. 85–125.

Hagen, Christian, Margareth Lanzinger and Janine Maegraith, "Verträge als Instrumente der Vermögensabsicherung im südlichen Tirol vom 14. bis zum 18. Jahrhundert", in: *Historische Anthropologie* 25, 2 (2017), pp. 188–212.

———"Competing Interests in Death-related Stipulations in South Tirol ca. 1350–1600", in: Mia Korpiola and AnuLahtinen(eds.), *Planning for Death: Wills, Inheritance and Property Strategies in Medieval and Reformation Europe*, Leiden and Boston 2018 [Brill], pp. 88–118.

Hamling, Tara and Catherine Richardson, *A Day at Home in Early Modern England. Material Culture and Domestic Life 1500–1700*, New Haven 2017 [Yale University Press].

Head-König, Anne-Lise (ed.), *Inheritance Practices, Marriage Strategies and Household Formation in European Rural Societies*, Turnhout 2012 [Brepols].

Hohkamp, Michaela, "Eine Tante für alle Fälle. Tanten-Nichten-Beziehungen und ihre Bedeutungen für die reichsfürstliche Gesellschaft der Frühen Neuzeit", in: Margareth Lanzinger and Edith Saurer (eds.), *Politiken der Verwandtschaft. Beziehungsnetze, Geschlecht und Recht*, Göttingen 2007 [V & R Unipress], pp. 147–169.

Howell, Martha C., "Movable/Immovable, What's in a Name? – The Case of Late Medieval Ghent", in: Lawrin Armstrong, Ivana Elbl and Martin M. Elbl (eds.), *Money, Markets and Trade in Late Medieval Europe*, Leiden and Boston 2007 [Brill], pp. 538–571.

Jaritz, Gerhard, "Arme Jungfrauen, Betten und das Seelenheil", in: *Beiträge zur Rechtsgeschichte Österreichs* 1 (2011), pp. 78–84.

Kühn, Sebastian, *Wissen, Arbeit, Freundschaft. Ökonomien und soziale Beziehungen in den Akademien von London, Paris und Berlin um 1700*, Göttingen 2011 [V & R Unipress].

———"Scholarly Households", in: Joachim Eibach and Margareth Lanzinger (eds.), The Routlegde History of the Domestic Sphere in Europe: 16th to 19th Century forthcoming [Routledge].

Langreiter, Nikola (ed.), *Tagebuch der Wett Teuschl (1870–1885)*, Cologne, Weimar and Vienna 2010 [Böhlau].

Lanzinger, Margareth, "Von der Macht der Linie zur Gegenseitigkeit. Heiratskontrakte in den Südtiroler Gerichten Welsberg und Innichen 1750–1850", in: Margareth Lanzinger, Gunda Barth-Scalmani, Ellinor Forster and Gertrude Langer-Ostrawsky, *Heiratsverträge der Neuzeit im europäischen Vergleich*, Cologne, Weimar and Vienna 2010 [Böhlau], pp. 205–367.

Lanzinger, Margareth and Janine Maegraith, "Konkurrenz um Vermögen im südlichen Tirol des 16. Jahrhunderts", in: *L'Homme. Z.F.G.* 27, 1 (2016), pp. 15–31.

———"Houses and the Range of Wealth in Early Modern Gender- and Intergenerational Relationships", in: *Jahrbuch für Europäische Geschichte/European History Yearbook* 18 (2017), pp. 14–34.

———"Vermögen als Medium der Herstellung von Verwandtschaftsräumen vom 16. bis zum 18. Jahrhundert – ein Projektbericht mit Objektperspektive", in: *Frühneuzeitinfo* 28 (2017), pp. 202–208.

Lanzinger, Margareth, Gunda Barth-Scalmani, Ellinor Forster and Gertrude Langer-Ostrawsky, *Aushandeln von Ehe. Heiratsverträge der Neuzeit im europäischen Vergleich*, Cologne, Weimar and Vienna 2010 (2nd ed., 2015) [Böhlau].

Levi, Giovanni, "On Microhistory", in: Peter Burke (ed.), *New Perspectives on Historical Writing*, Cambridge 1991 [Penn State University Press], pp. 93–113.

Lord Smail, Daniel, *Legal Plunder. Household and Debt Collection in Late Medieval Households in Europe*, Cambridge, MA and London 2016 [Harvard University Press].

Maegraith, Janine and Muldrew, Craig, "Consumption and Material Life", in: Hamish Scott (ed.), *Oxford Handbook of Early Modern European History*, Oxford 2015 [Oxford University Press], vol. I, ch. 14, pp. 369–397.

Mathieu, Jon, "Vermögensarrangements und Verwandtschaft im frühneuzeitlichen Graubünden. Grundmuster, Wandel, Einordnung", in: *Geschichte & Region / Storia e regione* 2 (2018), pp. 149–168.

Moring, Beatrice and Richard Wall, *Widows in European Economy and Society 1600–1920*, Woodbridge 2017 [Boydell & Brewer].

Morsel, Joseph, "Geschlecht und Repräsentation. Beobachtungen zur Verwandtschaftskonstruktion im fränkischen Adel", in: Otto G. Oexle and Andrea von Hülsen-Esch (eds.), *Die Repräsentation der Gruppen. Texte – Bilder – Objekte*, Göttingen 1998 [Vandenhoek & Ruprecht], pp. 259–325.

Muldrew, Craig, *Food, Energy and the Creation of Industriousness. Work and Material Culture in Agrarian England 1550–1780*, Cambridge 2011 [Cambridge University Press].

Ogilvie, Sheilagh, Markus Küpker and Janine Maegraith, "Household Debt in Early Modern Germany. Evidence from Personal Inventories", in: *Journal of Economic History* 3, 1 (2012), pp. 134–167.

Pennell, Sara, *The Birth of the English Kitchen 1600–1850*, London 2016 [Bloomsbury].

Pylkkänen, Anu, "Forming the Marital Economy in the Early Modern Finnish Countryside", in: Maria Ågren and Amy Louise Erickson (eds.), *The Marital Economy in Scandinavia and Britain 1400–1900*, Aldershot 2005 [Ashgate], pp. 57–73.

Roche, Daniel, *A History of Everyday Things. The Birth of Consumption in France, 1600–1800*, Cambridge 2000 [Johns Hopkins University Press].

Röckelein, Hedwig, "De feudofemineo – Über das Weiberlehen", in: Peter Aufgebauer and Christine van den Heuvel (eds.), *Herrschaftspraxis und soziale Ordnungen im Mittelalter und in der frühen Neuzeit. Ernst Schubert zum Gedenken*, Hannover 2006 [Hahnsche Buchhandlung], pp. 267–284.

Sarti, Raffaella, *Europe at Home. Family and Material Culture 1500–1800*, New Haven and London 1999 [Yale University Press].

Sassatelli, Roberta, *Consumer Culture. History, Theory and Politics*, Los Angeles 2007 [Sage].

Schäfer, Regina, "Inheritance Disputes from Ingelheim Court Records on the Threshold of the Early Modern Period (Fourteenth to Fifteenth Centuries)", in: Margareth Lanzinger, Janine Maegraith, Siglinde Clementi, Ellinor Forster and Christian Hagen (eds.), *Stipulating – Litigating – Mediating. Negotiations of Gender and Property*, Leiden and Boston 2020 [Brill].

Signori, Gabriela, *Vorsorgen – Vererben – Erinnern. Kinder- und familienlose Erblasser in der städtischen Gesellschaft des Spätmittelalters*, Göttingen 2001 [Vandenhoek & Ruprecht].

Štefanová, Dana, *Erbschaftspraxis, Besitztransfer und Handlungsspielräume von Untertanen in der Gutsherrschaft. Die Herrschaft Frýdlant in Nordböhmen 1558–1750*, Vienna 2009 [Böhlau].

Strobl, Oswald, *Geschichte des Kollegiatkapitels Innichen von 1690 bis 1785*, Innsbruck 1973 [PhD Dissertation], pp. 384–395.

Suter, Michael, "The Boundaries of Debt: Bankruptcy Between Local Practices and Liberal Rule in Nineteenth-Century Switzerland", in: Chia Yin Hsu, Thomas Luckett and Erika Vause (eds.), *The Cultural History of Money and Credit. A Global Perspective*, Lanham, MD 2016 [Lexington Books], pp. 51–65.

Suter, Mischa, *Rechtstrieb Schulden und Vollstreckung im liberalen Kapitalismus 1800–1900*, Konstanz 2016 [Konstanz University Press].

Whittle, Jane, "Enterprising Widows and Active Wives. Women's Unpaid Work in the Household Economy of Early Modern England", in: *The History of the Family* 19, 3 (2014), pp. 283–300.

INDEX OF OBJECTS

Note: Page numbers in *italics* indicate a figure and page numbers in **bold** indicate a table.

INDEX

Note: Page numbers in *italics* indicate a figure. General terms such as "property", "possession", "household", "widow", "mobile" or "immobile" are too numerous and are not included in the general index.